REAL Words
for SONGWRITERS

Alphabetical Word List and Abbreviated Rhyming Dictionary

by Linda A. Bell

First Edition

REAL Words for Songwriters
Alphabetical Word List and
Abbreviated Rhyming Dictionary

www.RealWordsForSongwriters.com

Copyright © 2014 Linda A. Bell
Bell Creative Studio
Las Vegas, Nevada
(702) 518-0552
www.BellCreativeStudio.com

Edited by Gina Dewees

Cover Design by Jeanne Quinn
www.SeeQuinn.com

Reference / Word Lists: real words for songwriters: alphabetical word list and abbreviated rhyming dictionary / Linda A. Bell.-1st. ed.

ISBN-13: 978-1502872463
ISBN-10: 1502872463

Printed in the United States of America

DISCLAIMER

This book is designed to provide you with information about the subject matter covered. The publisher and author are not rendering legal, accounting, or other professional services.

Every effort has been made to make this book as complete and as accurate as possible. For obvious reasons I cannot put every possible word (and variation of those words) in it.

The purpose of this book is to inspire you, educate you, and entertain you. Most importantly, it is intended to get your creativity in the form of a stream of words flowing.

There may be mistakes both typographical and in content. Therefore, this text should be used as only a general guide.

The author and publishing company shall have neither liability nor responsibility to any person or entity with respect to any loss or damage caused or alleged to be caused directly or indirectly by the information contained in this book.

TABLE OF CONTENTS

INTRODUCTION

I didn't plan to make a career out of writing lyrics, it just happened. In the past fifteen years I've sold 2,000 sets of lyrics to advertisers nationally! My husband, Linwood Bell, a highly regarded composer/arranger/producer, and the love of my life, produces the music. His arrangements are performed by some of the finest symphonies in the world. (See: www.LinwoodBell.com)

There have been times when I've had as many as seventy projects on my desk at once. Can you imagine?! Needless to say, I cannot afford to get stuck! While dictionaries, rhyming dictionaries, thesauruses, and word lists are great resources when you're at a loss for words, they fall short when it comes to using them as a tool for songwriting. They're not organized in a way that makes it easy to find the words (and sound-alike words) you need fast. They're also filled with thousands of words you would never use in lyrics, like *malapropos, usufruct, dishabille,* and *valetudinarian.* You just need **REAL Words;** words that people actually use in **real-life** conversations!

Frustrated with not being able to find precisely what I was searching for, I started jotting down my own list of words. This project, which was a labor of love, born of necessity, grew into two books:

> **REAL Words for Songwriters:** Alphabetical Word List and Abbreviated Rhyming Dictionary
>
> **REAL Words for Writers:** Alphabetical Word List (see p. 277)

In *this* book, you will find over 15,000 REAL Words, including base words and derivatives, sorted two different ways to help you get unstuck and keep your creativity flowing. I hope they bring you an abundance of creativity and success! - Linda Bell
www.RealWordsForSongwriters.com

HOW TO USE THIS BOOK
* TWO COMPLETE REFERENCE BOOKS IN ONE *

When you listen carefully to songs, you'll notice that the words at the end of the lines that rhyme have the **same Prominent Ending Vowel** [PEV] sound. This is what makes them pleasing to the ear and easy to recall. *(Keep in mind that when you're writing lyrics, imperfect rhymes often work perfectly fine!)*

PART ONE: Alphabetical Word List

Over 15,000 REAL Words are listed alphabetically. Each word is [PEV] coded by its prominent ending vowel sound to make it easy to find sound-alike words in Part Two. Long vowels are capitalized. As in *bag [a]* and *bake [A]*.

PART TWO: Abbreviated Rhyming Dictionary

REAL Words are sorted by their Prominent Ending Vowel sounds, then grouped together in a way that makes it easy to see a large selection of words that rhyme and/or sound-alike in one place.

If the prominent ending vowel is followed by a consonant that significantly alters the final sound of the word, *as in beer [E]r*, it is then placed into a subgroup. In most cases, words within the same [PEV] groups can be paired together, regardless of the subgroupings. Consonants with similar sounds have been combined. *As in: bang [a]ng/k* and *bank [a]ng/k.*

Alternate* pronunciations included!

Special consideration was given to the way vocalists and rap artists pronounce certain words. Lover, for example, is often pronounced *love-uh*, therefore you will find it listed as **lover [er]** *and* **lover [u]***.

PART ONE

Alphabetical Word List

A

a [A]
a [u]
aback [a]
abandon [e]m/n
abandoning [E]m/n
abandoning [e]m/n*
abbreviate [A]
abbreviated [e]
abbreviating [E]m/n
abbreviating [e]m/n*
abbreviation [u]m/n
abdomen [e]m/n
abdominal [u]l
abduct [u]
abducted [e]
abducting [E]m/n
abducting [e]m/n*
abduction [u]m/n
abductor [er]
abide [I]
abided [e]
abiding [E]m/n
abiding [e]m/n*
ability [E]
ablaze [A]
able [u]l
abnormal [u]l
abnormality [E]
abnormally [E]
aboard [O]r
abode [O]
abominable [u]l
abort [O]r
aborted [e]
aborting [E]m/n
aborting [e]m/n*
abortion [u]m/n
abound [ow]m/n
about [ow]
above [u]
abrasion [u]m/n

abrasive [i]
abreast [e]
abroad [o]
abrupt [u]
abruptly [E]
abscess [e]
absence [e]m/n
absent [e]m/n
absentee [E]
absolute [oo]
absolutely [E]
absolve [o]l
absorb [O]r
absorbance [e]m/n
absorbency [E]
absorbent [e]m/n
absorbing [E]m/n
absorbing [e]m/n*
absorption [u]m/n
abstain [A]m/n
abstaining [E]m/n
abstaining [e]m/n*
abstinence [e]m/n
abstract [a]
absurd [er]
absurdity [E]
abundance [e]m/n
abundant [e]m/n
abundantly [E]
abuse [oo]
abuser [er]
abusing [E]m/n
abusing [e]m/n*
abusive [i]
academic [i]
academically [E]
academy [E]
accelerate [A]
accelerated [e]
accelerating [E]m/n
accelerating [e]m/n*

acceleration [u]m/n
accelerator [er]
accent [e]m/n
accented [e]
accentuate [A]
accentuated [e]
accept [e]
acceptable [u]l
acceptance [e]m/n
accepting [E]m/n
accepting [e]m/n*
access [e]
accessible [u]l
accessing [E]m/n
accessing [e]m/n*
accessorize [I]
accessorizing [E]m/n
accessorizing [e]m/n*
accessory [E]
accident [e]m/n
accidental [u]l
accidentally [E]
acclaim [A]m/n
acclimate [A]
acclimated [e]
acclimating [E]m/n
acclimating [e]m/n*
accommodate [A]
accommodated [e]
accommodating [e]m/n*
accommodating [E]m/n
accommodation [u]m/n
accompaniment [e]m/n
accompany [E]
accompanying [E]m/n
accompanying [e]m/n*
accomplice [i]
accomplish [i]
accomplishing [E]m/n
accomplishing [e]m/n*
accomplishment [e]m/n

accord [O]r
accordance [e]m/n
according [E]m/n
according [e]m/n*
accordingly [E]
accordion [u]m/n
account [ow]m/n
accountability [E]
accountable [u]l
accountant [e]m/n
accounted [e]
accounting [E]m/n
accounting [e]m/n*
accumulate [A]
accumulated [e]
accumulating [E]m/n
accumulating [e]m/n*
accumulation [u]m/n
accuracy [E]
accurate [e]
accurately [E]
accusation [u]m/n
accusatory [E]
accuse [oo]
accuser [er]
accusing [E]m/n
accusing [e]m/n*
accustom [u]m/n
ace [A]
acetate [A]
ache [A]
achievable [u]l
achieve [E]
achievement [e]m/n
achiever [er]
achieving [E]m/n
achieving [e]m/n*
aching [E]m/n
aching [e]m/n*
achy [E]
acid [i]
acidic [i]
acidity [E]
acing [E]m/n
acing [e]m/n*

acknowledge [e]
acknowledging [E]m/n
acknowledging [e]m/n*
acne [E]
acorn [O]r
acoustic [i]
acoustically [E]
acquaint [A]m/n
acquaintance [e]m/n
acquainted [e]
acquire [I]r
acquiring [E]m/n
acquiring [e]m/n*
acre [er]
acreage [e]
acrobat [a]
acrobatic [i]
acrobatically [E]
across [o]
acrylic [i]
act [a]
acted [e]
acting [E]m/n
acting [e]m/n*
action [u]m/n
activate [A]
activated [e]
activating [E]m/n
activating [e]m/n*
activation [u]m/n
active [i]
actively [E]
activity [E]
actor [er]
actress [e]
actual [u]l
actuality [E]
actually [E]
acupressure [er]
acupuncture [er]
acute [oo]
acutely [E]
ad [a]
adamant [e]m/n
adamantly [E]

adapt [a]
adaptability [E]
adaptable [u]l
adaptation [u]m/n
adapted [e]
adapter [er]
adapting [E]m/n
adapting [e]m/n*
add [a]
added [e]
addendum [u]m/n
addict [i]
addicted [e]
addicting [E]m/n
addicting [e]m/n*
addiction [u]m/n
addictive [i]
adding [E]m/n
adding [e]m/n*
addition [u]m/n
additional [u]l
additionally [E]
additive [i]
address [e]
addressing [E]m/n
addressing [e]m/n*
adept [e]
adeptly [E]
adequacy [E]
adequate [e]
adequately [E]
adhere [E]r
adhering [E]m/n
adhering [e]m/n*
adhesive [i]
adjacent [e]m/n
adjoin [Oi]m/n
adjoining [E]m/n
adjoining [e]m/n*
adjourn [er]m/n
adjourning [E]m/n
adjourning [e]m/n*
adjust [u]
adjustable [u]l
adjusted [e]

adjuster [er]
adjusting [E]m/n
adjusting [e]m/n*
adjustment [e]m/n
administer [er]
administering [E]m/n
administering [e]m/n*
administrate [A]
administrated [e]
administration [u]m/n
administrative [i]
administrator [er]
admirable [u]l
admiral [u]l
admiration [u]m/n
admire [I]r
admiring [E]m/n
admiring [e]m/n*
admissible [u]l
admission [u]m/n
admit [i]
admitted [e]
admitting [E]m/n
admitting [e]m/n*
adobe [E]
adolesce
adolescent [e]m/n
adopt [o]
adoptable [u]l
adopted [e]
adopting [E]m/n
adopting [e]m/n*
adoption [u]m/n
adoptive [i]
adorable [u]l
adoration [u]m/n
adore [O]r
adoring [E]m/n
adoring [e]m/n*
adorn [O]r
adorning [E]m/n
adorning [e]m/n*
adrenaline [i]m/n
adrift [i]
adult [u]l

adultery [E]
advance [a]m/n
advancement [e]m/n
advancing [E]m/n
advancing [e]m/n*
advantage [e]
advantageous [e]
adventure [er]
adventuresome [u]m/n
adventurous [e]
adverb [er]
adversary [E]
adverse [er]
adversity [E]
advertise [I]
advertisement [e]m/n
advertiser [er]
advertising [E]m/n
advertising [e]m/n*
advice [I]
advisable [u]l
advise [I]
advisement [e]m/n
advising [E]m/n
advising [e]m/n*
advisor [er]
advisory [E]
advocate [A]
advocate [e]
advocated [e]
advocating [E]m/n
advocating [e]m/n*
aerate [A]
aerated [e]
aerial [u]l
aerobic [i]
aerodynamic [i]
aerodynamically [E]
aerosol [o]l
aesthetic [i]
aesthetically [E]
afar [o]r
affair [e]r
affect [e]
affecting [E]m/n

affecting [e]m/n*
affection [u]m/n
affectionate [e]
affiliate [e]
affiliated [e]
affiliation [u]m/n
affirm [er]m/n
affirmation [u]m/n
affirmative [i]
affirming [E]m/n
affirming [e]m/n*
affix [i]
affixing [E]m/n
affixing [e]m/n*
afflict [i]
afflicted [e]
afflicting [E]m/n
afflicting [e]m/n*
affliction [u]m/n
affluent [e]m/n
afford [O]r
affordable [u]l
affordably [E]
afire [I]r
afloat [O]
afoot [oo/]
afoul [ow]l
afraid [A]
after [er]
afterglow [O]
afterlife [I]
aftermath [a]
afternoon [oo]m/n
aftershave [A]
aftershock [o]
aftertaste [A]
afterthought [o]
afterward [er]
again [e]m/n
against [e]m/n
agape [A]
age [A]
ageless [e]
agency [E]
agenda [u]

aggravate [A]
aggravated [e]
aggravating [E]m/n
aggravating [e]m/n*
aggravation [u]m/n
aggression [u]m/n
aggressive [i]
aggressively [E]
agile [I]l
agility [E]
aging [E]m/n
aging [e]m/n*
agitate [A]
agitated [e]
agitation [u]m/n
agitator [er]
aglitter [er]
aglow [O]
ago [O]
agonize [I]
agonizing [E]m/n
agonizing [e]m/n*
agony [E]
agree [E]
agreeable [u]l
agreeing [E]m/n
agreeing [e]m/n*
agreement [e]m/n
agricultural [u]l
agriculture [er]
aground [ow]m/n
ah [o]
ahead [e]
ahem [e]m/n
ahoy [Oi]
aid [A]
aide [A]
aided [e]
aiding [E]m/n
aiding [e]m/n*
ailment [e]m/n
aim [A]m/n
aiming [E]m/n
aiming [e]m/n*
aimless [e]

aimlessly [E]
ain't [A]m/n
air [e]r
airborne [O]r
airbrush [u]
aircraft [a]
airfare [e]r
airflow [O]
airhead [e]
airline [I]m/n
airmail [A]l
airman [e]m/n
airplane [A]m/n
airport [O]r
airsick [i]
airstrip [i]
airtight [I]
airtime [I]m/n
airwave [A]
airway [A]
airy [E]
aisle [I]l
ajar [o]r
alarm [o]r
alarming [E]m/n
alarming [e]m/n*
alarmingly [E]
alarmist [i]
alas [a]
albino [O]
album [u]m/n
alcohol [o]l
alcoholic [i]
alcoholism [e]m/n
alcove [O]
ale [A]l
alert [er]
alerted [e]
alerting [E]m/n
alerting [e]m/n*
algae [E]
algebra [u]
alias [e]
alibi [I]
alien [e]m/n

alienate [A]
alienated [e]
align [I]m/n
aligning [E]m/n
aligning [e]m/n*
alignment [e]m/n
alike [I]
alimony [E]
alive [I]
alkaline [I]m/n
all [o]l
allegation [u]m/n
allege [e]
allegiance [e]m/n
alleging [E]m/n
alleging [e]m/n*
allergic [i]
allergy [E]
alleviate [A]
alleviated [e]
alleviating [E]m/n
alleviating [e]m/n*
alleviation [u]m/n
alley [E]
alliance [e]m/n
alligator [er]
allocate [A]
allocated [e]
allocating [E]m/n
allocating [e]m/n*
allocation [u]m/n
allot [o]
allotment [e]m/n
allotted [e]
allotting [E]m/n
allotting [e]m/n*
allow [ow]
allowable [u]l
allowance [e]m/n
allowing [E]m/n
allowing [e]m/n*
allude [oo]
alluded [e]
alluding [E]m/n
alluding [e]m/n*

allure [er]
alluring [E]m/n
alluring [e]m/n*
ally [I]
almanac [a]
almighty [E]
almond [e]m/n
almost [O]
aloe [O]
aloft [o]
alone [O]m/n
along [o]m/n
alongside [I]
aloud [ow]
alphabet [e]
alphabetical [u]l
alphabetize [I]
alpine [I]m/n
already [E]
already [e]*
alright [I]
also [O]
altar [er]
alter [er]
alteration [u]m/n
altering [E]m/n
altering [e]m/n*
alternate [A]
alternate [e]
alternated [e]
alternating [E]m/n
alternating [e]m/n*
alternative [i]
alternator [er]
although [O]
altitude [oo]
alto [O]
altogether [er]
aluminum [u]m/n
always [A]
amass [a]
amateur [er]
amateurish [i]
amaze [A]
amazement [e]m/n

amazing [E]m/n
amazing [e]m/n*
amazingly [E]
ambassador [er]
amber [er]
ambiance [e]m/n
ambient [e]m/n
ambition [u]m/n
ambitious [e]
ambitiously [E]
ambulance [e]m/n
ambush [oo/]
amen [e]m/n
amend [e]m/n
amended [e]
amending [E]m/n
amending [e]m/n*
amendment [e]m/n
amethyst [i]
amid [i]
amiss [i]
ammunition [u]m/n
amnesia [u]
amnesty [E]
amok [u]
among [u]m/n
amongst [u]m/n
amorous [e]
amount [ow]m/n
amounted [e]
amour [er]
ample [u]l
amplification [u]m/n
amplifier [I]r
amplify [I]
amplifying [E]m/n
amplifying [e]m/n*
amply [E]
amuse [oo]
amusement [e]m/n
amusing [E]m/n
amusing [e]m/n*
analog [o]
analysis [i]
analytical [u]l

analyze [I]
analyzer [er]
analyzing [E]m/n
analyzing [e]m/n*
anatomy [E]
ancestor [er]
ancestral [u]l
ancestry [E]
anchor [er]
anchoring [E]m/n
anchoring [e]m/n*
anchovy [E]
ancient [e]m/n
android [Oi]
anemia [u]
anemic [i]
anesthesia [u]
anesthetic [i]
anew [oo]
angel [u]l
angelfish [i]
angelic [i]
anger [er]
angering [E]m/n
angering [e]m/n*
angle [u]l
angrily [E]
angry [E]
anguish [i]
angular [er]
animal [u]l
animalistic [i]
animate [A]
animated [e]
animation [u]m/n
animator [er]
animosity [E]
ankle [u]l
anklet [e]
annex [e]
annihilate [A]
annihilated [e]
annihilating [E]m/n
annihilating [e]m/n*
annihilation [u]m/n

anniversary [E]
announce [ow]m/n
announcement [e]m/n
announcer [er]
announcing [E]m/n
announcing [e]m/n*
annoy [Oi]
annoyance [e]m/n
annoying [E]m/n
annoying [e]m/n*
annual [u]l
annually [E]
annul [u]l
anonymous [e]
anorexia [u]
anorexic [i]
another [er]
another [u]*
answer [er]
answerable [u]l
answering [E]m/n
answering [e]m/n*
ant [a]m/n
antacid [i]
antagonistic [i]
antagonize [I]
antagonizing [E]m/n
antagonizing [e]m/n*
ante [E]
antelope [O]
antenna [u]
anthem [e]m/n
anthill [i]l
anti [I]
antibiotic [i]
antibody [E]
antic [i]
anticipate [A]
anticipated [e]
anticipating [E]m/n
anticipating [e]m/n*
anticipation [u]m/n
anticlimactic [i]
antidote [O]
antifreeze [E]

antilock [o]
antioxidant [e]m/n
antiperspirant [e]m/n
antique [E]
antiseptic [i]
antisocial [u]l
antler [er]
antsy [E]
anxiety [E]
anxious [e]
anxiously [E]
any [E]
anybody [E]
anybody [e]*
anyhow [ow]
anymore [O]r
anyone [u]m/n
anyplace [A]
anything [E]m/n
anything [e]m/n*
anytime [I]m/n
anyway [A]
anywhere [e]r
apart [o]r
apartment [e]m/n
ape [A]
apiece [E]
apologetic [i]
apologize [I]
apologizing [E]m/n
apologizing [e]m/n*
apology [E]
apparatus [e]
apparel [u]l
apparent [e]m/n
apparently [E]
appeal [E]l
appealing [E]m/n
appealing [e]m/n*
appear [E]r
appearance [e]m/n
appearing [E]m/n
appearing [e]m/n*
appendix [i]
appetite [I]

appetizer [er]
appetizing [E]m/n
appetizing [e]m/n*
applaud [o]
applauded [e]
applauding [E]m/n
applauding [e]m/n*
applause [o]
apple [u]l
appliance [e]m/n
applicable [u]l
applicant [e]m/n
application [u]m/n
applicator [er]
apply [I]
applying [E]m/n
applying [e]m/n*
appoint [Oi]m/n
appointed [e]
appointing [E]m/n
appointing [e]m/n*
appointment [e]m/n
appraisal [u]l
appraise [A]
appraiser [er]
appraising [E]m/n
appraising [e]m/n*
appreciate [A]
appreciated [e]
appreciating [E]m/n
appreciating [e]m/n*
appreciation [u]m/n
appreciative [i]
apprehend [e]m/n
apprehended [e]
apprehending [E]m/n
apprehending [e]m/n*
apprehension [u]m/n
apprehensive [i]
apprentice [i]
apprenticeship [i]
approach [O]
approachable [u]l
approaching [E]m/n
approaching [e]m/n*

appropriate [A]
appropriate [e]
appropriated [e]
appropriately [E]
approval [u]l
approve [oo]
approving [E]m/n
approving [e]m/n*
approximate [e]
approximately [E]
approximation [u]m/n
apricot   [o]
April [u]l
apron [e]m/n
apt [a]
aptitude [oo]
aptly [E]
aqua [u]
aquamarine [E]m/n
aquarium [u]m/n
aquatic [i]
arbor [er]
arc [o]r
arcade [A]
arch [o]r
archery [E]
arching [E]m/n
arching [e]m/n*
architect [e]
architectural [u]l
architecture [er]
archival [u]l
archive [I]
archiving [E]m/n
archiving [e]m/n*
archway [A]
arctic [i]
are [o]r
area [u]
arena [u]
arguable [u]l
arguably [E]
argue [oo]
arguing [E]m/n
arguing [e]m/n*

argument [e]m/n
argumentative [i]
argyle [I]l
arise [I]
arisen [e]m/n
arising [E]m/n
arising [e]m/n*
ark [o]r
arm [o]r
armadillo [O]
armchair [e]r
armful [oo]l
armhole [O]l
armload [O]
armor [er]
armpit [i]
armrest [e]
army [E]
aroma [u]
aromatic [i]
around [ow]m/n
arousal [u]l
arouse [ow]
arousing [E]m/n
arousing [e]m/n*
arraign [A]m/n
arraigning [E]m/n
arraigning [e]m/n*
arraignment [e]m/n
arrange [A]m/n
arrangement [e]m/n
arranger [er]
arranging [E]m/n
arranging [e]m/n*
array [A]
arrest [e]
arresting [E]m/n
arresting [e]m/n*
arrival [u]l
arrive [I]
arriving [E]m/n
arriving [e]m/n*
arrogance [e]m/n
arrogant [e]m/n
arrogantly [E]

arrow [O]
arsenal [u]l
arsenic [i]
arson [e]m/n
art [o]r
artery [E]
artful [u]l
artfully [E]
arthritic [i]
arthritis [i]
artichoke [O]
article [u]l
artifact [a]
artificial [u]l
artificially [E]
artillery [E]
artisan [e]m/n
artist [i]
artistic [i]
artistically [E]
artistry [E]
artsy [E]
artwork [er]
ashamed [A]m/n
ashen [e]m/n
ashore [O]r
ashtray [A]
aside [I]
asinine [I]m/n
ask [a]
askew [oo]
asking [E]m/n
asking [e]m/n*
asleep [E]
asparagus [e]
aspect [e]
aspen [e]m/n
asphalt [o]l
aspire [I]r
aspirin [i]m/n
aspiring [E]m/n
aspiring [e]m/n*
ass [a]
assassin [i]m/n
assassinate [A]

assassinated [e]
assassinating [E]m/n
assassinating [e]m/n*
assassination [u]m/n
assault [o]l
assaulted [e]
assaulting [E]m/n
assaulting [e]m/n*
assemble [u]l
assembling [E]m/n
assembling [e]m/n*
assembly [E]
assert [er]
asserted [e]
asserting [E]m/n
asserting [e]m/n*
assertive [i]
assess [e]
assessing [E]m/n
assessing [e]m/n*
assessment [e]m/n
asset [e]
assign [I]m/n
assigning [E]m/n
assigning [e]m/n*
assignment [e]m/n
assist [i]
assistance [e]m/n
assistant [e]m/n
assisted [e]
assisting [E]m/n
assisting [e]m/n*
associate [A]
associate [e]
associated [e]
association [u]m/n
assort [O]r
assorted [e]
assorting [E]m/n
assorting [e]m/n*
assortment [e]m/n
assume [oo]m/n
assuming [E]m/n
assuming [e]m/n*
assumption [u]m/n

assurance [e]m/n
assure [er]
assuring [E]m/n
assuring [e]m/n*
asteroid [Oi]
asthma [u]
astonish [i]
astonishing [E]m/n
astonishing [e]m/n*
astonishingly [E]
astonishment [e]m/n
astound [ow]m/n
astounded [e]
astounding [E]m/n
astounding [e]m/n*
astoundingly [E]
astral [u]l
astray [A]
astride [I]
astringent [e]m/n
astrologer [er]
astrology [E]
astronaut [o]
astronomer [er]
astronomic [i]
astronomical [u]l
astronomically [E]
astronomy [E]
astute [oo]
astutely [E]
asylum [u]m/n
ate [A]
athlete [E]
athletic [i]
athletically [E]
atmosphere [E]r
atmospheric [i]
atom [u]m/n
atomic [i]
atone [O]m/n
atonement [e]m/n
atoning [E]m/n
atoning [e]m/n*
atop [o]
atrocious [e]

atrociously [E]
atrocity [E]
attach [a]
attaching [E]m/n
attaching [e]m/n*
attachment [e]m/n
attack [a]
attacker [er]
attacking [E]m/n
attacking [e]m/n*
attain [A]m/n
attainable [u]l
attaining [E]m/n
attaining [e]m/n*
attempt [e]m/n
attempted [e]
attempting [E]m/n
attempting [e]m/n*
attend [e]m/n
attendance [e]m/n
attendant [e]m/n
attended [e]
attendee [E]
attending [E]m/n
attending [e]m/n*
attention [u]m/n
attentive [i]
attentively [E]
attic [i]
attire [I]r
attitude [oo]
attorney [E]
attract [a]
attracted [e]
attracting [E]m/n
attracting [e]m/n*
attraction [u]m/n
attractive [i]
attractively [E]
attribute [oo]
attributed [e]
attributing [E]m/n
attributing [e]m/n*
atypical [u]l
auburn [er]m/n

auction [u]m/n
auctioning [E]m/n
auctioning [e]m/n*
audacity [E]
audible [u]l
audibly [E]
audience [e]m/n
audio [O]
audiovisual [u]l
audit [i]
audited [e]
auditing [E]m/n
auditing [e]m/n*
audition [u]m/n
auditorium [u]m/n
aught [o]
augment [e]m/n
augmentation [u]m/n
augmenting [E]m/n
augmenting [e]m/n*
August [e]
aunt [a]m/n
aunt [o]m/n
aura [u]
authentic [i]
authentically [E]
authenticate [A]
authenticated [e]
authenticity [E]
author [er]
authoring [E]m/n
authoring [e]m/n*
authority [E]
authorization [u]m/n
authorize [I]
authorizing [E]m/n

authorizing [e]m/n*
autism [e]m/n
autistic [i]
auto [O]
autobiography [E]
autograph [a]
autographing [E]m/n
autographing [e]m/n*
automate [A]
automated [e]
automatic [i]
automatically [E]
automating [E]m/n
automating [e]m/n*
automotive [i]
autumn [u]m/n
auxiliary [E]
avail [A]l
availability [E]
available [u]l
avalanche [a]m/n
avenge [e]m/n
avenger [er]
avenging [E]m/n
avenging [e]m/n*
avenue [oo]
avert [er]
averted [e]
averting [E]m/n
averting [e]m/n*
aviation [u]m/n
aviator [er]
avid [i]
avocado [O]
avoid [Oi]
avoidable [u]l

avoided [e]
avoiding [E]m/n
avoiding [e]m/n*
await [A]
awaited [e]
awaiting [E]m/n
awaiting [e]m/n*
awake [A]
awaken [e]m/n
awakening [E]m/n
awakening [e]m/n*
award [O]r
awarded [e]
awarding [E]m/n
awarding [e]m/n*
aware [e]r
away [A]
awe [o]
awesome [u]m/n
awestruck [u]
awful [u]l
awfully [E]
awhile [I]l
awkward [er]
awkwardly [E]
awning [E]m/n
awning [e]m/n*
awoke [O]
awoken [e]m/n
awry [I]
ax [a]
axle [u]l
aye [I]
azalea [u]

B

baboon [oo]m/n
baby [E]
baby [e]*
babysitter [er]

bachelor [er]
bachelorette [e]
back [a]
backache [A]

backbone [O]m/n
backbreaking [E]m/n
backbreaking [e]m/n*
backdoor [O]r

backdrop [o]
backer [er]
backfield [E]l
backfire [I]r
background [ow]m/n
backhand [a]m/n
backhanded [e]
backing [E]m/n
backing [e]m/n*
backlash [a]
backlog [o]
backpack [a]
backpacker [er]
backpacking [E]m/n
backpacking [e]m/n*
backrest [e]
backseat [E]
backside [I]
backslide [I]
backspace [A]
backstage [A]
backstairs [e]r
backstitch [i]
backstop [o]
backstretch [e]
backstroke [O]
backswing [E]m/n
backswing [e]m/n*
backtrack [a]
backup [u]
backward [er]
backwash [o]
backyard [o]r
bacon [e]m/n
bacteria [u]
bacterial [u]l
bad [a]
badge [a]
badger [er]
badly [E]
badly [e]*
baffle [u]l
baffling [E]m/n
baffling [e]m/n*
bag [a]

bagel [u]l
baggage [e]
bagger [er]
baggy [E]
bail [A]l
bailing [E]m/n
bailing [e]m/n*
bailout [ow]
bait [A]
baited [e]
baiting [E]m/n
baiting [e]m/n*
bake [A]
baker [er]
bakery [E]
baking [E]m/n
baking [e]m/n*
balance [e]m/n
balancing [E]m/n
balancing [e]m/n*
balcony [E]
bald [o]l
balding [E]m/n
balding [e]m/n*
bale [A]l
balk [o]l
balking [E]m/n
ball [o]l
ballad [e]
ballerina [u]
ballet [A]
balling [E]m/n
balling [e]m/n*
ballistic [i]
balloon [oo]m/n
ballot [e]
ballpark [o]r
ballpoint [Oi]m/n
ballroom [oo]m/n
balmy [E]
baloney [E]
bamboo [oo]
ban [a]m/n
banana [u]
band [a]m/n

bandage [e]
bandana [u]
banded [e]
banding [E]m/n
banding [e]m/n*
bandit [i]
bandstand [a]m/n
bandwagon [e]m/n
bandwidth [i]
bang [a]ng/k
banging [E]m/n
banging [e]m/n*
bangle [u]l
banish [i]
banishing [E]m/n
banishing [e]m/n*
banister [er]
banjo [O]
bank [a]ng/k
bankcard [o]r
banker [er]
banking [E]m/n
banking [e]m/n*
bankroll [O]l
bankrolling [E]m/n
bankrolling [e]m/n*
bankrupt [u]
bankruptcy [E]
bankrupted [e]
bankrupting [E]m/n
bankrupting [e]m/n*
banner [er]
banning [E]m/n
banning [e]m/n*
banquet [e]
banter [er]
bantering [E]m/n
bantering [e]m/n*
banzai [I]
baptism [e]m/n
baptize [I]
baptizing [E]m/n
baptizing [e]m/n*
bar [o]r
barbarian [e]m/n

barbaric [i]
barbecue [oo]
barbell [e]l
barber [er]
barbershop [o]
bare [e]r
bareback [a]
barefoot [oo/]
barely [E]
barely [e]*
bargain [i]m/n
baritone [O]m/n
bark [o]r
barking [E]m/n
barking [e]m/n*
barley [E]
barn [o]r
barnacle [u]l
barnyard [o]r
barrack [e]
barracuda [u]
barrel [u]l
barreling [E]m/n
barreling [e]m/n*
barren [e]m/n
barricade [A]
barricaded [e]
barricading [E]m/n
barricading [e]m/n*
barrier [er]
barring [E]m/n
barring [e]m/n*
barstool [oo]l
bartender [er]
barter [er]
bartering [E]m/n
bartering [e]m/n*
base [A]
baseball [o]l
baseboard [O]r
baseline [I]m/n
basement [e]m/n
bashful [u]l
basic [i]
basically [E]

basil [u]l
basin [i]m/n
basinet [e]
basis [i]
bask [a]
basket [e]
basketball [o]l
basking [E]m/n
basking [e]m/n*
bass [A]
bass [a]
bassinet [e]
bat [a]
batch [a]
bath [a]
bathe [A]
bathing [E]m/n
bathing [e]m/n*
bathrobe [O]
bathroom [oo]m/n
bathtub [u]
baton [o]m/n
batted [e]
batter [er]
battering [E]m/n
battering [e]m/n*
battery [E]
batting [E]m/n
batting [e]m/n*
battle [u]l
battlefield [E]l
batty [E]
bawl [o]l
bawling [E]m/n
bawling [e]m/n*
bay [A]
bayberry [E]
bazaar [o]r
be [E]
beach [E]
beachcomber [er]
beachfront [u]m/n
beacon [e]m/n
bead [E]
beaded [e]

beading [E]m/n
beading [e]m/n*
beadwork [er]
beady [E]
beagle [u]l
beaker [er]
beam [E]m/n
beaming [E]m/n
beaming [e]m/n*
bean [E]m/n
beanbag [a]
beanie [E]
beanstalk [o]
bear [e]r
bearable [u]l
beard [E]r
bearded [e]
bearing [E]m/n
bearing [e]m/n*
beast [E]
beat [E]
beaten [e]m/n
beating [E]m/n
beating [e]m/n*
beau [O]
beautician [u]m/n
beautiful [u]l
beautifully [E]
beautify [I]
beauty [E]
beaver [er]
became [A]m/n
because [u]
beckon [e]m/n
beckoning [E]m/n
beckoning [e]m/n*
become [u]m/n
becoming [E]m/n
becoming [e]m/n*
bed [e]
bedazzle [u]l
bedazzling [E]m/n
bedazzling [e]m/n*
bedbug [u]
bedding [E]m/n

bedding [e]m/n*
bedfellow [O]
bedridden [e]m/n
bedroom [oo]m/n
bedside [I]
bedspread [e]
bedtime [I]m/n
bee [E]
beef [E]
beefing [E]m/n
beefing [e]m/n*
beehive [I]
beeline [I]m/n
been [e]m/n
beep [E]
beeper [er]
beeping [E]m/n
beeping [e]m/n*
beer [E]r
beeswax [a]
beet [E]
beetle [u]l
before [O]r
beforehand [a]m/n
befriend [e]m/n
befriended [e]
befriending [E]m/n
befriending [e]m/n*
beg [e]
began [a]m/n
beggar [er]
begging [E]m/n
begging [e]m/n*
begin [i]m/n
beginner [er]
beginning [E]m/n
beginning [e]m/n*
begrudge [u]
begrudging [E]m/n
begrudging [e]m/n*
begun [u]m/n
behalf [a]
behave [A]
behaving [E]m/n
behaving [e]m/n*

behavior [er]
behind [I]m/n
behold [O]
beholding [E]m/n
beholding [e]m/n*
behoove [oo]
behooving [E]m/n
behooving [e]m/n*
beige [A]
being [E]m/n
being [e]m/n*
belated [e]
belief [E]
believable [u]l
believe [E]
believer [er]
believing [E]m/n
believing [e]m/n*
belittle [u]l
belittling [E]m/n
belittling [e]m/n*
bell [e]l
bellboy [Oi]
belle [e]l
bellhop [o]
belligerent [e]m/n
belligerently [E]
bellman [e]m/n
belly [E]
bellyache [A]
belong [o]m/n
belonging [E]m/n
belonging [e]m/n*
beloved [e]
below [O]
belt [e]l
belted [e]
belting [E]m/n
belting [e]m/n*
beltway [A]
bench [e]m/n
benching [E]m/n
benching [e]m/n*
benchmark [o]r
bend [e]m/n

bended [e]
bending [E]m/n
bending [e]m/n*
beneath [E]
beneficial [u]l
beneficiary [E]
benefit [i]
benefitted [e]
benefitting [E]m/n
benefitting [e]m/n*
benign [I]m/n
bent [e]m/n
bereavement [e]m/n
berry [E]
berserk [er]
beside [I]
best [e]
bestow [O]
bestowing [E]m/n
bestowing [e]m/n*
bestseller [er]
bet [e]
betray [A]
betrayal [u]l
betraying [E]m/n
betraying [e]m/n*
better [er]
betting [E]m/n
betting [e]m/n*
bettor [er]
between [E]m/n
bevel [u]l
beveling [E]m/n
beveling [e]m/n*
beverage [e]
beware [e]r
bewilder [er]
bewildering [E]m/n
bewildering [e]m/n*
bewitch [i]
bewitching [E]m/n
bewitching [e]m/n*
beyond [o]m/n
biannual [u]l
bias [e]

bib [i]
bible [u]l
biblical [u]l
biceps [e]
bicker [er]
bicycle [u]l
bid [i]
bidding [E]m/n
bidding [e]m/n*
bifocal [u]l
big [i]
bigamy [E]
bigger [er]
biggest [e]
bigot [e]
bike [I]
biker [er]
biking [E]m/n
biking [e]m/n*
bikini [E]
bilingual [u]l
bill [i]l
billboard [O]r
billfold [O]l
billiard [er]
billion [u]m/n
billionaire [e]r
bimonthly [E]
bin [i]m/n
bind [I]m/n
binder [er]
binding [E]m/n
binding [e]m/n*
binge [i]m/n
bingo [O]
binocular [er]
biodegradable [u]l
biography [E]
biology [E]
biosphere [E]r
bipartisan [e]m/n
bipolar [er]
bird [er]
birdbath [a]
birdbrain [A]m/n

birdhouse [ow]
birdie [E]
birdseed [E]
birth [er]
birthday [A]
birthing [E]m/n
birthing [e]m/n*
birthmark [o]r
birthplace [A]
birthstone [O]m/n
biscuit [i]
bishop [e]
bistro [O]
bit [i]
bitch [i]
bitchy [E]
bite [I]
biting [E]m/n
biting [e]m/n*
bitten [e]m/n
bitter [er]
bitterness [e]
bittersweet [E]
bitty [E]
biweekly [E]
bizarre [o]r
blab [a]
blabbing [E]m/n
blabbing [e]m/n*
black [a]
blackball [o]l
blackberry [E]
blackboard [O]r
blacken [e]m/n
blackjack [a]
blackmail [A]l
blackout [ow]
blacktop [o]
bladder [er]
blade [A]
blah [o]
blame [A]m/n
blaming [E]m/n
blaming [e]m/n*
bland [a]m/n

blank [a]ng/k
blanket [e]
blarney [E]
blasé [A]
blast [a]
blasted [e]
blasting [E]m/n
blasting [e]m/n*
blastoff [o]
blaze [A]
blazer [er]
blazing [E]m/n
blazing [e]m/n*
bleach [E]
bleacher [er]
bleaching [E]m/n
bleaching [e]m/n*
bled [e]
bleed [E]
bleeding [E]m/n
bleeding [e]m/n*
blemish [i]
blend [e]m/n
blended [e]
blender [er]
blending [E]m/n
blending [e]m/n*
bless [e]
blessing [E]m/n
blessing [e]m/n*
blew [oo]
blind [I]m/n
blinded [e]
blinder [er]
blindfold [O]l
blinding [E]m/n
blinding [e]m/n*
blindly [E]
blink [E]m/n
blinker [er]
blinking [E]m/n
blinking [e]m/n*
bliss [i]
blissful [u]l
blissfully [E]

blister [er]
blistering [E]m/n
blistering [e]m/n*
blizzard [er]
bloat [O]
bloated [e]
bloating [E]m/n
bloating [e]m/n*
blob [o]
block [o]
blockade [A]
blockbuster [er]
blocker [er]
blockhead [e]
blocking [E]m/n
blocking [e]m/n*
blond [o]m/n
blood [u]
bloodcurdling [E]m/n
bloodcurdling [e]m/n*
bloodshed [e]
bloodshot [o]
bloodstain [A]m/n
bloodsucker [er]
bloodthirsty [E]
bloody [E]
bloom [oo]m/n
bloomer [er]
blooming [E]m/n
blooming [e]m/n*
blooper [er]
blossom [u]m/n
blossoming [E]m/n
blossoming [e]m/n*
blot [o]
blotch [o]
blotchy [E]
blotted [e]
blotter [er]
blotting [E]m/n
blotting [e]m/n*
blouse [ow]
blow [O]
blower [er]
blowing [E]m/n

blowing [e]m/n*
blown [O]m/n
blowout [ow]
blowup [u]
bludgeon [e]m/n
bludgeoning [E]m/n
bludgeoning [e]m/n*
blue [oo]
blueberry [E]
bluebird [er]
bluegrass [a]
blueprint [i]m/n
bluer [er]
blues [oo]
bluff [u]
bluffing [E]m/n
bluffing [e]m/n*
bluish [i]
blunder [er]
blundering [E]m/n
blundering [e]m/n*
blunt [u]m/n
bluntly [E]
blur [er]
blurb [er]
blurring [E]m/n
blurring [e]m/n*
blurry [E]
blurt [er]
blurted [e]
blurting [E]m/n
blurting [e]m/n*
blush [u]
blustery [E]
board [O]r
boarded [e]
boarder [er]
boarding [E]m/n
boarding [e]m/n*
boardroom [oo]m/n
boardwalk [o]
boast [O]
boasted [e]
boasting [E]m/n
boasting [e]m/n*

boat [O]
boating [E]m/n
boating [e]m/n*
bob [o]
bobbing [E]m/n
bobbing [e]m/n*
bobsled [e]
bobsledding [E]m/n
bodice [i]
bodily [E]
body [E]
body [e]*
bogey [E]
boggle [u]l
boggling [E]m/n
boggling [e]m/n*
bogus [e]
boil [Oi]l
boiler [er]
boiling [E]m/n
boiling [e]m/n*
boisterous [e]
bold [O]l
bolder [er]
boldly [E]
bolt [O]l
bolted [e]
bolting [E]m/n
bolting [e]m/n*
bomb [o]m/n
bombard [o]r
bombarded [e]
bombarding [E]m/n
bombarding [e]m/n*
bomber [er]
bombing [E]m/n
bombing [e]m/n*
bombshell [e]l
bonanza [u]
bonbon [o]m/n
bond [o]m/n
bonded [e]
bonding [E]m/n
bonding [e]m/n*
bone [O]m/n

bonehead [e]
bonfire [I]r
bongo [O]
boniest [e]
bonnet [e]
bonsai [I]
bonus [e]
bony [E]
boo [oo]
boogie [E]
book [oo/]
bookcase [A]
bookend [e]m/n
bookie [E]
booking [E]m/n
booking [e]m/n*
bookkeeper [er]
bookkeeping [E]m/n
bookkeeping [e]m/n*
booklet [e]
bookmark [o]r
bookshelf [e]l
bookstore [O]r
bookworm [er]m/n
boom [oo]m/n
boomer [er]
boomerang [a]ng/k
booming [E]m/n
booming [e]m/n*
boondocks [o]
boost [oo]
boosted [e]
booster [er]
boosting [E]m/n
boosting [e]m/n*
boot [oo]
booted [e]
booth [oo]
bootie [E]
booting [E]m/n
booting [e]m/n*
bootleg [e]
bootlegger [er]
bootlegging [E]m/n
bootlegging [e]m/n*

booty [E]
booze [oo]
boozing [E]m/n
boozing [e]m/n*
border [er]
bordering [E]m/n
bordering [e]m/n*
borderline [I]m/n
bore [O]r
boredom [u]m/n
boring [E]m/n
boring [e]m/n*
born [O]r
borrow [O]
borrowing [E]m/n
borrowing [e]m/n*
bosom [u]m/n
boss [o]
bossiest [e]
bossing [E]m/n
bossing [e]m/n*
bossy [E]
botanic [i]
botanical [u]l
botany [E]
botch [o]
botching [E]m/n
botching [e]m/n*
both [O]
bother [er]
bothering [E]m/n
bothering [e]m/n*
bothersome [u]m/n
bottle [u]l
bottleneck [e]
bottlenecking [E]m/n
bottlenecking [e]m/n*
bottling [E]m/n
bottling [e]m/n*
bottom [u]m/n
bottomless [e]
boudoir [o]r
bought [o]
bouillon [o]m/n
boulder [er]

boulevard [o]r
bounce [ow]m/n
bouncer [er]
bounciest [e]
bouncing [E]m/n
bouncing [e]m/n*
bouncy [E]
bound [ow]m/n
boundary [E]
bounded [e]
bounding [E]m/n
bounding [e]m/n*
boundless [e]
bounty [E]
bouquet [A]
bourbon [u]m/n
boutique [E]
bow [O]
bow [ow]
bowel [ow]l
bowing [E]m/n
bowing [e]m/n*
bowl [O]l
bowler [er]
bowling [E]m/n
bowling [e]m/n*
box [o]
boxer [er]
boxing [E]m/n
boxing [e]m/n*
boy [Oi]
boycott [o]
boycotted [e]
boyfriend [e]m/n
boyish [i]
bra [o]
brace [A]
bracelet [e]
bracing [E]m/n
bracing [e]m/n*
bracket [e]
bracketing [E]m/n
brag [a]
bragger [er]
bragging [E]m/n

bragging [e]m/n*
braid [A]
braided [e]
braiding [E]m/n
braiding [e]m/n*
brain [A]m/n
brainchild [I]l
brainless [e]
brainpower [er]
brainstorm [O]r
brainstorming [E]m/n
brainstorming [e]m/n*
brainwash [o]
brainwashing [E]m/n
brainwashing [e]m/n*
brainy [E]
brake [A]
braking [E]m/n
braking [e]m/n*
bran [a]m/n
branch [a]m/n
branching [E]m/n
branching [e]m/n*
brand [a]m/n
branded [e]
branding [E]m/n
branding [e]m/n*
brandish [i]
brandy [E]
brass [a]
brassiere [E]r
brassy [E]
bratty [E]
bravado [O]
brave [A]
bravely [E]
bravery [E]
bravest [e]
bravo [O]
brawl [o]l
brawny [E]
brazen [e]m/n
brazenly [E]
breach [E]
breaching [E]m/n

breaching [e]m/n*
bread [e]
break [A]
breakable [u]l
breakdown [ow]m/n
breaker [er]
breakfast [e]
breaking [E]m/n
breaking [e]m/n*
breakneck [e]
breakout [ow]
breakthrough [oo]
breakup [u]
breast [e]
breastbone [O]m/n
breaststroke [O]
breath [e]
breathe [E]
breather [er]
breathing [E]m/n
breathing [e]m/n*
breathless [e]
breathtaking [E]m/n
breathtaking [e]m/n*
bred [e]
breed [E]
breeder [er]
breeding [E]m/n
breeding [e]m/n*
breeze [E]
breezeway [A]
breezing [E]m/n
breezing [e]m/n*
breezy [E]
brethren [e]m/n
brew [oo]
brewery [E]
brewing [E]m/n
brewing [e]m/n*
bribe [I]
bribery [E]
bribing [E]m/n
bribing [e]m/n*
brick [i]
brickyard [o]r

bridal [u]l
bride [I]
bridegroom [oo]m/n
bridesmaid [A]
bridge [i]
bridging [E]m/n
bridging [e]m/n*
bridle [u]l
brief [E]
briefcase [A]
briefing [E]m/n
briefing [e]m/n*
briefly [E]
brigade [A]
bright [I]
brighten [e]m/n
brightener [er]
brightening [E]m/n
brightening [e]m/n*
brighter [er]
brightest [e]
brightly [E]
brightness [e]
brilliance [e]m/n
brilliant [e]m/n
brilliantly [E]
brim [i]m/n
brimming [E]m/n
brimming [e]m/n*
brindle [u]l
bring [E]m/n
bringing [E]m/n
bringing [e]m/n*
brink [E]m/n
brisk [i]
briskly [E]
brittle [u]l
broach [O]
broaching [E]m/n
broaching [e]m/n*
broad [o]
broadband [a]m/n
broadcast [a]
broadcasted [e]
broadcaster [er]

broadcasting [E]m/n
broadcasting [e]m/n*
broaden [e]m/n
broadening [E]m/n
broadening [e]m/n*
broader [er]
broadside [I]
brocade [A]
broccoli [E]
brochure [er]
broil [Oi]l
broiler [er]
broiling [E]m/n
broiling [e]m/n*
broke [O]
broken [e]m/n
broker [er]
brokerage [e]
bronchial [u]l
bronchitis [i]
bronco [O]
bronze [o]m/n
bronzing [E]m/n
bronzing [e]m/n*
brooch [O]
brood [oo]
brooded [e]
brooding [E]m/n
brooding [e]m/n*
brook [oo/]
broom [oo]m/n
broomstick [i]
broth [o]
brother [er]
brother [u]*
brotherhood [oo/]
brotherly [E]
brought [o]
brow [ow]
brown [ow]m/n
brownie [E]
brownnose [O]
brownnosing [E]m/n
brownnosing [e]m/n*
brownstone [O]m/n

browse [ow]
browser [er]
browsing [E]m/n
browsing [e]m/n*
bruise [oo]
bruiser [er]
bruising [E]m/n
bruising [e]m/n*
brunch [u]m/n
brunette [e]
brunt [u]m/n
brush [u]
brushing [E]m/n
brushing [e]m/n*
brushwork [er]
brutal [u]l
brutality [E]
brutalize [I]
brutally [E]
brute [oo]
bubble [u]l
bubbler [er]
bubbling [E]m/n
bubbling [e]m/n*
buck [u]
bucket [e]
bucking [E]m/n
bucking [e]m/n*
buckle [u]l
buckshot [o]
buckwheat [E]
bud [u]
budded [e]
budding [E]m/n
budding [e]m/n*
buddy [E]
budge [u]
budget [e]
budgetary [E]
budgeting [E]m/n
budgeting [e]m/n*
buff [u]
buffalo [O]
buffer [er]
buffering [E]m/n

buffering [e]m/n*
buffet [A]
buffing [E]m/n
buffing [e]m/n*
buffoon [oo]m/n
bug [u]
bugger [er]
bugging [E]m/n
bugging [e]m/n*
buggy [E]
bugle [u]l
build [i]l
builder [er]
building [E]m/n
building [e]m/n*
buildup [u]
built [i]l
bulge [u]l
bulging [E]m/n
bulging [e]m/n*
bulk [u]l
bulky [E]
bull [oo]l
bulldog [o]
bulldoze [O]
bulldozer [er]
bulldozing [E]m/n
bulldozing [e]m/n*
bullet [e]
bulletin [i]m/n
bulletproof [oo]
bulletproofing [E]m/n
bulletproofing [e]m/n*
bullfight [I]
bullfighter [er]
bullfighting [E]m/n
bullfighting [e]m/n*
bullfrog [o]
bullhorn [O]r
bullion [u]m/n
bully [E]
bullying [E]m/n
bullying [e]m/n*
bum [u]m/n
bumblebee [E]

bummer [er]
bumming [E]m/n
bumming [e]m/n*
bump [u]m/n
bumper [er]
bumping [E]m/n
bumping [e]m/n*
bumpkin [i]m/n
bumpy [E]
bun [u]m/n
bunch [u]m/n
bunching [E]m/n
bunching [e]m/n*
bundle [u]l
bungalow [O]
bungee [E]
bunk [u]m/n
bunker [er]
bunking [E]m/n
bunking [e]m/n*
bunny [E]
buoy [E]
buoyant [e]m/n
burden [e]m/n
burdening [E]m/n
burdening [e]m/n*
burdensome [u]m/n
bureau [O]
bureaucracy [E]
bureaucrat [a]
burger [er]
burglar [er]
burglarize [I]
burglarizing [E]m/n
burglarizing [e]m/n*
burglarproof [oo]

burglary [E]
burgundy [E]
burial [u]l
burlap [a]
burlesque [e]
burn [er]m/n
burner [er]
burning [E]m/n
burning [e]m/n*
burnout [ow]
burp [er]
burping [E]m/n
burping [e]m/n*
burrito [O]
burrow [O]
burrowing [E]m/n
burrowing [e]m/n*
burst [er]
bursting [E]m/n
bursting [e]m/n*
bury [E]
bus [u]
busboy [Oi]
bush [oo/]
bushel [u]l
bushy [E]
busily [E]
business [e]
businessman [a]m/n
businesswoman [e]m/n
bust [u]
busted [e]
buster [er]
busting [E]m/n
busting [e]m/n*
bustle [u]l

bustling [E]m/n
bustling [e]m/n*
busty [E]
busy [E]
busybody [E]
but [u]
butane [A]m/n
butcher [er]
butler [er]
butt [u]
butter [er]
butterfly [I]
buttermilk [i]l
butterscotch [o]
buttery [E]
button [e]m/n
buttonhole [O]l
buxom [u]m/n
buy [I]
buyer [er]
buying [E]m/n
buying [e]m/n*
buzz [u]
buzzer [er]
buzzing [E]m/n
buzzing [e]m/n*
buzzword [er]
bye [I]
bygone [o]m/n
bylaw [o]
byline [I]m/n
bypass [a]
bypassing [E]m/n
bypassing [e]m/n*
bystander [er]
byte [I]

C

cab [a]
cabana [u]
cabaret [A]
cabbage [e]

cabby [E]
cabdriver [er]
cabin [i]m/n
cabinet [e]

cable [u]l
caboose [oo]
cache [a]
cacti [I]

cactus [e]
cad [a]
cadaver [er]
caddy [E]
cadet [e]
café [A]
cafeteria [u]
caffeine [E]m/n
cage [A]
cagey [E]
cake [A]
calamity [E]
calcification [u]m/n
calcify [I]
calcifying [E]m/n
calcifying [e]m/n*
calcium [u]m/n
calculate [A]
calculated [e]
calculating [E]m/n
calculating [e]m/n*
calculation [u]m/n
calculator [er]
calendar [er]
calf [a]
caliber [er]
calibrate [A]
calibrated [e]
calibrating [E]m/n
calibrating [e]m/n*
calibration [u]m/n
calico [O]
call [o]l
callback [a]
caller [er]
calligraphy [E]
calling [E]m/n
calling [e]m/n*
callous [e]
calm [o]l
calmer [er]
calmly [E]
calmness [e]
caloric [i]
calorie [E]

camaraderie [E]
came [A]m/n
camel [u]l
cameo [O]
camera [u]
camisole [O]l
camouflage [o]
camouflaging [E]m/n
camouflaging [e]m/n*
camp [a]m/n
campaign [A]m/n
campaigning [E]m/n
campaigning [e]m/n*
camper [er]
campground [ow]m/n
camping [E]m/n
camping [e]m/n*
campsite [I]
campus [e]
can [a]m/n
canal [a]l
canary [E]
cancel [u]l
cancellation [u]m/n
canceling [E]m/n
canceling [e]m/n*
cancer [er]
candelabra [u]
candid [i]
candidate [A]
candidly [E]
candle [u]l
candlelight [I]
candlestick [i]
candor [er]
candy [E]
cane [A]m/n
canine [I]m/n
canister [er]
canker [er]
cannery [E]
canning [E]m/n
canning [e]m/n*
cannon [e]m/n
cannot [o]

canoe [oo]
canoeing [E]m/n
canoeing [e]m/n*
canon [e]m/n
canopy [E]
cantaloupe [O]
cantankerous [e]
canteen [E]m/n
canvas [e]
canvassing [E]m/n
canvassing [e]m/n*
canyon [u]m/n
cap [a]
capability [E]
capable [u]l
capacity [E]
cape [A]
caper [er]
capital [u]l
capitalism [e]m/n
capitalist [i]
capitalize [I]
capitalizing [E]m/n
capitalizing [e]m/n*
capitol [u]l
capping [E]m/n
capping [e]m/n*
cappuccino [O]
capsize [I]
capsizing [E]m/n
capsizing [e]m/n*
capsule [oo]l
captain [e]m/n
caption [u]m/n
captivate [A]
captivated [e]
captivating [E]m/n
captivating [e]m/n*
captive [i]
captivity [E]
captor [er]
capture [er]
capturing [E]m/n
capturing [e]m/n*
car [o]r

carafe [a]
caramel [e]l
caramelize [l]
caramelizing [E]m/n
caramelizing [e]m/n*
caravan [a]m/n
carbohydrate [A]
carbon [e]m/n
carbonated [e]
carburetor [er]
card [o]r
cardboard [O]r
carded [e]
cardiac [a]
cardigan [a]m/n
cardinal [u]l
cardiologist [i]
cardiology [E]
care [e]r
careen [E]m/n
careening [E]m/n
careening [e]m/n*
career [E]r
carefree [E]
careful [u]l
carefully [E]
caregiver [er]
careless [e]
carelessly [E]
caress [e]
caressing [E]m/n
caressing [e]m/n*
caretaker [er]
cargo [O]
caricature [er]
caring [E]m/n
caring [e]m/n*
carload [O]
carnation [u]m/n
carnival [u]l
carob [e]
carol [u]l
caroler [er]
caroling [E]m/n
caroling [e]m/n*

carousel [e]l
carpenter [er]
carpentry [E]
carpet [e]
carpeting [E]m/n
carpeting [e]m/n*
carpool [oo]l
carpooling [E]m/n
carpooling [e]m/n*
carport [O]r
carriage [e]
carrier [er]
carrot [e]
carry [E]
carrying [E]m/n
carrying [e]m/n*
carsick [i]
cart [o]r
carted [e]
cartel [e]l
carting [E]m/n
carting [e]m/n*
carton [e]m/n
cartoon [oo]m/n
cartridge [i]
carve [o]r
carver [er]
carving [E]m/n
carving [e]m/n*
carwash [o]
cascade [A]
cascaded [e]
cascading [E]m/n
cascading [e]m/n*
case [A]
caseload [O]
cash [a]
cashew [oo]
cashier [E]r
cashing [E]m/n
cashing [e]m/n*
cashmere [E]r
casing [E]m/n
casing [e]m/n*
casino [O]

casket [e]
casserole [O]l
cassette [e]
cast [a]
castaway [A]
casting [E]m/n
casting [e]m/n*
castle [u]l
castoff [o]
castrate [A]
castrated [e]
castrating [E]m/n
castrating [e]m/n*
casual [u]l
casually [E]
casualty [E]
cat [a]
catalog [o]
cataloging [E]m/n
cataloging [e]m/n*
cataract [a]
catastrophe [E]
catch [a]
catchall [o]l
catcher [er]
catching [E]m/n
catching [e]m/n*
catchy [E]
categorize [l]
categorizing [E]m/n
categorizing [e]m/n*
category [E]
cater [er]
catering [E]m/n
catering [e]m/n*
caterpillar [er]
catfish [i]
cathedral [u]l
catnap [a]
catnip [i]
cattail [A]l
cattle [u]l
catty [E]
caught [o]
cauldron [e]m/n

cauliflower [er]
caulk [o]l
caulking [E]m/n
caulking [e]m/n*
cause [o]
causeway [A]
causing [E]m/n
causing [e]m/n*
caustic [i]
caution [u]m/n
cautionary [E]
cautioning [E]m/n
cautioning [e]m/n*
cautious [e]
cautiously [E]
cavalier [E]r
cavalry [E]
cave [A]
cavern [er]m/n
caviar [o]r
caving [E]m/n
caving [e]m/n*
cavity [E]
cavort [O]r
cavorted [e]
cavorting [E]m/n
cavorting [e]m/n*
cayenne [e]m/n
cease [E]
ceasing [E]m/n
ceasing [e]m/n*
cedar [er]
ceiling [E]m/n
ceiling [e]m/n*
celebrate [A]
celebrated [e]
celebrating [E]m/n
celebrating [e]m/n*
celebration [u]m/n
celebrity [E]
celery [E]
celestial [u]l
celibate [e]
cell [e]l
cellar [er]

cellblock [o]
cello [O]
cellophane [A]m/n
cellular [er]
cellulite [I]
cement [e]m/n
cemented [e]
cementing [E]m/n
cementing [e]m/n*
cemetery [E]
censor [er]
censoring [E]m/n
censoring [e]m/n*
censorship [i]
census [e]
cent [e]m/n
centennial [u]l
center [er]
centering [E]m/n
centering [e]m/n*
centerpiece [E]
centimeter [er]
centipede [E]
central [u]l
centralize [I]
centralizing [E]m/n
centralizing [e]m/n*
century [E]
ceramic [i]
cereal [u]l
cerebral [u]l
ceremonial [u]l
ceremony [E]
certain [e]m/n
certainly [E]
certainty [E]
certificate [e]
certification [u]m/n
certify [I]
cervix [i]
cesspool [oo]l
chain [A]m/n
chaining [E]m/n
chaining [e]m/n*
chair [e]r

chairman [e]m/n
chalet [A]
chalk [o]
chalky [E]
challenge [e]m/n
challenger [er]
challenging [E]m/n
challenging [e]m/n*
chamber [er]
chambray [A]
chameleon [e]m/n
chamois [E]
champ [a]m/n
champagne [A]m/n
champion [e]m/n
championship [i]
chance [a]m/n
change [A]m/n
changing [E]m/n
changing [e]m/n*
channel [u]l
channeling [E]m/n
channeling [e]m/n*
chant [a]m/n
chanted [e]
chanting [E]m/n
chanting [e]m/n*
chaos [o]
chaotic [i]
chaotically [E]
chap [a]
chapel [u]l
chaperon [O]m/n
chaperoning [E]m/n
chaperoning [e]m/n*
chaplain [i]m/n
chapter [er]
character [er]
characteristic [i]
characterize [I]
charade [A]
charcoal [O]l
charge [o]r
charger [er]
charging [E]m/n

charging [e]m/n*
charisma [u]
charismatic [i]
charitable [u]l
charitably [E]
charity [E]
charm [o]r
charmer [er]
charming [E]m/n
charming [e]m/n*
chart [o]r
charted [e]
charter [er]
chartering [E]m/n
chartering [e]m/n*
charting [E]m/n
charting [e]m/n*
chase [A]
chaser [er]
chasing [E]m/n
chasing [e]m/n*
chassis [E]
chastise [I]
chateau [O]
chatter [er]
chatterbox [o]
chattering [E]m/n
chattering [e]m/n*
chatty [E]
chauffeur [er]
chauvinism [e]m/n
chauvinist [i]
chauvinistic [i]
cheap [E]
cheapen [e]m/n
cheapening [E]m/n
cheapening [e]m/n*
cheaper [er]
cheaply [E]
cheapskate [A]
cheat [E]
cheated [e]
cheater [er]
cheating [E]m/n
cheating [e]m/n*

check [e]
checkbook [oo/]
checker [er]
checking [E]m/n
checking [e]m/n*
checklist [i]
checkmate [A]
checkout [ow]
checkpoint [Oi]m/n
checkup [u]
cheddar [er]
cheek [E]
cheekbone [O]m/n
cheeky [E]
cheer [E]r
cheerful [u]l
cheerfully [E]
cheering [E]m/n
cheering [e]m/n*
cheery [E]
cheese [E]
cheeseburger [er]
cheesecake [A]
cheesecloth [o]
cheesy [E]
chef [e]
chemical [u]l
chemist [i]
chemistry [E]
chenille [i]l
cherish [i]
cherishing [E]m/n
cherishing [e]m/n*
cherry [E]
cherub [u]
chess [e]
chestnut [u]
chew [oo]
chewing [E]m/n
chewing [e]m/n*
chewy [E]
chick [i]
chicken [e]m/n
chickpea [E]
chief [E]

chiefly [E]
chiffon [o]m/n
child [I]l
childbearing [E]m/n
childbearing [e]m/n*
childbirth [er]
childhood [oo/]
childish [i]
childlike [I]
childproof [oo]
childproofing [E]m/n
childproofing [e]m/n*
children [e]m/n
chili [E]
chill [i]l
chilling [E]m/n
chilling [e]m/n*
chime [I]m/n
chiming [E]m/n
chiming [e]m/n*
chimney [E]
chimpanzee [E]
chin [i]m/n
chintzy [E]
chip [i]
chipmunk [u]m/n
chipping [E]m/n
chipping [e]m/n*
chiropractic [i]
chiropractor [er]
chirp [er]
chirping [E]m/n
chirping [e]m/n*
chisel [u]l
chiseling [E]m/n
chiseling [e]m/n*
chitchat [a]
chloride [I]
chlorine [E]m/n
chock [o]
chocolate [e]
choice [Oi]
choicest [e]
choir [I]r
choke [O]

choker [er]
choking [E]m/n
choking [e]m/n*
cholesterol [o]l
choose [oo]
chooser [er]
choosing [E]m/n
choosing [e]m/n*
choosy [E]
chop [o]
chopper [er]
chopping [E]m/n
chopping [e]m/n*
choppy [E]
chopstick [i]
choral [u]l
chord [O]r
chore [O]r
choreographer [er]
choreography [E]
chorus [e]
chose [O]
chosen [e]m/n
chow [ow]
chowder [er]
christen [e]m/n
Christian [e]m/n
Christmas [e]
chromatic [i]
chrome [O]m/n
chronic [i]
chronicle [u]l
chubby [E]
chuck [u]
chuckle [u]l
chuckling [E]m/n
chuckling [e]m/n*
chug [u]
chugging [E]m/n
chugging [e]m/n*
chum [u]m/n
chummy [E]
chunk [u]m/n
chunky [E]
church [er]

churn [er]m/n
churning [E]m/n
churning [e]m/n*
chute [oo]
chutney [E]
cider [er]
cigar [o]r
cigarette [e]
cinch [i]m/n
cinching [E]m/n
cinching [e]m/n*
cinder [er]
cinema [u]
cinematic [i]
cinematography [E]
cinnamon [u]m/n
circle [u]l
circling [E]m/n
circling [e]m/n*
circuit [i]
circuiting [E]m/n
circuiting [e]m/n*
circuitry [E]
circular [er]
circulate [A]
circulated [e]
circulating [E]m/n
circulating [e]m/n*
circulation [u]m/n
circulatory [E]
circumference [e]m/n
circumstance [a]m/n
circumstantial [u]l
circus [e]
citation [u]m/n
cite [I]
cited [e]
citizen [e]m/n
citizenship [i]
citrus [e]
city [E]
civic [i]
civil [u]l
civilian [e]m/n
civilization [u]m/n

civilize [l]
civilizing [E]m/n
civilizing [e]m/n*
clack [a]
clacking [E]m/n
clacking [e]m/n*
claim [A]m/n
claiming [E]m/n
claiming [e]m/n*
clairvoyance [e]m/n
clairvoyant [e]m/n
clam [a]m/n
clammy [E]
clamp [a]m/n
clamping [E]m/n
clamping [e]m/n*
clamshell [e]l
clan [a]m/n
clang [a]ng/k
clanging [E]m/n
clanging [e]m/n*
clap [a]
clapping [E]m/n
clapping [e]m/n*
clarification [u]m/n
clarify [I]
clarinet [e]
clarity [E]
clash [a]
clashing [E]m/n
clashing [e]m/n*
clasp [a]
clasping [E]m/n
clasping [e]m/n*
class [a]
classic [i]
classical [u]l
classification [u]m/n
classify [I]
classmate [A]
classroom [oo]m/n
classy [E]
clatter [er]
clattering [E]m/n
clattering [e]m/n*

clause [o]
claustrophobia [u]
claustrophobic [i]
claw [o]
clawing [E]m/n
clawing [e]m/n*
clay [A]
clean [E]m/n
cleaner [er]
cleanest [e]
cleaning [E]m/n
cleaning [e]m/n*
cleanliness [e]
cleanse [e]m/n
cleanser [er]
cleansing [E]m/n
cleansing [e]m/n*
cleanup [u]
clear [E]r
clearance [e]m/n
clearer [er]
clearest [e]
clearing [E]m/n
clearing [e]m/n*
clearly [E]
cleavage [e]
cleaver [er]
clergy [E]
clerical [u]l
clerk [er]
clever [er]
cliché [A]
click [i]
clicker [er]
clicking [E]m/n
clicking [e]m/n*
client [e]m/n
clientele [e]l
cliff [i]
cliffhanger [er]
climactic [i]
climate [e]
climax [a]
climb [I]m/n
climber [er]

climbing [E]m/n
climbing [e]m/n*
clinch [i]m/n
clincher [er]
cling [E]m/n
clinging [E]m/n
clinging [e]m/n*
clingy [E]
clinic [i]
clinical [u]l
clinically [E]
clip [i]
clipper [er]
clipping [E]m/n
clipping [e]m/n*
clique [i]
cloak [O]
cloaking [E]m/n
cloaking [e]m/n*
clobber [er]
clock [o]
clocking [E]m/n
clocking [e]m/n*
clockwise [I]
clockwork [er]
clog [o]
clogging [E]m/n
clogging [e]m/n*
clone [O]m/n
cloning [E]m/n
cloning [e]m/n*
close [O]
closeness [e]
closer [er]
closest [e]
closet [e]
closing [E]m/n
closing [e]m/n*
closure [er]
clot [o]
cloth [o]
clothes [O]
clothesline [l]m/n
clothespin [i]m/n
clotted [e]

clotting [E]m/n
cloud [ow]
clouded [e]
cloudy [E]
clout [ow]
clove [O]
clover [er]
clown [ow]m/n
clowning [E]m/n
clowning [e]m/n*
club [u]
clubbing [E]m/n
clubbing [e]m/n*
clubhouse [ow]
cluck [u]
clucking [E]m/n
clucking [e]m/n*
clue [oo]
clueless [e]
cluing [E]m/n
cluing [e]m/n*
clump [u]m/n
clumping [E]m/n
clumping [e]m/n*
clumpy [E]
clumsy [E]
clunk [u]m/n
clunker [er]
clunky [E]
cluster [er]
clutch [u]
clutching [E]m/n
clutching [e]m/n*
clutter [er]
cluttering [E]m/n
cluttering [e]m/n*
coach [O]
coaching [E]m/n
coaching [e]m/n*
coal [O]l
coarse [O]r
coarsely [E]
coast [O]
coasted [e]
coaster [er]

coasting [E]m/n
coasting [e]m/n*
coastline [I]m/n
coat [O]
coated [e]
coating [E]m/n
coating [e]m/n*
coattail [A]l
coax [O]
coaxing [E]m/n
coaxing [e]m/n*
cob [o]
cobalt [o]l
cobbler [er]
cobblestone [O]m/n
cobra [u]
cobweb [e]
cocaine [A]m/n
cock [o]
cocker [er]
cockeyed [I]
cockfight [I]
cockney [E]
cockpit [i]
cockroach [O]
cocktail [A]l
cocky [E]
cocoa [O]
coconut [u]
cocoon [oo]m/n
code [O]
coded [e]
codeine [E]m/n
coding [E]m/n
coding [e]m/n*
coed [e]
coexist [i]
coexisting [E]m/n
coexisting [e]m/n*
coffee [E]
coffeepot [o]
coffin [i]m/n
cog [o]
cognac [a]
cohort [O]r

coil [Oi]l
coiling [E]m/n
coiling [e]m/n*
coin [Oi]m/n
coincide [I]
coincidence [e]m/n
coincident [e]m/n
coincidental [u]l
coining [E]m/n
coining [e]m/n*
colander [er]
cold [O]l
colder [er]
coldest [e]
coleslaw [o]
colic [i]
colicky [E]
coliseum [u]m/n
collaborate [A]
collaborated [e]
collaborating [E]m/n
collaborating [e]m/n*
collaboration [u]m/n
collaborator [er]
collage [o]
collapse [a]
collapsible [u]l
collapsing [E]m/n
collapsing [e]m/n*
collar [er]
collarbone [O]m/n
collateral [u]l
colleague [E]
collect [e]
collectible [u]l
collecting [E]m/n
collecting [e]m/n*
collection [u]m/n
collective [i]
collector [er]
college [e]
collegiate [e]
collide [I]
collided [e]
colliding [E]m/n

colliding [e]m/n*
collie [E]
collision [u]m/n
cologne [O]m/n
colon [u]m/n
colonel [u]l
colonial [u]l
colonize [I]
colonizing [E]m/n
colonizing [e]m/n*
colony [E]
color [er]
colorfast [a]
colorful [u]l
coloring [E]m/n
coloring [e]m/n*
colorless [e]
colossal [u]l
column [u]m/n
columnist [i]
coma [u]
comatose [O]
comb [O]m/n
combat [a]
combated [e]
combating [E]m/n
combating [e]m/n*
combination [u]m/n
combine [I]m/n
combing [E]m/n
combing [e]m/n*
combining [E]m/n
combining [e]m/n*
combo [O]
combustible [u]l
combustion [u]m/n
come [u]m/n
comeback [a]
comedian [e]m/n
comedic [i]
comedienne [e]m/n
comedy [E]
comet [e]
comfort [er]
comfortable [u]l

comforted [e]
comforter [er]
comforting [E]m/n
comforting [e]m/n*
comfy [E]
comic [i]
comical [ʊ]l
comically [E]
coming [E]m/n
coming [e]m/n*
comma [ʊ]
command [a]m/n
commanded [e]
commandeer [E]r
commandeering [E]m/n
commandeering [e]m/n*
commander [er]
commanding [E]m/n
commanding [e]m/n*
commandment [e]m/n
commando [O]
commemorate [A]
commemorated [e]
commemorating [E]m/n
commemorating [e]m/n*
commemoration [ʊ]m/n
commemorative [i]
commence [e]m/n
commencement [e]m/n
commencing [E]m/n
commencing [e]m/n*
commend [e]m/n
commendable [ʊ]l
commended [e]
commending [E]m/n
commending [e]m/n*
comment [e]m/n
commentary [E]
commentate [A]
commentated [e]
commentator [er]
commented [e]
commenting [E]m/n
commenting [e]m/n*
commerce [er]

commercial [ʊ]l
commercialism [e]m/n
commercialize [I]
commiserate [A]
commiserated [e]
commission [ʊ]m/n
commissioner [er]
commissioning [E]m/n
commissioning [e]m/n*
commit [i]
commitment [e]m/n
committed [e]
committee [E]
committing [E]m/n
committing [e]m/n*
commode [O]
commodity [E]
common [e]m/n
commoner [er]
commonplace [A]
commonsense [e]m/n
commotion [ʊ]m/n
commune [oo]m/n
communicate [A]
communicated [e]
communicating [E]m/n
communicating [e]m/n*
communication [ʊ]m/n
communicative [i]
communion [ʊ]m/n
communism [e]m/n
communist [i]
community [E]
commute [oo]
commuted [e]
commuter [er]
commuting [E]m/n
commuting [e]m/n*
compact [a]
compacted [e]
compacting [E]m/n
compacting [e]m/n*
compactor [er]
companion [ʊ]m/n
companionship [i]

company [E]
comparable [ʊ]l
comparative [i]
comparatively [E]
compare [e]r
comparing [E]m/n
comparing [e]m/n*
comparison [e]m/n
compartment [e]m/n
compass [e]
compassion [ʊ]m/n
compassionate [e]
compassionately [E]
compatibility [E]
compatible [ʊ]l
compatibly [E]
compel [e]l
compelling [E]m/n
compelling [e]m/n*
compensate [A]
compensated [e]
compensating [E]m/n
compensating [e]m/n*
compensation [ʊ]m/n
compete [E]
competed [e]
competent [e]m/n
competing [E]m/n
competing [e]m/n*
competition [ʊ]m/n
competitive [i]
competitor [er]
compilation [ʊ]m/n
compile [I]l
compiling [E]m/n
compiling [e]m/n*
complain [A]m/n
complainer [er]
complaining [E]m/n
complaining [e]m/n*
complaint [A]m/n
complete [E]
completed [e]
completely [E]
completing [E]m/n

completing [e]m/n*
complex [e]
complexion [u]m/n
complexity [E]
compliant [e]m/n
complicate [A]
complicated [e]
complicating [E]m/n
complicating [e]m/n*
complication [u]m/n
compliment [e]m/n
complimentary [E]
complimented [e]
complimenting [E]m/n
complimenting [e]m/n*
comply [I]
complying [E]m/n
complying [e]m/n*
component [e]m/n
compose [O]
composer [er]
composing [E]m/n
composing [e]m/n*
composite [i]
composition [u]m/n
compost [O]
composted [e]
composting [E]m/n
composting [e]m/n*
composure [er]
compound [ow]m/n
compounded [e]
compounding [E]m/n
compounding [e]m/n*
comprehend [e]m/n
comprehended [e]
comprehending [E]m/n
comprehending [e]m/n*
comprehension [u]m/n
comprehensive [i]
compress [e]
compressing [E]m/n
compressing [e]m/n*
compression [u]m/n
comprise [I]

comprising [E]m/n
comprising [e]m/n*
compromise [I]
compromising [E]m/n
compromising [e]m/n*
compulsion [u]m/n
compulsive [i]
compulsively [E]
compute [oo]
computed [e]
computer [er]
computerize [I]
computerizing [E]m/n
computerizing [e]m/n*
computing [E]m/n
computing [e]m/n*
comrade [a]
con [o]m/n
concave [A]
conceal [E]l
concealing [E]m/n
concealing [e]m/n*
concede [E]
conceded [e]
conceding [E]m/n
conceding [e]m/n*
conceit [E]
conceited [e]
conceivable [u]l
conceive [E]
conceiving [E]m/n
conceiving [e]m/n*
concentrate [A]
concentrated [e]
concentrating [E]m/n
concentrating [e]m/n*
concentration [u]m/n
concept [e]
conceptual [u]l
conceptualize [I]
concern [er]m/n
concerning [E]m/n
concerning [e]m/n*
concert [er]
concerto [O]

concession [u]m/n
concessionaire [e]r
concierge [e]r
concise [I]
concisely [E]
conclude [oo]
concluded [e]
concluding [E]m/n
concluding [e]m/n*
conclusion [u]m/n
conclusive [i]
conclusively [E]
concoct [o]
concocted [e]
concocting [E]m/n
concocting [e]m/n*
concrete [E]
concussion [u]m/n
condemn [e]m/n
condemning [E]m/n
condemning [e]m/n*
condensation [u]m/n
condense [e]m/n
condensing [E]m/n
condensing [e]m/n*
condescend [e]m/n
condescended [e]
condescending [E]m/n
condescending [e]m/n*
condiment [e]m/n
condition [u]m/n
conditional [u]l
conditionally [E]
condo [O]
condolence [e]m/n
condom [u]m/n
condone [O]m/n
condoning [E]m/n
condoning [e]m/n*
conducive [i]
conduct [u]
conducted [e]
conducting [E]m/n
conducting [e]m/n*
conductor [er]

cone [O]m/n
confection [u]m/n
confectionery [E]
confederate [e]
confer [er]
conference [e]m/n
confess [e]
confessing [E]m/n
confessing [e]m/n*
confession [u]m/n
confessional [u]l
confetti [E]
confidante [o]m/n
confide [I]
confided [e]
confidence [e]m/n
confident [e]m/n
confidential [u]l
confidentiality [E]
confidentially [E]
confidently [E]
confiding [E]m/n
confiding [e]m/n*
configuration [u]m/n
configure [er]
configuring [E]m/n
configuring [e]m/n*
confine [I]m/n
confinement [e]m/n
confining [E]m/n
confining [e]m/n*
confirm [er]m/n
confirmation [u]m/n
confirming [E]m/n
confirming [e]m/n*
confiscate [A]
confiscated [e]
confiscating [E]m/n
confiscating [e]m/n*
conflict [i]
conflicted [e]
conflicting [E]m/n
conflicting [e]m/n*
conform [O]r
conforming [E]m/n

conforming [e]m/n*
conformity [E]
confront [u]m/n
confrontation [u]m/n
confronted [e]
confronting [E]m/n
confronting [e]m/n*
confuse [oo]
confusing [E]m/n
confusing [e]m/n*
confusion [u]m/n
congest [e]
congestion [u]m/n
conglomerate [e]
conglomeration [u]m/n
congratulate [A]
congratulated [e]
congratulating [E]m/n
congratulating [e]m/n*
congratulation [u]m/n
congregate [A]
congregated [e]
congregating [E]m/n
congregating [e]m/n*
congregation [u]m/n
congress [e]
congressional [u]l
conical [u]l
conjure [er]
conjuring [E]m/n
conjuring [e]m/n*
connect [e]
connecting [E]m/n
connecting [e]m/n*
connection [u]m/n
conning [E]m/n
conning [e]m/n*
connive [I]
conniving [E]m/n
conniving [e]m/n*
connoisseur [er]
conquer [er]
conquering [E]m/n
conquering [e]m/n*
conquest [e]

conscience [e]m/n
conscientious [e]
conscientiously [E]
conscious [e]
consciously [E]
consciousness [e]
consensual [u]l
consent [e]m/n
consented [e]
consenting [E]m/n
consenting [e]m/n*
consequence [e]m/n
consequential [u]l
conservation [u]m/n
conservative [i]
conservatory [E]
conserve [er]
conserving [E]m/n
conserving [e]m/n*
consider [er]
considerable [u]l
considerate [e]
consideration [u]m/n
considering [E]m/n
considering [e]m/n*
consign [I]m/n
consigning [E]m/n
consigning [e]m/n*
consignment [e]m/n
consist [i]
consisted [e]
consistency [E]
consistent [e]m/n
consistently [E]
consisting [E]m/n
consisting [e]m/n*
consolation [u]m/n
console [O]l
consolidate [A]
consolidated [e]
consolidating [E]m/n
consolidating [e]m/n*
consolidation [u]m/n
consoling [E]m/n
consoling [e]m/n*

conspicuous [e]
conspicuously [E]
conspiracy [E]
conspirator [er]
conspire [I]r
conspiring [E]m/n
conspiring [e]m/n*
constable [u]l
constant [e]m/n
constantly [E]
constellation [u]m/n
constipate [A]
constipated [e]
constipation [u]m/n
constrain [A]m/n
constraining [E]m/n
constraining [e]m/n*
constrict [i]
constricted [e]
constricting [E]m/n
constricting [e]m/n*
constriction [u]m/n
constrictive [i]
construct [u]
constructed [e]
constructing [E]m/n
constructing [e]m/n*
construction [u]m/n
constructive [i]
construe [oo]
consult [u]l
consultation [u]m/n
consulted [e]
consulting [E]m/n
consulting [e]m/n*
consumable [u]l
consume [oo]m/n
consumer [er]
consuming [E]m/n
consuming [e]m/n*
consummate [A]
consummate [e]
consummated [e]
contact [a]
contacted [e]

contacting [E]m/n
contacting [e]m/n*
contagion [u]m/n
contagious [e]
contain [A]m/n
container [er]
containing [E]m/n
containing [e]m/n*
containment [e]m/n
contaminant [e]m/n
contaminate [A]
contaminated [e]
contaminating [E]m/n
contaminating [e]m/n*
contamination [u]m/n
contemporary [E]
contempt [e]m/n
contemptible [u]l
contend [e]m/n
contended [e]
contender [er]
contending [E]m/n
contending [e]m/n*
content [e]m/n
contently [E]
contest [e]
contestant [e]m/n
contesting [E]m/n
contesting [e]m/n*
context [e]
contextual [u]l
continent [e]m/n
continental [u]l
continual [u]l
continually [E]
continuation [u]m/n
continue [oo]
continuity [E]
continuous [e]
contort [O]r
contorted [e]
contorting [E]m/n
contorting [e]m/n*
contour [er]
contraception [u]m/n

contract [a]
contracted [e]
contracting [E]m/n
contracting [e]m/n*
contraction [u]m/n
contractor [er]
contractual [u]l
contradict [i]
contradicted [e]
contradicting [E]m/n
contradicting [e]m/n*
contradiction [u]m/n
contraption [u]m/n
contrary [E]
contrast [a]
contrasted [e]
contrasting [E]m/n
contrasting [e]m/n*
contribute [oo]
contributed [e]
contributing [E]m/n
contributing [e]m/n*
contribution [u]m/n
contributor [er]
control [O]l
controller [er]
controlling [E]m/n
controlling [e]m/n*
controversial [u]l
controversy [E]
convalescence [e]m/n
convalescent [e]m/n
convene [E]m/n
convenient [e]m/n
conveniently [E]
convening [E]m/n
convening [e]m/n*
convent [e]m/n
convention [u]m/n
conventional [u]l
converge [er]
converging [E]m/n
converging [e]m/n*
conversation [u]m/n
converse [er]

conversing [E]m/n
conversing [e]m/n*
convert [er]
converted [e]
convertible [u]l
converting [E]m/n
converting [e]m/n*
convex [e]
convey [A]
conveying [E]m/n
conveying [e]m/n*
convict [i]
convicted [e]
convicting [E]m/n
convicting [e]m/n*
conviction [u]m/n
convince [i]m/n
convincing [E]m/n
convincing [e]m/n*
convoy [Oi]
convulse [u]l
convulsion [u]m/n
coo [oo]
cooing [E]m/n
cooing [e]m/n*
cook [oo/]
cookie [E]
cooking [E]m/n
cooking [e]m/n*
cookout [ow]
cool [oo]l
coolant [e]m/n
cooler [er]
coolest [e]
cooling [E]m/n
cooling [e]m/n*
cooperate [A]
cooperated [e]
cooperating [E]m/n
cooperating [e]m/n*
cooperation [u]m/n
cooperative [i]
coordinate [A]
coordinate [e]
coordinated [e]

coordinating [E]m/n
coordinating [e]m/n*
coordination [u]m/n
coordinator [er]
cootie [E]
cop [o]
cope [O]
copier [er]
coping [E]m/n
coping [e]m/n*
copper [er]
copping [E]m/n
copping [e]m/n*
copy [E]
copycat [a]
copying [E]m/n
copying [e]m/n*
copyright [I]
copywriter [er]
coral [u]l
cord [O]r
corded [e]
cordial [u]l
cordially [E]
corduroy [Oi]
core [O]r
coring [E]m/n
coring [e]m/n*
cork [O]r
corkscrew [oo]
corn [O]r
cornball [o]l
cornbread [e]
corncob [o]
cornea [u]
corner [er]
cornering [E]m/n
cornering [e]m/n*
cornerstone [O]m/n
cornflake [A]
cornflower [er]
cornmeal [E]l
cornstalk [o]
cornstarch [o]r
corny [E]

coronary [E]
coroner [er]
corporate [e]
corporation [u]m/n
corpse [O]r
corral [a]l
corralling [E]m/n
corralling [e]m/n*
correct [e]
correcting [E]m/n
correcting [e]m/n*
correction [u]m/n
corrective [i]
correspond [o]m/n
corresponded [e]
correspondence [e]m/n
correspondent [e]m/n
corresponding [E]m/n
corresponding [e]m/n*
corridor [O]r
corrode [O]
corroded [e]
corroding [E]m/n
corroding [e]m/n*
corrosion [u]m/n
corrosive [i]
corrupt [u]
corrupted [e]
corrupting [E]m/n
corrupting [e]m/n*
corruption [u]m/n
corsage [o]
cosign [I]m/n
cosigning [E]m/n
cosigning [e]m/n*
cosmetic [i]
cosmetically [E]
cosmetologist [i]
cosmetology [E]
cosmic [i]
cosmically [E]
cosmopolitan [e]m/n
cosmos [O]
cost [o]
costing [E]m/n

costing [e]m/n*
costume [oo]m/n
cot [o]
cottage [e]
cotton [e]m/n
couch [ow]
cougar [er]
cough [o]
coughing [E]m/n
coughing [e]m/n*
could [oo/]
couldn't [e]m/n
council [u]l
counsel [u]l
counseling [E]m/n
counseling [e]m/n*
counselor [er]
count [ow]m/n
countdown [ow]m/n
counted [e]
counter [er]
counteract [a]
counteracted [e]
counteracting [E]m/n
counteracting [e]m/n*
counterclockwise [I]
counterfeit [i]
counterfeited [e]
counterfeiting [E]m/n
counterfeiting [e]m/n*
countertop [o]
counting [E]m/n
counting [e]m/n*
countless [e]
country [E]
countryside [I]
county [E]
couple [u]l
coupon [o]m/n
courage [i]
courageous [e]
courageously [E]
courier [er]
course [O]r
court [O]r

courted [e]
courteous [e]
courteously [E]
courtesy [E]
courthouse [ow]
courting [E]m/n
courting [e]m/n*
courtroom [oo]m/n
courtship [i]
courtyard [o]r
cousin [i]m/n
cove [O]
cover [er]
covering [E]m/n
covering [e]m/n*
covert [er]
cow [ow]
cowbell [e]l
cowboy [Oi]
cower [er]
cowering [E]m/n
cowering [e]m/n*
cowgirl [er]l
cowhide [I]
cowlick [i]
coworker [er]
cowpoke [O]
coy [Oi]
coyly [E]
coyote [E]
cozy [E]
crab [a]
crabby [E]
crabgrass [a]
crack [a]
crackdown [ow]m/n
cracker [er]
cracking [E]m/n
cracking [e]m/n*
crackle [u]l
crackling [E]m/n
crackling [e]m/n*
crackpot [o]
crackup [u]
cradle [u]l

cradling [E]m/n
cradling [e]m/n*
craft [a]
crafted [e]
crafting [E]m/n
crafting [e]m/n*
craftsman [a]m/n
crafty [E]
cram [a]m/n
cramming [E]m/n
cramming [e]m/n*
cramp [a]m/n
cramping [E]m/n
cramping [e]m/n*
cranberry [E]
cranium [u]m/n
crank [a]ng/k
cranking [E]m/n
cranking [e]m/n*
cranky [E]
cranny [E]
crap [a]
crappy [E]
crash [a]
crasher [er]
crashing [E]m/n
crashing [e]m/n*
crass [a]
crate [A]
crated [e]
crater [er]
crating [E]m/n
crating [e]m/n*
crave [A]
craving [E]m/n
craving [e]m/n*
crawl [o]l
crawler [er]
crawling [E]m/n
crawling [e]m/n*
crayon [o]m/n
craze [A]
crazily [E]
crazy [E]
crazy [e]*

creak [E]
creaking [E]m/n
creaking [e]m/n*
creaky [E]
cream [E]m/n
creamer [er]
creaminess [e]
creamy [E]
create [A]
created [e]
creating [E]m/n
creating [e]m/n*
creation [u]m/n
creative [i]
creator [er]
creature [er]
credential [u]l
credibility [E]
credible [u]l
credit [i]
credited [e]
creditor [er]
creek [E]
creep [E]
creeping [E]m/n
creeping [e]m/n*
creepy [E]
cremate [A]
cremated [e]
cremating [E]m/n
cremating [e]m/n*
crepe [A]
crescent [e]m/n
crevice [i]
crew [oo]
crib [i]
cricket [e]
crier [l]r
crime [l]m/n
criminal [u]l
criminally [E]
crimson [e]m/n
cringe [i]m/n
cringing [E]m/n
cringing [e]m/n*

crinkle [u]l
crinkling [E]m/n
crinkling [e]m/n*
cripple [u]l
crippling [E]m/n
crippling [e]m/n*
crisis [i]
crisp [i]
crisper [er]
crispy [E]
crisscross [o]
crisscrossing [E]m/n
crisscrossing [e]m/n*
criteria [u]
critic [i]
critical [u]l
critically [E]
criticism [e]m/n
criticize [l]
criticizing [E]m/n
criticizing [e]m/n*
critique [E]
critiquing [E]m/n
critiquing [e]m/n*
critter [er]
croak [O]
croaking [E]m/n
croaking [e]m/n*
croaky [E]
crochet [A]
crocheting [E]m/n
crocheting [e]m/n*
crocodile [l]l
croissant [o]m/n
crony [E]
crooked [e]
crookedly [E]
crooner [er]
crop [o]
cropping [E]m/n
cropping [e]m/n*
croquet [A]
croquette [e]
cross [o]
crossbred [e]

crossbreed [E]
crossbreeding [E]m/n
crossbreeding [e]m/n*
crossing [E]m/n
crossing [e]m/n*
crossroad [O]
crosswalk [o]
crosswise [l]
croup [oo]
croupy [E]
crouton [o]m/n
crow [O]
crowbar [o]r
crowd [ow]
crowded [e]
crowding [E]m/n
crowding [e]m/n*
crowing [E]m/n
crowing [e]m/n*
crown [ow]m/n
crowning [E]m/n
crowning [e]m/n*
crucial [u]l
crucially [E]
crucifix [i]
crucify [l]
crucifying [E]m/n
crucifying [e]m/n*
crud [u]
cruddy [E]
crude [oo]
crudely [E]
cruel [oo]l
cruelly [E]
cruelty [E]
cruise [oo]
cruiser [er]
cruising [E]m/n
cruising [e]m/n*
crumb [u]m/n
crumble [u]l
crumbling [E]m/n
crumbling [e]m/n*
crummy [E]
crumple [u]l

crumpling [E]m/n
crumpling [e]m/n*
crunch [u]m/n
crunching [E]m/n
crunching [e]m/n*
crunchy [E]
crusade [A]
crusaded [e]
crusading [E]m/n
crusading [e]m/n*
crush [u]
crusher [er]
crushing [E]m/n
crushing [e]m/n*
crust [u]
crusted [e]
crusty [E]
cry [I]
crying [E]m/n
crying [e]m/n*
crypt [i]
cryptic [i]
cryptically [E]
crystal [u]l
crystallize [I]
crystallizing [E]m/n
crystallizing [e]m/n*
cub [u]
cubby [E]
cube [oo]
cubic [i]
cubicle [u]l
cuckoo [oo]
cucumber [er]
cud [u]
cuddle [u]l
cuddling [E]m/n
cuddling [e]m/n*
cue [oo]
cueing [E]m/n
cueing [e]m/n*
cuff [u]
cuffing [E]m/n
cuffing [e]m/n*
cuisine [E]m/n

culinary [E]
culprit [i]
cultivate [A]
cultivated [e]
cultivating [E]m/n
cultivating [e]m/n*
cultural [u]l
culture [er]
cumbersome [u]m/n
cumin [i]m/n
cumulative [i]
cup [u]
cupboard [er]
cupcake [A]
cupful [oo]l
cupid [i]
cupping [E]m/n
cupping [e]m/n*
curable [u]l
curb [er]
curbing [E]m/n
curbing [e]m/n*
curbside [I]
curdle [u]l
curdling [E]m/n
curdling [e]m/n*
cure [er]
curfew [oo]
curing [E]m/n
curing [e]m/n*
curiosity [E]
curious [e]
curiously [E]
curl [er]l
curler [er]
curling [E]m/n
curling [e]m/n*
currency [E]
current [e]m/n
currently [E]
curriculum [u]m/n
curry [E]
curse [er]
cursing [E]m/n
cursing [e]m/n*

cursive [i]
cursor [er]
curtail [A]l
curtailing [E]m/n
curtailing [e]m/n*
curtain [e]m/n
curtsy [E]
curtsying [E]m/n
curtsying [e]m/n*
curve [er]
curving [E]m/n
curving [e]m/n*
curvy [E]
cushion [u]m/n
cushioning [E]m/n
cushioning [e]m/n*
cushy [E]
custard [er]
custodial [u]l
custodian [e]m/n
custody [E]
custom [u]m/n
customary [E]
customer [er]
customize [I]
customizing [E]m/n
customizing [e]m/n*
cut [u]
cutback [a]
cute [oo]
cutely [E]
cuter [er]
cutest [e]
cutesy [E]
cuticle [u]l
cutie [E]
cutlery [E]
cutlet [e]
cutoff [o]
cutter [er]
cutthroat [O]
cutting [E]m/n
cutting [e]m/n*
cyber [er]
cyberspace [A]

cycle [u]l
cycler [er]
cycling [E]m/n
cycling [e]m/n*

cyclist [i]
cyclone [O]m/n
cylinder [er]
cynic [i]

cynical [u]l
cynically [E]
cynicism [e]m/n
cyst [i]

D

dab [a]
dabbing [E]m/n
dabbing [e]m/n*
dabble [u]l
dabbling [E]m/n
dabbling [e]m/n*
dad [a]
daddy [E]
daddy [e]*
daffodil [i]l
daffy [E]
dagger [er]
daily [E]
daintily [E]
dainty [E]
dairy [E]
daisy [E]
dally [E]
dam [a]m/n
damage [e]
damaging [E]m/n
damaging [e]m/n*
damn [a]m/n
damp [a]m/n
dampen [e]m/n
dampening [E]m/n
dampening [e]m/n*
damper [er]
dance [a]m/n
dancer [er]
dancing [E]m/n
dancing [e]m/n*
dandelion [u]m/n
dander [er]
dandruff [u]
dandy [E]

dang [a]ng/k
danger [er]
dangerous [e]
dangerously [E]
dangle [u]l
dangling [E]m/n
dangling [e]m/n*
dare [e]r
daredevil [u]l
daresay [A]
daring [E]m/n
daring [e]m/n*
dark [o]r
darken [e]m/n
darkening [E]m/n
darkening [e]m/n*
darker [er]
darkness [e]
darkroom [oo]m/n
darling [E]m/n
darling [e]m/n*
darn [o]r
darning [E]m/n
darning [e]m/n*
dart [o]r
darted [e]
darting [E]m/n
darting [e]m/n*
dash [a]
dashboard [O]r
dasher [er]
dashing [E]m/n
dashing [e]m/n*
data [u]
database [A]
date [A]

dated [e]
dateline [l]m/n
dating [E]m/n
dating [e]m/n*
daughter [er]
daunting [E]m/n
daunting [e]m/n*
dawn [o]m/n
dawning [E]m/n
dawning [e]m/n*
day [A]
daybed [e]
daybreak [A]
daydream [E]m/n
daydreaming [E]m/n
daydreaming [e]m/n*
daylight [l]
daytime [l]m/n
daze [A]
dazzle [u]l
dazzling [E]m/n
dazzling [e]m/n*
dead [e]
deaden [e]m/n
deadening [E]m/n
deadening [e]m/n*
deadhead [e]
deadline [l]m/n
deadlock [o]
deadly [E]
deadpan [a]m/n
deaf [e]
deafen [e]m/n
deafening [E]m/n
deafening [e]m/n*
deal [E]l

dealer [er]
dealing [E]m/n
dealing [e]m/n*
dealt [e]l
dear [E]r
dearly [E]
death [e]
deathbed [e]
deathly [E]
deathtrap [a]
debatable [u]l
debate [A]
debated [e]
debating [E]m/n
debating [e]m/n*
debit [i]
debonair [e]r
debrief [E]
debriefing [E]m/n
debriefing [e]m/n*
debris [E]
debt [e]
debug [u]
debugging [E]m/n
debugging [e]m/n*
debunk [u]m/n
debunking [E]m/n
debunking [e]m/n*
debut [oo]
debutante [o]m/n
debuting [E]m/n
debuting [e]m/n*
decade [A]
decadence [e]m/n
decadent [e]m/n
decaffeinated [e]
decal [a]l
decanter [er]
decay [A]
decaying [E]m/n
decaying [e]m/n*
deceased [E]
deceit [E]
deceitful [u]l
deceive [E]

deceiving [E]m/n
deceiving [e]m/n*
December [er]
decency [E]
decent [e]m/n
decently [E]
deception [u]m/n
deceptive [i]
decide [I]
decided [e]
deciding [E]m/n
deciding [e]m/n*
decimal [u]l
decipher [er]
deciphering [E]m/n
deciphering [e]m/n*
decision [u]m/n
decisive [i]
decisively [E]
deck [e]
decking [E]m/n
decking [e]m/n*
declaration [u]m/n
declare [e]r
declaring [E]m/n
declaring [e]m/n*
decline [I]m/n
declining [E]m/n
declining [e]m/n*
deco [O]
decode [O]
decoded [e]
decoder [er]
decoding [E]m/n
decoding [e]m/n*
decongestant [e]m/n
decontaminate [A]
decontaminated [e]
decontaminating [E]m/n
decontaminating
[e]m/n*
decontamination [u]m/n
decor [O]r
decorate [A]
decorated [e]

decorating [E]m/n
decorating [e]m/n*
decoration [u]m/n
decorative [i]
decorator [er]
decoy [Oi]
decrease [E]
decreasing [E]m/n
decreasing [e]m/n*
decree [E]
decrepit [i]
dedicate [A]
dedicated [e]
dedicating [E]m/n
dedicating [e]m/n*
dedication [u]m/n
deduct [u]
deducted [e]
deductible [u]l
deducting [E]m/n
deducting [e]m/n*
deduction [u]m/n
deed [E]
deejay [A]
deep [E]
deepen [e]m/n
deeper [er]
deepest [e]
deeply [E]
deer [E]r
deface [A]
defacing [E]m/n
defacing [e]m/n*
default [o]l
defaulted [e]
defaulting [E]m/n
defaulting [e]m/n*
defeat [E]
defeated [e]
defeating [E]m/n
defeating [e]m/n*
defect [e]
defecting [E]m/n
defecting [e]m/n*
defective [i]

defend [e]m/n
defendant [e]m/n
defended [e]
defender [er]
defending [E]m/n
defending [e]m/n*
defense [e]m/n
defensive [i]
defensively [E]
defer [er]
deferring [E]m/n
deferring [e]m/n*
defiance [e]m/n
defiant [e]m/n
defiantly [E]
deficiency [E]
deficient [e]m/n
deficiently [E]
deficit [i]
define [I]m/n
defining [E]m/n
defining [e]m/n*
definite [i]
definition [u]m/n
definitive [i]
deflate [A]
deflated [e]
deflating [E]m/n
deflating [e]m/n*
deflect [e]
deflecting [E]m/n
deflecting [e]m/n*
deforestation [u]m/n
deform [O]r
deformity [E]
defrost [o]
defrosted [e]
defroster [er]
defrosting [E]m/n
defrosting [e]m/n*
defunct [u]m/n
defy [I]
defying [E]m/n
defying [e]m/n*
degenerate [A]

degenerate [e]
degenerated [e]
degenerating [E]m/n
degenerative [i]
degrade [A]
degraded [e]
degrading [E]m/n
degrading [e]m/n*
degree [E]
dehydrate [A]
dehydrated [e]
dehydrating [E]m/n
dehydrating [e]m/n*
dehydration [u]m/n
dehydrator [er]
delay [A]
delaying [E]m/n
delaying [e]m/n*
delectable [u]l
delegate [A]
delegate [e]
delegated [e]
delegating [E]m/n
delegating [e]m/n*
delegation [u]m/n
delete [E]
deleted [e]
deleting [E]m/n
deleting [e]m/n*
deli [E]
deliberate [A]
deliberate [e]
deliberated [e]
deliberately [E]
deliberating [E]m/n
deliberating [e]m/n*
deliberation [u]m/n
delicacy [E]
delicate [e]
delicately [E]
delicious [e]
delight [I]
delighted [e]
delightful [u]l
delightfully [E]

delighting [E]m/n
delighting [e]m/n*
delinquency [E]
delinquent [e]m/n
delinquently [E]
delirious [e]
deliriously [E]
deliver [er]
delivering [E]m/n
delivering [e]m/n*
dell [e]l
delude [oo]
deluded [e]
deluding [E]m/n
deluding [e]m/n*
delusion [u]m/n
delusional [u]l
deluxe [u]
demand [a]m/n
demanded [e]
demanding [E]m/n
demanding [e]m/n*
demean [E]m/n
demeaning [E]m/n
demeaning [e]m/n*
demeanor [er]
demented [e]
dementia [u]
demerit [i]
demise [I]
democracy [E]
democratic [i]
democratically [E]
demographic [i]
demography [E]
demolish [i]
demolishing [E]m/n
demolishing [e]m/n*
demolition [u]m/n
demon [e]m/n
demonic [i]
demonstrate [A]
demonstrated [e]
demonstrating [E]m/n
demonstrating [e]m/n*

demonstration [u]m/n
demonstrative [i]
demonstrator [er]
demote [O]
demoted [e]
demoting [E]m/n
demoting [e]m/n*
den [e]m/n
denial [u]l
denim [i]m/n
denomination [u]m/n
denominator [er]
denounce [ow]m/n
denouncing [E]m/n
denouncing [e]m/n*
dense [e]m/n
densely [E]
density [E]
dent [e]m/n
dental [u]l
dented [e]
denting [E]m/n
denting [e]m/n*
dentist [i]
dentistry [E]
denture [er]
deny [I]
denying [E]m/n
denying [e]m/n*
deodorant [e]m/n
deodorize [I]
deodorizer [er]
deodorizing [E]m/n
deodorizing [e]m/n*
depart [o]r
departed [e]
departing [E]m/n
departing [e]m/n*
department [e]m/n
departure [er]
depend [e]m/n
dependability [E]
dependable [u]l
depended [e]
dependence [e]m/n

dependent [e]m/n
depending [E]m/n
depending [e]m/n*
depict [i]
depicted [e]
depicting [E]m/n
depicting [e]m/n*
deplete [E]
depleted [e]
depleting [E]m/n
depleting [e]m/n*
deplorable [u]l
deplore [O]r
deploring [E]m/n
deploring [e]m/n*
deploy [Oi]
deploying [E]m/n
deploying [e]m/n*
deport [O]r
deportation [u]m/n
deported [e]
deporting [E]m/n
deporting [e]m/n*
deposit [i]
deposited [e]
depositing [E]m/n
depositing [e]m/n*
deposition [u]m/n
depot [O]
depreciate [A]
depreciated [e]
depreciating [E]m/n
depreciating [e]m/n*
depreciation [u]m/n
depress [e]
depressing [E]m/n
depressing [e]m/n*
depression [u]m/n
depressurize [I]
deprive [I]
depriving [E]m/n
depriving [e]m/n*
deputize [I]
deputizing [E]m/n
deputizing [e]m/n*

deputy [E]
derail [A]l
derailing [E]m/n
derailing [e]m/n*
deranged [A]m/n
derby [E]
derelict [i]
derive [I]
deriving [E]m/n
deriving [e]m/n*
dermatology [E]
derogatory [E]
descend [e]m/n
descendant [e]m/n
descending [E]m/n
descending [e]m/n*
descent [e]m/n
describe [I]
describing [E]m/n
describing [e]m/n*
description [u]m/n
descriptive [i]
desensitize [I]
desensitizing [E]m/n
desensitizing [e]m/n*
desert [er]
deserted [e]
deserter [er]
deserting [E]m/n
deserting [e]m/n*
deserve [er]
deservedly [E]
deserving [E]m/n
deserving [e]m/n*
design [I]m/n
designate [A]
designated [e]
designation [u]m/n
designer [er]
designing [E]m/n
designing [e]m/n*
desirable [u]l
desire [I]r
desiring [E]m/n
desiring [e]m/n*

desk [e]
desktop [o]
desolate [e]
desolation [u]m/n
despair [e]r
despairing [E]m/n
despairing [e]m/n*
desperate [e]
desperately [E]
desperation [u]m/n
despicable [u]l
despicably [E]
despise [I]
despising [E]m/n
despising [e]m/n*
despite [I]
dessert [er]
destination [u]m/n
destined [e]m/n
destiny [E]
destitute [oo]
destroy [Oi]
destroyer [er]
destroying [E]m/n
destroying [e]m/n*
destruct [u]
destructible [u]l
destruction [u]m/n
destructive [i]
destructively [E]
detach [a]
detaching [E]m/n
detaching [e]m/n*
detail [A]l
detailing [E]m/n
detailing [e]m/n*
detain [A]m/n
detainee [E]
detaining [E]m/n
detaining [e]m/n*
detect [e]
detectable [u]l
detecting [E]m/n
detecting [e]m/n*
detection [u]m/n

detective [i]
detention [u]m/n
deter [er]
detergent [e]m/n
deteriorate [A]
deteriorated [e]
deteriorating [E]m/n
deteriorating [e]m/n*
deterioration [u]m/n
determination [u]m/n
determine [i]m/n
determining [E]m/n
determining [e]m/n*
deterrent [e]m/n
deterring [E]m/n
deterring [e]m/n*
detest [e]
detestable [u]l
dethrone [O]m/n
dethroning [E]m/n
dethroning [e]m/n*
detonate [A]
detonated [e]
detonating [E]m/n
detonating [e]m/n*
detonator [er]
detour [er]
detouring [E]m/n
detouring [e]m/n*
detriment [e]m/n
detrimental [u]l
devastate [A]
devastated [e]
devastating [E]m/n
devastating [e]m/n*
develop [u]
developer [er]
developing [E]m/n
developing [e]m/n*
development [e]m/n
deviate [A]
deviated [e]
deviating [E]m/n
deviating [e]m/n*
deviation [u]m/n

device [I]
devious [e]
devise [I]
devising [E]m/n
devising [e]m/n*
devoid [Oi]
devote [O]
devoted [e]
devoting [E]m/n
devoting [e]m/n*
devotion [u]m/n
devotional [u]l
devour [er]
devouring [E]m/n
devouring [e]m/n*
dew [oo]
dewdrop [o]
dewy [E]
dexterity [E]
diabetes [e]
diabetic [i]
diabolic [i]
diabolical [u]l
diagnose [O]
diagnosing [E]m/n
diagnosing [e]m/n*
diagnosis [i]
diagnostic [i]
diagonal [u]l
diagonally [E]
diagram [a]m/n
dial [I]l
dialing [E]m/n
dialing [e]m/n*
dialogue [o]
dialysis [i]
diameter [er]
diametric [i]
diametrically [E]
diamond [e]m/n
diaper [er]
diarrhea [u]
diary [E]
dice [I]
dicing [E]m/n

dicing [e]m/n*
dicker [er]
dickering [E]m/n
dickering [e]m/n*
dictate [A]
dictated [e]
dictating [E]m/n
dictating [e]m/n*
dictation [u]m/n
dictator [er]
diction [u]m/n
dictionary [E]
did [i]
die [I]
diesel [u]l
diet [e]
dietary [E]
dieting [E]m/n
dieting [e]m/n*
dietitian [u]m/n
differ [er]
difference [e]m/n
different [e]m/n
differentiate [A]
differentiated [e]
differentiating [E]m/n
differentiating [e]m/n*
differently [E]
differing [E]m/n
differing [e]m/n*
difficult [u]l
difficulty [E]
diffuse [oo]
diffusing [E]m/n
diffusing [e]m/n*
dig [i]
digest [e]
digestible [u]l
digesting [E]m/n
digesting [e]m/n*
digestion [u]m/n
digging [E]m/n
digging [e]m/n*
digit [i]
digital [u]l

digitize [I]
digitizing [E]m/n
digitizing [e]m/n*
dignify [I]
dignifying [E]m/n
dignifying [e]m/n*
dignity [E]
digress [e]
digressing [E]m/n
digressing [e]m/n*
dike [I]
dilate [A]
dilated [e]
dilating [E]m/n
dilating [e]m/n*
dilemma [u]
diligence [e]m/n
diligent [e]m/n
diligently [E]
dilly [E]
dilute [oo]
diluted [e]
diluting [E]m/n
diluting [e]m/n*
dim [i]m/n
dime [I]m/n
dimension [u]m/n
dimensional [u]l
diminish [i]
diminishing [E]m/n
diminishing [e]m/n*
dimly [E]
dimmer [er]
dimming [E]m/n
dimming [e]m/n*
dimple [u]l
dimply [E]
dimwit [i]
dimwitted [e]
din [i]m/n
dine [I]m/n
diner [er]
dinette [e]
dingy [E]
dining [E]m/n

dining [e]m/n*
dinky [E]
dinner [er]
dinnerware [e]r
dinosaur [O]r
dip [i]
diploma [u]
diplomacy [E]
diplomat [a]
diplomatic [i]
diplomatically [E]
dipper [er]
dipping [E]m/n
dipping [e]m/n*
dippy [E]
dipstick [i]
dire [I]r
direct [e]
directing [E]m/n
directing [e]m/n*
direction [u]m/n
directive [i]
directly [E]
director [er]
directory [E]
dirt [er]
dirty [E]
disability [E]
disable [u]l
disabling [E]m/n
disabling [e]m/n*
disadvantage [e]
disagree [E]
disagreeable [u]l
disagreeing [E]m/n
disagreeing [e]m/n*
disagreement [e]m/n
disappear [E]r
disappearance [e]m/n
disappearing [E]m/n
disappearing [e]m/n*
disappoint [Oi]m/n
disappointed [e]
disappointing [E]m/n
disappointing [e]m/n*

disappointment [e]m/n
disapproval [u]l
disapprove [oo]
disapproving [E]m/n
disapproving [e]m/n*
disarm [o]r
disarming [E]m/n
disarming [e]m/n*
disassemble [u]l
disassembling [E]m/n
disassembling [e]m/n*
disaster [er]
disastrous [e]
disband [a]m/n
disbanded [e]
disbanding [E]m/n
disbanding [e]m/n*
disbar [o]r
disbarring [E]m/n
disbarring [e]m/n*
disbelief [E]
disbelieve [E]
disbeliever [er]
disbelieving [E]m/n
disbelieving [e]m/n*
disburse [er]
disbursement [e]m/n
disbursing [E]m/n
disbursing [e]m/n*
disc [i]
discard [o]r
discarded [e]
discarding [E]m/n
discarding [e]m/n*
discharge [o]r
discharging [E]m/n
discharging [e]m/n*
disciplinary [E]
discipline [i]m/n
disciplining [E]m/n
disciplining [e]m/n*
disclaim [A]m/n
disclaimer [er]
disclaiming [E]m/n
disclaiming [e]m/n*

disclose [O]
disclosing [E]m/n
disclosing [e]m/n*
disclosure [er]
disco [O]
discolor [er]
discoloration [u]m/n
discoloring [E]m/n
discoloring [e]m/n*
discomfort [er]
discomforting [E]m/n
discomforting [e]m/n*
disconnect [e]
disconnecting [E]m/n
disconnecting [e]m/n*
disconnection [u]m/n
discontinue [oo]
discontinuing [E]m/n
discontinuing [e]m/n*
discount [ow]m/n
discounted [e]
discounting [E]m/n
discounting [e]m/n*
discourage [e]
discouragement [e]m/n
discouraging [E]m/n
discouraging [e]m/n*
discourse [O]r
discover [er]
discovering [E]m/n
discovering [e]m/n*
discovery [E]
discredit [i]
discredited [e]
discrediting [E]m/n
discrediting [e]m/n*
discreet [E]
discreetly [E]
discrepancy [E]
discretion [u]m/n
discriminate [A]
discriminated [e]
discriminating [E]m/n
discriminating [e]m/n*
discrimination [u]m/n

discuss [u]
discussing [E]m/n
discussing [e]m/n*
discussion [u]m/n
disdain [A]m/n
disease [E]
disfigure [er]
disfiguring [E]m/n
disfiguring [e]m/n*
disgrace [A]
disgraceful [u]l
disgracefully [E]
disgruntle [u]l
disguise [I]
disguising [E]m/n
disguising [e]m/n*
disgust [u]
disgusted [e]
disgusting [E]m/n
disgusting [e]m/n*
dish [i]
dishcloth [o]
dishing [E]m/n
dishing [e]m/n*
dishonest [e]
dishonestly [E]
dishonor [er]
dishonorable [u]l
dishonorably [E]
dishonoring [E]m/n
dishonoring [e]m/n*
dishpan [a]m/n
dishrag [a]
dishtowel [ow]l
dishwasher [er]
dishwater [er]
disillusion [u]m/n
disillusionment [e]m/n
disinfect [e]
disinfectant [e]m/n
disinfecting [E]m/n
disinfecting [e]m/n*
disk [i]
diskette [e]
dislike [I]

disliking [E]m/n

disliking [e]m/n*

dislocate [A]

dislocated [e]

dislocating [E]m/n

dislocating [e]m/n*

dislocation [u]m/n

dislodge [o]

dislodging [E]m/n

dislodging [e]m/n*

disloyal [u]l

disloyally [E]

dismantle [u]l

dismantling [E]m/n

dismantling [e]m/n*

dismay [A]

dismiss [i]

dismissing [E]m/n

dismissing [e]m/n*

dismount [ow]m/n

dismounted [e]

dismounting [E]m/n

dismounting [e]m/n*

disobedience [e]m/n

disobedient [e]m/n

disobediently [E]

disobey [A]

disobeying [E]m/n

disobeying [e]m/n*

disorder [er]

disorderly [E]

disorganize [I]

disorganizing [E]m/n

disorganizing [e]m/n*

disown [O]m/n

disowning [E]m/n

disowning [e]m/n*

dispatch [a]

dispatching [E]m/n

dispatching [e]m/n*

dispel [e]l

dispelling [E]m/n

dispelling [e]m/n*

dispense [e]m/n

dispensing [E]m/n

dispensing [e]m/n*

disperse [er]

dispersing [E]m/n

dispersing [e]m/n*

displace [A]

displacing [E]m/n

displacing [e]m/n*

display [A]

displaying [E]m/n

displaying [e]m/n*

displease [E]

displeasing [E]m/n

displeasing [e]m/n*

disposable [u]l

disposal [u]l

dispose [O]

disposing [E]m/n

disposing [e]m/n*

disposition [u]m/n

disproportionate [e]

disprove [oo]

disproving [E]m/n

disproving [e]m/n*

dispute [oo]

disputed [e]

disputing [E]m/n

disputing [e]m/n*

disqualify [I]

disqualifying [E]m/n

disqualifying [e]m/n*

disregard [o]r

disregarded [e]

disregarding [E]m/n

disregarding [e]m/n*

disrepair [e]r

disrespect [e]

disrespectful [u]l

disrespecting [E]m/n

disrespecting [e]m/n*

disrobe [O]

disrobing [E]m/n

disrobing [e]m/n*

disrupt [u]

disrupted [e]

disrupting [E]m/n

disrupting [e]m/n*

dissatisfaction [u]m/n

dissatisfactory [E]

dissatisfied [I]

dissect [e]

dissecting [E]m/n

dissecting [e]m/n*

disservice [i]

dissipate [A]

dissipated [e]

dissipating [E]m/n

dissipating [e]m/n*

dissolve [o]l

dissolving [E]m/n

dissolving [e]m/n*

distance [e]m/n

distant [e]m/n

distantly [E]

distemper [er]

distill [i]l

distilling [E]m/n

distilling [e]m/n*

distinct [E]m/n

distinction [u]m/n

distinctive [i]

distinctly [E]

distinguish [i]

distort [O]r

distorted [e]

distorting [E]m/n

distorting [e]m/n*

distract [a]

distracted [e]

distracting [E]m/n

distracting [e]m/n*

distraught [o]

distress [e]

distribute [oo]

distributed [e]

distributing [E]m/n

distributing [e]m/n*

distribution [u]m/n

disturb [er]

disturbing [E]m/n

disturbing [e]m/n*

ditto [O]
ditty [E]
dive [I]
diver [er]
diverse [er]
diversity [E]
divert [er]
diverted [e]
diverting [E]m/n
diverting [e]m/n*
divide [I]
divided [e]
dividend [e]m/n
divider [er]
dividing [E]m/n
dividing [e]m/n*
divine [I]m/n
divinely [E]
diving [E]m/n
diving [e]m/n*
divorce [O]r
divorcing [E]m/n
divorcing [e]m/n*
divulge [u]l
divulging [E]m/n
divulging [e]m/n*
divvy [E]
divvying [E]m/n
divvying [e]m/n*
dizzy [E]
do [oo]
doc [o]
docile [u]l
dock [o]
docking [E]m/n
docking [e]m/n*
dockside [I]
doctor [er]
doctorate [e]
doctoring [E]m/n
doctoring [e]m/n*
document [e]m/n
documentary [E]
documentation [u]m/n
documented [e]

documenting [E]m/n
documenting [e]m/n*
dodge [o]
dodger [er]
dodging [E]m/n
dodging [e]m/n*
dodgy [E]
doer [er]
does [u]
dog [o]
dogcatcher [er]
dogfight [I]
dogging [E]m/n
dogging [e]m/n*
doggone [o]m/n
doggy [E]
doghouse [ow]
doily [E]
doing [E]m/n
doing [e]m/n*
doll [o]l
dollar [er]
dollop [u]
dolly [E]
dolphin [i]m/n
domain [A]m/n
dome [O]m/n
domestic [i]
domesticate [A]
domesticated [e]
domesticating [E]m/n
domesticating [e]m/n*
dominance [e]m/n
dominant [e]m/n
dominate [A]
dominated [e]
dominating [E]m/n
dominating [e]m/n*
domination [u]m/n
dominatrix [i]
domineer [E]r
domineering [E]m/n
domineering [e]m/n*
dominion [e]m/n
domino [O]

don't [O]m/n
donate [A]
donated [e]
donating [E]m/n
donating [e]m/n*
donation [u]m/n
done [u]m/n
donkey [E]
donor [er]
doodad [a]
doodler [er]
doomsday [A]
door [O]r
doorbell [e]l
doorjamb [a]m/n
doorknob [o]
doorman [a]m/n
doormat [a]
doornail [A]l
doorstep [e]
doorstop [o]
doorway [A]
dope [O]
dopey [E]
dorm [O]r
dormant [e]m/n
dormitory [E]
dot [o]
dote [O]
doted [e]
doting [E]m/n
doting [e]m/n*
dotted [e]
dotting [E]m/n
dotting [e]m/n*
double [u]l
doubling [E]m/n
doubling [e]m/n*
doubt [ow]
doubted [e]
doubtful [u]l
doubtfully [E]
doubting [E]m/n
doubting [e]m/n*
doubtless [e]

doubtlessly [E]
dough [O]
doughnut [u]
doughy [E]
douse [ow]
dousing [E]m/n
dousing [e]m/n*
dove [u]
dovetail [A]l
dowdy [E]
dowel [u]l
down [ow]m/n
downbeat [E]
downcast [a]
downer [er]
downfall [o]l
downgrade [A]
downgraded [e]
downgrading [E]m/n
downgrading [e]m/n*
downhill [i]l
download [O]
downloaded [e]
downloading [E]m/n
downloading [e]m/n*
downplay [A]
downplaying [E]m/n
downplaying [e]m/n*
downpour [O]r
downright [I]
downside [I]
downsize [I]
downsizing [E]m/n
downsizing [e]m/n*
downstairs [e]r
downtime [I]m/n
downtown [ow]m/n
downturn [er]m/n
downward [er]
downwind [i]m/n
downy [E]
dowry [E]
doze [O]
dozen [e]m/n
dozing [E]m/n

dozing [e]m/n*
drab [a]
draft [a]
drafted [e]
draftee [E]
drafting [E]m/n
drafting [e]m/n*
draftsman [e]m/n
drafty [E]
drag [a]
dragging [E]m/n
dragging [e]m/n*
dragnet [e]
dragon [e]m/n
dragonfly [I]
drain [A]m/n
drainage [e]
draining [E]m/n
draining [e]m/n*
drainpipe [I]
drama [u]
dramatic [i]
dramatize [I]
dramatizing [E]m/n
dramatizing [e]m/n*
drank [a]ng/k
drape [A]
drapery [E]
draping [E]m/n
draping [e]m/n*
drastic [i]
drastically [E]
draw [o]
drawback [a]
drawbridge [i]
drawer [O]r
drawing [E]m/n
drawing [e]m/n*
drawl [o]l
drawn [o]m/n
dread [e]
dreadful [u]l
dreadfully [E]
dreading [E]m/n
dreading [e]m/n*

dream [E]m/n
dreamboat [O]
dreamer [er]
dreaming [E]m/n
dreaming [e]m/n*
dreamland [a]m/n
dreamy [E]
dreary [E]
dredge [e]
dredging [E]m/n
dredging [e]m/n*
drench [e]m/n
drenching [E]m/n
drenching [e]m/n*
dress [e]
dresser [er]
dressing [E]m/n
dressing [e]m/n*
dressmaker [er]
dressy [E]
drew [oo]
dribble [u]l
dribbler [er]
dribbling [E]m/n
dribbling [e]m/n*
drift [i]
drifted [e]
drifter [er]
drifting [E]m/n
drifting [e]m/n*
driftwood [oo/]
drill [i]l
driller [er]
drilling [E]m/n
drilling [e]m/n*
drink [E]m/n
drinkable [u]l
drinker [er]
drinking [E]m/n
drinking [e]m/n*
drip [i]
dripping [E]m/n
dripping [e]m/n*
drippy [E]
drive [I]

driven [e]m/n
driver [er]
driveway [A]
driving [E]m/n
driving [e]m/n*
drizzle [u]l
drizzling [E]m/n
drizzling [e]m/n*
drone [O]m/n
droning [E]m/n
droning [e]m/n*
drool [oo]l
drooling [E]m/n
drooling [e]m/n*
droop [oo]
drooping [E]m/n
drooping [e]m/n*
droopy [E]
drop [o]
dropkick [i]
dropkicking [E]m/n
dropkicking [e]m/n*
dropper [er]
dropping [E]m/n
dropping [e]m/n*
drought [ow]
drove [O]
drown [ow]m/n
drowning [E]m/n
drowning [e]m/n*
drowsy [E]
drudge [u]
drudgery [E]
drudging [E]m/n
drudging [e]m/n*
drug [u]
drugging [E]m/n
drugging [e]m/n*
drugstore [O]r
drum [u]m/n
drumbeat [E]
drummer [er]
drumming [E]m/n
drumming [e]m/n*
drumstick [i]

drunk [u]m/n
drunkard [er]
drunken [e]m/n
drunker [er]
druthers [er]
dry [I]
dryer [er]
drying [E]m/n
drying [e]m/n*
dryness [e]
drywall [o]l
dual [oo]l
duality [E]
dub [u]
dubbing [E]m/n
dubbing [e]m/n*
dubious [e]
duck [u]
ducking [E]m/n
duckling [e]m/n*
ducktail [A]l
ducky [E]
dud [u]
dude [oo]
due [oo]
duet [e]
dug [u]
dugout [ow]
dull [u]l
duller [er]
dullest [e]
dulling [E]m/n
dulling [e]m/n*
duly [E]
dumb [u]m/n
dumbbell [e]l
dumber [er]
dumbstruck [u]
dumdum [u]m/n
dummy [E]
dump [u]m/n
dumping [E]m/n
dumping [e]m/n*
dumpling [E]m/n
dumpling [e]m/n*

dumpster [er]
dumpy [E]
dungeon [e]m/n
dunk [u]m/n
dunking [E]m/n
dunking [e]m/n*
duo [O]
duplex [e]
duplicate [A]
duplicate [e]
duplicated [e]
duplicating [E]m/n
duplicating [e]m/n*
duplication [u]m/n
duplicator [er]
durability [E]
durable [u]l
duration [u]m/n
during [E]m/n
during [e]m/n*
dusky [E]
dust [u]
dusted [e]
duster [er]
dusting [E]m/n
dusting [e]m/n*
dustpan [a]m/n
dusty [E]
duty [E]
dwell [e]l
dweller [er]
dwelling [E]m/n
dwelling [e]m/n*
dwindle [u]l
dwindling [E]m/n
dwindling [e]m/n*
dye [I]
dying [E]m/n
dying [e]m/n*
dynamic [i]
dynamite [I]
dynamo [O]
dynasty [E]
dysfunction [u]m/n
dysfunctional [u]l

E

each [E]
eager [er]
eagerly [E]
eagle [u]l
ear [E]r
earache [A]
eardrop [o]
eardrum [u]m/n
earlier [er]
earliest [e]
earlobe [O]
early [E]
earmuff [u]
earn [er]m/n
earnest [e]
earnestly [E]
earning [E]m/n
earning [e]m/n*
earphone [O]m/n
earplug [u]
earring [E]m/n
earshot [o]
earth [er]
earthling [E]m/n
earthling [e]m/n*
earthly [E]
earthquake [A]
earthworm [er]m/n
earthy [E]
earwax [a]
ease [E]
easel [u]l
easier [er]
easiest [e]
easily [E]
easing [E]m/n
easing [e]m/n*
east [E]
eastern [er]m/n
easy [E]
easygoing [E]m/n

easygoing [e]m/n*
eat [E]
eatable [u]l
eaten [e]m/n
eating [E]m/n
eating [e]m/n*
eaves [E]
eavesdrop [o]
eavesdropping [E]m/n
eavesdropping [e]m/n*
ebony [E]
eccentric [i]
eccentricity [E]
echo [O]
eclipse [i]
eclipsing [E]m/n
eclipsing [e]m/n*
ecological [u]l
ecologically [E]
ecology [E]
economic [i]
economical [u]l
economically [E]
economist [i]
economize [I]
economy [E]
ecosystem [e]m/n
ecstasy [E]
ecstatic [i]
eczema [u]
edge [e]
edger [er]
edgewise [I]
edging [E]m/n
edging [e]m/n*
edgy [E]
edible [u]l
edit [i]
editing [E]m/n
editing [e]m/n*
edition [u]m/n

editor [er]
editorial [u]l
educate [A]
educated [e]
educating [E]m/n
educating [e]m/n*
education [u]m/n
educational [u]l
educator [er]
eerie [E]
eerily [E]
effect [e]
effective [i]
effectively [E]
efficiency [E]
efficient [e]m/n
efficiently [E]
effort [er]
effortless [e]
effortlessly [E]
egg [e]
egghead [e]
egging [E]m/n
egging [e]m/n*
eggnog [o]
eggplant [a]m/n
eggshell [e]l
ego [O]
eight [A]
eighteen [E]m/n
eighty [E]
either [er]
eject [e]
ejecting [E]m/n
ejecting [e]m/n*
elaborate [A]
elaborate [e]
elaborated [e]
elaborating [E]m/n
elaborating [e]m/n*
elastic [i]

elasticity [E]
elate [A]
elated [e]
elation [u]m/n
elbow [O]
elbowing [E]m/n
elbowing [e]m/n*
elbowroom [oo]m/n
elder [er]
eldest [e]
elect [e]
electing [E]m/n
electing [e]m/n*
election [u]m/n
elective [i]
electric [i]
electrical [u]l
electrician [u]m/n
electricity [E]
electrify [I]
electrifying [E]m/n
electrifying [e]m/n*
electrocute [oo]
electrocuting [E]m/n
electrocuting [e]m/n*
electrocution [u]m/n
electronic [i]
elegance [e]m/n
elegant [e]m/n
elegantly [E]
element [e]m/n
elemental [u]l
elementary [E]
elephant [e]m/n
elevate [A]
elevated [e]
elevating [E]m/n
elevating [e]m/n*
elevation [u]m/n
elevator [er]
eleven [e]m/n
elf [e]l
eligibility [E]
eligible [u]l
eliminate [A]

eliminated [e]
eliminating [E]m/n
eliminating [e]m/n*
elimination [u]m/n
elite [E]
elitist [i]
elongate [A]
elongated [e]
elongating [E]m/n
elongating [e]m/n*
elope [O]
eloping [E]m/n
eloping [e]m/n*
eloquence [e]m/n
eloquent [e]m/n
eloquently [E]
else [e]l
elsewhere [e]r
elude [oo]
eluded [e]
eluding [E]m/n
eluding [e]m/n*
elusive [i]
embark [o]r
embarking [E]m/n
embarking [e]m/n*
embarrass [e]
embarrassing [E]m/n
embarrassing [e]m/n*
embarrassment [e]m/n
embassy [E]
embed [e]
embedding [E]m/n
embedding [e]m/n*
embellish [i]
embellishing [E]m/n
embellishing [e]m/n*
ember [er]
embezzle [u]l
embezzling [E]m/n
embezzling [e]m/n*
emblem [e]m/n
embody [E]
emboss [o]
embossing [E]m/n

embossing [e]m/n*
embrace [A]
embracing [E]m/n
embracing [e]m/n*
embroidery [E]
embryo [O]
embryonic [i]
emcee [E]
emceeing [E]m/n
emceeing [e]m/n*
emerald [u]l
emerge [er]
emergency [E]
emerging [E]m/n
emerging [e]m/n*
emission [u]m/n
emit [i]
emitted [e]
emitting [E]m/n
emitting [e]m/n*
emotion [u]m/n
emotional [u]l
emotive [i]
empathetic [i]
empathy [E]
emphasis [i]
emphasize [I]
empire [I]r
employ [Oi]
employee [E]
employing [E]m/n
employing [e]m/n*
employment [e]m/n
emporium [u]m/n
empower [er]
empowering [E]m/n
empowering [e]m/n*
empty [E]
emptying [E]m/n
emptying [e]m/n*
enable [u]l
enabler [er]
enabling [E]m/n
enabling [e]m/n*
enact [a]

enacted [e]
enacting [E]m/n
enacting [e]m/n*
enamel [u]l
enchant [a]m/n
enchanted [e]
enchanting [E]m/n
enchanting [e]m/n*
enchantment [e]m/n
enchilada [u]
enclose [O]
enclosing [E]m/n
enclosing [e]m/n*
enclosure [er]
encode [O]
encoded [e]
encoding [E]m/n
encoding [e]m/n*
encompass [e]
encompassing [E]m/n
encompassing [e]m/n*
encore [O]r
encounter [er]
encountering [E]m/n
encountering [e]m/n*
encourage [e]
encouragement [e]m/n
encouraging [E]m/n
encouraging [e]m/n*
encrypt [i]
encrypted [e]
encrypting [E]m/n
encrypting [e]m/n*
end [e]m/n
endanger [er]
endangering [E]m/n
endangering [e]m/n*
endeavor [er]
endeavoring [E]m/n
endeavoring [e]m/n*
ended [e]
ending [E]m/n
ending [e]m/n*
endless [e]
endlessly [E]

endorse [O]r
endorsing [E]m/n
endorsing [e]m/n*
endurance [e]m/n
endure [er]
enduring [E]m/n
enduring [e]m/n*
enemy [E]
energetic [i]
energize [I]
energizer [er]
energizing [E]m/n
energizing [e]m/n*
energy [E]
enforce [O]r
enforceable [u]l
enforcing [E]m/n
enforcing [e]m/n*
engage [A]
engagement [e]m/n
engaging [E]m/n
engaging [e]m/n*
engine [i]m/n
engineer [E]r
engineering [E]m/n
engineering [e]m/n*
engrave [A]
engraving [E]m/n
engraving [e]m/n*
enhance [a]m/n
enhancing [E]m/n
enhancing [e]m/n*
enjoy [Oi]
enjoyable [u]l
enjoying [E]m/n
enjoying [e]m/n*
enlarge [o]r
enlargement [e]m/n
enlarging [E]m/n
enlarging [e]m/n*
enlighten [e]m/n
enlightening [E]m/n
enlightening [e]m/n*
enlightenment [e]m/n
enlist [i]

enlisted [e]
enlisting [E]m/n
enlisting [e]m/n*
enormity [E]
enormous [e]
enormously [E]
enough [u]
enrage [A]
enraging [E]m/n
enraging [e]m/n*
enrich [i]
enriching [E]m/n
enriching [e]m/n*
enroll [O]l
enrolling [E]m/n
enrolling [e]m/n*
enrollment [e]m/n
ensemble [u]l
ensure [er]
entail [A]l
entailing [E]m/n
entailing [e]m/n*
entangle [u]l
entangling [E]m/n
entangling [e]m/n*
enter [er]
entering [E]m/n
entering [e]m/n*
enterprise [I]
enterprising [E]m/n
enterprising [e]m/n*
entertain [A]m/n
entertaining [E]m/n
entertaining [e]m/n*
entertainment [e]m/n
enthrall [o]l
enthralling [E]m/n
enthralling [e]m/n*
enthused [oo]
enthusiasm [e]m/n
enthusiast [e]
enthusiastic [i]
entice [I]
enticing [E]m/n
enticing [e]m/n*

entire [I]r
entirely [E]
entitle [u]l
entitling [E]m/n
entitling [e]m/n*
entity [E]
entourage [o]
entrance [e]m/n
entrap [a]
entrapment [e]m/n
entrapping [E]m/n
entrapping [e]m/n*
entrée [A]
entrepreneur [er]
entrepreneurial [u]l
entry [E]
entwine [I]m/n
entwining [E]m/n
entwining [e]m/n*
enunciate [A]
enunciated [e]
enunciating [E]m/n
enunciating [e]m/n*
envelope [O]
enveloping [E]m/n
enveloping [e]m/n*
envious [e]
enviously [E]
environment [e]m/n
environmental [u]l
environmentally [E]
envision [u]m/n
envisioning [E]m/n
envisioning [e]m/n*
envoy [Oi]
envy [E]
envying [E]m/n
envying [e]m/n*
enzyme [I]m/n
eon [o]m/n
epic [i]
epidemic [i]
epiphany [E]
episode [O]
episodic [i]

equal [u]l
equaling [E]m/n
equaling [e]m/n*
equality [E]
equalize [I]
equally [E]
equate [A]
equated [e]
equating [E]m/n
equating [e]m/n*
equation [u]m/n
equator [er]
equestrian [e]m/n
equilibrium [u]m/n
equine [I]m/n
equip [i]
equipment [e]m/n
equipping [E]m/n
equipping [e]m/n*
equivalent [e]m/n
era [u]
eradicate [A]
eradicated [e]
eradicating [E]m/n
eradicating [e]m/n*
eradication [u]m/n
erase [A]
eraser [er]
erasing [E]m/n
erasing [e]m/n*
erect [e]
erecting [E]m/n
erecting [e]m/n*
erode [O]
eroded [e]
eroding [E]m/n
eroding [e]m/n*
erosion [u]m/n
erosive [i]
erotic [i]
erotically [E]
errand [e]m/n
erratic [i]
erratically [E]
error [er]

erupt [u]
erupted [e]
erupting [E]m/n
erupting [e]m/n*
eruption [u]m/n
escalate [A]
escalated [e]
escalating [E]m/n
escalating [e]m/n*
escalator [er]
escape [A]
escaping [E]m/n
escaping [e]m/n*
escort [O]r
escorted [e]
escorting [E]m/n
escorting [e]m/n*
escrow [O]
esophagus [e]
esoteric [i]
espresso [O]
essay [A]
essence [e]m/n
essential [u]l
essentially [E]
establish [i]
establishing [E]m/n
establishing [e]m/n*
establishment [e]m/n
estate [A]
esteem [E]m/n
estimate [A]
estimate [e]
estimating [E]m/n
estimating [e]m/n*
estrogen [e]m/n
etch [e]
etching [E]m/n
etching [e]m/n*
eternal [u]l
eternally [E]
eternity [E]
ether [er]
ethical [u]l
ethically [E]

ethics [i]
ethnic [i]
etiquette [e]
eulogy [E]
euphoric [i]
evacuate [A]
evacuated [e]
evacuating [E]m/n
evacuating [e]m/n*
evacuation [u]m/n
evade [A]
evaded [e]
evading [E]m/n
evading [e]m/n*
evaluate [A]
evaluated [e]
evaluating [E]m/n
evaluating [e]m/n*
evaluation [u]m/n
evaporate [A]
evaporated [e]
evaporating [E]m/n
evaporating [e]m/n*
evaporation [u]m/n
evasive [i]
evasively [E]
eve [E]
even [e]m/n
evening [E]m/n
evening [e]m/n*
evenly [E]
event [e]m/n
eventful [u]l
eventual [u]l
eventually [E]
ever [er]
everlasting [E]m/n
everlasting [e]m/n*
evermore [O]r
every [E]
everybody [E]
everybody [e]*
everyday [A]
everyone [u]m/n
everyplace [A]

everything [E]m/n
everything [e]m/n*
everywhere [e]r
evict [i]
evicted [e]
evidence [e]m/n
evident [e]m/n
evidently [E]
evoke [O]
evoking [E]m/n
evoking [e]m/n*
evolution [u]m/n
evolve [o]l
evolving [E]m/n
evolving [e]m/n*
exact [a]
exactly [E]
exaggerate [A]
exaggerated [e]
exaggerating [E]m/n
exaggerating [e]m/n*
exaggeration [u]m/n
exam [a]m/n
examination [u]m/n
examine [i]m/n
examining [E]m/n
examining [e]m/n*
example [u]l
exceed [E]
exceeded [e]
exceeding [E]m/n
exceeding [e]m/n*
excel [e]l
excellence [e]m/n
excellent [e]m/n
excelling [E]m/n
excelling [e]m/n*
except [e]
exception [u]m/n
exceptional [u]l
exceptionally [E]
excess [e]
excessive [i]
excessively [E]
exchange [A]m/n

exchanging [E]m/n
exchanging [e]m/n*
excitable [u]l
excite [I]
excited [e]
excitement [e]m/n
exciting [E]m/n
exciting [e]m/n*
exclaim [A]m/n
exclaiming [E]m/n
exclaiming [e]m/n*
exclamation [u]m/n
exclude [oo]
excluded [e]
excluding [E]m/n
excluding [e]m/n*
exclusive [i]
exclusively [E]
exclusivity [E]
excursion [u]m/n
excuse [oo]
excusing [E]m/n
excusing [e]m/n*
execute [oo]
executed [e]
executing [E]m/n
executing [e]m/n*
executive [i]
exemplary [E]
exempt [e]m/n
exempting [E]m/n
exempting [e]m/n*
exemption [u]m/n
exercise [I]
exercising [E]m/n
exercising [e]m/n*
exert [er]
exerted [e]
exerting [E]m/n
exerting [e]m/n*
exertion [u]m/n
exhale [A]l
exhaling [E]m/n
exhaling [e]m/n*
exhaust [o]

exhausted [e]
exhausting [E]m/n
exhausting [e]m/n*
exhaustion [u]m/n
exhaustive [i]
exhibit [i]
exhibited [e]
exhibiting [E]m/n
exhibiting [e]m/n*
exhibition [u]m/n
exile [l]l
exist [i]
existed [e]
existence [e]m/n
existing [E]m/n
existing [e]m/n*
exit [i]
exited [e]
exiting [E]m/n
exiting [e]m/n*
exotic [i]
exotically [E]
expand [a]m/n
expanded [e]
expanding [E]m/n
expanding [e]m/n*
expanse [a]m/n
expansive [i]
expect [e]
expectant [e]m/n
expectation [u]m/n
expecting [E]m/n
expecting [e]m/n*
expedient [e]m/n
expedite [I]
expedited [e]
expediting [E]m/n
expediting [e]m/n*
expedition [u]m/n
expel [e]l
expelling [E]m/n
expelling [e]m/n*
expense [e]m/n
expensive [i]
expensively [E]

experience [e]m/n
experiencing [E]m/n
experiencing [e]m/n*
experiment [e]m/n
experimental [u]l
experimented [e]
experimenting [E]m/n
experimenting [e]m/n*
expert [er]
expertise [E]
expertly [E]
expiration [u]m/n
expire [I]r
expiring [E]m/n
expiring [e]m/n*
explain [A]m/n
explaining [E]m/n
explaining [e]m/n*
explanation [u]m/n
explanatory [E]
explicit [i]
explicitly [E]
explode [O]
exploded [e]
exploding [E]m/n
exploding [e]m/n*
exploit [Oi]
exploited [e]
exploiting [E]m/n
exploiting [e]m/n*
exploration [u]m/n
exploratory [E]
explore [O]r
exploring [E]m/n
exploring [e]m/n*
explosion [u]m/n
explosive [i]
expo [O]
export [O]r
exported [e]
exporting [E]m/n
exporting [e]m/n*
expose [O]
exposing [E]m/n
exposing [e]m/n*

exposure [er]
express [e]
expressing [E]m/n
expressing [e]m/n*
expression [u]m/n
expressive [i]
expressively [E]
expulsion [u]m/n
exquisite [i]
exquisitely [E]
extend [e]m/n
extended [e]
extending [E]m/n
extending [e]m/n*
extension [u]m/n
extensive [i]
extensively [E]
extent [e]m/n
exterior [er]
exterminate [A]
exterminated [e]
exterminating [E]m/n
exterminating [e]m/n*
exterminator [er]
external [u]l
externally [E]
extinct [E]m/n
extinction [u]m/n
extinguish [i]
extinguishing [E]m/n
extinguishing [e]m/n*
extort [O]r
extorted [e]
extorting [E]m/n
extorting [e]m/n*
extract [a]
extracted [e]
extracting [E]m/n
extracting [e]m/n*
extraction [u]m/n
extracurricular [er]
extraordinarily [E]
extraordinary [E]
extravagance [e]m/n
extravagant [e]m/n

extravagantly [E]
extravaganza [u]
extreme [E]m/n
extremely [E]
extremity [E]
extrude [oo]
extruded [e]
extruding [E]m/n

extruding [e]m/n*
exuberant [e]m/n
exuberantly [E]
eye [I]
eyeball [o]l
eyebrow [ow]
eyedropper [er]
eyeglasses [e]

eyeing [E]m/n
eyeing [e]m/n*
eyelash [a]
eyelid [i]
eyesight [I]
eyesore [O]r
eyestrain [A]m/n
eyewitness [e]

F

fabric [i]
fabricate [A]
fabricated [e]
fabrication [u]m/n
fabulous [e]
fabulously [E]
face [A]
facet [e]
facial [u]l
facilitate [A]
facilitated [e]
facilitating [E]m/n
facilitating [e]m/n*
facility [E]
facing [E]m/n
facing [e]m/n*
fact [a]
factor [er]
factory [E]
factual [u]l
faculty [E]
fad [a]
fade [A]
faded [e]
fading [E]m/n
fading [e]m/n*
fail [A]l
failing [E]m/n
failing [e]m/n*
failure [er]
faint [A]m/n
fainted [e]

faintly [E]
fair [e]r
fairly [E]
fairway [A]
fairy [E]
fairytale [A]l
faith [A]
faithful [u]l
faithfully [E]
fake [A]
faker [er]
faking [E]m/n
faking [e]m/n*
fall [o]l
fallen [e]m/n
falling [E]m/n
falling [e]m/n*
false [o]l
falsely [E]
falsie [E]
falsify [I]
falsifying [E]m/n
falsifying [e]m/n*
falter [er]
faltering [E]m/n
faltering [e]m/n*
fame [A]m/n
familiar [er]
familiarize [I]
familiarizing [E]m/n
familiarizing [e]m/n*
family [E]

famine [i]m/n
famous [e]
famously [E]
fan [a]m/n
fanatic [i]
fanatical [u]l
fanatically [E]
fanciful [u]l
fancy [E]
fanning [E]m/n
fanning [e]m/n*
fanny [E]
fantasize [I]
fantasizing [E]m/n
fantasizing [e]m/n*
fantastic [i]
fantastically [E]
fantasy [E]
far [o]r
farce [o]r
fare [e]r
farewell [e]l
farfetched [e]
farm [o]r
farmer [er]
farmhouse [ow]
farming [E]m/n
farming [e]m/n*
farmland [a]m/n
farmstead [e]
farsighted [e]
farther [er]

farthest [e]
fascinate [A]
fascinated [e]
fascinating [E]m/n
fascinating [e]m/n*
fascination [u]m/n
fashion [u]m/n
fashionable [u]l
fashionably [E]
fast [a]
fasted [e]
fastener [er]
faster [er]
fasting [E]m/n
fasting [e]m/n*
fat [a]
fate [A]
fated [e]
father [er]
father [u]*
fathering [E]m/n
fathering [e]m/n*
fatherly [E]
fathom [u]m/n
fatigue [E]
fatten [e]m/n
fattening [E]m/n
fattening [e]m/n*
fatter [er]
fatty [E]
faucet [e]
fault [o]l
faulting [E]m/n
faulting [e]m/n*
faulty [E]
favor [er]
favorable [u]l
favoring [E]m/n
favoring [e]m/n*
favorite [i]
favoritism [e]m/n
fawn [o]m/n
fawning [E]m/n
fawning [e]m/n*
fax [a]

faxing [E]m/n
faxing [e]m/n*
fear [E]r
fearful [u]l
fearfully [E]
fearless [e]
fearlessly [E]
fearsome [u]m/n
feasible [u]l
feasibly [E]
feast [E]
feasting [E]m/n
feasting [e]m/n*
feat [E]
feather [er]
feathering [E]
feathery [E]
feature [er]
featuring [E]m/n
featuring [e]m/n*
February [E]
fed [e]
fee [E]
feeble [u]l
feebly [E]
feed [E]
feedback [a]
feeder [er]
feeding [E]m/n
feeding [e]m/n*
feel [E]l
feeler [er]
feeling [E]m/n
feeling [e]m/n*
feet [E]
feisty [E]
feline [I]m/n
fell [e]l
fellow [O]
felon [e]m/n
felony [E]
felt [e]l
female [A]l
feminine [i]m/n
femininity [E]

femme [e]m/n
femur [er]
fence [e]m/n
fencing [E]m/n
fencing [e]m/n*
fender [er]
ferment [e]m/n
fermented [e]
fermenting [E]m/n
fermenting [e]m/n*
fern [er]m/n
ferocious [e]
ferociously [E]
ferret [e]
ferry [E]
fertile [u]l
fertility [E]
fertilization [u]m/n
fertilize [l]
fertilizer [er]
fertilizing [E]m/n
fertilizing [e]m/n*
fester [er]
festering [E]m/n
festering [e]m/n*
festival [u]l
festive [i]
festivity [E]
fetch [e]
fetching [E]m/n
fetching [e]m/n*
fetish [i]
fetus [e]
feud [oo]
feuding [E]m/n
feuding [e]m/n*
fever [er]
feverish [i]
few [oo]
fewer [er]
fiancé [A]
fiasco [O]
fib [i]
fibbing [E]m/n
fibbing [e]m/n*

fiber [er]
fiberglass [a]
fickle [u]l
fiction [u]m/n
fictional [u]l
fictitious [e]
fiddle [u]l
fiddler [er]
fiddling [E]m/n
fiddling [e]m/n*
fidelity [E]
fidgety [E]
field [E]l
fielding [E]m/n
fielding [e]m/n*
fieldwork [er]
fiend [E]m/n
fiendish [i]
fierce [E]r
fiercely [E]
fiery [E]
fiesta [u]
fifteen [E]m/n
fifth [i]
fifty [E]
fig [i]
fight [I]
fighter [er]
fighting [E]m/n
fighting [e]m/n*
figment [e]m/n
figurative [i]
figure [er]
figurine [E]m/n
file [I]l
fill [i]l
filler [er]
fillet [A]
filling [E]m/n
filling [e]m/n*
filly [E]
filmmaker [er]
filmstrip [i]
filmy [E]
filter [er]

filtering [E]m/n
filtering [e]m/n*
filthy [E]
filtrate [A]
filtrated [e]
filtration [u]m/n
fin [i]
finagle [u]l
final [u]l
finale [E]
finale [e]*
finalist [i]
finality [E]
finalize [I]
finalizing [E]m/n
finalizing [e]m/n*
finally [E]
finance [a]m/n
financial [u]l
financing [E]m/n
financing [e]m/n*
find [I]m/n
finder [er]
finding [E]m/n
finding [e]m/n*
fine [I]m/n
finely [E]
finer [er]
finesse [e]
finest [e]
finger [er]
fingering [E]m/n
fingering [e]m/n*
fingertip [i]
finicky [E]
finish [i]
finishing [E]m/n
finishing [e]m/n*
finite [I]
fire [I]r
fireball [o]l
firecracker [er]
firefly [I]
fireman [e]m/n
fireplace [A]

fireproof [oo]
fireproofing [E]m/n
fireproofing [e]m/n*
fireside [I]
firetrap [a]
fireworks [er]
firing [E]m/n
firing [e]m/n*
firm [er]m/n
firmly [E]
first [er]
firstborn [O]r
fiscal [u]l
fish [i]
fishbowl [O]l
fisherman [e]m/n
fisheye [I]
fishing [E]m/n
fishing [e]m/n*
fishnet [e]
fishy [E]
fistfight [I]
fit [i]
fitness [e]
fitted [e]
fitting [E]m/n
fitting [e]m/n*
five [I]
fix [i]
fixate [A]
fixated [e]
fixation [u]m/n
fixer [er]
fixing [E]m/n
fixing [e]m/n*
fixture [er]
fizzle [u]l
fizzling [E]m/n
fizzling [e]m/n*
fizzy [E]
flab [a]
flabby [E]
flack [a]
flag [a]
flagpole [O]l

flagship [i]
flagstone [O]m/n
flair [e]r
flake [A]
flaking [E]m/n
flaking [e]m/n*
flaky [E]
flamboyant [e]m/n
flamboyantly [E]
flame [A]m/n
flaming [E]m/n
flaming [e]m/n*
flannel [u]l
flap [a]
flapjack [a]
flapping [E]m/n
flapping [e]m/n*
flare [e]r
flaring [E]m/n
flaring [e]m/n*
flash [a]
flashback [a]
flashing [E]m/n
flashing [e]m/n*
flashlight [I]
flashy [E]
flask [a]
flat [a]
flatbed [e]
flathead [e]
flatly [E]
flatten [e]m/n
flatter [er]
flattering [E]m/n
flattering [e]m/n*
flattery [E]
flattop [o]
flaunt [o]m/n
flaunted [e]
flaunter [er]
flaunting [E]m/n
flaunting [e]m/n*
flaunty [E]
flavor [er]
flavorful [u]l

flaw [o]
flawless [e]
flea [E]
fleabag [a]
fleabite [I]
fleck [e]
fled [e]
flee [E]
fleece [E]
fleecy [E]
fleeing [E]m/n
fleeing [e]m/n*
fleet [E]
fleeting [E]m/n
fleeting [e]m/n*
flesh [e]
fleshy [E]
flew [oo]
flex [e]
flexibility [E]
flexible [u]l
flexibly [E]
flexing [E]m/n
flexing [e]m/n*
flick [i]
flicker [er]
flickering [E]m/n
flickering [e]m/n*
flicking [E]m/n
flicking [e]m/n*
flier [I]r
flight [I]
flighty [E]
flimsy [E]
flinch [i]m/n
flinching [E]m/n
flinching [e]m/n*
fling [E]m/n
flip [i]
flipper [er]
flipping [E]m/n
flipping [e]m/n*
flirt [er]
flirtatious [e]
flirted [e]

flirting [E]m/n
flirting [e]m/n*
flirty [E]
float [O]
floated [e]
floater [er]
floating [E]m/n
floating [e]m/n*
flock [o]
flocking [E]m/n
flocking [e]m/n*
flood [u]
flooded [e]
floodgate [A]
flooding [E]m/n
flooding [e]m/n*
floodlight [I]
floor [O]r
flooring [E]m/n
flooring [e]m/n*
floozy [E]
flop [o]
flopping [E]m/n
flopping [e]m/n*
floppy [E]
floral [u]l
florist [i]
floss [o]
flossing [E]m/n
flossing [e]m/n*
flossy [E]
flouncy [E]
flounder [er]
floundering [E]m/n
floundering [e]m/n*
flour [er]
flourish [i]
flourishing [E]m/n
flourishing [e]m/n*
flow [O]
flower [er]
flowerpot [o]
flowery [E]
flowing [E]m/n
flowing [e]m/n*

flown [O]m/n
flu [oo]
flub [u]
flubbing [E]m/n
flubbing [e]m/n*
fluctuate [A]
fluctuated [e]
fluctuating [E]m/n
fluctuating [e]m/n*
fluent [e]m/n
fluently [E]
fluff [u]
fluffing [E]m/n
fluffing [e]m/n*
fluffy [E]
fluid [i]
fluke [oo]
flunk [u]m/n
flunking [E]m/n
flunking [e]m/n*
flunky [E]
fluoride [I]
flurry [E]
flush [u]
flushing [E]m/n
flushing [e]m/n*
fluster [er]
flustering [E]m/n
flustering [e]m/n*
flute [oo]
flutter [er]
fluttering [E]m/n
fluttering [e]m/n*
fly [I]
flyer [er]
flying [E]m/n
flying [e]m/n*
foal [O]l
foam [O]m/n
foaming [E]m/n
foaming [e]m/n*
foamy [E]
focal [u]l
focus [e]
focusing [E]m/n

focusing [e]m/n*
fog [o]
foggy [E]
foghorn [O]r
fogy [E]
foil [Oi]l
fold [O]l
folded [e]
folder [er]
folding [E]m/n
folding [e]m/n*
folk [O]l
folklore [O]r
folksy [E]
follow [O]
follower [er]
following [E]m/n
following [e]m/n*
folly [E]
fond [o]m/n
fondly [E]
font [o]m/n
food [oo]
fool [oo]l
fooling [E]m/n
fooling [e]m/n*
foolish [i]
foolishly [E]
foolproof [oo]
foot [oo/]
football [o]l
footer [er]
foothill [i]l
footing [E]m/n
footing [e]m/n*
footnote [O]
footstep [e]
footstool [oo]l
footwork [er]
for [O]r
forbid [i]
forbidden [e]m/n
forbidding [E]m/n
forbidding [e]m/n*
force [O]r

forceful [u]l
forcefully [E]
forcing [E]m/n
forcing [e]m/n*
fore [O]r
forecast [a]
forecasted [e]
forecasting [E]m/n
forecasting [e]m/n*
foreclose [O]
foreclosing [E]m/n
foreclosing [e]m/n*
foreclosure [er]
forefront [u]m/n
forego [O]
foregoing [E]m/n
foregoing [e]m/n*
foregone [o]m/n
forehead [e]
foreign [e]lm/n
foreigner [er]
foreman [e]m/n
foreplay [A]
foresee [E]
foreseeing [E]m/n
foreseeing [e]m/n*
foresight [I]
forest [e]
foretell [e]l
foretelling [E]m/n
foretelling [e]m/n*
forethought [o]
forever [er]
forevermore [O]r
forewarn [O]r
forewarning [E]m/n
forewarning [e]m/n*
forfeit [i]
forfeited [e]
forfeiting [E]m/n
forfeiting [e]m/n*
forgave [A]
forget [e]
forgettable [u]l
forgetting [E]m/n

forgetting [e]m/n*
forgive [i]
forgiven [e]
forgiveness [e]
forgiving [E]m/n
forgiving [e]m/n*
forgot [o]
forgotten [e]m/n
fork [O]r
forlorn [O]r
form [O]r
formal [u]l
formality [E]
formalize [I]
formalizing [E]m/n
formalizing [e]m/n*
formally [E]
format [a]
formation [u]m/n
formatted [e]
formatting [E]m/n
formatting [e]m/n*
former [er]
forming [E]m/n
forming [e]m/n*
formula [u]
formulate [A]
formulated [e]
formulating [E]m/n
formulating [e]m/n*
forsake [A]
forsaken [e]m/n
forsaking [E]m/n
forsaking [e]m/n*
fort [O]r
forth [O]r
forthcoming [E]m/n
forthcoming [e]m/n*
forthright [I]
fortify [I]
fortifying [E]m/n
fortifying [e]m/n*
fortitude [oo]
fortnight [I]
fortunate [e]

fortunately [E]
fortune [e]m/n
forty [E]
forum [u]m/n
forward [er]
forwarding [E]m/n
forwarding [e]m/n*
fossil [u]l
foster [er]
fostering [E]m/n
fostering [e]m/n*
fought [o]
foul [ow]l
fouling [E]m/n
fouling [e]m/n*
found [ow]m/n
foundation [u]m/n
founded [e]
founder [er]
founding [E]m/n
founding [e]m/n*
fountain [e]m/n
four [O]r
fourscore [O]r
foursome [u]m/n
fourteen [E]m/n
fourth [O]r
fowl [ow]l
fox [o]
foxhole [O]l
foxtrot [o]
foxy [E]
foyer [er]
fraction [u]m/n
fractional [u]l
fracture [er]
fracturing [E]m/n
fracturing [e]m/n*
fragile [u]l
fragment [e]m/n
fragmented [e]
fragmenting [E]m/n
fragmenting [e]m/n*
fragrance [e]m/n
fragrant [e]m/n

frail [A]l
frame [A]m/n
framer [er]
framework [er]
framing [E]m/n
framing [e]m/n*
franchise [I]
frank [a]ng/k
frankly [E]
frantic [i]
frantically [E]
fraught [o]
freak [E]
freaking [E]m/n
freaking [e]m/n*
freaky [E]
freckle [u]l
free [E]
freebie [E]
freedom [u]m/n
freeing [E]m/n
freeing [e]m/n*
freeloader [er]
freeloading [E]m/n
freeloading [e]m/n*
freer [er]
freestyle [I]l
freeway [A]
freewill [i]l
freeze [E]
freezer [er]
freezing [E]m/n
freezing [e]m/n*
freight [A]
freighter [er]
frenzy [E]
frequency [E]
frequent [e]m/n
frequented [e]
frequently [E]
fresh [e]
freshen [e]m/n
freshening [E]m/n
freshening [e]m/n*
fresher [er]

freshly [E]
freshman [e]m/n
fret [e]
fretting [E]m/n
fretting [e]m/n*
friction [u]m/n
Friday [A]
fridge [i]
friend [e]m/n
friendlier [er]
friendly [E]
friendship [i]
fright [I]
frighten [e]m/n
frightening [E]m/n
frightening [e]m/n*
frightful [u]l
frightfully [E]
frigid [i]
frigidly [E]
frill [i]l
frilly [E]
fringe [i]m/n
friskier [er]
frisky [E]
fritter [er]
frivolous [e]
frivolously [E]
frizz [i]
frizzy [E]
fro [O]
frock [o]
frog [o]
frolic [i]
frolicking [E]m/n
frolicking [e]m/n*
from [u]m/n
front [u]m/n
frontal [u]l
frost [o]
frostbite [I]
frosted [e]
frosting [E]m/n

frosting [e]m/n*
frosty [E]
frothy [E]
frown [ow]m/n
frowning [E]m/n
frowning [e]m/n*
froze [O]
frozen [e]m/n
frugal [u]l
frugally [E]
fruit [oo]
fruitcake [A]
fruity [E]
frumpy [E]
frustrate [A]
frustrated [e]
frustrating [E]m/n
frustrating [e]m/n*
frustration [u]m/n
fry [I]
fryer [er]
frying [E]m/n
frying [e]m/n*
fudge [u]
fudging [E]m/n
fudging [e]m/n*
fuel [oo]l
fueling [E]m/n
fueling [e]m/n*
fugitive [i]
fulfill [i]l
fulfilling [E]m/n
fulfilling [e]m/n*
full [oo]l
fullback [a]
fuller [er]
fumble [u]l
fumbling [E]m/n
fumbling [e]m/n*
fumigate [A]
fumigated [e]
fumigating [E]m/n
fumigating [e]m/n*

fumy [E]
fun [u]m/n
function [u]m/n
functional [u]l
functioning [E]m/n
functioning [e]m/n*
fund [u]m/n
fundamental [u]l
fundamentally [E]
funded [e]
funding [E]m/n
funding [e]m/n*
funeral [u]l
fungus [e]
funky [E]
funnel [u]l
funny [E]
funny [e]*
fur [er]
furious [e]
furiously [E]
furlough [O]
furnace [e]
furnish [i]
furnishing [E]m/n
furnishing [e]m/n*
furniture [er]
furrow [O]
furry [E]
further [er]
furthermore [O]r
fury [E]
fusion [u]m/n
fuss [u]
fussing [E]m/n
fussing [e]m/n*
fussy [E]
futile [u]l
futility [E]
future [er]
futuristic [i]
fuzz [u]
fuzzy [E]

G

gab [a]
gabby [E]
gadget [e]
gag [a]
gagging [E]m/n
gagging [e]m/n*
gain [A]m/n
gainful [u]l
gaining [E]m/n
gaining [e]m/n*
gait [A]
gaited [e]
gal [a]l
galaxy [E]
gall [o]l
gallant [e]m/n
gallantly [E]
gallery [E]
galley [E]
gallon [u]m/n
gallop [u]
galloping [E]m/n
galloping [e]m/n*
gallstone [O]m/n
galore [O]r
gamble [u]l
gambler [er]
gambling [E]m/n
gambling [e]m/n*
game [A]m/n
gamer [er]
gamey [E]
gaming [E]m/n
gaming [e]m/n*
gamut [u]
gang [a]ng/k
gangster [er]
gap [a]
gape [A]
gaping [E]m/n
gaping [e]m/n*

garage [o]
garbage [e]
garden [e]m/n
gardenia [u]
gardening [E]m/n
gardening [e]m/n*
gargle [u]l
gargling [E]m/n
gargling [e]m/n*
garland [e]m/n
garlic [i]
garlicky [E]
garment [e]m/n
garner [er]
garnish [i]
garnishing [E]m/n
garnishing [e]m/n*
garter [er]
gas [a]
gaslight [l]
gasoline [E]m/n
gassy [E]
gate [A]
gated [e]
gateway [A]
gather [er]
gathering [E]m/n
gathering [e]m/n*
gator [er]
gaudy [E]
gauge [A]
gauging [E]m/n
gauging [e]m/n*
gauze [o]
gave [A]
gavel [u]l
gawk [o]
gawking [E]m/n
gawking [e]m/n*
gay [A]
gaze [A]

gazebo [O]
gazelle [e]l
gazer [er]
gazette [e]
gazing [E]m/n
gazing [e]m/n*
gear [E]r
gearbox [o]
gearing [E]m/n
gearing [e]m/n*
gecko [O]
gee [E]
geezer [er]
gel [e]l
gem [e]m/n
gemstone [O]m/n
gender [er]
general [u]l
generally [E]
generate [A]
generated [e]
generating [E]m/n
generating [e]m/n*
generation [u]m/n
generator [er]
generic [i]
generosity [E]
generous [e]
generously [E]
genie [E]
genius [e]
gentile [l]l
gentle [u]l
gentler [er]
gently [E]
gently [e]*
genuine [i]m/n
genuinely [E]
geranium [u]m/n
germ [er]m/n
gesture [er]

gesturing [E]m/n
gesturing [e]m/n*
get [e]
getting [E]m/n
getting [e]m/n*
geyser [er]
ghetto [O]
ghost [O]
ghostly [E]
ghostwrite [I]
ghoul [oo]l
ghoulish [i]
giant [e]m/n
gibberish [i]
giddy [E]
gift [i]
gifted [e]
gifting [E]m/n
gifting [e]m/n*
gig [i]
gigantic [i]
giggle [u]l
giggling [E]m/n
giggling [e]m/n*
gill [i]l
gimmick [i]
gimmicky [E]
gin [i]m/n
ginger [er]
gingerly [E]
gingham [e]m/n
giraffe [a]
girl [er]l
girlfriend [e]m/n
girlish [i]
girly [E]
give [i]
given [e]m/n
giver [er]
giving [E]m/n
giving [e]m/n*
gizmo [O]
glacier [er]
glad [a]
glade [A]

gladly [E]
glamorous [e]
glamorously [E]
glamour [er]
glance [a]m/n
glancing [E]m/n
glancing [e]m/n*
gland [a]m/n
glare [e]r
glaring [E]m/n
glaring [e]m/n*
glass [a]
glassy [E]
glaze [A]
glazing [E]m/n
glazing [e]m/n*
glee [E]
glen [e]m/n
glide [I]
glided [e]
glider [er]
gliding [E]m/n
gliding [e]m/n*
glimmer [er]
glimmering [E]m/n
glimmering [e]m/n*
glimpse [i]m/n
glimpsing [E]m/n
glimpsing [e]m/n*
glisten [e]m/n
glistening [E]m/n
glistening [e]m/n*
glitch [i]
glitter [er]
glittering [E]m/n
glittering [e]m/n*
glittery [E]
glitzy [E]
gloat [O]
gloated [e]
gloating [E]m/n
gloating [e]m/n*
glob [o]
global [u]l
globally [E]

globe [O]
globetrotting [E]m/n
globetrotting [e]m/n*
globular [er]
gloom [oo]m/n
gloomy [E]
glorify [I]
glorifying [E]m/n
glorifying [e]m/n*
glorious [e]
glory [E]
gloss [o]
glossing [E]m/n
glossing [e]m/n*
glossy [E]
glove [u]
glow [O]
glowing [E]m/n
glowing [e]m/n*
glue [oo]
glum [u]m/n
glumly [E]
gnaw [o]
gnawing [E]m/n
gnawing [e]m/n*
gnome [O]m/n
go [O]
goad [O]
goaded [e]
goading [E]m/n
goading [e]m/n*
goal [O]l
goalie [E]
goat [O]
goatee [E]
gob [o]
gobble [u]l
goblet [e]
goblin [i]m/n
godchild [I]l
goddess [e]
goes [O]
going [E]m/n
going [e]m/n*
gold [O]l

golden [e]m/n
golf [o]l
golfer [er]
golfing [E]m/n
golfing [e]m/n*
golly [E]
gondola [u]
gone [o]m/n
goner [er]
good [oo/]
goodbye [I]
goodness [e]
goodnight [I]
goodwill [i]l
goody [E]
gooey [E]
goof [oo]
goofball [o]l
goofing [E]m/n
goofing [e]m/n*
goofy [E]
gooseneck [e]
gore [O]r
gorgeous [e]
gorgeously [E]
gorilla [u]
gory [E]
gosh [o]
gossip [i]
gossiping [E]m/n
gossiping [e]m/n*
got [o]
gothic [i]
gotten [e]m/n
gourmet [A]
govern [er]m/n
governing [E]m/n
governing [e]m/n*
governor [er]
gown [ow]m/n
grab [a]
grabbing [E]m/n
grabbing [e]m/n*
grace [A]
graceful [u]l

gracefully [E]
gracious [e]
graciously [E]
grad [a]
grade [A]
graded [e]
grader [er]
grading [E]m/n
grading [e]m/n*
gradual [u]l
gradually [E]
graduate [A]
graduate [e]
graduated [e]
graduating [E]m/n
graduating [e]m/n*
graduation [u]m/n
grain [A]m/n
grainy [E]
gram [a]m/n
grammar [er]
grand [a]m/n
grandchild [I]l
grandchildren [e]m/n
granddaughter [er]
grander [er]
grandfather [er]
grandly [E]
grandma [o]
grandmother [er]
grandpa [o]
grandson [u]m/n
grandstand [a]m/n
grandstanded [e]
grandstanding [E]m/n
grandstanding [e]m/n*
granite [i]
granny [E]
grant [a]m/n
granted [e]
granting [E]m/n
granting [e]m/n*
grantor [er]
grape [A]
grapevine [I]m/n

graph [a]
graphic [i]
graphically [E]
graphite [I]
grasp [a]
grasping [E]m/n
grasping [e]m/n*
grass [a]
grassy [E]
grate [A]
grated [e]
grater [er]
gratify [I]
gratifying [E]m/n
gratifying [e]m/n*
grating [E]m/n
grating [e]m/n*
gratitude [oo]
grave [A]
gravel [u]l
gravely [E]
gravitate [A]
gravitated [e]
gravitating [E]m/n
gravitating [e]m/n*
gravitation [u]m/n
gravitational [u]l
gravity [E]
gravy [E]
gray [A]
graying [E]m/n
graying [e]m/n*
graze [A]
grazing [E]m/n
grazing [e]m/n*
grease [E]
greasy [E]
great [A]
greater [er]
greatly [E]
greed [E]
greedy [E]
green [E]m/n
greenback [a]
greener [er]

greenhouse [ow]
greet [E]
greeted [e]
greeter [er]
greeting [E]m/n
greeting [e]m/n*
grew [oo]
grey [A]
grid [i]
griddle [u]l
gridlock [o]
grill [i]l
grilling [E]m/n
grilling [e]m/n*
grim [i]m/n
grime [I]m/n
grimy [E]
grin [i]m/n
grind [I]m/n
grinder [er]
grinding [E]m/n
grinding [e]m/n*
grinning [E]m/n
grinning [e]m/n*
grip [i]
gripe [I]
gripping [E]m/n
gripping [e]m/n*
gristle [u]l
grit [i]
gritted [e]
gritting [E]m/n
gritting [e]m/n*
gritty [E]
grizzly [E]
groan [O]m/n
groaning [E]m/n
groaning [e]m/n*
grocer [er]
grocery [E]
groggy [E]
groin [Oi]m/n
groom [oo]m/n
groomer [er]
grooming [E]m/n

grooming [e]m/n*
groomsman [e]m/n
groove [oo]
grooving [E]m/n
grooving [e]m/n*
groovy [E]
grope [O]
groping [E]m/n
groping [e]m/n*
gross [O]
grossly [E]
grotto [O]
grouchy [E]
ground [ow]m/n
grounded [e]
groundhog [o]
grounding [E]m/n
grounding [e]m/n*
group [oo]
groupie [E]
grouping [E]m/n
grouping [e]m/n*
grove [O]
grovel [u]l
grow [O]
grower [er]
growing [E]m/n
growing [e]m/n*
growl [ow]l
growling [E]m/n
growling [e]m/n*
grown [O]m/n
grownup [u]
growth [O]
grub [u]
grubby [E]
grudge [u]
grudgingly [E]
gruel [oo]l
grueling [E]m/n
grueling [e]m/n*
gruesome [u]m/n
gruff [u]
gruffly [E]
grumble [u]l

grumbling [E]m/n
grumbling [e]m/n*
grumpy [E]
grungy [E]
grunt [u]m/n
grunted [e]
grunting [E]m/n
grunting [e]m/n*
guacamole [E]
guarantee [E]
guarantor [O]r
guard [o]r
guarded [e]
guardian [e]m/n
guarding [E]m/n
guarding [e]m/n*
guess [e]
guesswork [er]
guest [e]
guide [I]
guided [e]
guideline [I]m/n
guiding [E]m/n
guiding [e]m/n*
guild [i]l
guilt [i]l
guilty [E]
guitar [o]r
gulf [u]l
gum [u]m/n
gumbo [O]
gumdrop [o]
gumming [E]m/n
gumming [e]m/n*
gummy [E]
gumption [u]m/n
gun [u]m/n
gunfight [I]
gunk [u]m/n
gunman [e]m/n
gunning [E]m/n
gunning [e]m/n*
gunshot [o]
guppy [E]
gurney [E]

gush [u]
gusher [er]
gushing [E]m/n
gushing [e]m/n*
gushy [E]
gusto [O]
gusty [E]
gut [u]
gutsy [E]

gutter [er]
guy [I]
guzzle [u]l
guzzler [er]
guzzling [E]m/n
guzzling [e]m/n*
gym [i]m/n
gymnasium [u]m/n
gymnastic [i]

gypsum [u]m/n
gypsy [E]
gyrate [A]
gyrated [e]
gyrating [E]m/n
gyrating [e]m/n*
gyro [O]

H

habit [i]
habitat [a]
habitual [u]l
habitually [E]
hack [a]
hacker [er]
hacking [E]m/n
hacking [e]m/n*
hacksaw [o]
had [a]
hag [a]
haggle [u]l
haggling [E]m/n
haggling [e]m/n*
hah [o]
hail [A]l
hailing [E]m/n
hailing [e]m/n*
hair [e]r
hairball [o]l
haircut [u]
hairdo [oo]
hairless [e]
hairline [I]m/n
hairpin [i]m/n
hairstyle [I]l
hairstyling [E]m/n
hairstyling [e]m/n*
hairstylist [i]
hairy [E]
half [a]

halfback [a]
halftime [I]m/n
halftone [O]m/n
halfway [A]
hall [o]l
Halloween [E]m/n
hallucinate [A]
hallucinated [e]
hallucinating [E]m/n
hallucinating [e]m/n*
hallway [A]
halo [O]
halt [o]l
halted [e]
halter [er]
halting [E]m/n
halting [e]m/n*
ham [a]m/n
hamburger [er]
hammer [er]
hammering [E]m/n
hammering [e]m/n*
hamming [E]m/n
hamming [e]m/n*
hammock [e]
hamper [er]
hampering [E]m/n
hampering [e]m/n*
hamster [er]
hand [a]m/n
handbag [a]

handball [o]l
handbook [oo/]
handcrafted [e]
handcuff [u]
handcuffing [E]m/n
handcuffing [e]m/n*
handed [e]
handful [oo]l
handgun [u]m/n
handicap [a]
handing [E]m/n
handing [e]m/n*
handiwork [er]
handle [u]l
handlebar [o]r
handler [er]
handling [E]m/n
handling [e]m/n*
handmade [A]
handpick [i]
handset [e]
handshake [A]
handsome [u]m/n
handsomely [E]
handwriting [E]m/n
handwriting [e]m/n*
handwritten [e]m/n
handy [E]
hang [a]ng/k
hangar [er]
hanger [er]

hanging [E]m/n
hanging [e]m/n*
hanky [E]
Hanukkah [u]
haphazard [er]
haphazardly [E]
happen [e]m/n
happening [E]m/n
happening [e]m/n*
happenstance [a]m/n
happily [E]
happiness [e]
happy [E]
happy [e]*
harass [a]
harassing [E]m/n
harassing [e]m/n*
harbor [er]
harboring [E]m/n
harboring [e]m/n*
hard [o]r
hardback [a]
hardball [o]l
hardcore [O]r
harden [e]m/n
hardener [er]
hardening [E]m/n
hardening [e]m/n*
harder [er]
hardest [e]
hardhead [e]
hardly [E]
hardship [i]
hardtop [o]
hardy [E]
harem [e]m/n
harm [o]r
harmful [u]l
harming [E]m/n
harming [e]m/n*
harmonize [I]
harmonizing [E]m/n
harmonizing [e]m/n*
harmony [E]
harness [e]

harnessing [E]m/n
harnessing [e]m/n*
harp [o]r
harping [E]m/n
harping [e]m/n*
harsh [o]r
harsher [er]
harshly [E]
harvest [e]
harvesting [E]m/n
harvesting [e]m/n*
has [a]
hassle [u]l
hassling [E]m/n
hassling [e]m/n*
haste [A]
hasten [e]m/n
hastening [E]m/n
hastening [e]m/n*
hastily [E]
hasty [E]
hat [a]
hatbox [o]
hatch [a]
hatchback [a]
hatching [E]m/n
hatching [e]m/n*
hate [A]
hated [e]
hating [E]m/n
hating [e]m/n*
hatred [e]
haul [o]l
hauling [E]m/n
hauling [e]m/n*
haunt [o]m/n
haunted [e]
haunting [E]m/n
haunting [e]m/n*
have [a]
haven [e]m/n
having [E]m/n
having [e]m/n*
havoc [e]
hawk [o]

hawking [E]m/n
hawking [e]m/n*
hay [A]
hayride [I]
haystack [a]
hazard [er]
hazardous [e]
hazardously [E]
haze [A]
hazel [u]l
hazing [E]m/n
hazing [e]m/n*
hazy [E]
he [E]
head [e]
headache [A]
headdress [e]
heading [E]m/n
heading [e]m/n*
headlight [I]
headline [I]m/n
headlock [o]
headphone [O]m/n
headset [e]
headstone [O]m/n
headway [A]
heal [E]l
healer [er]
healing [E]m/n
healing [e]m/n*
health [e]l
healthy [E]
heap [E]
heaping [E]m/n
heaping [e]m/n*
hear [E]r
heard [er]
hearing [E]m/n
hearing [e]m/n*
hearsay [A]
heart [o]r
heartache [A]
heartbreak [A]
heartbreaking [E]m/n
heartbreaking [e]m/n*

heartbroken [e]m/n
heartburn [er]m/n
heartfelt [e]l
heartily [E]
heartsick [i]
heartthrob [o]
hearty [E]
heat [E]
heated [e]
heater [er]
heathen [e]m/n
heather [er]
heating [E]m/n
heating [e]m/n*
heatstroke [O]
heave [E]
heaven [e]m/n
heavenly [E]
heavier [er]
heaving [E]m/n
heaving [e]m/n*
heavy [E]
heavy [e]*
heavyweight [A]
heck [e]
heckle [u]l
heckling [E]m/n
heckling [e]m/n*
hectic [i]
hedge [e]
hedging [E]m/n
hedging [e]m/n*
heed [E]
heeded [e]
heeding [E]m/n
heeding [e]m/n*
heel [E]l
heeler [er]
heeling [E]m/n
heeling [e]m/n*
hefty [E]
heifer [er]
height [I]
heighten [e]m/n
heightening [E]m/n

heightening [e]m/n*
heirloom [oo]m/n
held [e]l
helicopter [er]
helium [u]m/n
hell [e]l
hellhole [O]l
hellish [i]
hello [O]
helmet [e]
help [e]l
helper [er]
helpful [u]l
helping [E]m/n
helping [e]m/n*
helpless [e]
helplessly [E]
hem [e]m/n
hemline [I]m/n
hemlock [o]
hemming [E]m/n
hemming [e]m/n*
hemorrhoid [Oi]
hen [e]m/n
her [er]
herb [er]
herbal [u]l
herd [er]
herded [e]
herding [E]m/n
herding [e]m/n*
here [E]r
hereby [I]
hereditary [E]
herein [i]m/n
hermit [i]
hero [O]
heroic [i]
heroically [E]
heroism [e]m/n
herself [e]l
hesitant [e]m/n
hesitantly [E]
hesitate [A]
hesitated [e]

hesitating [E]m/n
hesitating [e]m/n*
hesitation [u]m/n
hex [e]
hexagon [o]m/n
hey [A]
hi [I]
hiatus [e]
hibernate [A]
hibernated [e]
hibernating [E]m/n
hibernating [e]m/n*
hiccup [u]
hiccuping [E]m/n
hiccuping [e]m/n*
hick [i]
hickey [E]
hid [i]
hidden [e]m/n
hide [I]
hiding [E]m/n
hiding [e]m/n*
high [I]
highball [o]l
higher [er]
highlight [I]
highlighter [er]
highlighting [E]m/n
highlighting [e]m/n*
highly [E]
highness [e]
highway [A]
hijack [a]
hijacking [E]m/n
hijacking [e]m/n*
hike [I]
hiker [er]
hiking [E]m/n
hiking [e]m/n*
hilarious [e]
hilariously [E]
hill [i]l
hillside [I]
hilltop [o]
hilly [E]

him [i]m/n
himself [e]l
hind [I]m/n
hinder [er]
hindering [E]m/n
hindering [e]m/n*
hindsight [I]
hinge [i]m/n
hinging [E]m/n
hinging [e]m/n*
hint [i]m/n
hinted [e]
hinting [E]m/n
hinting [e]m/n*
hip [i]
hipbone [O]m/n
hippie [E]
hippo [O]
hipster [er]
hire [I]r
hiring [E]m/n
hiring [e]m/n*
his [i]
Hispanic [i]
hiss [i]
hissing [E]m/n
hissing [e]m/n*
historic [i]
historically [E]
history [E]
hit [i]
hitch [i]
hitchhike [I]
hitchhiking [E]m/n
hitchhiking [e]m/n*
hitter [er]
hitting [E]m/n
hitting [e]m/n*
hive [I]
hoagie [E]
hoard [O]r
hoarded [e]
hoarding [E]m/n
hoarding [e]m/n*
hoarse [O]r

hoarsely [E]
hoax [O]
hobby [E]
hobnob [o]
hobnobbing [E]m/n
hobnobbing [e]m/n*
hock [o]
hockey [E]
hocking [E]m/n
hocking [e]m/n*
hoe [O]
hog [o]
hogging [E]m/n
hogging [e]m/n*
hoist [Oi]
hoisted [e]
hoisting [E]m/n
hoisting [e]m/n*
hokey [E]
hold [O]l
holder [er]
holding [E]m/n
holding [e]m/n*
holdup [u]
hole [O]l
holiday [A]
holistic [i]
holistically [E]
holler [er]
hollering [E]m/n
hollering [e]m/n*
hollow [O]
holly [E]
holy [E]
home [O]m/n
homegrown [O]m/n
homelike [I]
homemade [A]
homeopath [a]
homeopathic [i]
homer [er]
homesick [i]
homespun [u]m/n
hometown [ow]m/n
homework [er]

homey [E]
homing [E]m/n
homing [e]m/n*
honcho [O]
hone [O]m/n
honest [e]
honestly [E]
honesty [E]
honey [E]
honeymoon [oo]m/n
honeymooning [E]m/n
honeymooning [e]m/n*
honeysuckle [u]l
honing [E]m/n
honing [e]m/n*
honk [o]m/n
honker [er]
honking [E]m/n
honking [e]m/n*
honky [E]
honor [er]
honorable [u]l
honorably [E]
honorary [E]
honoring [E]m/n
honoring [e]m/n*
hood [oo/]
hooded [e]
hook [oo/]
hooker [er]
hooking [E]m/n
hooking [e]m/n*
hooky [E]
hoop [oo]
hoopla [o]
hooray [A]
hop [o]
hope [O]
hopeful [u]l
hopefully [E]
hopeless [e]
hopelessly [E]
hoping [E]m/n
hoping [e]m/n*
hopping [E]m/n

hopping [e]m/n*
horizon [e]m/n
horizontal [u]l
horizontally [E]
hormonal [u]l
hormone [O]m/n
horn [O]r
hornet [e]
horny [E]
horoscope [O]
horrible [u]l
horribly [E]
horrid [i]
horrific [i]
horrify [I]
horrifying [E]
horror [er]
horse [O]r
horseback [a]
horsefly [I]
horseplay [A]
hose [O]
hosiery [E]
hospitable [u]l
hospital [u]l
hospitality [E]
host [O]
hostage [e]
hosted [e]
hostess [e]
hostile [u]l
hostility [E]
hosting [E]m/n
hosting [e]m/n*
hot [o]
hotcake [A]
hotel [e]l
hotly [E]
hotshot [o]
hotter [er]
hound [ow]m/n
hounded [e]
hounding [E]m/n
hounding [e]m/n*
hour [er]

hourglass [a]
hourly [E]
house [ow]
houseboat [O]
housebreak [A]
housebreaking [E]m/n
housebreaking [e]m/n*
housebroken [e]m/n
housecoat [O]
housefly [I]
household [O]
housesit [i]
housework [er]
housing [E]m/n
housing [e]m/n*
hover [er]
hovering [E]m/n
hovering [e]m/n*
how [ow]
howdy [E]
however [er]
howl [ow]l
howling [E]m/n
howling [e]m/n*
hub [u]
hubbub [u]
hubby [E]
hubcap [a]
huddle [u]l
huddling [E]m/n
huddling [e]m/n*
hue [oo]
huff [u]
huffy [E]
hug [u]
huge [oo]
hugely [E]
huggable [u]l
hugger [er]
hugging [E]m/n
hugging [e]m/n*
hum [u]m/n
human [e]m/n
humane [A]m/n
humanely [E]

humanly [E]
humble [u]l
humbly [E]
humbug [u]
humdrum [u]m/n
humid [i]
humidify [I]
humidity [E]
humiliate [A]
humiliated [e]
humiliating [E]m/n
humiliating [e]m/n*
humiliation [u]m/n
humility [E]
humming [E]m/n
humming [e]m/n*
humor [er]
humoring [E]m/n
humoring [e]m/n*
humorous [e]
humpback [a]
hunch [u]m/n
hunchback [a]
hunching [E]m/n
hunching [e]m/n*
hundred [e]
hunger [er]
hungry [E]
hungry [e]*
hunk [u]m/n
hunker [er]
hunkering [E]m/n
hunkering [e]m/n*
hunt [u]m/n
hunted [e]
hunter [er]
hunting [E]m/n
hunting [e]m/n*
hurdle [u]l
hurdling [E]m/n
hurdling [e]m/n*
hurl [er]l
hurrah [o]
hurricane [A]m/n
hurry [E]

hurry [e]*
hurrying [E]m/n
hurrying [e]m/n*
hurt [er]
hurting [E]m/n
hurting [e]m/n*
husband [e]m/n
hush [u]
hushing [E]m/n
hushing [e]m/n*
husky [E]
hussy [E]

hustle [u]l
hustler [er]
hustling [E]m/n
hustling [e]m/n*
hut [u]
hutch [u]
hybrid [i]
hydrate [A]
hydrated [e]
hydrating [E]m/n
hydrating [e]m/n*
hydraulic [i]

hygiene [E]m/n
hymn [i]m/n
hype [I]
hyper [er]
hypnosis [i]
hypnotic [i]
hypnotically [E]
hypnotize [I]
hypnotizing [E]m/n
hypnotizing [e]m/n*

I

I [I]
ice [I]
icebox [o]
icecap [a]
icepack [a]
icicle [u]l
icing [E]m/n
icing [e]m/n*
icky [E]
icon [o]m/n
icy [E]
idea [u]
ideal [E]l
idealize [I]
ideally [E]
identical [u]l
identify [I]
identifying [E]m/n
identifying [e]m/n*
identity [E]
idiot [e]
idiotic [i]
idle [u]l
idling [E]m/n
idling [e]m/n*
idol [u]l
idolize [I]
iffy [E]

ignite [I]
ignited [e]
igniting [E]m/n
igniting [e]m/n*
ignorance [e]m/n
ignorant [e]m/n
ignore [O]r
ignoring [E]m/n
ignoring [e]m/n*
ill [i]l
illegal [u]l
illegally [E]
illness [e]
illuminate [A]
illuminated [e]
illuminating [E]m/n
illuminating [e]m/n*
illusion [u]m/n
illustrate [A]
illustrated [e]
illustrating [E]m/n
illustrating [e]m/n*
illustration [u]m/n
image [e]
imaginary [E]
imagination [u]m/n
imaginative [i]
imagine [i]m/n

imagining [E]m/n
imagining [e]m/n*
imbalance [e]m/n
imbecile [u]l
imitate [A]
imitated [e]
imitating [E]m/n
imitating [e]m/n*
imitation [u]m/n
immaculate [e]
immaculately [E]
immature [er]
immediate [e]
immediately [E]
immense [e]m/n
immensely [E]
immerse [er]
immersing [E]m/n
immersing [e]m/n*
immoral [u]l
immortal [u]l
immortality [E]
immortalize [I]
immune [oo]m/n
immunity [E]
impact [a]
impacted [e]
impacting [E]m/n

impacting [e]m/n*
impair [e]r
impairing [E]m/n
impairing [e]m/n*
impasse [a]
impatient [e]m/n
impatiently [E]
impeccable [u]l
impeccably [E]
imperfect [e]
imperfection [u]m/n
imperfectly [E]
imperial [u]l
imperialistic [i]
implant [a]m/n
implanted [e]
implement [e]m/n
implemented [e]
implementing [E]m/n
implementing [e]m/n*
implode [O]
imploded [e]
imploding [E]m/n
imploding [e]m/n*
implore [O]r
imploring [E]m/n
imploring [e]m/n*
imply [I]
implying [E]m/n
implying [e]m/n*
impolite [I]
impolitely [E]
import [O]r
important [e]m/n
importantly [E]
imported [e]
importing [E]m/n
importing [e]m/n*
impose [O]
imposing [E]m/n
imposing [e]m/n*
imposition [u]m/n
impossibility [E]
impossible [u]l
impostor [er]

impractical [u]l
impress [e]
impressing [E]m/n
impressing [e]m/n*
impression [u]m/n
impressive [i]
impressively [E]
improper [er]
improperly [E]
improve [oo]
improvement [e]m/n
improving [E]m/n
improving [e]m/n*
improvise [I]
improvising [E]m/n
improvising [e]m/n*
impulsive [i]
impulsively [E]
in [i]m/n
inaccurate [e]
inaccurately [E]
inactive [i]
inadequate [e]
inadequately [E]
incentive [i]
inch [i]m/n
inching [E]m/n
inching [e]m/n*
inchworm [er]m/n
incident [e]m/n
incidental [u]l
incidentally [E]
inclination [u]m/n
incline [I]m/n
inclining [E]m/n
inclining [e]m/n*
include [oo]
included [e]
including [E]m/n
including [e]m/n*
income [u]m/n
incomplete [E]
inconsiderate [e]
incorporate [A]
incorporated [e]

increase [E]
increasing [E]m/n
increasing [e]m/n*
incur [er]
incurring [E]m/n
incurring [e]m/n*
indebted [e]
indecent [e]m/n
indecently [E]
indecision [u]m/n
indeed [E]
indent [e]m/n
indentation [u]m/n
indented [e]
indenting [E]m/n
indenting [e]m/n*
indestructible [u]l
indestructibly [E]
index [e]
indexing [E]m/n
indexing [e]m/n*
indicate [A]
indicated [e]
indicating [E]m/n
indicating [e]m/n*
indication [u]m/n
indicator [er]
indict [I]
indicted [e]
indicting [E]m/n
indicting [e]m/n*
indigestion [u]m/n
indigo [O]
indirect [e]
indirectly [E]
individual [u]l
individually [E]
indoor [O]r
indulge [u]l
indulging [E]m/n
indulging [e]m/n*
industrial [u]l
industry [E]
ineffective [i]
ineffectively [E]

inefficient [e]m/n
inefficiently [E]
inevitable [u]l
inevitably [E]
inexpensive [i]
inexpensively [E]
infant [e]m/n
infantile [I]l
infect [e]
infecting [E]m/n
infecting [e]m/n*
infection [u]m/n
inferior [er]
infinite [i]
infinitely [E]
inflame [A]m/n
inflaming [E]m/n
inflaming [e]m/n*
inflammation [u]m/n
inflate [A]
inflated [e]
inflating [E]m/n
inflating [e]m/n*
inflation [u]m/n
inflict [i]
inflicted [e]
inflicting [E]m/n
inflicting [e]m/n*
infliction [u]m/n
influence [e]m/n
influencing [E]m/n
influencing [e]m/n*
influential [u]l
info [O]
inform [O]r
informal [u]l
informally [E]
information [u]m/n
informative [i]
informing [E]m/n
informing [e]m/n*
infrared [e]
ingenious [e]
ingrown [O]m/n
inhale [A]l

inhaling [E]m/n
inhaling [e]m/n*
inherit [i]
inherited [e]
inheriting [E]m/n
inheriting [e]m/n*
inhibit [i]
inhibited [e]
inhibiting [E]m/n
inhibiting [e]m/n*
inhibition [u]m/n
initial [u]l
initiate [A]
initiated [e]
initiating [E]m/n
initiating [e]m/n*
inject [e]
injecting [E]m/n
injecting [e]m/n*
injection [u]m/n
injure [er]
injuring [E]m/n
injuring [e]m/n*
injury [E]
ink [E]m/n
inkblot [o]
inlaid [A]
inlay [A]
inmate [A]
inn [i]m/n
inner [er]
innermost [O]
inning [E]m/n
inning [e]m/n*
innocence [e]m/n
innocent [e]m/n
innocently [E]
innovate [A]
innovated [e]
innovation [u]m/n
innovative [i]
input [oo/]
inquire [I]r
inquiring [E]m/n
inquiring [e]m/n*

insane [A]m/n
insanely [E]
insanity [E]
insect [e]
insert [er]
inserted [e]
inserting [E]m/n
inserting [e]m/n*
insertion [u]m/n
inside [I]
insider [er]
insight [I]
insincere [E]r
insincerity [E]
insist [i]
insisted [e]
insisting [E]m/n
insisting [e]m/n*
insole [O]l
inspect [e]
inspecting [E]m/n
inspecting [e]m/n*
inspection [u]m/n
inspector [er]
inspiration [u]m/n
inspirational [u]l
inspire [I]r
inspiring [E]m/n
inspiring [e]m/n*
install [o]l
installation [u]m/n
installer [er]
installing [E]m/n
installing [e]m/n*
installment [e]m/n
instant [e]m/n
instantly [E]
instead [e]
instep [e]
instill [i]l
instilling [E]m/n
instilling [e]m/n*
instinct [E]m/n
instinctive [i]
instinctively [E]

institute [oo]
institution [u]m/n
institutional [u]l
institutionalize [l]
instruct [u]
instructed [e]
instructing [E]m/n
instructing [e]m/n*
instruction [u]m/n
instructional [u]l
instructor [er]
instrument [e]m/n
instrumental [u]l
instrumentation [u]m/n
insufficient [e]m/n
insulate [A]
insulated [e]
insulation [u]m/n
insult [u]l
insulted [e]
insulting [E]m/n
insulting [e]m/n*
insurance [e]m/n
insure [er]
intact [a]
intake [A]
integrity [E]
intellect [e]
intellectual [u]l
intellectually [E]
intelligence [e]m/n
intelligent [e]m/n
intelligently [E]
intend [e]m/n
intended [e]
intending [E]m/n
intending [e]m/n*
intense [e]m/n
intensely [E]
intensify [l]
intensifying [E]m/n
intensifying [e]m/n*
intent [e]m/n
intention [u]m/n
intentional [u]l

intently [E]
intercom [o]m/n
interest [e]
interesting [E]m/n
interesting [e]m/n*
interior [er]
intermediate [e]
intermission [u]m/n
intern [er]m/n
internal [u]l
internally [E]
interning [E]m/n
interning [e]m/n*
interpret [e]
interpretation [u]m/n
interpreting [E]m/n
interpreting [e]m/n*
interrupt [u]
interrupted [e]
interrupting [E]m/n
interrupting [e]m/n*
interruption [u]m/n
intersect [e]
intersecting [E]m/n
intersecting [e]m/n*
intersection [u]m/n
interview [oo]
interviewing [E]m/n
interviewing [e]m/n*
intestinal [u]l
intestine [i]m/n
intimacy [E]
intimate [e]
intimately [E]
intimidate [A]
intimidated [e]
intimidating [E]m/n
intimidating [e]m/n*
intimidation [u]m/n
into [oo]
intoxicate [A]
intoxicated [e]
intoxicating [E]m/n
intoxicating [e]m/n*
intoxication [u]m/n

intravenous [e]
intravenously [E]
intricate [e]
intricately [E]
intrigue [E]
intriguing [E]m/n
intriguing [e]m/n*
introduce [oo]
introducing [E]m/n
introducing [e]m/n*
introduction [u]m/n
intrude [oo]
intruding [E]m/n
intruding [e]m/n*
intrusion [u]m/n
intuition [u]m/n
intuitive [i]
intuitively [E]
inundate [A]
inundated [e]
invade [A]
invaded [e]
invading [E]m/n
invading [e]m/n*
invasion [u]m/n
invent [e]m/n
invented [e]
inventing [E]m/n
inventing [e]m/n*
invention [u]m/n
inventory [E]
inverse [er]
invert [er]
inverted [e]
inverting [E]m/n
inverting [e]m/n*
invest [e]
investigate [A]
investigated [e]
investigating [E]m/n
investigating [e]m/n*
investigation [u]m/n
investing [E]m/n
investing [e]m/n*
investment [e]m/n

invincible [u]l

invisible [u]l

invisibly [E]

invitation [u]m/n

invite [I]

invited [e]

inviting [E]m/n

inviting [e]m/n*

invoice [Oi]

invoicing [E]m/n

invoicing [e]m/n*

involuntarily [E]

involuntary [E]

involve [o]l

involving [E]m/n

involving [e]m/n*

inward [er]

irate [A]

irk [er]

irking [E]m/n

irking [e]m/n*

iron [er]m/n

ironic [i]

ironing [E]m/n

ironing [e]m/n*

irony [E]

irrational [u]l

irrationally [E]

irregular [er]

irregularity [E]

irregularly [E]

irrelevant [e]m/n

irresistible [u]l

irresistibly [E]

irresponsible [u]l

irresponsibly [E]

irreversible [u]l

irrigate [A]

irrigated [e]

irrigating [E]m/n

irrigating [e]m/n*

irrigation [u]m/n

irritable [u]l

irritate [A]

irritated [e]

irritating [E]m/n

irritating [e]m/n*

irritation [u]m/n

island [e]m/n

isle [I]l

isolate [A]

isolated [e]

isolating [E]m/n

isolating [e]m/n*

isolation [u]m/n

issue [oo]

issuing [E]m/n

issuing [e]m/n*

itch [i]

itching [E]m/n

itching [e]m/n*

itchy [E]

item [e]m/n

itemize [I]

itemizing [E]m/n

itemizing [e]m/n*

itself [e]l

ivory [E]

ivy [E]

J

jab [a]

jabbing [E]m/n

jabbing [e]m/n*

jack [a]

jackass [a]

jacket [e]

jackpot [o]

jade [A]

jaded [e]

jagged [e]

jaggedly [E]

jailbait [A]

jailbreak [A]

jailhouse [ow]

jam [a]m/n

jamboree [E]

jamming [E]m/n

jamming [e]m/n*

janitor [er]

janitorial [u]l

January [E]

jar [o]r

jarring [E]m/n

jarring [e]m/n*

jasmine [i]m/n

jaw [o]

jawbone [O]m/n

jaywalk [o]

jaywalking [E]m/n

jaywalking [e]m/n*

jazz [a]

jazzy [E]

jealous [e]

jealously [E]

jelly [E]

jeopardize [I]

jeopardizing [E]m/n

jeopardizing [e]m/n*

jeopardy [E]

jerk [er]

jerking [E]m/n

jerking [e]m/n*

jerky [E]

jester [er]

jet [e]

jetting [E]m/n

jetting [e]m/n*

jewel [u]l

jeweler [er]

jewelry [E]

jiff [i]

jiffy [E]
jig [i]
jiggle [u]l
jiggling [E]m/n
jiggling [e]m/n*
jigsaw [o]
jilt [i]l
jilted [e]
jilting [E]m/n
jilting [e]m/n*
jingle [u]l
jinx [E]m/n
jinxing [E]m/n
jinxing [e]m/n*
jitter [er]
jittery [E]
job [o]
jock [o]
jockey [E]
jog [o]
jogger [er]
jogging [E]m/n
jogging [e]m/n*
join [Oi]m/n
joining [E]m/n
joining [e]m/n*
joint [Oi]m/n
jointly [E]
joke [O]
joker [er]
joking [E]m/n
joking [e]m/n*

jolly [E]
jolt [O]l
jolted [e]
jolting [E]m/n
jolting [e]m/n*
jot [o]
jotted [e]
jotting [E]m/n
jotting [e]m/n*
journal [u]l
journalism [e]m/n
journalist [i]
journalistic [i]
journey [E]
joy [Oi]
joyful [u]l
joyous [e]
joyride [I]
joyriding [E]m/n
joyriding [e]m/n*
jubilant [e]m/n
jubilantly [E]
jubilee [E]
judge [u]
judging [E]m/n
judging [e]m/n*
jug [u]
juggle [u]l
juggler [er]
juggling [E]m/n
juggling [e]m/n*
juice [oo]

juicer [er]
juicy [E]
July [I]
jumble [u]l
jumbling [E]m/n
jumbling [e]m/n*
jumbo [O]
jump [u]m/n
jumper [er]
jumping [E]m/n
jumping [e]m/n*
jumpy [E]
junction [e]m/n
June [oo]m/n
jungle [u]l
junior [er]
junk [u]m/n
junkie [E]
junky [E]
juror [er]
jury [E]
just [u]
justice [i]
justify [I]
justly [E]
jut [u]
jutted [e]
juvenile [I]l

K

kaleidoscope [O]
kangaroo [oo]
karate [E]
karmic [i]
kayak [a]
kayaking [E]m/n
kayaking [e]m/n*
keen [E]m/n

keener [er]
keenly [E]
keep [E]
keeper [er]
keeping [E]m/n
keeping [e]m/n*
keepsake [A]
keg [e]

kennel [u]l
kenneling [E]m/n
kenneling [e]m/n*
kept [e]
ketchup [u]
key [E]
keyboard [O]r
keyhole [O]l

keynote [O]
keypad [a]
keystone [O]m/n
keystroke [O]
khaki [E]
kick [i]
kickback [a]
kicker [er]
kicking [E]m/n
kicking [e]m/n*
kickoff [o]
kid [i]
kidded [e]
kidding [E]m/n
kidding [e]m/n*
kidnap [a]
kidnapping [E]m/n
kidnapping [e]m/n*
kidney [E]
kill [i]l
killer [er]
killing [E]m/n
killing [e]m/n*
killjoy [Oi]
kilo [O]
kilometer [er]
kilter [er]
kin [i]m/n
kind [I]m/n
kinder [er]
kindergarten [e]m/n
kindhearted [e]

kindheartedly [E]
kindly [E]
kindly [e]*
kindness [e]
king [E]m/n
kingdom [u]m/n
kink [E]m/n
kinky [E]
kinship [i]
kismet [e]
kiss [i]
kisser [er]
kissing [E]m/n
kissing [e]m/n*
kit [i]
kitchen [e]m/n
kite [I]
kitten [e]m/n
kitty [E]
kiwi [E]
klutzy [E]
knack [a]
knapsack [a]
knead [E]
kneaded [e]
kneading [E]m/n
kneading [e]m/n*
knee [E]
kneecap [a]
kneel [E]l
kneeling [E]m/n
kneeling [e]m/n*

knew [oo]
knickknack [a]
knife [I]
knight [I]
knighted [e]
knit [i]
knitted [e]
knitting [E]m/n
knitting [e]m/n*
knob [o]
knobby [E]
knock [o]
knockdown [ow]m/n
knocker [er]
knocking [E]m/n
knocking [e]m/n*
knockoff [o]
knoll [O]l
knot [o]
knothole [O]l
knotted [e]
knotty [E]
know [O]
knowing [E]m/n
knowing [e]m/n*
knowledge [e]
knowledgeable [u]l
known [O]m/n
knuckle [u]l
kook [oo]
kooky [E]
kosher [er]

L

lab [a]
label [u]l
labor [er]
laboratory [E]
laborer [er]
laboring [E]m/n
laboring [e]m/n*
lace [A]

lacing [E]m/n
lacing [e]m/n*
lack [a]
lackluster [er]
lacquer [er]
lacquering [E]m/n
lacquering [e]m/n*
lacy [E]

lad [a]
ladder [er]
lady [E]
lady [e]*
ladybug [u]
lag [a]
lagging [E]m/n
lagging [e]m/n*

lagoon [oo]m/n
laid [A]
lake [A]
lamb [a]m/n
lame [A]m/n
lamebrain [A]m/n
laminate [A]
laminate [e]
laminated [e]
laminating [E]m/n
laminating [e]m/n*
lamp [a]m/n
lamplight [I]
lampshade [A]
land [a]m/n
landed [e]
landfall [o]l
landfill [i]l
landing [E]m/n
landing [e]m/n*
landlord [O]r
landmark [o]r
landscape [A]
landscaping [E]m/n
landscaping [e]m/n*
landslide [I]
lane [A]m/n
language [e]
lanky [E]
lantern [er]m/n
lap [a]
lapdog [o]
lapel [e]l
lapping [E]m/n
lapping [e]m/n*
lapse [a]
larceny [E]
large [o]r
largely [E]
larger [er]
largest [e]
laser [er]
lass [a]
lasso [O]
last [a]

lasted [e]
lasting [E]m/n
lasting [e]m/n*
lastly [E]
latch [a]
latching [E]m/n
latching [e]m/n*
late [A]
lately [E]
lately [e]*
later [er]
latest [e]
lather [er]
lathering [E]m/n
lathering [e]m/n*
latitude [oo]
lattice [i]
laugh [a]
laughable [u]l
laughing [E]m/n
laughing [e]m/n*
laughter [er]
launch [o]m/n
launcher [er]
launching [E]m/n
launching [e]m/n*
launder [er]
laundering [E]m/n
laundering [e]m/n*
laundry [E]
lavender [er]
lavish [i]
lavishly [E]
law [o]
lawful [u]l
lawfully [E]
lawn [o]m/n
lawsuit [oo]
lawyer [er]
lay [A]
layer [er]
layering [E]m/n
layering [e]m/n*
layette [e]
laying [E]m/n

laying [e]m/n*
layoff [o]
lazily [E]
lazy [E]
lazy [e]*
lead [E]
lead [e]
leader [er]
leadership [i]
leading [E]m/n
leading [e]m/n*
leaf [E]
leafy [E]
league [E]
leak [E]
leaking [E]m/n
leaking [e]m/n*
leaky [E]
lean [E]m/n
leaner [er]
leanest [e]
leaning [E]m/n
leaning [e]m/n*
leap [E]
leapfrog [o]
leaping [E]m/n
leaping [e]m/n*
learn [er]m/n
learning [E]m/n
learning [e]m/n*
lease [E]
leasing [E]m/n
leasing [e]m/n*
least [E]
leather [er]
leave [E]
leaving [E]m/n
leaving [e]m/n*
lecture [er]
lecturing [E]m/n
lecturing [e]m/n*
led [e]
ledge [e]
ledger [er]
leer [E]r

leering [E]m/n
leering [e]m/n*
leery [E]
left [e]
lefty [E]
leg [e]
legal [u]l
legalize [I]
legalizing [E]m/n
legalizing [e]m/n*
legally [E]
legend [e]m/n
legendary [E]
legible [u]l
legit [i]
legitimate [e]
legitimately [E]
legwork [er]
leisure [er]
leisurely [E]
lemon [e]m/n
lemonade [A]
lemony [E]
lend [e]m/n
lender [er]
lending [E]m/n
lending [e]m/n*
length [e]m/n
lengthen [e]m/n
lengthening [E]m/n
lengthening [e]m/n*
lengthy [E]
lenient [e]m/n
lens [e]m/n
lent [e]m/n
leopard [er]
leper [er]
less [e]
lessen [e]m/n
lessening [E]m/n
lessening [e]m/n*
lesser [er]
lesson [e]m/n
let [e]
letdown [ow]m/n

lethal [u]l
lethally [E]
letter [er]
letterhead [e]
lettering [E]m/n
lettering [e]m/n*
letting [E]m/n
letting [e]m/n*
lettuce [e]
levee [E]
level [u]l
leveling [E]m/n
leveling [e]m/n*
lever [er]
leverage [e]
leveraging [E]m/n
leveraging [e]m/n*
lewd [oo]
liability [E]
liable [u]l
liar [I]r
liberal [u]l
liberally [E]
liberate [A]
liberated [e]
liberating [E]m/n
liberating [e]m/n*
libido [O]
librarian [e]m/n
library [E]
license [e]m/n
licensing [E]m/n
licensing [e]m/n*
lick [i]
licking [E]m/n
licking [e]m/n*
licorice [i]
lid [i]
lie [I]
lien [E]m/n
life [I]
lifeboat [O]
lifeguard [o]r
lifeline [I]m/n
lifelong [o]m/n

lifestyle [I]l
lifetime [I]m/n
lift [i]
lifting [E]m/n
lifting [e]m/n*
liftoff [o]
light [I]
lighten [e]m/n
lightening [E]m/n
lightening [e]m/n*
lighter [er]
lighthearted [e]
lightheartedly [E]
lighthouse [ow]
lightly [E]
lightning [E]m/n
lightning [e]m/n*
lightweight [A]
likable [u]l
like [I]
likelihood [oo/]
likely [E]
likeness [e]
likewise [I]
lilac [a]
lily [E]
limb [i]m/n
limber [er]
limbo [O]
lime [I]m/n
limeade [A]
limerick [i]
limestone [O]m/n
limit [i]
limitation [u]m/n
limiting [E]m/n
limiting [e]m/n*
limitless [e]
limo [O]
limousine [E]m/n
limp [i]m/n
limping [E]m/n
limping [e]m/n*
line [I]m/n
linen [e]m/n

liner [er]
lineup [u]
linger [er]
lingering [E]m/n
lingering [e]m/n*
lingo [O]
linguine [E]
lining [E]m/n
lining [e]m/n*
link [E]m/n
linking [E]m/n
linking [e]m/n*
linoleum [u]m/n
lion [e]m/n
lioness [e]
lip [i]
lipstick [i]
liqueur [er]
liquid [i]
liquidate [A]
liquidated [e]
liquidating [E]m/n
liquidating [e]m/n*
liquidation [u]m/n
liquor [er]
list [i]
listed [e]
listen [e]m/n
listener [er]
listening [E]m/n
listening [e]m/n*
listing [E]m/n
listing [e]m/n*
listless [e]
lit [i]
liter [er]
literally [E]
literature [er]
litter [er]
littering [E]m/n
littering [e]m/n*
little [u]l
live [l]
live [i]
lively [E]

liven [e]m/n
liver [er]
livid [i]
living [E]m/n
living [e]m/n*
load [O]
loaded [e]
loading [E]m/n
loading [e]m/n*
loaf [O]
loafer [er]
loafing [E]m/n
loafing [e]m/n*
loan [O]m/n
loaner [er]
loaning [E]m/n
loaning [e]m/n*
loathsome [u]m/n
lob [o]
lobby [E]
lobbying [E]m/n
lobbying [e]m/n*
lobster [er]
local [u]l
locale [a]l
locally [E]
locate [A]
located [e]
locating [E]m/n
locating [e]m/n*
location [u]m/n
lock [o]
locker [er]
locket [e]
locking [E]m/n
locking [e]m/n*
loco [O]
lodge [o]
lodger [er]
lodging [E]m/n
lodging [e]m/n*
loft [o]
lofty [E]
log [o]
logger [er]

logging [E]m/n
logging [e]m/n*
logic [i]
logical [u]l
logically [E]
logo [O]
loin [Oi]m/n
loiter [er]
loitering [E]m/n
loitering [e]m/n*
lollipop [o]
lone [O]m/n
loneliness [e]
lonely [E]
lonely [e]*
loner [er]
lonesome [u]m/n
long [o]m/n
longer [er]
longest [e]
longhorn [O]r
longing [E]m/n
longing [e]m/n*
look [oo/]
looker [er]
looking [E]m/n
looking [e]m/n*
loony [E]
loop [oo]
loophole [O]l
looping [E]m/n
looping [e]m/n*
loopy [E]
loose [oo]
loosely [E]
loosen [e]m/n
loosening [E]m/n
loosening [e]m/n*
looser [er]
loot [oo]
looted [e]
looting [E]m/n
looting [e]m/n*
lop [o]
lopping [E]m/n

lopping [e]m/n*
lose [oo]
loser [er]
losing [E]m/n
losing [e]m/n*
loss [o]
lost [o]
lot [o]
lotion [ʊ]m/n
lottery [E]
lotto [O]
loud [ow]
louder [er]
loudest [e]
loudly [E]
lounge [ow]m/n
lounger [er]
lounging [E]m/n
lounging [e]m/n*
louse [ow]
lousier [er]
lousiest [e]
lousy [E]
lousy [e]*
lovable [ʊ]l
love [ʊ]
lovelorn [O]r
lovely [E]
lovely [e]*
lover [er]
lover [ʊ]*

lovesick [i]
loving [E]m/n
loving [e]m/n*
low [O]
lowdown [ow]m/n
lower [er]
lowering [E]m/n
lowering [e]m/n*
lowly [E]
lox [o]
loyal [ʊ]l
loyally [E]
loyalty [E]
luau [ow]
lube [oo]
lubricant [e]m/n
lubricate [A]
lubricated [e]
lubricating [E]m/n
lubricating [e]m/n*
lucid [i]
lucidity [E]
lucidly [E]
luck [ʊ]
luckily [E]
lucky [E]
lug [ʊ]
luggage [e]
lugging [E]m/n
lugging [e]m/n*
lukewarm [O]r

lullaby [I]
lumber [er]
lumbering [E]m/n
lumbering [e]m/n*
luminous [e]
lump [ʊ]m/n
lumping [E]m/n
lumping [e]m/n*
lumpy [E]
lunar [er]
lunatic [i]
lunch [ʊ]m/n
luncheon [e]m/n
lurk [er]
lurking [E]m/n
lurking [e]m/n*
luscious [e]
lusciously [E]
lush [ʊ]
lust [ʊ]
lusted [e]
luster [er]
lustful [ʊ]l
lustrous [e]
luxurious [e]
luxury [E]
lying [E]m/n
lying [e]m/n*
lyric [i]
lyrical [ʊ]l

M

ma [o]
ma'am [a]m/n
macaroni [E]
machine [E]m/n
macho [O]
macro [O]
mad [a]
madam [e]m/n
maddening [E]m/n

maddening [e]m/n*
made [A]
madhouse [ow]
madly [E]
madman [a]m/n
maestro [O]
magazine [E]m/n
magic [i]
magical [ʊ]l

magically [E]
magician [e]m/n
magistrate [A]
magnet [e]
magnetic [i]
magnetism [e]m/n
magnificent [e]m/n
magnificently [E]
magnify [I]

magnifying [E]m/n
magnifying [e]m/n*
maid [A]
maiden [e]m/n
mail [A]l
mailbag [a]
mailbox [o]
mailer [er]
mailing [E]m/n
mailing [e]m/n*
mailman [a]m/n
main [A]m/n
mainframe [A]m/n
mainline [I]m/n
mainly [E]
mainstay [A]
mainstream [E]m/n
mainstreaming [E]m/n
mainstreaming [e]m/n*
maintain [A]m/n
maintaining [E]m/n
maintaining [e]m/n*
majestic [i]
majestically [E]
majesty [E]
major [er]
majoring [E]m/n
majoring [e]m/n*
majority [E]
make [A]
maker [er]
makeup [u]
making [E]m/n
making [e]m/n*
male [A]l
mall [o]l
malt [o]l
mama [u]
man [a]m/n
manage [e]
management [e]m/n
managing [E]m/n
managing [e]m/n*
manatee [E]
mandate [A]

mandated [e]
mandating [E]m/n
mandating [e]m/n*
mandatory [E]
mane [A]m/n
maneuver [er]
maneuvering [E]m/n
maneuvering [e]m/n*
mango [O]
maniac [a]
maniacal [u]l
manic [i]
manicure [er]
manicuring [E]m/n
manicuring [e]m/n*
manipulate [A]
manipulated [e]
manipulating [E]m/n
manipulating [e]m/n*
mankind [I]m/n
manly [E]
manmade [A]
mannequin [e]m/n
manner [er]
mannerism [e]m/n
manor [er]
mansion [e]m/n
manufacture [er]
manufacturing [E]m/n
manufacturing [e]m/n*
manure [er]
manuscript [i]
many [E]
map [a]
mapping [E]m/n
mapping [e]m/n*
mar [o]r
marathon [o]m/n
marble [u]l
march [o]r
marching [E]m/n
marching [e]m/n*
margarine [i]m/n
margin [i]m/n
marginal [u]l

marigold [O]l
marine [E]m/n
marital [u]l
mark [o]r
markdown [ow]m/n
marker [er]
market [e]
marketing [E]m/n
marketing [e]m/n*
marking [E]m/n
marking [e]m/n*
marksman [e]m/n
marquee [E]
marriage [e]
marring [E]m/n
marring [e]m/n*
marry [E]
marry [e]*
marrying [E]m/n
marrying [e]m/n*
marshmallow [O]
martini [E]
martyr [er]
marvelous [e]
marvelously [E]
mascot [o]
masculine [i]m/n
masculinity [E]
mask [a]
masking [E]m/n
masking [e]m/n*
masquerade [A]
masqueraded [e]
masquerading [E]m/n
masquerading [e]m/n*
mass [a]
massage [o]
massaging [E]m/n
massaging [e]m/n*
massive [i]
massively [E]
mast [a]
master [er]
mastering [E]m/n
mastering [e]m/n*

masterpiece [E]
mat [a]
match [a]
matcher [er]
matching [E]m/n
matching [e]m/n*
mate [A]
mated [e]
material [u]l
materialistic [i]
materialize [I]
materializing [E]m/n
materializing [e]m/n*
maternal [u]l
maternally [E]
maternity [E]
math [a]
mathematical [u]l
mathematician [e]m/n
mathematics [i]
matrimonial [u]l
matrimony [E]
matrix [i]
matron [e]m/n
matronly [E]
matted [e]
matter [er]
matting [E]m/n
matting [e]m/n*
mattress [e]
mature [er]
maturely [E]
maturing [E]m/n
maturing [e]m/n*
maturity [E]
maul [o]l
mauling [E]m/n
mauling [e]m/n*
mauve [o]
maverick [i]
maxi [E]
maximize [I]
maximizing [E]m/n
maximizing [e]m/n*
maximum [u]m/n

may [A]
maybe [E]
mayday [A]
mayhem [e]m/n
mayo [O]
mayor [er]
maze [A]
me [E]
meadow [O]
meager [er]
meal [E]l
mealtime [I]m/n
mealy [E]
mean [E]m/n
meaner [er]
meanest [e]
meaning [E]m/n
meaning [e]m/n*
meant [e]m/n
meantime [I]m/n
meanwhile [I]l
measles [u]l
measly [E]
measure [er]
measurement [e]m/n
measuring [E]m/n
measuring [e]m/n*
meat [E]
meatball [o]l
meaty [E]
mechanic [i]
mechanical [u]l
mechanically [E]
medal [u]l
medallion [u]m/n
meddle [u]l
meddler [er]
meddling [E]m/n
meddling [e]m/n*
media [u]
mediate [A]
mediated [e]
mediating [E]
mediation [u]m/n
medic [i]

medical [u]l
medically [E]
medicate [A]
medicated [e]
medication [u]m/n
medicine [i]m/n
medieval [u]l
mediocre [er]
meditate [A]
meditated [e]
meditating [E]m/n
meditating [e]m/n*
meditation [u]m/n
medium [u]m/n
medley [E]
meet [E]
meeting [E]m/n
meeting [e]m/n*
melancholy [E]
mellow [O]
melodic [i]
melodically [E]
melodrama [o]
melodramatic [i]
melodramatically [E]
melody [E]
melon [e]m/n
melt [e]l
meltdown [ow]m/n
melted [e]
melting [E]m/n
melting [e]m/n*
member [er]
membership [i]
membrane [A]m/n
memo [O]
memoir [o]r
memorable [u]l
memorial [u]l
memorialize [I]
memorize [I]
memory [E]
men [e]m/n
menace [e]
menacing [E]m/n

menacing [e]m/n*
mend [e]m/n
mended [e]
mending [E]m/n
mending [e]m/n*
mental [u]l
mentality [E]
mentally [E]
menthol [o]l
mention [u]m/n
mentioning [E]m/n
mentioning [e]m/n*
mentor [O]r
mentoring [E]m/n
mentoring [e]m/n*
menu [oo]
merchandise [I]
merchandising [E]m/n
merchandising [e]m/n*
merchant [e]m/n
merciful [u]l
mercifully [E]
mercy [E]
mercy [e]*
mere [E]r
merely [E]
merge [er]
merger [er]
merging [E]m/n
merging [e]m/n*
merit [i]
mermaid [A]
merriment [e]
merry [E]
mesmerize [I]
mesmerizing [E]m/n
mesmerizing [e]m/n*
mess [e]
message [e]
messenger [er]
messing [E]m/n
messing [e]m/n*
messy [E]
met [e]
metal [u]l

metallic [i]
meteor [O]r
meteorite [I]
meter [er]
metering [E]m/n
metering [e]m/n*
method [e]
methodical [u]l
methodically [E]
meticulous [e]
meticulously [E]
metric [i]
metro [O]
metronome [O]m/n
mew [oo]
mewing [E]m/n
mewing [e]m/n*
micro [O]
microphone [O]m/n
microscope [O]
microscopic [i]
microwave [A]
microwaving [E]m/n
microwaving [e]m/n*
mid [i]
middle [u]l
midnight [I]
midterm [er]m/n
midway [A]
might [I]
mighty [E]
migraine [A]m/n
migrate [A]
migrated [e]
migrating [E]m/n
migrating [e]m/n*
mild [I]l
milder [er]
mildest [e]
mildew [oo]
mildly [E]
mile [I]l
mileage [e]
milestone [O]m/n
military [E]

milk [i]l
milking [E]m/n
milking [e]m/n*
milkman [a]m/n
milkshake [A]
milky [E]
mill [i]l
millennium [u]m/n
milling [E]m/n
milling [e]m/n*
million [u]m/n
millionaire [e]r
mimic [i]
mimicking [E]m/n
mimicking [e]m/n*
mince [i]m/n
mincing [E]m/n
mincing [e]m/n*
mind [I]m/n
minded [e]
minding [E]m/n
minding [e]m/n*
mine [I]m/n
miner [er]
mineral [u]l
mingle [u]l
mingling [E]m/n
mingling [e]m/n*
mini [E]
miniature [er]
miniaturize [I]
miniaturizing [E]m/n
miniaturizing [e]m/n*
minimal [u]l
minimalist [i]
minimalistic [i]
minimize [I]
minimizing [E]m/n
minimizing [e]m/n*
minimum [u]m/n
mining [E]m/n
mining [e]m/n*
minor [er]
minority [E]
mint [i]m/n

minted [e]

minty [E]

minus [e]

minute [e]

minute [oo]

miracle [u]l

miraculous [e]

mirage [o]

mirror [er]

mirroring [E]m/n

mirroring [e]m/n*

misbehave [A]

misbehaving [E]m/n

misbehaving [e]m/n*

miscast [a]

miscellaneous [e]

mischief [i]

mischievous [e]

misconstrue [oo]

misconstruing [E]m/n

misconstruing [e]m/n*

miser [er]

miserable [u]l

miserably [E]

miserly [E]

misery [E]

misfile [I]l

misfire [I]r

misfit [i]

misfortune [e]m/n

misguide [I]

misguided [e]

misguiding [E]m/n

misguiding [e]m/n*

mishap [a]

misjudge [u]

misjudging [E]m/n

misjudging [e]m/n*

mislaid [A]

mislead [E]

misleading [E]m/n

misleading [e]m/n*

misled [e]

misplace [A]

misplacing [E]m/n

misplacing [e]m/n*

misread [e]

misreading [E]m/n

misreading [e]m/n*

miss [i]

misshape [A]

misshapen [e]m/n

missile [u]l

missing [E]m/n

missing [e]m/n*

mission [u]m/n

missionary [E]

misspell [e]l

misspelling [E]m/n

misspelling [e]m/n*

misstep [e]

mist [i]

mistake [A]

mistaken [e]m/n

mistakenly [E]

mister [er]

misting [E]m/n

misting [e]m/n*

mistletoe [O]

mistress [e]

misty [E]

mitt [i]

mitten [e]m/n

mix [i]

mixer [er]

mixing [E]m/n

mixing [e]m/n*

mixture [er]

moan [O]m/n

moaning [E]m/n

moaning [e]m/n*

moat [O]

mob [o]

mobbing [E]m/n

mobbing [e]m/n*

mobile [u]l

mobilize [I]

mobilizing [E]m/n

mobilizing [e]m/n*

mobster [er]

moccasin [i]m/n

mocha [u]

mock [o]

mockery [E]

mocking [E]m/n

mocking [e]m/n*

modality [E]

mode [O]

model [u]l

modeling [E]m/n

modeling [e]m/n*

modem [e]m/n

moderate [A]

moderate [e]

moderated [e]

moderately [E]

moderation [u]m/n

moderator [er]

modern [er]m/n

modernize [I]

modest [e]

modestly [E]

modesty [E]

modify [I]

modifying [E]m/n

modifying [e]m/n*

modular [er]

module [oo]l

moist [Oi]

moisten [e]m/n

moistening [E]m/n

moistening [e]m/n*

moisture [er]

moisturize [I]

moisturizing [E]m/n

moisturizing [e]m/n*

molar [er]

mold [O]l

molded [e]

molding [E]m/n

molding [e]m/n*

moldy [E]

mole [O]l

molecular [er]

molecule [oo]l

molehill [i]l
molest [e]
molestation [u]m/n
molesting [E]m/n
molesting [e]m/n*
molten [e]m/n
mom [o]m/n
moment [e]m/n
momentarily [E]
momentary [E]
momentum [u]m/n
mommy [E]
Monday [A]
monetary [E]
money [E]
money [e]*
monitor [er]
monitoring [E]m/n
monitoring [e]m/n*
monk [u]m/n
monkey [E]
mono [O]
monogram [a]m/n
monogramming [E]m/n
monogramming [e]m/n*
monopoly [E]
monotonous [e]
monotony [E]
monster [er]
monstrosity [E]
monstrous [e]
month [u]m/n
monument [e]m/n
monumental [u]l
monumentally [E]
mood [oo]
moody [E]
moon [oo]m/n
mooning [E]m/n
mooning [e]m/n*
moonlight [I]
moonlit [i]
moonrise [I]
moonshine [I]m/n
moonstone [O]m/n

moonwalk [o]
moose [oo]
moot [oo]
mop [o]
mope [O]
moped [e]
moping [E]m/n
moping [e]m/n*
mopping [E]m/n
mopping [e]m/n*
moral [u]l
morale [a]l
morally [E]
morbid [i]
morbidity [E]
morbidly [E]
more [O]r
morning [E]m/n
morning [e]m/n*
moron [o]m/n
moronic [i]
morsel [e]l
mortal [u]l
mortality [E]
mortally [E]
mortgage [e]
mosaic [i]
mosquito [O]
moss [o]
mossy [E]
most [O]
mostly [E]
motel [e]l
mothball [o]l
mother [er]
mother [u]*
mothering [E]m/n
mothering [e]m/n*
motherly [E]
motif [E]
motion [u]m/n
motioning [E]m/n
motioning [e]m/n*
motivate [A]
motivated [e]

motivating [E]m/n
motivating [e]m/n*
motivation [u]m/n
motivational [u]l
motive [i]
motley [E]
motor [er]
motorcycle [u]l
motorcycling [E]m/n
motorcycling [e]m/n*
motto [O]
mound [ow]m/n
mounding [E]m/n
mounding [e]m/n*
mountain [i]m/n
mountaintop [o]
mourn [O]r
mourning [E]m/n
mourning [e]m/n*
mouse [ow]
mousetrap [a]
mousy [E]
mouth [ow]
mouthful [oo]l
mouthwash [o]
mouthwatering [E]m/n
mouthwatering [e]m/n*
mouthy [E]
move [oo]
movement [e]m/n
mover [er]
movie [E]
moving [E]m/n
moving [e]m/n*
mow [O]
mower [er]
mowing [E]m/n
mowing [e]m/n*
moxie [E]
mozzarella [u]
much [u]
muck [u]
mucking [E]m/n
mucking [e]m/n*
mud [u]

muddle [ʊ]l
muddy [E]
muffin [i]m/n
muffle [ʊ]l
muffler [er]
muffling [E]m/n
muffling [e]m/n*
mug [ʊ]
mugger [er]
mugging [E]m/n
mugging [e]m/n*
muggy [E]
mule [oo]l
multi [E]
multilevel [ʊ]l
multimedia [ʊ]
multiple [ʊ]l
multiply [I]
multiplying [E]m/n
multiplying [e]m/n*
multitude [oo]
mum [ʊ]m/n
mumbo [O]
mummy [E]
munch [ʊ]m/n
munchies [E]
munching [E]m/n
munching [e]m/n*
mundane [A]m/n

mural [ʊ]l
murder [er]
murdering [E]m/n
murdering [e]m/n*
murderous [e]
murky [E]
murmur [er]
murmuring [E]m/n
murmuring [e]m/n*
muscle [ʊ]l
muscular [er]
museum [ʊ]m/n
mush [ʊ]
mushroom [oo]m/n
mushy [E]
music [i]
musical [ʊ]l
musicality [E]
musically [E]
musician [ʊ]m/n
musk [ʊ]
musky [E]
muslin [i]m/n
must [ʊ]
mustache [a]
mustang [a]ng/k
mustard [er]
muster [er]
mustering [E]m/n

mustering [e]m/n*
musty [E]
mutate [A]
mutated [e]
mutating [E]m/n
mutating [e]m/n*
mutation [ʊ]m/n
mute [oo]
mutiny [E]
mutt [ʊ]
mutter [er]
muttering [E]m/n
muttering [e]m/n*
mutual [ʊ]l
mutually [E]
muzzle [ʊ]l
my [I]
myself [e]l
mysterious [e]
mysteriously [E]
mystery [E]
mystic [i]
mystical [ʊ]l
mystically [E]
mystify [I]
mystique [E]
myth [i]

N

nab [a]
nabbing [E]m/n
nabbing [e]m/n*
nag [a]
nagging [E]m/n
nagging [e]m/n*
nail [A]l
nailing [E]m/n
nailing [e]m/n*
naive [E]
naively [E]

naiveté [A]
naked [e]
name [A]m/n
nameless [e]
namely [E]
nameplate [A]
namesake [A]
naming [E]m/n
naming [e]m/n*
nanny [E]
nap [a]

napkin [i]m/n
napping [E]m/n
napping [e]m/n*
nappy [E]
narcotic [i]
narrate [A]
narrated [e]
narrating [E]m/n
narrating [e]m/n*
narration [ʊ]m/n
narrow [O]

narrower [er]
narrowing [E]m/n
narrowing [e]m/n*
narrowly [E]
nasal [u]l
nasally [E]
nastily [E]
nasty [E]
nasty [e]*
nation [u]m/n
national [u]l
nationality [E]
nationally [E]
nationwide [I]
native [i]
natural [u]l
naturally [E]
nature [er]
naught [o]
naughty [E]
nausea [u]
nautical [u]l
naval [u]l
navigate [A]
navigated [e]
navigating [E]m/n
navigating [e]m/n*
navigation [u]m/n
navy [E]
nay [A]
naysayer [er]
Neanderthal [o]l
near [E]r
nearby [I]
nearer [er]
nearing [E]m/n
nearing [e]m/n*
nearly [E]
nearsighted [e]
neat [E]
neater [er]
neatly [E]
nebula [u]
necessarily [E]
necessary [E]

necessity [E]
neck [e]
necking [E]m/n
necking [e]m/n*
necklace [e]
neckline [I]m/n
necktie [I]
nectar [er]
nectarine [E]m/n
need [E]
needed [e]
needing [E]m/n
needing [e]m/n*
needle [u]l
needlepoint [Oi]m/n
needling [E]m/n
needling [e]m/n*
needy [E]
negative [i]
negatively [E]
negativity [E]
neglect [e]
neglecting [E]m/n
neglecting [e]m/n*
negligee [A]
negotiate [A]
negotiated [e]
negotiating [E]m/n
negotiating [e]m/n*
negotiation [u]m/n
neighbor [er]
neighborhood [oo/]
neighboring [E]m/n
neighboring [e]m/n*
neighborly [E]
neither [er]
neon [o]m/n
nephew [oo]
nerd [er]
nerdy [E]
nerve [er]
nervous [e]
nervously [E]
nervy [E]
net [e]

netting [E]m/n
netting [e]m/n*
network [er]
networking [E]m/n
networking [e]m/n*
neurosis [E]
neurosis [i]
neurotic [i]
neurotically [E]
neuter [er]
neutering [E]m/n
neutering [e]m/n*
neutral [u]l
neutralize [I]
neutralizing [E]m/n
neutralizing [e]m/n*
never [er]
new [oo]
newborn [O]r
newer [er]
newest [e]
newly [E]
newlywed [e]
newscast [a]
newscaster [er]
newsletter [er]
newspaper [er]
next [e]
nibble [u]l
nibbling [E]m/n
nibbling [e]m/n*
nice [I]
nicely [E]
nicer [er]
nicest [e]
niche [E]
niche [i]
nick [i]
nickel [u]l
nicking [E]m/n
nicking [e]m/n*
nickname [A]m/n
nicotine [E]m/n
niece [E]
nifty [E]

night [I]
nightcap [a]
nightclub [u]
nightfall [o]l
nightgown [ow]m/n
nighthawk [o]
nightingale [A]l
nightly [E]
nightmare [e]r
nightspot [o]
nighttime [I]
nil [i]l
nimble [u]l
nimbly [E]
nine [I]m/n
nineteen [E]m/n
ninety [E]
ninny [E]
ninth [I]m/n
nip [i]
nipping [E]m/n
nipping [e]m/n*
nippy [E]
nit [i]
nitpick [i]
nitpicking [E]m/n
nitpicking [e]m/n*
nitrogen [e]m/n
nitwit [i]
nix [i]
nixing [E]m/n
nixing [e]m/n*
no [O]
nobility [E]
noble [u]l
nobly [E]
nobody [E]
nobody [e]*
nocturnal [u]l
nocturnally [E]
nod [o]
nodded [e]
nodding [E]m/n
nodding [e]m/n*
node [O]

nodule [oo]l
Noel [e]l
noggin [i]m/n
noise [Oi]
noisily [E]
noisy [E]
nomad [a]
nomadic [i]
nominal [u]l
nominally [E]
nominate [A]
nominated [e]
nominating [E]m/n
nominating [e]m/n*
nominee [E]
nonchalant [o]m/n
nonchalantly [E]
none [u]m/n
nonetheless [e]
nonfat [a]
nonfiction [u]m/n
nonsense [e]m/n
nonskid [i]
nonstop [o]
nonverbal [u]l
nonviolent [e]m/n
noodle [u]l
nook [oo/]
noon [oo]m/n
nope [O]
nor [O]r
norm [O]r
normal [u]l
normalcy [E]
normalize [I]
normalizing [E]m/n
normalizing [e]m/n*
normally [E]
north [O]r
northerly [E]
northern [er]m/n
nose [O]
nosedive [I]
nostalgia [u]
nostalgic [i]

nostril [u]l
nosy [E]
nosy [e]*
not [o]
notate [A]
notated [e]
notating [E]m/n
notating [e]m/n*
notation [u]m/n
notch [o]
note [O]
notebook [oo/]
noted [e]
notepad [a]
nothing [E]m/n
nothing [e]m/n*
notice [i]
noticeable [u]l
noticing [E]m/n
noticing [e]m/n*
notification [u]m/n
notify [I]
notifying [E]m/n
notifying [e]m/n*
noting [E]m/n
noting [e]m/n*
notion [u]m/n
notorious [e]
notoriously [E]
noun [ow]m/n
nourish [i]
nourishing [E]m/n
nourishing [e]m/n*
nourishment [e]m/n
novel [u]l
novelist [i]
novelty [E]
November [er]
novice [i]
now [ow]
nowadays [A]
nowhere [e]r
nub [u]
nubby [E]
nucleus [e]

nude [oo]
nudge [u]
nudging [E]m/n
nudging [e]m/n*
nudity [E]
nugget [e]
nuisance [e]m/n
nuke [oo]
nuking [E]m/n
nuking [e]m/n*
numb [u]m/n
number [er]
numbing [E]m/n
numbing [e]m/n*

numeric [i]
numerical [u]l
numerically [E]
numerous [e]
numskull [u]l
nun [u]m/n
nurse [er]
nursemaid [A]
nursery [E]
nursing [E]m/n
nursing [e]m/n*
nurture [er]
nurturing [E]m/n
nurturing [e]m/n*

nut [u]
nuthouse [ow]
nutmeg [e]
nutrient [e]m/n
nutrition [u]m/n
nutritious [e]
nutshell [e]l
nutty [E]
nuzzle [u]l
nuzzling [E]m/n
nuzzling [e]m/n*
nylon [o]m/n

O

o'clock [o]
oaf [O]
oak [O]
oar [O]r
oasis [i]
oath [O]
obedience [e]m/n
obedient [e]m/n
obediently [E]
obese [E]
obesity [E]
obey [A]
obeying [E]m/n
obeying [e]m/n*
obituary [E]
object [e]
objecting [E]m/n
objecting [e]m/n*
objection [u]m/n
objective [i]
objectively [E]
objectivity [E]
obligate [A]
obligated [e]
obligation [u]m/n
obligatory [E]

oblivion [u]m/n
oblivious [e]
oblong [o]m/n
obscene [E]m/n
obscenely [E]
obscenity [E]
obscure [er]
obscuring [E]m/n
obscuring [e]m/n*
obscurity [E]
observant [e]m/n
observation [u]m/n
observatory [E]
observe [er]
observing [E]m/n
observing [e]m/n*
obsess [e]
obsessing [E]m/n
obsessing [e]m/n*
obsession [u]m/n
obsessive [i]
obsessively [E]
obsolete [E]
obstacle [u]l
obstetric [i]
obstetrician [e]m/n

obstruct [u]
obstructing [E]m/n
obstructing [e]m/n*
obstruction [u]m/n
obtain [A]m/n
obtaining [E]m/n
obtaining [e]m/n*
obvious [e]
obviously [E]
occasion [u]m/n
occasional [u]l
occasionally [E]
occult [u]l
occupancy [E]
occupant [e]m/n
occupation [u]m/n
occupy [I]
occupying [E]m/n
occupying [e]m/n*
occur [er]
occurrence [e]m/n
occurring [E]m/n
occurring [e]m/n*
ocean [e]m/n
oceanic [i]
octagon [o]m/n

octane [A]m/n
octave [e]
October [er]
octopus [oo/]
odd [o]
oddball [o]l
oddity [E]
oddly [E]
ode [O]
odor [er]
of [u]
off [o]
offbeat [E]
offend [e]m/n
offended [e]
offending [E]m/n
offending [e]m/n*
offense [e]m/n
offensive [i]
offensively [E]
offer [er]
offering [E]m/n
offering [e]m/n*
office [i]
officer [er]
official [u]l
officially [E]
offset [e]
offsetting [E]m/n
offsetting [e]m/n*
offshore [O]r
often [e]m/n
ogre [er]
oh [O]
oil [Oi]l
oily [E]
okay [A]
okaying [E]m/n
okaying [e]m/n*
old [O]l
olden [e]m/n
older [er]
oldest [e]
oldie [E]
olive [i]

omelet [e]
omen [e]m/n
ominous [e]
ominously [E]
omit [i]
omitting [E]m/n
omitting [e]m/n*
on [o]m/n
one [u]m/n
ongoing [E]m/n
ongoing [e]m/n*
onion [e]m/n
online [I]m/n
only [E]
only [e]*
onset [e]
onslaught [o]
onyx [i]
ooze [oo]
oozing [E]m/n
oozing [e]m/n*
oozy [E]
opacity [E]
opaque [A]
open [e]m/n
opening [E]m/n
opening [e]m/n*
openly [E]
opera [u]
operate [A]
operated [e]
operatic [i]
operating [E]m/n
operating [e]m/n*
operation [u]m/n
operational [u]l
operator [er]
opinion [e]m/n
opponent [e]m/n
opportune [oo]m/n
opportunity [E]
oppose [O]
opposing [E]m/n
opposing [e]m/n*
opposite [i]

opposition [u]m/n
opt [o]
optic [i]
optical [u]l
optician [e]m/n
optimal [u]l
optimism [e]m/n
optimistic [i]
optimize [I]
optimum [u]m/n
opting [E]m/n
opting [e]m/n*
option [u]m/n
optional [u]l
or [O]r
oral [u]l
orally [E]
orange [e]m/n
orb [O]r
orbit [i]
orbital [u]l
orchard [er]
orchestra [u]
orchestral [u]l
orchestrate [A]
orchestrated [e]
orchestration [u]m/n
orchid [i]
ordeal [E]l
order [er]
ordering [E]m/n
ordering [e]m/n*
orderly [E]
ordinance [e]m/n
ordinarily [E]
ordinary [E]
ore [O]r
organ [e]m/n
organic [i]
organically [E]
organization [u]m/n
organize [I]
organizer [er]
organizing [E]m/n
organizing [e]m/n*

orgy [E]
orient [e]m/n
oriental [u]l
orientation [u]m/n
oriented [e]
origin [i]m/n
original [u]l
originally [E]
originate [A]
originated [e]
originating [E]m/n
originating [e]m/n*
ornament [e]m/n
ornamental [u]l
ornate [A]
ornery [E]
orphan [e]m/n
orphanage [e]
orthodox [o]
orthopedic [i]
oscillate [A]
oscillating [E]m/n
oscillating [e]m/n*
osmosis [i]
other [er]
otherwise [l]
ouch [ow]
ought [o]
ounce [ow]m/n
our [er]
ourselves [e]l
oust [ow]
ousting [E]m/n
ousting [e]m/n*
out [ow]
outback [a]
outbid [i]
outbidding [E]m/n
outbidding [e]m/n*
outbox [o]
outbreak [A]
outburst [er]
outcast [a]
outclass [a]
outcome [u]m/n

outdid [i]
outdo [oo]
outdone [u]m/n
outdoor [O]r
outer [er]
outfield [E]l
outfit [i]
outfitted [e]
outfox [o]
outfoxing [E]m/n
outfoxing [e]m/n*
outgrew [oo]
outgrow [O]
outgrowing [E]m/n
outgrowing [e]m/n*
outgrown [O]m/n
outhouse [ow]
outing [E]m/n
outing [e]m/n*
outlast [a]
outlasted [e]
outlasting [E]m/n
outlasting [e]m/n*
outlaw [o]
outlet [e]
outline [l]m/n
outlining [E]m/n
outlining [e]m/n*
outlive [i]
outliving [E]m/n
outliving [e]m/n*
outlook [oo/]
outmaneuver [er]
outmaneuvering [E]m/n
outmaneuvering [e]m/n*
outnumber [er]
outnumbering [E]m/n
outnumbering [e]m/n*
outpour [O]r
outpouring [E]m/n
outpouring [e]m/n*
outrage [A]
outrageous [e]
outrageously [E]
outran [a]m/n

outright [l]
outrun [u]m/n
outscore [O]r
outsell [e]l
outselling [E]m/n
outselling [e]m/n*
outshine [l]m/n
outshining [E]m/n
outshining [e]m/n*
outside [l]
outsider [er]
outsmart [o]r
outsmarting [E]m/n
outsmarting [e]m/n*
outspoken [e]m/n
outstanding [E]m/n
outstanding [e]m/n*
outward [er]
outweigh [A]
outweighing [E]m/n
outweighing [e]m/n*
outwit [i]
outwitted [e]
outwitting [E]m/n
outwitting [e]m/n*
outworn [O]r
oval [u]l
ovation [u]m/n
oven [e]m/n
over [er]
overall [o]l
overboard [O]r
overcame [A]m/n
overcast [a]
overcharge [o]r
overcharging [E]m/n
overcharging [e]m/n*
overcoat [O]
overcome [u]m/n
overcoming [E]m/n
overcoming [e]m/n*
overdraft [a]
overdraw [o]
overdrawing [E]m/n
overdrawing [e]m/n*

overdrawn [o]m/n
overdue [oo]
overeat [E]
overeating [E]m/n
overeating [e]m/n*
overflow [O]
overflowing [E]m/n
overflowing [e]m/n*
overgrow [O]
overgrowing [E]m/n
overgrowing [e]m/n*
overgrown [O]m/n
overhaul [o]l
overhead [e]
overhear [E]r
overheard [er]
overindulge [u]l
overjoyed [Oi]
overlap [a]
overload [O]

overlook [oo/]
overly [E]
overnight [I]
overpaid [A]
overpass [a]
overpay [A]
overpower [er]
overpowering [E]m/n
overpowering [e]m/n*
overrule [oo]l
overruling [E]m/n
overruling [e]m/n*
overseas [E]
oversee [E]
overseeing [E]m/n
overseeing [e]m/n*
oversensitive [i]
oversight [I]
oversize [I]
overture [er]

overview [oo]
overweight [A]
overwhelm [e]l
overwhelming [E]m/n
overwhelming [e]m/n*
overzealous [e]
ow [ow]
owe [O]
owing [E]m/n
owing [e]m/n*
owl [ow]l
own [O]m/n
owner [er]
owning [E]m/n
owning [e]m/n*
ox [o]
oxen [e]m/n
oxygen [e]m/n
oyster [er]
ozone [O]m/n

P

pa [o]
pace [A]
pacifier [I]r
pacify [I]
pacing [E]m/n
pacing [e]m/n*
pack [a]
package [e]
packaging [E]m/n
packaging [e]m/n*
packet [e]
packing [E]m/n
packing [e]m/n*
pad [a]
padded [e]
padding [E]m/n
padding [e]m/n*
paddle [u]l
paddling [E]m/n
paddling [e]m/n*

padlock [o]
page [A]
pager [er]
paging [E]m/n
paging [e]m/n*
paid [A]
pail [A]l
pain [A]m/n
painful [u]l
painfully [E]
painkiller [er]
painstaking [E]m/n
painstaking [e]m/n*
painstakingly [E]
paint [A]m/n
paintbrush [u]
painted [e]
painter [er]
painterly [E]
painting [E]m/n

painting [e]m/n*
pair [e]r
pairing [E]m/n
pairing [e]m/n*
paisley [E]
pajama [u]
pal [a]l
palace [e]
palatable [u]l
palate [e]
pale [A]l
palette [e]
pallet [e]
palm [o]l
palpable [u]l
palpitate [A]
palpitated [e]
palpitation [u]m/n
pamper [er]
pampering [E]m/n

pampering [e]m/n*
pan [a]m/n
pancake [A]
pane [A]m/n
panel [u]l
paneling [E]m/n
paneling [e]m/n*
panelist [i]
panhandle [u]l
panhandling [E]m/n
panhandling [e]m/n*
panic [i]
panicking [E]m/n
panicking [e]m/n*
panicky [E]
panorama [u]
panoramic [i]
pansy [E]
pant [a]m/n
panted [e]
panther [er]
panting [E]m/n
panting [e]m/n*
pantry [E]
panty [E]
pap [a]
papa [u]
papaya [u]
paper [er]
paperless [e]
paperweight [A]
paperwork [er]
papoose [oo]
par [o]r
parachute [oo]
parachuting [E]m/n
parachuting [e]m/n*
parade [A]
paraded [e]
parading [E]m/n
parading [e]m/n*
paradise [I]
paraffin [i]m/n
paragraph [a]
parakeet [E]

paralegal [u]l
parallel [e]l
paralysis [i]
paralyze [I]
paralyzing [E]m/n
paralyzing [e]m/n*
paramedic [i]
parasite [I]
parcel [u]l
parchment [e]m/n
pardon [u]m/n
pardoning [E]m/n
pardoning [e]m/n*
parent [e]m/n
parental [u]l
parenthood [oo/]
parenting [E]m/n
parenting [e]m/n*
parfait [A]
parish [i]
parishioner [er]
park [o]r
parking [E]m/n
parking [e]m/n*
parkway [A]
parlay [A]
parliament [e]m/n
parlor [er]
Parmesan [o]m/n
parody [E]
parole [O]l
paroling [E]m/n
paroling [e]m/n*
parrot [e]
parsley [E]
parsnip [i]
part [o]r
partake [A]
partaking [E]m/n
partaking [e]m/n*
partial [u]l
partially [E]
participant [e]m/n
participate [A]
participated [e]

participating [E]m/n
participating [e]m/n*
participation [u]m/n
particle [u]l
particular [er]
particularly [E]
parting [E]m/n
parting [e]m/n*
partition [u]m/n
partly [E]
partner [er]
partnering [E]m/n
partnering [e]m/n*
partnership [i]
partridge [i]
partway [A]
party [E]
party [e]*
pass [a]
passage [e]
passageway [A]
passenger [er]
passerby [I]
passing [E]m/n
passing [e]m/n*
passion [u]m/n
passionate [e]
passionately [E]
passive [i]
passively [E]
passport [O]r
password [er]
past [a]
pasta [u]
paste [A]
pasted [e]
pastel [e]l
pasteurize [I]
pasteurizing [E]m/n
pasteurizing [e]m/n*
pastime [I]m/n
pasting [E]m/n
pasting [e]m/n*
pastor [er]
pastrami [E]

pastry [E]
pasture [er]
pasty [E]
pat [a]
patch [a]
patching [E]m/n
patching [e]m/n*
patchwork [er]
patchy [E]
patent [e]m/n
patenting [E]m/n
patenting [e]m/n*
paternal [u]l
paternally [E]
paternity [E]
path [a]
pathetic [i]
pathetically [E]
pathway [A]
patience [e]m/n
patient [e]m/n
patiently [E]
patriot [e]
patriotic [i]
patriotism [e]m/n
patrol [O]l
patrolling [E]m/n
patrolling [e]m/n*
patron [e]m/n
patronize [I]
patsy [E]
patted [e]
patter [er]
pattern [er]m/n
patting [E]m/n
patting [e]m/n*
paunch [o]m/n
pauper [er]
pause [o]
pausing [E]m/n
pausing [e]m/n*
pave [A]
paver [er]
pavilion [e]m/n
paving [E]m/n

paving [e]m/n*
paw [o]
pawing [E]m/n
pawing [e]m/n*
pawn [o]m/n
pawning [E]m/n
pawning [e]m/n*
pawnshop [o]
pay [A]
payback [a]
paycheck [e]
payday [A]
payee [E]
paying [E]m/n
paying [e]m/n*
payload [O]
payment [e]m/n
payoff [o]
payroll [O]l
pea [E]
peace [E]
peaceful [u]l
peacefully [E]
peacetime [l]m/n
peach [E]
peachy [E]
peacock [o]
peak [E]
peaking [E]m/n
peaking [e]m/n*
peanut [u]
pear [e]r
pearl [er]l
peasant [e]m/n
pebble [u]l
pecan [a]m/n
pecan [o]m/n
peck [e]
pecker [er]
pecking [E]m/n
pecking [e]m/n*
peculiar [er]
peculiarity [E]
peculiarly [E]
pedal [u]l

pedaling [E]m/n
pedaling [e]m/n*
peddle [u]l
peddler [er]
peddling [E]m/n
peddling [e]m/n*
pedestal [u]l
pedestrian [e]m/n
pediatrician [e]m/n
pediatrics [i]
pedicure [er]
pedigree [E]
pedometer [er]
pee [E]
peeing [E]m/n
peeing [e]m/n*
peek [E]
peeking [E]m/n
peeking [e]m/n*
peel [E]l
peeler [er]
peeling [E]m/n
peeling [e]m/n*
peeper [er]
peephole [O]l
peer [E]r
peering [E]m/n
peering [e]m/n*
peeve [E]
peewee [E]
peg [e]
pegging [E]m/n
pegging [e]m/n*
pelican [e]m/n
pellet [e]
pelvic [i]
pelvis [i]
pen [e]m/n
penal [u]l
penalize [I]
penalty [E]
penchant [e]m/n
pencil [u]l
pendant [e]m/n
pendent [e]m/n

pendulum [u]m/n
penetrate [A]
penetrated [e]
penetrating [E]m/n
penetrating [e]m/n*
penguin [i]m/n
penicillin [i]m/n
penlight [I]
pennant [e]m/n
penniless [e]
penny [E]
pension [u]m/n
pent [e]
pentagon [o]m/n
penthouse [ow]
people [u]l
pep [e]
pepper [er]
peppercorn [O]r
peppermint [i]m/n
pepperoni [E]
peppy [E]
per [er]
perceive [E]
perceiving [E]m/n
perceiving [e]m/n*
percent [e]m/n
percentile [I]l
perceptible [u]l
perception [u]m/n
perceptive [i]
perceptual [oo]l
perch [er]
perching [E]m/n
perching [e]m/n*
percussion [u]m/n
perennial [u]l
perfect [e]
perfecting [E]m/n
perfecting [e]m/n*
perfection [u]m/n
perfectly [E]
perforate [A]
perforated [e]
perforation [u]m/n

perform [O]r
performance [e]m/n
performing [E]m/n
performing [e]m/n*
perfume [oo]m/n
perhaps [a]
peril [u]l
perilous [e]
period [i]
periodic [i]
peripheral [u]l
periphery [E]
periscope [O]
perish [i]
perishable [u]l
perishing [E]m/n
perishing [e]m/n*
perjure [er]
perjuring [E]m/n
perjuring [e]m/n*
perjury [E]
perk [er]
perking [E]m/n
perking [e]m/n*
perky [E]
perm [er]m/n
permanent [e]m/n
permanently [E]
permeate [A]
permeated [e]
permeating [E]m/n
permeating [e]m/n*
permissible [u]l
permission [u]m/n
permissive [i]
permit [i]
permitting [E]m/n
permitting [e]m/n*
peroxide [I]
perpetrate [A]
perpetrating [E]m/n
perpetrating [e]m/n*
perpetual [u]l
perpetually [E]
perplex [e]

perplexing [E]m/n
perplexing [e]m/n*
persecute [oo]
persecuting [E]m/n
persecuting [e]m/n*
persecution [u]m/n
perseverance [e]m/n
persevere [E]r
persevering [E]m/n
persevering [e]m/n*
persist [i]
persistence [e]m/n
persistent [e]m/n
persistently [E]
persisting [E]m/n
persisting [e]m/n*
person [e]m/n
personal [u]l
personality [E]
personalize [I]
personally [E]
personnel [e]l
perspective [i]
perspiration [u]m/n
perspire [I]r
perspiring [E]m/n
perspiring [e]m/n*
persuade [A]
persuaded [e]
persuading [E]m/n
persuading [e]m/n*
persuasion [u]m/n
persuasive [i]
pertain [A]m/n
pertaining [E]m/n
pertaining [e]m/n*
perturb [er]
perturbing [E]m/n
perturbing [e]m/n*
perverse [er]
perversion [u]m/n
pervert [er]
perverted [e]
pesky [E]
pessimism [e]m/n

pessimistic [i]
pest [e]
pester [er]
pestering [E]m/n
pestering [e]m/n*
pesticide [I]
pet [e]
petal [u]l
petite [E]
petition [u]m/n
petitioning [E]m/n
petitioning [e]m/n*
petroleum [u]m/n
petting [E]m/n
petting [e]m/n*
petty [E]
petunia [u]
pew [oo]
pewter [er]
phantom [u]m/n
pharmaceutical [u]l
pharmacist [i]
pharmacy [E]
phase [A]
phasing [E]m/n
phasing [e]m/n*
pheasant [e]m/n
phenomenal [u]l
phenomenally [E]
phenomenon [o]m/n
philosopher [er]
philosophical [u]l
philosophy [E]
phlegm [e]m/n
phobia [u]
phobic [i]
phone [O]m/n
phonetic [i]
phonics [i]
phoning [E]m/n
phoning [e]m/n*
phony [E]
phooey [E]
photo [O]
photocopy [E]

photogenic [i]
photograph [a]
photographer [er]
photographic [i]
photographing [E]m/n
photographing [e]m/n*
photography [E]
phrase [A]
phrasing [E]m/n
phrasing [e]m/n*
physical [u]l
physically [E]
physician [e]m/n
physics [i]
physique [E]
pianist [i]
piano [O]
piccolo [O]
pick [i]
picker [er]
picket [e]
picketing [E]m/n
picketing [e]m/n*
picking [E]m/n
picking [e]m/n*
pickle [u]l
pickling [E]m/n
pickling [e]m/n*
picky [E]
picnic [i]
picture [er]
picturing [E]m/n
picturing [e]m/n*
pie [I]
piece [E]
piecework [er]
piecing [E]m/n
piecing [e]m/n*
piecrust [u]
pier [E]r
pierce [E]r
piercing [E]m/n
piercing [e]m/n*
pig [i]
pigeon [e]m/n

piggy [E]
piggyback [a]
pigment [e]m/n
pigsty [I]
pike [I]
pilaf [o]
pile [I]l
pilgrim [i]m/n
pilgrimage [e]
piling [E]m/n
piling [e]m/n*
pill [i]l
pillar [er]
pillbox [o]
pilling [E]m/n
pilling [e]m/n*
pillow [O]
pillowcase [A]
pilot [e]
pimento [O]
pimp [i]m/n
pimping [E]m/n
pimping [e]m/n*
pimple [u]l
pin [i]m/n
piñata [u]
pinball [o]l
pinch [i]m/n
pinching [E]m/n
pinching [e]m/n*
pincushion [u]m/n
pine [I]m/n
pineapple [u]l
pinecone [O]m/n
pinhead [e]
pinhole [O]l
pink [E]m/n
pinkeye [I]
pinkish [i]
pinky [E]
pinnacle [u]l
pinning [E]m/n
pinning [e]m/n*
pinpoint [Oi]m/n
pinpointing [E]m/n

pinpointing [e]m/n*
pinprick [i]
pinstripe [I]
pioneer [E]r
pioneering [E]m/n
pioneering [e]m/n*
pip [i]
pipe [I]
pipeline [I]m/n
piper [er]
piping [E]m/n
piping [e]m/n*
pistachio [O]
pistol [u]l
piston [e]m/n
pit [i]
pitch [i]
pitcher [er]
pitchfork [O]r
pitching [E]m/n
pitching [e]m/n*
pitchy [E]
pitfall [o]l
pitiful [u]l
pitifully [E]
pitting [E]m/n
pitting [e]m/n*
pity [E]
pitying [E]m/n
pitying [e]m/n*
pivot [i]
pivotal [u]l
pivoting [E]m/n
pivoting [e]m/n*
pixel [u]l
pixie [E]
pizza [u]
pizzazz [a]
pizzeria [u]
place [A]
placebo [O]
placement [e]m/n
placing [E]m/n
placing [e]m/n*
plague [A]

plaguing [E]m/n
plaguing [e]m/n*
plaid [a]
plain [A]m/n
plainly [E]
plaintiff [i]
plan [a]m/n
plane [A]m/n
planet [e]
planetarium [u]m/n
planetary [E]
plank [a]ng/k
plankton [e]m/n
planner [er]
planning [E]m/n
planning [e]m/n*
plant [a]m/n
plantation [u]m/n
planted [e]
planter [er]
planting [E]m/n
planting [e]m/n*
plaque [a]
plaster [er]
plastering [E]m/n
plastering [e]m/n*
plastic [i]
plate [A]
plateau [O]
plated [e]
plated [e]
platform [O]r
platinum [u]m/n
platonic [i]
platoon [oo]m/n
platter [er]
play [A]
playback [a]
playboy [Oi]
player [er]
playful [u]l
playfully [E]
playgirl [er]l
playground [ow]m/n
playhouse [ow]

playing [E]m/n
playing [e]m/n*
playmate [A]
playoff [o]
playpen [e]m/n
plaything [E]m/n
playtime [I]m/n
playwright [I]
plaza [u]
plea [E]
plead [E]
pleading [E]m/n
pleading [e]m/n*
pleasant [e]m/n
pleasantly [E]
pleasantries [E]
please [E]
pleaser [er]
pleasing [E]m/n
pleasing [e]m/n*
pleasurable [u]l
pleasure [er]
pleat [E]
pleated [e]
pleating [E]m/n
pleating [e]m/n*
pled [e]
pledge [e]
pledging [E]m/n
pledging [e]m/n*
plentiful [u]l
plenty [E]
pliable [u]l
pliers [I]r
plight [I]
plod [o]
plodded [e]
plodding [E]m/n
plodding [e]m/n*
plop [o]
plopping [E]m/n
plopping [e]m/n*
plot [o]
plotted [e]
plotting [E]m/n

plotting [e]m/n*
ploy [Oi]
plug [u]
plugging [E]m/n
plugging [e]m/n*
plum [u]m/n
plumber [er]
plumbing [E]m/n
plumbing [e]m/n*
plume [oo]m/n
plump [u]m/n
plumper [er]
plumping [E]m/n
plumping [e]m/n*
plunder [er]
plundering [E]m/n
plundering [e]m/n*
plunge [u]m/n
plunger [er]
plunging [E]m/n
plunging [e]m/n*
plunk [u]m/n
plural [u]l
plus [u]
plush [u]
ply [I]
plying [E]m/n
plying [e]m/n*
plywood [oo/]
pneumonia [u]
poach [O]
poaching [E]m/n
poaching [e]m/n*
pocket [e]
podiatrist [i]
podiatry [E]
podium [u]m/n
poem [e]m/n
poet [e]
poetic [i]
poetry [E]
point [Oi]m/n
pointed [e]
pointer [er]
pointing [E]m/n

pointing [e]m/n*
pointless [e]
pointy [E]
poise [Oi]
poison [e]m/n
poisonous [e]
poke [O]
poker [er]
poking [E]m/n
poking [e]m/n*
poky [E]
polar [er]
polarize [I]
polarizing [E]m/n
polarizing [e]m/n*
pole [O]l
police [E]
policeman [e]m/n
policewoman [e]m/n
policy [E]
polish [i]
polishing [E]m/n
polishing [e]m/n*
polite [I]
politely [E]
political [u]l
politically [E]
politician [e]m/n
politics [i]
polka [u]
poll [O]l
pollen [e]m/n
pollinate [A]
pollinated [e]
pollinating [E]m/n
pollinating [e]m/n*
polling [E]m/n
polling [e]m/n*
pollute [oo]
polluting [E]m/n
polluting [e]m/n*
pollution [u]m/n
polo [O]
poltergeist [I]
polyp [i]

pomegranate [e]
pompous [e]
pompously [E]
poncho [O]
pond [o]m/n
ponder [er]
pondering [E]m/n
pondering [e]m/n*
pony [E]
poodle [u]l
pool [oo]l
pooling [E]m/n
pooling [e]m/n*
poolside [I]
poor [O]r
poorhouse [ow]
poorly [E]
pop [o]
popcorn [O]r
popper [er]
popping [E]m/n
popping [e]m/n*
poppy [E]
popular [er]
popularity [E]
populate [A]
populated [e]
populating [E]m/n
populating [e]m/n*
population [u]m/n
porcelain [i]m/n
porcupine [I]m/n
pore [O]r
pork [O]r
porky [E]
porn [O]r
porno [O]
pornography [E]
porous [e]
porpoise [i]
porridge [i]
port [O]r
portable [u]l
portal [u]l
porter [er]

portfolio [O]
portion [u]m/n
portrait [i]
portray [A]
portraying [E]m/n
portraying [e]m/n*
pose [O]
poser [er]
posing [E]m/n
posing [e]m/n*
position [u]m/n
positioning [E]m/n
positioning [e]m/n*
positive [i]
positively [E]
posse [E]
possess [e]
possessing [E]m/n
possessing [e]m/n*
possession [u]m/n
possessive [i]
possessively [E]
possibility [E]
possible [u]l
possibly [E]
possum [u]m/n
post [O]
postage [e]
postal [u]l
postcard [o]r
postdate [A]
postdated [e]
poster [er]
posterior [er]
posterity [E]
posting [E]m/n
posting [e]m/n*
postman [e]m/n
postpartum [u]m/n
postpone [O]m/n
postponing [E]m/n
postponing [e]m/n*
posture [er]
posturing [E]m/n
posturing [e]m/n*

postwar [O]r
posy [E]
pot [o]
potassium [u]m/n
potato [O]
potency [E]
potent [e]m/n
potential [u]l
potentially [E]
pothead [e]
pothole [O]l
potion [u]m/n
potluck [u]
potpie [I]
potpourri [E]
potshot [o]
potter [er]
pottery [E]
potting [E]m/n
potting [e]m/n*
potty [E]
pouch [ow]
poultry [E]
pound [ow]m/n
pounded [e]
pounding [E]m/n
pounding [e]m/n*
pour [O]r
pouring [E]m/n
pouring [e]m/n*
pout [ow]
pouting [E]m/n
pouting [e]m/n*
poverty [E]
powder [er]
powdery [E]
power [er]
powerful [u]l
powerfully [E]
powering [E]m/n
powering [e]m/n*
powerless [e]
pox [o]
practical [u]l
practically [E]

practice [i]
practitioner [er]
pragmatic [i]
prairie [E]
praise [A]
praising [E]m/n
praising [e]m/n*
prank [a]ng/k
prankster [er]
prawn [o]m/n
pray [A]
prayer [er]
praying [E]m/n
praying [e]m/n*
preach [E]
preacher [er]
preaching [E]m/n
preaching [e]m/n*
preachy [E]
precarious [e]
precariously [E]
precaution [u]m/n
precede [E]
precedent [e]m/n
preceding [E]m/n
preceding [e]m/n*
precinct [E]m/n
precious [e]
precipitate [A]
precipitating [E]m/n
precipitating [e]m/n*
precipitation [u]m/n
precise [I]
precisely [E]
precision [u]m/n
preconceive [E]
preconception [u]m/n
predator [er]
predatory [E]
predawn [o]m/n
predecessor [er]
predetermine [i]m/n
predicament [e]m/n
predict [i]
predictable [u]l

predicting [E]m/n
predicting [e]m/n*
prediction [U]m/n
predispose [O]
predisposing [E]m/n
predisposing [e]m/n*
predominance [e]m/n
predominant [e]m/n
predominantly [E]
preemie [E]
preempt [e]m/n
preempting [E]m/n
preempting [e]m/n*
preexist [i]
preexisting [E]m/n
preexisting [e]m/n*
prefab [a]
preface [e]
prefacing [E]m/n
prefacing [e]m/n*
prefer [er]
preferable [U]l
preferably [E]
preference [e]m/n
preferential [U]l
preferring [E]m/n
preferring [e]m/n*
prefix [i]
pregame [A]m/n
pregnant [e]m/n
preheat [E]
preheating [E]m/n
preheating [e]m/n*
prehistoric [i]
prejudice [i]
prejudicial [U]l
preliminary [E]
prelude [oo]
premature [er]
prematurely [E]
premed [e]
premeditate [A]
premeditated [e]
premeditation [U]m/n
premier [E]r

premiering [E]m/n
premiering [e]m/n*
premise [i]
premium [U]m/n
premonition [U]m/n
prenatal [U]l
preoccupy [I]
prep [e]
preparation [U]m/n
preparatory [E]
prepare [e]r
preparing [E]m/n
preparing [e]m/n*
prepay [A]
prepaying [E]m/n
prepaying [e]m/n*
preplan [a]m/n
preplanning [E]m/n
preplanning [e]m/n*
prepping [E]m/n
prepping [e]m/n*
preppy [E]
preregister [er]
preschool [oo]l
preschooler [er]
prescribe [I]
prescribing [E]m/n
prescribing [e]m/n*
prescription [U]m/n
presence [e]m/n
present [e]m/n
presentable [U]l
presentation [U]m/n
presenting [E]m/n
presenting [e]m/n*
presently [E]
preservation [U]m/n
preserve [er]
preserving [E]m/n
preserving [e]m/n*
preset [e]
preshrink [E]m/n
preshrinking [E]m/n
preshrinking [e]m/n*
preshrunk [U]m/n

preside [I]
presidency [E]
president [e]m/n
presiding [E]m/n
presiding [e]m/n*
presoak [O]
presoaking [E]m/n
presoaking [e]m/n*
press [e]
pressing [E]m/n
pressing [e]m/n*
pressure [er]
pressuring [E]m/n
pressuring [e]m/n*
pressurize [I]
pressurizing [E]m/n
pressurizing [e]m/n*
prestige [E]
prestigious [e]
presto [O]
presumable [U]l
presumably [E]
presume [oo]m/n
presuming [E]m/n
presuming [e]m/n*
presumption [U]m/n
presumptuous [e]
pretend [e]m/n
pretending [E]m/n
pretending [e]m/n*
pretense [e]m/n
prettier [er]
pretty [E]
pretty [e]*
pretzel [U]l
prevail [A]l
prevailing [E]m/n
prevailing [e]m/n*
prevalence [e]m/n
prevalent [e]m/n
prevent [e]m/n
preventative [i]
preventing [E]m/n
preventing [e]m/n*
prevention [U]m/n

preventive [i]
preview [oo]
previewing [E]m/n
previewing [e]m/n*
previous [e]
previously [E]
prey [A]
preying [E]m/n
preying [e]m/n*
price [I]
priceless [e]
pricing [E]m/n
pricing [e]m/n*
prick [i]
pricking [E]m/n
pricking [e]m/n*
prickle [u]l
prickling [E]m/n
prickling [e]m/n*
prickly [E]
pride [I]
priest [E]
priestess [e]
prim [i]m/n
primarily [E]
primary [E]
primate [A]
prime [I]m/n
primer [er]
primeval [u]l
priming [E]m/n
priming [e]m/n*
primitive [i]
primitively [E]
primrose [O]
prince [i]m/n
princess [e]
principal [u]l
principle [u]l
print [i]m/n
printable [u]l
printer [er]
printing [E]m/n
printing [e]m/n*
prior [I]r

priority [E]
prism [i]m/n
prison [e]m/n
prisoner [er]
prissy [E]
pristine [E]m/n
privacy [E]
private [e]
privately [E]
privilege [e]
privy [E]
prize [I]
prizefight [I]
pro [O]
probability [E]
probable [u]l
probably [E]
probate [A]
probation [u]m/n
probe [O]
probing [E]m/n
probing [e]m/n*
problem [e]m/n
problematic [i]
procedural [u]l
procedure [er]
proceed [E]
proceeding [E]m/n
proceeding [e]m/n*
process [e]
processing [E]m/n
processing [e]m/n*
proclaim [A]m/n
proclaiming [E]m/n
proclaiming [e]m/n*
procrastinate [A]
procrastinated [e]
procrastinating [E]m/n
procrastinating [e]m/n*
procrastination [u]m/n
procrastinator [er]
prod [o]
prodding [E]m/n
prodding [e]m/n*
prodigy [E]

produce [oo]
producer [er]
producing [E]m/n
producing [e]m/n*
product [u]
production [u]m/n
productive [i]
productively [E]
productivity [E]
profane [A]m/n
profanity [E]
profess [e]
professing [E]m/n
professing [e]m/n*
professional [u]l
professionalism [e]m/n
professionally [E]
professor [er]
proficient [e]m/n
proficiently [E]
profile [I]l
profiling [E]m/n
profiling [e]m/n*
profit [i]
profitable [u]l
profiting [E]m/n
profiting [e]m/n*
profound [ow]m/n
profoundly [E]
prognosis [i]
program [a]m/n
programming [E]m/n
programming [e]m/n*
progress [e]
progressing [E]m/n
progressing [e]m/n*
progression [u]m/n
progressive [i]
progressively [E]
prohibit [i]
prohibiting [E]m/n
prohibiting [e]m/n*
prohibitive [i]
project [e]
projectile [I]l

projecting [E]m/n
projecting [e]m/n*
projector [er]
prolific [i]
prologue [o]
prolong [o]m/n
prolonging [E]m/n
prolonging [e]m/n*
prom [o]m/n
promenade [A]
promenaded [e]
promenading [E]m/n
promenading [e]m/n*
prominence [e]m/n
prominent [e]m/n
prominently [E]
promiscuity [E]
promiscuous [e]
promise [i]
promising [E]m/n
promising [e]m/n*
promissory [E]
promote [O]
promoter [er]
promoting [E]m/n
promoting [e]m/n*
promotion [u]m/n
promotional [u]l
prompt [o]m/n
prompter [er]
prompting [E]m/n
prompting [e]m/n*
prone [O]m/n
pronoun [ow]m/n
pronounce [ow]m/n
pronouncing [E]m/n
pronouncing [e]m/n*
pronto [O]
pronunciation [u]m/n
proof [oo]
proofing [E]m/n
proofing [e]m/n*
proofread [E]
proofreading [E]m/n
proofreading [e]m/n*

prop [o]
propaganda [u]
propane [A]m/n
propel [e]l
propellant [e]m/n
propeller [er]
propelling [E]m/n
propelling [e]m/n*
proper [er]
properly [E]
property [E]
prophecy [E]
proportion [u]m/n
proportionate [e]
proportionately [E]
proposal [u]l
propose [O]
proposing [E]m/n
proposing [e]m/n*
proposition [u]m/n
propositioning [E]m/n
propositioning [e]m/n*
propping [E]m/n
propping [e]m/n*
proprietary [E]
proprietor [er]
propulsion [u]m/n
prorate [A]
prorated [e]
prorating [E]m/n
prorating [e]m/n*
prose [O]
prosecute [oo]
prosecuting [E]m/n
prosecuting [e]m/n*
prosecution [u]m/n
prosecutor [er]
prospect [e]
prospective [i]
prospector [er]
prosper [er]
prospering [E]m/n
prospering [e]m/n*
prosperity [E]
prosperous [e]

prostate [A]
prosthetic [i]
prostitute [oo]
prostitution [u]m/n
prostrate [A]
protagonist [i]
protect [e]
protecting [E]m/n
protecting [e]m/n*
protection [u]m/n
protector [er]
protégé [A]
protein [E]m/n
protest [e]
protestant [e]m/n
protesting [E]m/n
protesting [e]m/n*
protocol [o]l
prototype [I]
protrude [oo]
protruding [E]m/n
protruding [e]m/n*
protrusion [u]m/n
proud [ow]
prouder [er]
proudly [E]
prove [oo]
proven [e]m/n
proverb [er]
proverbial [u]l
provide [I]
provided [e]
provider [er]
providing [E]m/n
providing [e]m/n*
provincial [u]l
proving [E]m/n
proving [e]m/n*
provision [u]m/n
provisional [u]l
provocation [u]m/n
provocative [i]
provoke [O]
prowl [u]l
prowler [er]

prowling [E]m/n
prowling [e]m/n*
proximity [E]
proxy [E]
prude [oo]
prudish [i]
prune [oo]m/n
pruning [E]m/n
pruning [e]m/n*
pry [I]
prying [E]m/n
prying [e]m/n*
psyche [E]
psychiatric [i]
psychiatry [E]
psychic [i]
psycho [O]
psychological [u]l
psychologically [E]
psychology [E]
psychotic [i]
psychotically [E]
pub [u]
puberty [E]
pubic [i]
public [i]
publication [u]m/n
publicist [i]
publicity [E]
publicize [I]
publicly [E]
publish [i]
publisher [er]
publishing [E]m/n
publishing [e]m/n*
puck [u]
pucker [er]
puckering [E]m/n
puckering [e]m/n*
pudding [E]m/n
pudding [e]m/n*
puddle [u]l
pudgy [E]
pueblo [O]
puff [u]

puffing [E]m/n
puffing [e]m/n*
puffy [E]
pug [u]
puke [oo]
puking [E]m/n
puking [e]m/n*
pull [oo]l
pulley [E]
pulling [E]m/n
pulling [e]m/n*
pulp [u]l
pulsate [A]
pulsated [e]
pulsating [E]m/n
pulsating [e]m/n*
pulse [u]l
pulverize [I]
pulverizing [E]m/n
pulverizing [e]m/n*
pummel [u]l
pummeling [E]m/n
pummeling [e]m/n*
pump [u]m/n
pumpernickel [u]l
pumping [E]m/n
pumping [e]m/n*
pumpkin [i]m/n
pun [u]m/n
punch [u]m/n
puncher [er]
punching [E]m/n
punching [e]m/n*
punchy [E]
punctual [u]l
punctuality [E]
punctually [E]
punctuate [A]
punctuated [e]
punctuating [E]m/n
punctuating [e]m/n*
punctuation [u]m/n
puncture [er]
puncturing [E]m/n
puncturing [e]m/n*

pungent [e]m/n
punish [i]
punishable [u]l
punishing [E]m/n
punishing [e]m/n*
punishment [e]m/n
punitive [i]
punk [u]m/n
punt [u]m/n
punting [E]m/n
punting [e]m/n*
puny [E]
pup [u]
pupil [u]l
puppet [e]
puppetry [E]
puppy [E]
purchase [e]
purchasing [E]m/n
purchasing [e]m/n*
pure [er]
purebred [e]
puree [A]
purely [E]
purely [e]*
purge [er]
purging [E]m/n
purging [e]m/n*
purification [u]m/n
purify [I]
purifying [E]m/n
purifying [e]m/n*
purist [i]
purity [E]
purple [u]l
purplish [i]
purpose [e]
purposely [E]
purr [er]
purring [E]m/n
purring [e]m/n*
purse [er]
pursing [E]m/n
pursing [e]m/n*
pursuant [e]m/n

pursue [oo]
pursuing [E]m/n
pursuing [e]m/n*
pursuit [oo]
push [oo/]
pusher [er]
pushing [E]m/n
pushing [e]m/n*
pushup [u]

pushy [E]
put [oo/]
putdown [ow]m/n
putrid [i]
putt [u]
putter [er]
putting [E]m/n
putting [e]m/n*
putty [E]

puzzle [u]l
puzzling [E]m/n
puzzling [e]m/n*
pygmy [E]
pylon [o]m/n
pyramid [i]
python [o]m/n

Q

quack [a]
quackery [E]
quacking [E]m/n
quacking [e]m/n*
quadrant [e]m/n
quadruple [u]l
quail [A]l
quaint [A]m/n
quaintly [E]
qualification [u]m/n
qualify [I]
qualifying [E]m/n
qualifying [e]m/n*
quality [E]
qualm [o]l
quantity [E]
quantum [u]m/n
quarantine [E]m/n
quarrel [e]l
quarreling [E]m/n
quarreling [e]m/n*
quart [O]r
quarter [er]
quarterback [a]

quartering [E]m/n
quartering [e]m/n*
quartet [e]
quartz [O]r
queasy [E]
queen [E]m/n
quell [e]l
query [E]
question [u]m/n
questionable [u]l
questioning [E]m/n
questioning [e]m/n*
questionnaire [e]r
quick [i]
quicken [e]m/n
quicker [er]
quickie [E]
quickly [E]
quiet [e]
quietly [E]
quilt [i]l
quilted [e]
quilting [E]m/n
quilting [e]m/n*

quintessential [u]l
quintet [e]
quintuplet [e]
quip [i]
quirk [er]
quirky [E]
quit [i]
quite [I]
quitter [er]
quitting [E]m/n
quitting [e]m/n*
quiver [er]
quivering [E]m/n
quivering [e]m/n*
quiz [i]
quizzical [u]l
quizzing [E]m/n
quizzing [e]m/n*
quota [u]
quotation [u]m/n
quote [O]
quoting [E]m/n

R

rabbi [I]
rabbit [i]

rabid [i]
rabies [E]

raccoon [oo]m/n
race [A]

racehorse [O]r
racer [er]
racetrack [a]
raceway [A]
racial [u]l
racially [E]
racing [E]m/n
racing [e]m/n*
racism [e]m/n
rack [a]
racket [e]
racketeer [E]r
racketeering [E]m/n
racketeering [e]m/n*
racking [E]m/n
racking [e]m/n*
racy [E]
radar [o]r
radial [u]l
radiance [e]m/n
radiant [e]m/n
radiantly [E]
radiate [A]
radiated [e]
radiating [E]m/n
radiating [e]m/n*
radiation [u]m/n
radiator [er]
radical [u]l
radically [E]
radio [O]
radiology [E]
radish [i]
radius [e]
raffle [u]l
raffling [E]m/n
raffling [e]m/n*
raft [a]
rafted [e]
rafter [er]
rafting [E]m/n
rafting [e]m/n*
rag [a]
rage [A]
ragged [e]

raggedy [E]
raging [E]m/n
raging [e]m/n*
ragweed [E]
raid [A]
raided [e]
raider [er]
raiding [E]m/n
raiding [e]m/n*
rail [A]l
railing [E]m/n
railing [e]m/n*
railroad [O]
railway [A]
rain [A]m/n
rainbow [O]
raincoat [O]
raindrop [o]
rainfall [o]l
raining [E]m/n
raining [e]m/n*
rainy [E]
raise [A]
raisin [i]m/n
raising [E]m/n
raising [e]m/n*
rake [A]
raking [E]m/n
raking [e]m/n*
rally [E]
rally [e]*
ram [a]m/n
ramble [u]l
rambler [er]
rambling [E]m/n
rambling [e]m/n*
rambunctious [e]
ramification [u]m/n
ramming [E]m/n
ramming [e]m/n*
ramp [a]m/n
rampant [e]m/n
rampantly [E]
ramping [E]m/n
ramping [e]m/n*

ramshackle [u]l
ran [a]m/n
ranch [a]m/n
rancher [er]
rancid [i]
random [u]m/n
randomly [E]
rang [a]ng/k
range [A]m/n
ranger [er]
ranging [E]m/n
ranging [e]m/n*
rank [a]ng/k
ranking [E]m/n
ranking [e]m/n*
ransack [a]
ransacking [E]m/n
ransacking [e]m/n*
ransom [u]m/n
rap [a]
rape [A]
rapid [i]
rapidly [E]
raping [E]m/n
raping [e]m/n*
rappel [e]l
rappelling [E]m/n
rappelling [e]m/n*
rapper [er]
rapping [E]m/n
rapping [e]m/n*
rapport [O]r
rapt [a]
rapture [er]
rare [e]r
rarely [E]
rarely [e]*
rarity [E]
rascal [u]l
rash [a]
rashly [E]
raspberry [E]
raspy [E]
rat [a]
ratchet [e]

ratcheting [E]m/n
ratcheting [e]m/n*
rate [A]
rated [e]
rather [er]
rating [E]m/n
rating [e]m/n*
ratio [O]
ration [u]m/n
rational [u]l
rationale [a]l
rationalize [I]
rationalizing [E]m/n
rationalizing [e]m/n*
rationing [E]m/n
rationing [e]m/n*
rattan [a]m/n
ratted [e]
rattle [u]l
rattler [er]
rattlesnake [A]
rattling [E]m/n
rattling [e]m/n*
ratty [E]
raunchy [E]
ravage [e]
ravaging [E]m/n
ravaging [e]m/n*
rave [A]
ravel [u]l
raveling [E]m/n
raveling [e]m/n*
raven [e]m/n
ravenous [e]
ravenously [E]
ravine [E]m/n
raving [E]m/n
raving [e]m/n*
ravioli [E]
raw [o]
rawhide [I]
ray [A]
rayon [o]m/n
razor [er]
reach [E]

reaching [E]m/n
reaching [e]m/n*
react [a]
reacted [e]
reacting [E]m/n
reacting [e]m/n*
reaction [u]m/n
reactor [er]
read [E]
read [e]
reader [er]
readily [E]
reading [E]m/n
reading [e]m/n*
ready [E]
ready [e]*
real [E]l
realistic [i]
reality [E]
realization [u]m/n
realize [I]
realizing [E]m/n
realizing [e]m/n*
really [E]
really [e]*
realm [e]l
realty [E]
rear [E]r
rearing [E]m/n
rearing [e]m/n*
rearrange [A]m/n
rearranging [E]m/n
rearranging [e]m/n*
reason [u]m/n
reasonable [u]l
reasonably [E]
reasoning [E]m/n
reasoning [e]m/n*
reassurance [e]m/n
reassure [er]
reassuring [E]m/n
reassuring [e]m/n*
rebate [A]
rebated [e]
rebating [E]m/n

rebating [e]m/n*
rebel [u]l
rebelling [E]m/n
rebelling [e]m/n*
rebellion [e]m/n
rebellious [e]
reborn [O]r
rebuild [i]l
rebuilding [E]m/n
rebuilding [e]m/n*
rebuilt [i]l
rebuttal [u]l
recall [o]l
recalling [E]m/n
recalling [e]m/n*
recant [a]m/n
recanted [e]
recanting [E]m/n
recanting [e]m/n*
recap [a]
recapping [E]m/n
recapping [e]m/n*
recapture [er]
recast [a]
recede [E]
receded [e]
receding [E]m/n
receding [e]m/n*
receipt [E]
receive [E]
receiver [er]
receiving [E]m/n
receiving [e]m/n*
recent [e]m/n
recently [E]
receptacle [u]l
reception [u]m/n
receptionist [i]
receptive [i]
recess [e]
recessing [E]m/n
recessing [e]m/n*
recession [u]m/n
recheck [e]
rechecking [E]m/n

rechecking [e]m/n*
recipe [E]
recipient [e]m/n
reciprocal [u]l
reciprocate [A]
reciprocated [e]
reciprocating [E]m/n
reciprocating [e]m/n*
recital [u]l
recite [I]
recited [e]
reciting [E]m/n
reciting [e]m/n*
reckless [e]
recklessly [E]
reckon [e]m/n
reckoning [E]m/n
reckoning [e]m/n*
reclaim [A]m/n
reclaiming [E]m/n
reclaiming [e]m/n*
recline [I]m/n
recliner [er]
reclining [E]m/n
reclining [e]m/n*
recognition [u]m/n
recognize [I]
recognizing [E]m/n
recognizing [e]m/n*
recoil [Oi]l
recoiling [E]m/n
recoiling [e]m/n*
recollect [e]
recollecting [E]m/n
recollecting [e]m/n*
recommend [e]m/n
recommendation [u]m/n
recommended [e]
recommending [E]m/n
recommending [e]m/n*
reconcile [I]l
reconciliation [u]m/n
reconciling [E]m/n
reconciling [e]m/n*
recondition [u]m/n

reconfirm [er]m/n
reconfirming [E]m/n
reconfirming [e]m/n*
reconsider [er]
reconsidering [E]m/n
reconsidering [e]m/n*
record [er]
record [O]r
recorded [e]
recording [E]m/n
recording [e]m/n*
recoup [oo]
recouping [E]m/n
recouping [e]m/n*
recourse [O]r
recover [er]
recovering [E]m/n
recovering [e]m/n*
recovery [E]
recreation [u]m/n
recreational [u]l
recruit [oo]
recruited [e]
recruiting [E]m/n
recruiting [e]m/n*
rectangle [u]l
rectangular [er]
recuperate [A]
recuperated [e]
recuperating [E]m/n
recuperating [e]m/n*
recur [er]
recurring [E]m/n
recurring [e]m/n*
recycle [u]l
recycling [E]m/n
recycling [e]m/n*
red [e]
redecorate [A]
redecorated [e]
redecorating [E]m/n
redecorating [e]m/n*
redeem [E]m/n
redeeming [E]m/n
redeeming [e]m/n*

redefine [I]m/n
redefining [E]m/n
redefining [e]m/n*
redemption [u]m/n
redhead [e]
redid [i]
redneck [e]
redo [oo]
redoing [E]m/n
redoing [e]m/n*
redone [u]m/n
reduce [oo]
reducing [E]m/n
reducing [e]m/n*
reduction [u]m/n
redundant [e]m/n
reef [E]
reefer [er]
reek [E]
reeking [E]m/n
reeking [e]m/n*
reel [E]l
reeling [E]m/n
reeling [e]m/n*
refer [er]
referee [E]
reference [e]m/n
referral [u]l
referring [E]m/n
referring [e]m/n*
refill [i]l
refilling [E]m/n
refilling [e]m/n*
refine [I]m/n
refining [E]m/n
refining [e]m/n*
reflect [e]
reflecting [E]m/n
reflecting [e]m/n*
reflection [u]m/n
reflective [i]
reflector [er]
reflex [e]
reform [O]r
reforming [E]m/n

reforming [e]m/n*
refrain [A]m/n
refraining [E]m/n
refraining [e]m/n*
refresh [e]
refreshing [E]m/n
refreshing [e]m/n*
refreshment [e]m/n
refried [I]
refrigerate [A]
refrigerated [e]
refrigerating [E]m/n
refrigerating [e]m/n*
refrigeration [u]m/n
refrigerator [er]
refry [I]
refrying [E]m/n
refrying [e]m/n*
refuel [oo]l
refueling [E]m/n
refueling [e]m/n*
refuge [oo]
refugee [E]
refund [u]m/n
refunded [e]
refunding [E]m/n
refunding [e]m/n*
refurbish [i]
refurbishing [E]m/n
refurbishing [e]m/n*
refusal [u]l
refuse [oo]
refusing [E]m/n
refusing [e]m/n*
refute [oo]
regain [A]m/n
regaining [E]m/n
regaining [e]m/n*
regal [u]l
regard [o]r
regarded [e]
regarding [E]m/n
regarding [e]m/n*
regardless [e]
reggae [A]

regime [E]m/n
regimen [e]m/n
region [e]m/n
regional [u]l
register [er]
registering [E]m/n
registering [e]m/n*
registrar [o]r
registration [u]m/n
registry [E]
regress [e]
regressing [E]m/n
regressing [e]m/n*
regression [u]m/n
regret [e]
regretting [E]m/n
regretting [e]m/n*
regular [er]
regularly [E]
regulate [A]
regulated [e]
regulation [u]m/n
regulator [er]
rehab [a]
rehabilitate [A]
rehabilitated [e]
rehabilitating [E]m/n
rehabilitating [e]m/n*
rehabilitation [u]m/n
rehearsal [u]l
rehearse [er]
rehearsing [E]m/n
rehearsing [e]m/n*
reign [A]m/n
reigning [E]m/n
reigning [e]m/n*
reimburse [er]
reimbursement [e]m/n
reimbursing [E]m/n
reimbursing [e]m/n*
rein [A]m/n
reincarnation [u]m/n
reindeer [E]r
reinforce [O]r
reinforcement [e]m/n

reinforcing [E]m/n
reinforcing [e]m/n*
reining [E]m/n
reining [e]m/n*
reinstate [A]
reinstated [e]
reinstating [E]m/n
reinstating [e]m/n*
reject [e]
rejecting [E]m/n
rejecting [e]m/n*
rejection [u]m/n
rejoice [Oi]
rejoicing [E]m/n
rejoicing [e]m/n*
rejoin [Oi]m/n
rejoining [E]m/n
rejoining [e]m/n*
rejuvenate [A]
rejuvenated [e]
rejuvenating [E]m/n
rejuvenating [e]m/n*
relapse [a]
relapsing [E]m/n
relapsing [e]m/n*
relate [A]
related [e]
relating [E]m/n
relating [e]m/n*
relation [u]m/n
relationship [i]
relative [i]
relatively [E]
relativity [E]
relax [a]
relaxation [u]m/n
relaxing [E]m/n
relaxing [e]m/n*
relay [A]
relaying [E]m/n
relaying [e]m/n*
release [E]
releasing [E]m/n
releasing [e]m/n*
relent [e]

relentless [e]
relentlessly [E]
relevance [e]m/n
relevant [e]m/n
reliability [E]
reliable [u]l
reliably [E]
relic [i]
relief [E]
relieve [E]
relieving [E]m/n
relieving [e]m/n*
religion [e]m/n
religious [e]
relish [i]
relishing [E]m/n
relishing [e]m/n*
relive [i]
reliving [E]m/n
reliving [e]m/n*
reload [O]
reloaded [e]
reloading [E]m/n
reloading [e]m/n*
reluctance [e]m/n
reluctant [e]m/n
reluctantly [E]
rely [I]
relying [E]m/n
relying [e]m/n*
remain [A]m/n
remainder [er]
remaining [E]m/n
remaining [e]m/n*
remake [A]
remaking [E]m/n
remaking [e]m/n*
remark [o]r
remarkable [u]l
remarking [E]m/n
remarking [e]m/n*
remedial [u]l
remediation [u]m/n
remedy [E]
remember [er]

remembering [E]m/n
remembering [e]m/n*
remembrance [e]m/n
remind [I]m/n
reminded [e]
reminding [E]m/n
reminding [e]m/n*
reminisce [i]
reminiscent [e]m/n
reminiscing [E]m/n
reminiscing [e]m/n*
remit [i]
remitted [e]
remitting [E]m/n
remitting [e]m/n*
remnant [e]m/n
remodel [u]l
remodeling [E]m/n
remodeling [e]m/n*
remorse [O]r
remorseful [u]l
remote [O]
remotely [E]
removable [u]l
removal [u]l
remove [oo]
removing [E]m/n
removing [e]m/n*
renaissance [o]m/n
rename [A]m/n
renaming [E]m/n
renaming [e]m/n*
render [er]
rendering [E]m/n
rendering [e]m/n*
rendezvous [oo]
renew [oo]
renewing [E]m/n
renewing [e]m/n*
renovate [A]
renovated [e]
renovating [E]m/n
renovating [e]m/n*
renovation [u]m/n
renown [ow]m/n

rent [e]m/n
rental [u]l
rented [e]
renter [er]
renting [E]m/n
renting [e]m/n*
reorganize [I]
reorganizing [E]m/n
reorganizing [e]m/n*
repack [a]
repacking [E]m/n
repacking [e]m/n*
repaid [A]
repair [e]r
repairing [E]m/n
repairing [e]m/n*
repay [A]
repaying [E]m/n
repaying [e]m/n*
repeal [E]l
repealing [E]m/n
repealing [e]m/n*
repeat [E]
repeated [e]
repeating [E]m/n
repeating [e]m/n*
repel [e]l
repelling [E]m/n
repelling [e]m/n*
repetition [u]m/n
repetitious [e]
repetitive [i]
replace [A]
replacement [e]m/n
replacing [E]m/n
replacing [e]m/n*
replay [A]
replaying [E]m/n
replaying [e]m/n*
replenish [i]
replenishing [E]m/n
replenishing [e]m/n*
replica [u]
reply [I]
replying [E]m/n

replying [e]m/n*
report [O]r
reported [e]
reporter [er]
reporting [E]m/n
reporting [e]m/n*
represent [e]m/n
represented [e]
representing [E]m/n
representing [e]m/n*
repress [e]
repressing [E]m/n
repressing [e]m/n*
reprisal [u]l
reprise [I]
reprising [E]m/n
reprising [e]m/n*
reproduce [oo]
reproducing [E]m/n
reproducing [e]m/n*
reptile [I]l
republic [i]
republican [e]m/n
repulse [u]l
repulsion [u]m/n
repulsive [i]
reputable [u]l
reputation [u]m/n
reputed [e]
request [e]
requesting [E]m/n
requesting [e]m/n*
require [I]r
requirement [e]m/n
requiring [E]m/n
requiring [e]m/n*
rerun [u]m/n
rerunning [E]m/n
rerunning [e]m/n*
rescue [oo]
rescuing [E]m/n
rescuing [e]m/n*
research [er]
researching [E]m/n
researching [e]m/n*

resell [e]l
reselling [E]m/n
reselling [e]m/n*
resemble [u]l
resembling [E]m/n
resembling [e]m/n*
resent [e]m/n
resented [e]
resentful [u]l
resenting [E]m/n
resenting [e]m/n*
resentment [e]m/n
reservation [u]m/n
reserve [er]
reserving [E]m/n
reserving [e]m/n*
reservoir [O]r
reset [e]
resetting [E]m/n
resetting [e]m/n*
reshape [A]
reshaping [E]m/n
reshaping [e]m/n*
reside [I]
resided [e]
residence [e]m/n
resident [e]m/n
residential [u]l
residing [E]m/n
residing [e]m/n*
residual [oo]l
residue [oo]
resign [I]m/n
resigning [E]m/n
resigning [e]m/n*
resin [i]m/n
resist [i]
resistance [e]m/n
resisted [e]
resisting [E]m/n
resisting [e]m/n*
resolve [o]l
resolving [E]m/n
resolving [e]m/n*
resort [O]r

resorted [e]
resorting [E]m/n
resorting [e]m/n*
resource [O]r
resourceful [u]l
respect [e]
respectable [u]l
respectful [u]l
respectfully [E]
respecting [E]m/n
respecting [e]m/n*
respond [o]m/n
responded [e]
responding [E]m/n
responding [e]m/n*
response [o]m/n
responsibility [E]
responsible [u]l
responsibly [E]
rest [e]
restart [o]r
restarted [e]
restarting [E]m/n
restarting [e]m/n*
restate [A]
restated [e]
restaurant [o]m/n
resting [E]m/n
resting [e]m/n*
restless [e]
restlessly [E]
restoration [u]m/n
restore [O]r
restoring [E]m/n
restoring [e]m/n*
restrain [A]m/n
restraining [E]m/n
restraining [e]m/n*
restraint [A]m/n
restrict [i]
restricted [e]
restricting [E]m/n
restricting [e]m/n*
restriction [u]m/n
restroom [oo]m/n

result [u]l
resulted [e]
resulting [E]m/n
resulting [e]m/n*
resume [A]
resume [oo]m/n
resuming [E]m/n
resuming [e]m/n*
retail [A]l
retailer [er]
retailing [E]m/n
retailing [e]m/n*
retain [A]m/n
retainer [er]
retaining [E]m/n
retaining [e]m/n*
retake [A]
retaking [E]m/n
retaking [e]m/n*
retaliate [A]
retaliated [e]
retaliating [E]m/n
retaliating [e]m/n*
retaliation [u]m/n
retention [u]m/n
rethink [E]m/n
rethinking [E]m/n
rethinking [e]m/n*
retina [u]
retinal [u]l
retire [I]r
retirement [e]m/n
retiring [E]m/n
retiring [e]m/n*
retouch [u]
retouching [E]m/n
retouching [e]m/n*
retrace [A]
retracing [E]m/n
retracing [e]m/n*
retract [a]
retracted [e]
retracting [E]m/n
retracting [e]m/n*
retreat [E]

retreated [e]
retreating [E]m/n
retreating [e]m/n*
retrieve [E]
retrieving [E]m/n
retrieving [e]m/n*
retrospect [e]
retrospective [i]
return [er]m/n
returning [E]m/n
returning [e]m/n*
reunion [e]m/n
reunite [I]
reunited [e]
reuniting [E]m/n
reuniting [e]m/n*
reuse [oo]
reusing [E]m/n
reusing [e]m/n*
reveal [E]l
revealing [E]m/n
revealing [e]m/n*
revelation [u]m/n
revenge [e]m/n
revenging [E]m/n
revenging [e]m/n*
revenue [oo]
reverence [e]m/n
reverend [e]m/n
reverent [e]m/n
reversal [u]l
reverse [er]
reversible [u]l
reversing [E]m/n
reversing [e]m/n*
revert [er]
reverted [e]
reverting [E]m/n
reverting [e]m/n*
review [oo]
reviewing [E]m/n
reviewing [e]m/n*
revise [I]
revising [E]m/n
revising [e]m/n*

revision [u]m/n
revitalize [I]
revitalizing [E]m/n
revitalizing [e]m/n*
revival [u]l
revive [I]
revocable [u]l
revoke [O]
revoking [E]m/n
revoking [e]m/n*
revolt [O]l
revolted [e]
revolting [E]m/n
revolting [e]m/n*
revolution [u]m/n
revolutionary [E]
revolutionize [I]
revolutionizing [E]m/n
revolutionizing [e]m/n*
revolve [o]l
revolving [E]m/n
revolving [e]m/n*
revue [oo]
reward [O]r
rewarded [e]
rewarding [E]m/n
rewarding [e]m/n*
rewind [I]m/n
rewinding [E]m/n
rewinding [e]m/n*
rewrite [I]
rewriting [E]m/n
rewriting [e]m/n*
rewrote [O]
rhinestone [O]m/n
rhinoceros [i]
rhubarb [o]r
rhyme [I]m/n
rhyming [E]m/n
rhyming [e]m/n*
rhythm [e]m/n
rhythmic [i]
rhythmically [E]
rib [i]
ribbing [E]m/n

ribbing [e]m/n*
ribbon [e]m/n
rich [i]
richer [er]
rickety [E]
rickrack [a]
ricochet [A]
ricocheting [E]m/n
ricocheting [e]m/n*
rid [i]
ridden [e]m/n
ridding [E]m/n
ridding [e]m/n*
riddle [u]l
ride [I]
rider [er]
ridge [i]
ridicule [oo]l
ridiculous [e]
ridiculously [E]
riding [E]m/n
riding [e]m/n*
riff [i]
riffraff [a]
rifle [u]l
rifling [E]m/n
rifling [e]m/n*
rig [i]
rigging [E]m/n
rigging [e]m/n*
right [I]
righteous [e]
rightful [u]l
rightfully [E]
righting [E]m/n
righting [e]m/n*
rigid [i]
rigidly [E]
rigorous [e]
rigorously [E]
rile [I]l
rim [i]m/n
rind [I]m/n
ring [E]m/n
ringer [er]

ringing [E]m/n
ringing [e]m/n*
ringside [I]
rink [E]m/n
rinse [i]m/n
rinsing [E]m/n
rinsing [e]m/n*
rip [i]
ripe [I]
ripen [e]m/n
ripening [E]m/n
ripening [e]m/n*
riper [er]
ripping [E]m/n
ripping [e]m/n*
ripple [u]l
rippling [E]m/n
rippling [e]m/n*
riptide [I]
rise [I]
risen [e]m/n
riser [er]
rising [E]m/n
rising [e]m/n*
risk [i]
risking [E]m/n
risking [e]m/n*
risky [E]
risqué [A]
rite [I]
ritzy [E]
rival [u]l
rivaling [E]m/n
rivaling [e]m/n*
rivalry [E]
river [er]
road [O]
roadblock [o]
roadie [E]
roadside [I]
roadway [A]
roadwork [er]
roam [O]m/n
roaming [E]m/n
roaming [e]m/n*

roar [O]r
roaring [E]m/n
roaring [e]m/n*
roast [O]
roasted [e]
roaster [er]
roasting [E]m/n
roasting [e]m/n*
rob [o]
robber [er]
robbery [E]
robbing [E]m/n
robbing [e]m/n*
robe [O]
robin [i]m/n
robot [o]
robotic [i]
robust [u]
rock [o]
rocker [er]
rocket [e]
rocketing [E]m/n
rocketing [e]m/n*
rocking [E]m/n
rocking [e]m/n*
rocky [E]
rod [o]
rode [O]
rodent [e]m/n
rodeo [O]
rogue [O]
role [O]l
roll [O]l
rollback [a]
roller [er]
rolling [E]m/n
rolling [e]m/n*
romance [a]m/n
romancing [E]m/n
romancing [e]m/n*
romantic [i]
romantically [E]
romp [o]m/n
romper [er]
romping [E]m/n

romping [e]m/n*
roof [oo]
roofer [er]
roofing [E]m/n
roofing [e]m/n*
rooftop [o]
rookie [E]
room [oo]m/n
rooming [E]m/n
rooming [e]m/n*
roommate [A]
roomy [E]
roost [oo]
roosted [e]
rooster [er]
roosting [E]m/n
roosting [e]m/n*
root [oo]
rooting [E]m/n
rooting [e]m/n*
rope [O]
roper [er]
roping [E]m/n
roping [e]m/n*
rosary [E]
rose [O]
rosebud [u]
rosette [e]
roster [er]
rosy [E]
rot [o]
rotary [E]
rotate [A]
rotated [e]
rotating [E]m/n
rotating [e]m/n*
rotation [u]m/n
rotted [e]
rotten [e]m/n
rotting [E]m/n
rotting [e]m/n*
rotunda [u]
rouge [oo]
rough [u]
roughage [e]

roughen [e]m/n
roughening [E]m/n
roughening [e]m/n*
rougher [er]
roughhouse [ow]
roughing [E]m/n
roughing [e]m/n*
roughly [E]
roughneck [e]
roulette [e]
round [ow]m/n
rounded [e]
rounder [er]
rounding [E]m/n
rounding [e]m/n*
roundup [u]
route [oo]
route [ow]
router [er]
routine [E]m/n
routinely [E]
rove [O]
rover [er]
roving [E]m/n
roving [e]m/n*
row [O]
rowboat [O]
rowdy [E]
rowdy [e]*
rowing [E]m/n
rowing [e]m/n*
royal [u]l
royally [E]
royalty [E]
rub [u]
rubber [er]
rubbing [E]m/n
rubbing [e]m/n*
rubbish [i]
rubble [u]l
rubdown [ow]m/n
ruby [E]
rudder [er]
rude [oo]
rudely [E]

ruffle [u]l
ruffling [E]m/n
ruffling [e]m/n*
rug [u]
rugby [E]
rugged [e]
ruggedly [E]
ruin [i]m/n
ruining [E]m/n
ruining [e]m/n*
rule [oo]l
ruler [er]
ruling [E]m/n
ruling [e]m/n*
rum [u]m/n
rumble [u]l
rumbling [E]m/n
rumbling [e]m/n*
rummage [e]
rummaging [E]m/n
rummaging [e]m/n*
rumor [er]
run [u]m/n
rundown [ow]m/n
rung [u]m/n
runner [er]
running [E]m/n
running [e]m/n*
runny [E]
runway [A]
rupture [er]
rupturing [E]m/n
rupturing [e]m/n*
rural [u]l
rush [u]
rushing [E]m/n
rushing [e]m/n*
rust [u]
rustic [i]
rusting [E]m/n
rusting [e]m/n*
rustle [u]l
rustler [er]
rustling [E]m/n
rustling [e]m/n*

rusty [E]   rut [ʊ]   rye [I]
rusty [e]*   ruthless [e]

S

saber [er]   saggy [E]   sampling [e]m/n*
sabotage [o]   said [e]   sanction [ʊ]m/n
sabotaging [E]m/n   sail [A]l   sanctioning [E]m/n
sabotaging [e]m/n*   sailboat [O]   sanctioning [e]m/n*
sac [a]   sailing [E]m/n   sanctuary [E]
sachet [A]   sailing [e]m/n*   sand [a]m/n
sack [a]   sailor [er]   sandal [ʊ]l
sacking [E]m/n   saint [A]m/n   sandbag [a]
sacking [e]m/n*   saintly [E]   sandbar [o]r
sacred [e]   sake [A]   sandblast [a]
sacredly [E]   salad [e]   sandblasted [e]
sacrifice [I]   salary [E]   sandblasting [E]m/n
sacrificing [E]m/n   sale [A]l   sandblasting [e]m/n*
sacrificing [e]m/n*   salesclerk [er]   sandbox [o]
sad [a]   salesgirl [er]l   sanded [e]
sadden [e]m/n   salesman [e]m/n   sanding [E]m/n
sadder [er]   salesperson [e]m/n   sanding [e]m/n*
saddest [e]   saline [E]m/n   sandman [a]m/n
saddle [ʊ]l   saliva [ʊ]   sandpaper [er]
saddling [E]m/n   salmon [e]m/n   sandstone [O]m/n
saddling [e]m/n*   salon [o]m/n   sandwich [i]
sadly [E]   saloon [oo]m/n   sandy [E]
safe [A]   salt [o]l   sane [A]m/n
safeguard [o]r   salted [e]   sang [a]ng/k
safeguarded [e]   saltine [E]m/n   sanitary [E]
safeguarding [E]m/n   salty [E]   sanitation [ʊ]m/n
safeguarding [e]m/n*   salute [oo]   sanity [E]
safelight [I]   saluted [e]   sank [a]ng/k
safely [E]   saluting [E]m/n   sap [a]
safely [e]*   saluting [e]m/n*   sapped [e]
safer [er]   salvage [e]   sapphire [I]r
safest [e]   salvaging [E]m/n   sapping [E]m/n
safety [E]   salvaging [e]m/n*   sapping [e]m/n*
saffron [o]m/n   salvation [ʊ]m/n   sappy [E]
sag [a]   same [A]m/n   sarcasm [e]m/n
saga [ʊ]   sample [ʊ]l   sarcastic [i]
sagging [E]m/n   sampler [er]   sarcastically [E]
sagging [e]m/n*   sampling [E]m/n   sardine [E]m/n

sashay [A]
sashaying [E]m/n
sashaying [e]m/n*
sass [a]
sassafras [a]
sassy [E]
sat [a]
satellite [I]
satin [i]m/n
satire [I]r
satisfaction [u]m/n
satisfactory [E]
satisfy [I]
satisfying [E]m/n
satisfying [e]m/n*
saturate [A]
saturated [e]
saturating [E]m/n
saturating [e]m/n*
saturation [u]m/n
Saturday [A]
sauce [o]
saucepan [a]m/n
saucer [er]
saucy [E]
sauna [u]
saunter [er]
sauntering [E]m/n
sauntering [e]m/n*
sauté [A]
sautéing [E]m/n
sautéing [e]m/n*
savage [e]
savagely [E]
save [A]
saving [E]m/n
saving [e]m/n*
savior [er]
savor [er]
savoring [E]m/n
savoring [e]m/n*
savory [E]
savvy [E]
saw [o]
sawhorse [O]r

sawing [E]m/n
sawing [e]m/n*
sawmill [i]l
say [A]
saying [E]m/n
saying [e]m/n*
says [e]
scab [a]
scabbing [E]m/n
scabbing [e]m/n*
scaffold [O]l
scaffolding [E]m/n
scaffolding [e]m/n*
scald [o]l
scalded [e]
scalding [E]m/n
scalding [e]m/n*
scale [A]l
scaling [E]m/n
scaling [e]m/n*
scallion [e]m/n
scallop [u]
scalloping [E]m/n
scalloping [e]m/n*
scalpel [u]l
scam [a]m/n
scamming [E]m/n
scamming [e]m/n*
scamper [er]
scampering [E]m/n
scampering [e]m/n*
scampi [E]
scan [a]m/n
scandal [u]l
scandalize [I]
scandalous [e]
scanner [er]
scanning [E]m/n
scanning [e]m/n*
scantily [E]
scanty [E]
scapegoat [O]
scar [o]r
scarce [e]r
scarcely [E]

scare [e]r
scarecrow [O]
scarf [o]r
scaring [E]m/n
scaring [e]m/n*
scarlet [e]
scarring [E]m/n
scarring [e]m/n*
scary [E]
scary [e]*
scathing [E]m/n
scathing [e]m/n*
scatter [er]
scattering [E]m/n
scattering [e]m/n*
scavenge [e]m/n
scavenger [er]
scavenging [E]m/n
scavenging [e]m/n*
scenario [O]
scene [E]m/n
scenery [E]
scenic [i]
scenically [E]
scent [e]m/n
scented [e]
schedule [u]l
scheduling [E]m/n
scheduling [e]m/n*
schematic [i]
scheme [E]m/n
scheming [E]m/n
scheming [e]m/n*
schizophrenic [i]
schlep [e]
schlepping [E]m/n
schlepping [e]m/n*
schmuck [u]
scholar [er]
scholarly [E]
scholarship [i]
scholastic [i]
scholastically [E]
school [oo]l
schoolbag [a]

schoolboy [Oi]
schoolgirl [er]l
schoolhouse [ow]
schooling [E]m/n
schooling [e]m/n*
schoolmate [A]
schoolwork [er]
science [e]m/n
scientific [i]
scientifically [E]
scientist [i]
scintillate [A]
scintillating [E]m/n
scintillating [e]m/n*
scissors [er]
scoff [o]
scoffing [E]m/n
scoffing [e]m/n*
scold [O]l
scolded [e]
scolding [E]m/n
scolding [e]m/n*
scone [O]m/n
scoop [oo]
scooping [E]m/n
scooping [e]m/n*
scoot [oo]
scooted [e]
scooter [er]
scooting [E]m/n
scooting [e]m/n*
scope [O]
scoping [E]m/n
scoping [e]m/n*
scorch [O]r
scorcher [er]
scorching [E]m/n
scorching [e]m/n*
score [O]r
scoreboard [O]r
scoring [E]m/n
scoring [e]m/n*
scorn [O]r
scorning [E]m/n
scorning [e]m/n*

scorpion [e]m/n
scoundrel [u]l
scour [er]
scouring [E]m/n
scouring [e]m/n*
scout [ow]
scouted [e]
scouting [E]m/n
scouting [e]m/n*
scowl [ow]l
scowling [E]m/n
scowling [e]m/n*
scram [a]m/n
scramble [u]l
scrambling [E]m/n
scrambling [e]m/n*
scrap [a]
scrapbook [oo/]
scrape [A]
scraping [E]m/n
scraping [e]m/n*
scrapping [E]m/n
scrapping [e]m/n*
scrappy [E]
scratch [a]
scratcher [er]
scratching [E]m/n
scratching [e]m/n*
scratchpad [a]
scratchy [E]
scrawl [o]l
scrawling [E]m/n
scrawling [e]m/n*
scrawny [E]
scream [E]m/n
screamer [er]
screaming [E]m/n
screaming [e]m/n*
screech [E]
screeching [E]m/n
screeching [e]m/n*
screechy [E]
screen [E]m/n
screener [er]
screening [E]m/n

screening [e]m/n*
screenplay [A]
screw [oo]
screwball [o]l
screwing [E]m/n
screwing [e]m/n*
screwy [E]
scribble [u]l
scribbler [er]
scribbling [E]m/n
scribbling [e]m/n*
scrimp [i]m/n
scrimping [E]m/n
scrimping [e]m/n*
scrimpy [E]
script [i]
scripted [e]
scripture [er]
scroll [O]l
scrolling [E]m/n
scrolling [e]m/n*
scrooge [oo]
scrounge [ow]m/n
scrounger [er]
scrounging [E]m/n
scrounging [e]m/n*
scrub [u]
scrubber [er]
scrubbing [E]m/n
scrubbing [e]m/n*
scruff [u]
scruffy [E]
scrumptious [e]
scrunch [u]m/n
scrunching [E]m/n
scrunching [e]m/n*
scrutinize [I]
scrutinizing [E]m/n
scrutinizing [e]m/n*
scrutiny [E]
scuff [u]
scuffing [E]m/n
scuffing [e]m/n*
scuffle [u]l
scuffling [E]m/n

scuffling [e]m/n*
sculptor [er]
sculpture [er]
scum [u]m/n
scummy [E]
scurry [E]
scurrying [E]m/n
scurrying [e]m/n*
sea [E]
seabed [e]
seafood [oo]
seagull [u]l
seahorse [O]r
seal [E]l
sealer [er]
sealing [E]m/n
sealing [e]m/n*
seam [E]m/n
seamy [E]
sear [E]r
search [er]
searching [E]m/n
searching [e]m/n*
searchlight [I]
searing [E]m/n
searing [e]m/n*
seascape [A]
seashell [e]l
seashore [O]r
seasick [i]
seaside [I]
season [e]m/n
seasonal [u]l
seasoning [E]m/n
seasoning [e]m/n*
seat [E]
seated [e]
seating [E]m/n
seating [e]m/n*
seclude [oo]
secluded [e]
seclusion [u]m/n
second [e]m/n
secondary [E]
seconding [E]m/n

seconding [e]m/n*
secrecy [E]
secret [e]
secretary [E]
secretive [i]
secretly [E]
section [u]m/n
sectional [u]l
sector [er]
secure [er]
securely [E]
securing [E]m/n
securing [e]m/n*
security [E]
sedan [a]m/n
sedate [A]
sedated [e]
sedately [E]
sedating [E]m/n
sedating [e]m/n*
sedation [u]m/n
sedative [i]
sediment [e]m/n
seduce [oo]
seducing [E]m/n
seducing [e]m/n*
seduction [u]m/n
seductive [i]
see [E]
seed [E]
seeded [e]
seeding [E]m/n
seeding [e]m/n*
seedy [E]
seeing [E]m/n
seeing [e]m/n*
seek [E]
seeker [er]
seeking [E]m/n
seeking [e]m/n*
seem [E]m/n
seeming [E]m/n
seeming [e]m/n*
seemingly [E]
seen [E]m/n

seer [er]
segment [e]m/n
segmented [e]
segmenting [E]m/n
segmenting [e]m/n*
segregate [A]
segregated [e]
segregating [E]m/n
segregating [e]m/n*
segregation [u]m/n
seismic [i]
seize [E]
seizing [E]m/n
seizing [e]m/n*
seizure [er]
seldom [u]m/n
select [e]
selecting [E]m/n
selecting [e]m/n*
selection [u]m/n
selective [i]
selectively [E]
self [e]l
selfish [i]
sell [e]l
seller [er]
selling [E]m/n
selling [e]m/n*
seltzer [er]
semblance [e]m/n
semester [er]
semiformal [u]l
seminar [o]r
senate [e]
senator [er]
senatorial [u]l
send [e]m/n
sender [er]
sending [E]m/n
sending [e]m/n*
sendoff [o]
senile [I]l
senility [E]
senior [er]
seniority [E]

sensation [u]m/n
sensational [u]l
sensationalize [l]
sensationalizing [E]m/n
sensationalizing [e]m/n*
sense [e]m/n
senseless [e]
sensibilities [E]
sensible [u]l
sensibly [E]
sensing [E]m/n
sensing [e]m/n*
sensitive [i]
sensitively [E]
sensitivity [E]
sensitize [l]
sensor [er]
sensory [E]
sensual [u]l
sensuality [E]
sensually [E]
sensuous [e]
sensuously [E]
sent [e]m/n
sentence [e]m/n
sentencing [E]m/n
sentencing [e]m/n*
sentiment [e]m/n
sentimental [u]l
sentimentally [E]
sentry [E]
separate [A]
separate [e]
separated [e]
separately [E]
separating [E]m/n
separating [e]m/n*
separation [u]m/n
September [er]
septic [i]
sequel [u]l
sequence [e]m/n
sequencing [E]m/n
sequencing [e]m/n*
sequential [u]l

sequin [i]m/n
serenade [A]
serenaded [e]
serenading [E]m/n
serenading [e]m/n*
serendipity [E]
serene [E]m/n
serenely [E]
serenity [E]
serial [u]l
series [E]
serious [e]
seriously [E]
sermon [u]m/n
serpent [e]m/n
serum [u]m/n
serve [er]
server [er]
service [i]
serving [E]m/n
serving [e]m/n*
session [u]m/n
set [e]
setback [a]
setter [er]
setting [E]m/n
setting [e]m/n*
settle [u]l
settlement [e]m/n
settler [er]
settling [E]m/n
settling [e]m/n*
setup [u]
seven [e]m/n
seventeen [E]m/n
seventh [e]m/n
seventy [E]
sever [er]
several [u]l
severance [e]m/n
severe [E]r
severely [E]
severing [E]m/n
severing [e]m/n*
severity [E]

sew [O]
sewage [e]
sewer [er]
sewing [E]m/n
sewing [e]m/n*
sex [e]
sexpot [o]
sexual [u]l
sexuality [E]
sexually [E]
sexy [E]
sexy [e]*
shabby [E]
shack [a]
shacking [E]m/n
shacking [e]m/n*
shackle [u]l
shade [A]
shaded [e]
shading [E]m/n
shading [e]m/n*
shadow [O]
shadowy [E]
shady [E]
shady [e]*
shag [a]
shagging [E]m/n
shagging [e]m/n*
shaggy [E]
shake [A]
shakedown [ow]m/n
shaken [e]m/n
shaker [er]
shakeup [u]
shaking [E]m/n
shaking [e]m/n*
shaky [E]
shall [a]l
shallow [O]
sham [a]m/n
shamble [u]l
shame [A]m/n
shameful [u]l
shameless [e]
shampoo [oo]

shampooing [E]m/n
shampooing [e]m/n*
shamrock [o]
shape [A]
shapely [E]
shaping [E]m/n
shaping [e]m/n*
share [e]r
sharing [E]m/n
sharing [e]m/n*
shark [o]r
sharp [o]r
sharpen [e]m/n
sharpening [E]m/n
sharpening [e]m/n*
sharper [er]
sharpie [E]
shatter [er]
shattering [E]m/n
shattering [e]m/n*
shave [A]
shaven [e]m/n
shaver [er]
shaving [E]m/n
shaving [e]m/n*
shawl [o]l
shear [E]r
shearing [E]m/n
shearing [e]m/n*
shed [e]
shedding [E]m/n
shedding [e]m/n*
sheen [E]m/n
sheepish [i]
sheer [E]r
sheet [E]
sheeting [E]m/n
sheeting [e]m/n*
shelf [e]l
shell [e]l
shellac [a]
shellfish [i]
shelling [E]m/n
shelling [e]m/n*
shelter [er]

sheltering [E]m/n
sheltering [e]m/n*
shelving [E]m/n
shelving [e]m/n*
sheriff [i]
shield [E]l
shielded [e]
shielding [E]m/n
shielding [e]m/n*
shift [i]
shifted [e]
shifting [E]m/n
shifting [e]m/n*
shifty [E]
shill [i]l
shilling [E]m/n
shilling [e]m/n*
shimmer [er]
shimmering [E]m/n
shimmering [e]m/n*
shimmy [E]
shin [i]m/n
shinbone [O]m/n
shindig [i]
shine [I]m/n
shining [E]m/n
shining [e]m/n*
shiny [E]
shiny [e]*
ship [i]
shipload [O]
shipper [er]
shipping [E]m/n
shipping [e]m/n*
shipshape [A]
shipwreck [e]
shirk [er]
shirking [E]m/n
shirking [e]m/n*
shirt [er]
shirtless [e]
shiver [er]
shivering [E]m/n
shivering [e]m/n*
shock [o]

shocker [er]
shocking [E]m/n
shocking [e]m/n*
shockwave [A]
shoddy [E]
shoe [oo]
shoelace [A]
shook [oo/]
shoot [oo]
shooter [er]
shooting [E]m/n
shooting [e]m/n*
shop [o]
shopper [er]
shopping [E]m/n
shopping [e]m/n*
shore [O]r
shoreline [I]m/n
short [O]r
shortage [e]
shortbread [e]
shortcake [A]
shortcut [u]
shorted [e]
shorten [e]m/n
shortening [E]m/n
shortening [e]m/n*
shorter [er]
shortfall [o]l
shorting [E]m/n
shorting [e]m/n*
shortwave [A]
shot [o]
shotgun [u]m/n
should [oo/]
shoulder [er]
shout [ow]
shouter [er]
shouting [E]m/n
shouting [e]m/n*
shove [u]
shovel [u]l
shoveling [E]m/n
shoveling [e]m/n*
shoving [E]m/n

shoving [e]m/n*
show [O]
showboat [O]
showdown [ow]m/n
shower [er]
showing [E]m/n
showing [e]m/n*
showoff [o]
showroom [oo]m/n
showy [E]
shred [e]
shredder [er]
shrewd [oo]
shrewder [er]
shrewdly [E]
shriek [E]
shrieking [E]m/n
shrieking [e]m/n*
shrill [i]l
shrilly [E]
shrimp [i]m/n
shrine [I]m/n
shrink [E]m/n
shrinkage [e]
shrinking [E]m/n
shrinking [e]m/n*
shrivel [u]l
shriveling [E]m/n
shriveling [e]m/n*
shroud [ow]
shrouded [e]
shrub [u]
shrubbery [E]
shrug [u]
shrugging [E]m/n
shrugging [e]m/n*
shrunk [u]m/n
shrunken [e]m/n
shtick [i]
shudder [er]
shuddering [E]m/n
shuddering [e]m/n*
shuffle [u]l
shuffling [E]m/n
shuffling [e]m/n*

shun [u]m/n
shunning [E]m/n
shunning [e]m/n*
shut [u]
shutdown [ow]m/n
shuteye [I]
shutoff [o]
shutter [er]
shutting [E]m/n
shutting [e]m/n*
shy [I]
shyly [E]
shyster [er]
sibling [E]m/n
sibling [e]m/n*
sick [i]
sickbed [e]
sicken [e]m/n
sickening [E]m/n
sickening [e]m/n*
sicker [er]
sickly [E]
sickness [e]
side [I]
sideburn [er]
sidekick [i]
sideline [I]m/n
sidelining [E]m/n
sidelining [e]m/n*
sideman [a]m/n
sideshow [O]
sidestep [e]
sidestepping [E]m/n
sidestepping [e]m/n*
sidetrack [a]
sidetracking [E]m/n
sidetracking [e]m/n*
sidewalk [o]
sideways [A]
siding [E]m/n
siding [e]m/n*
siege [E]
siesta [u]
sieve [i]
sifter [er]

sigh [I]
sighing [E]m/n
sighing [e]m/n*
sight [I]
sighted [e]
sighting [E]m/n
sighting [e]m/n*
sightsee [E]
sightseeing [E]m/n
sightseeing [e]m/n*
sign [I]m/n
signal [u]l
signaling [E]m/n
signaling [e]m/n*
signature [er]
signer [er]
significance [e]m/n
significant [e]m/n
significantly [E]
signify [I]
signifying [E]m/n
signifying [e]m/n*
signing [E]m/n
signing [e]m/n*
silent [e]m/n
silently [E]
silhouette [e]
silk [i]l
silken [e]m/n
sill [i]l
silly [E]
silly [e]*
silo [O]
silver [er]
silverware [e]r
silvery [E]
similar [er]
similarity [E]
similarly [E]
simmer [er]
simmering [E]m/n
simmering [e]m/n*
simple [u]l
simpler [er]
simpleton [e]m/n

simplicity [E]
simplify [I]
simplifying [E]m/n
simplifying [e]m/n*
simply [E]
simulate [A]
simulated [e]
simulating [E]m/n
simulating [e]m/n*
simulation [u]m/n
simultaneous [e]
simultaneously [E]
sin [i]m/n
since [i]m/n
sincere [E]r
sincerely [E]
sincerely [e]*
sincerity [E]
sinful [u]l
sinfully [E]
sing [E]m/n
singe [i]m/n
singer [er]
singing [E]m/n
singing [e]m/n*
single [u]l
singular [er]
singularity [E]
sinister [er]
sinisterly [E]
sink [E]m/n
sinkhole [O]l
sinking [E]m/n
sinking [e]m/n*
sinner [er]
sinning [E]m/n
sinning [e]m/n*
sinus [e]
sip [i]
siphon [e]m/n
siphoning [E]m/n
siphoning [e]m/n*
sipping [E]m/n
sipping [e]m/n*
sir [er]

siren [e]m/n
sirloin [Oi]m/n
sissy [E]
sister [er]
sister [u]*
sisterly [E]
sit [i]
sitcom [o]m/n
site [I]
sitter [er]
sitting [E]m/n
sitting [e]m/n*
situate [A]
situated [e]
situation [u]m/n
six [i]
sixteen [E]m/n
sixty [E]
sizable [u]l
size [I]
sizing [E]m/n
sizing [e]m/n*
sizzle [u]l
sizzler [er]
sizzling [E]m/n
sizzling [e]m/n*
skate [A]
skateboard [O]r
skated [e]
skater [er]
skating [E]m/n
skating [e]m/n*
skeletal [u]l
skeleton [e]m/n
skeptic [i]
skeptical [u]l
skeptically [E]
sketch [e]
sketcher [er]
sketching [E]m/n
sketching [e]m/n*
sketchy [E]
skew [oo]
skewer [er]
skewing [E]m/n

skewing [e]m/n*
ski [E]
skid [i]
skidded [e]
skidding [E]m/n
skidding [e]m/n*
skier [er]
skiing [E]m/n
skiing [e]m/n*
skill [i]l
skillful [u]l
skillfully [E]
skim [i]m/n
skimmer [er]
skimming [E]m/n
skimming [e]m/n*
skimp [i]m/n
skimping [E]m/n
skimping [e]m/n*
skimpy [E]
skin [i]m/n
skinhead [e]
skinning [E]m/n
skinning [e]m/n*
skinny [E]
skintight [I]
skip [i]
skipper [er]
skipping [E]m/n
skipping [e]m/n*
skirmish [i]
skirt [er]
skirted [e]
skirting [E]m/n
skirting [e]m/n*
skis [E]
skit [i]
skittish [i]
skivvy [E]
skull [u]l
skullcap [a]
skunk [u]m/n
sky [I]
skydive [I]
skydiving [E]m/n

skydiving [e]m/n*
skylight [l]
skyline [l]m/n
skyrocket [e]
skyrocketing [E]m/n
skyrocketing [e]m/n*
skywrite [l]
skywriting [E]m/n
skywriting [e]m/n*
slab [a]
slack [a]
slacken [e]m/n
slackening [E]m/n
slackening [e]m/n*
slacker [er]
slacking [E]m/n
slacking [e]m/n*
slain [A]m/n
slam [a]m/n
slammer [er]
slamming [E]m/n
slamming [e]m/n*
slander [er]
slandering [E]m/n
slandering [e]m/n*
slant [a]m/n
slanted [e]
slanting [E]m/n
slanting [e]m/n*
slap [a]
slapjack [a]
slapper [er]
slapping [E]m/n
slapping [e]m/n*
slapstick [i]
slate [A]
slated [e]
slaughter [er]
slaughtering [E]m/n
slaughtering [e]m/n*
slave [A]
slavery [E]
slaving [E]m/n
slaving [e]m/n*
slay [A]

slayer [er]
slaying [E]m/n
slaying [e]m/n*
sleazy [E]
sled [e]
sledding [E]m/n
sledding [e]m/n*
sleek [E]
sleep [E]
sleeper [er]
sleeping [E]m/n
sleeping [e]m/n*
sleepless [e]
sleepwalk [o]
sleepwalking [E]m/n
sleepwalking [e]m/n*
sleepy [E]
sleeve [E]
sleeveless [e]
sleigh [A]
slender [er]
slenderizing [E]m/n
slenderizing [e]m/n*
slept [e]
slice [l]
slicer [er]
slicing [E]m/n
slicing [e]m/n*
slick [i]
slicker [er]
slid [i]
slide [l]
slider [er]
slideshow [O]
sliding [E]m/n
sliding [e]m/n*
slight [l]
slighted [e]
slim [i]m/n
slime [l]m/n
slimmer [er]
slimming [E]m/n
slimming [e]m/n*
slimy [E]
slingshot [o]

slink [E]
slinking [E]m/n
slinking [e]m/n*
slinky [E]
slip [i]
slipknot [o]
slipper [er]
slippery [E]
slipping [E]m/n
slipping [e]m/n*
slit [i]
slither [er]
slithering [E]m/n
slithering [e]m/n*
slitting [E]m/n
slitting [e]m/n*
sliver [er]
slivery [E]
slob [o]
slobber [er]
slobbering [E]m/n
slobbering [e]m/n*
slogan [e]m/n
slope [O]
sloping [E]m/n
sloping [e]m/n*
sloppy [E]
slot [o]
slotted [e]
slouch [ow]
slouching [E]m/n
slouching [e]m/n*
slow [O]
slowdown [ow]m/n
slower [er]
slowly [E]
slowly [e]*
slowpoke [O]
sludge [u]
slug [u]
slugger [er]
slugging [E]m/n
slugging [e]m/n*
sluggish [i]
slum [u]m/n

slumber [er]
slumming [E]m/n
slumming [e]m/n*
slummy [E]
slump [u]m/n
slumping [E]m/n
slumping [e]m/n*
slunk [u]m/n
slur [er]
slurring [E]m/n
slurring [e]m/n*
slurry [E]
slush [u]
slushy [E]
slut [u]
slutty [E]
sly [I]
slyly [E]
smack [a]
smacking [E]m/n
smacking [e]m/n*
small [o]l
smaller [er]
smallest [e]
smart [o]r
smarten [e]m/n
smarter [er]
smartest [e]
smartly [E]
smarty [E]
smash [a]
smashing [E]m/n
smashing [e]m/n*
smatter [er]
smattering [E]m/n
smattering [e]m/n*
smear [E]r
smearing [E]m/n
smearing [e]m/n*
smell [e]l
smelling [E]m/n
smelling [e]m/n*
smile [I]l
smiley [E]
smiling [E]m/n

smiling [e]m/n*
smirk [er]
smirking [E]m/n
smirking [e]m/n*
smite [I]
smithereens [E]m/n
smitten [e]m/n
smock [o]
smog [o]
smoggy [E]
smoke [O]
smokehouse [ow]
smoker [er]
smokestack [a]
smoking [E]m/n
smoking [e]m/n*
smoky [E]
smolder [er]
smoldering [E]m/n
smoldering [e]m/n*
smooth [oo]
smoother [er]
smoothing [E]m/n
smoothing [e]m/n*
smoothly [E]
smother [er]
smothering [E]m/n
smothering [e]m/n*
smudge [u]
smudging [E]m/n
smudging [e]m/n*
smug [u]
smuggle [u]l
smugly [E]
smut [u]
smutty [E]
snack [a]
snacking [E]m/n
snacking [e]m/n*
snafu [oo]
snag [a]
snagging [E]m/n
snagging [e]m/n*
snail [A]l
snake [A]

snakebite [I]
snaking [E]m/n
snaking [e]m/n*
snap [a]
snapper [er]
snapping [E]m/n
snapping [e]m/n*
snappy [E]
snapshot [o]
snatch [a]
snatcher [er]
snatching [E]m/n
snatching [e]m/n*
snazzy [E]
sneak [E]
sneaker [er]
sneaking [E]m/n
sneaking [e]m/n*
sneaky [E]
sneer [E]r
sneering [E]m/n
sneering [e]m/n*
sneeze [E]
sneezing [E]m/n
sneezing [e]m/n*
snicker [er]
snickering [E]m/n
snickering [e]m/n*
snide [I]
sniff [i]
sniffing [E]m/n
sniffing [e]m/n*
snifter [er]
snip [i]
snipe [I]
sniper [er]
snipping [E]m/n
snipping [e]m/n*
snippy [E]
snob [o]
snobbish [i]
snobby [E]
snoot [oo]
snooty [E]
snooze [oo]

snoozing [E]m/n
snoozing [e]m/n*
snore [O]r
snoring [E]m/n
snoring [e]m/n*
snorkel [ʊ]l
snorkeling [E]m/n
snorkeling [e]m/n*
snort [O]r
snorting [E]m/n
snorting [e]m/n*
snot [o]
snotty [E]
snow [O]
snowcap [a]
snowfall [o]l
snowflake [A]
snowing [E]m/n
snowing [e]m/n*
snowman [a]m/n
snowstorm [O]r
snowy [E]
snub [ʊ]
snubbing [E]m/n
snubbing [e]m/n*
snuff [ʊ]
snuffing [E]m/n
snuffing [e]m/n*
snug [ʊ]
snuggle [ʊ]l
snuggling [E]m/n
snuggling [e]m/n*
snugly [E]
so [O]
soak [O]
soaking [E]m/n
soaking [e]m/n*
soap [O]
soapbox [o]
soaping [E]m/n
soaping [e]m/n*
soapy [E]
soar [O]r
soaring [E]m/n
soaring [e]m/n*

sober [er]
sobering [E]m/n
sobering [e]m/n*
soccer [er]
sociable [ʊ]l
social [ʊ]l
socialize [I]
socially [E]
society [E]
sock [o]
socket [e]
socking [E]m/n
socking [e]m/n*
sod [o]
soda [ʊ]
sodium [ʊ]m/n
soft [o]
softball [o]l
soften [e]m/n
softening [E]m/n
softening [e]m/n*
softer [er]
softie [E]
softly [E]
soggy [E]
soil [Oi]l
soiling [E]m/n
soiling [e]m/n*
solar [er]
sold [O]l
solder [er]
soldering [E]m/n
soldering [e]m/n*
soldier [er]
sole [O]l
solely [E]
solemn [e]m/n
solemnly [E]
solicit [i]
solicitation [ʊ]m/n
solicited [e]
soliciting [E]m/n
soliciting [e]m/n*
solicitor [er]
solid [i]

solidarity [E]
solidify [I]
solidly [E]
solitaire [e]r
solitary [E]
solitude [oo]
solo [O]
soloing [E]m/n
soloing [e]m/n*
solstice [i]
solution [ʊ]m/n
solve [o]l
solver [er]
solving [E]m/n
solving [e]m/n*
somber [er]
somberly [E]
some [ʊ]m/n
somebody [E]
somebody [e]*
someday [A]
somehow [ow]
someone [ʊ]m/n
something [E]m/n
something [e]m/n*
sometime [I]m/n
someway [A]
somewhat [ʊ]
somewhere [e]r
son [ʊ]m/n
sonar [o]r
song [o]m/n
sonic [i]
soon [oo]m/n
sooner [er]
soot [oo/]
soothe [oo]
soothing [E]m/n
soothing [e]m/n*
sophisticated [e]
sophistication [ʊ]m/n
sophomore [O]r
soprano [O]
sorcerer [er]
sorcery [E]

sordid [i]
sore [O]r
sorely [E]
sorority [E]
sorrow [O]
sorrowful [u]l
sorrowfully [E]
sorry [E]
sort [O]r
sorted [e]
sorting [E]m/n
sorting [e]m/n*
soufflé [A]
sought [o]
soul [O]l
soulful [u]l
sound [ow]m/n
sounded [e]
sounding [E]m/n
sounding [e]m/n*
soundproof [oo]
soundtrack [a]
soup [oo]
soupy [E]
sour [er]
source [O]r
sourdough [O]
south [ow]
southerly [E]
southern [er]m/n
southpaw [o]
souvenir [E]r
sow [O]
sowing [E]m/n
sowing [e]m/n*
sown [O]m/n
soy [Oi]
soybean [E]m/n
spa [o]
space [A]
spaceflight [I]
spaceman [a]m/n
spaceship [i]
spacewalk [o]
spacing [E]m/n

spacing [e]m/n*
spacious [e]
spaghetti [E]
span [a]m/n
spanning [E]m/n
spanning [e]m/n*
spar [o]r
spare [e]r
sparing [E]m/n
sparing [e]m/n*
spark [o]r
sparking [E]m/n
sparking [e]m/n*
sparkle [u]l
sparkler [er]
sparkly [E]
sparring [E]m/n
sparring [e]m/n*
sparrow [O]
spasm [e]m/n
spastic [i]
spatter [er]
spattering [E]m/n
spattering [e]m/n*
spatula [u]
spawn [o]m/n
spawning [E]m/n
spawning [e]m/n*
spay [A]
spaying [E]m/n
spaying [e]m/n*
speak [E]
speaker [er]
speaking [E]m/n
speaking [e]m/n*
spear [E]r
spearhead [e]
spearing [E]m/n
spearing [e]m/n*
spearmint [i]m/n
spec [e]
special [u]l
specialist [i]
specialize [I]
specializing [E]m/n

specializing [e]m/n*
specialty [E]
species [E]
specific [i]
specifically [E]
specification [u]m/n
specify [I]
specifying [E]m/n
specifying [e]m/n*
specimen [e]m/n
speck [e]
speckle [u]l
spectacle [u]l
spectacular [er]
spectacularly [E]
spectrum [u]m/n
speculate [A]
speculated [e]
speculating [E]m/n
speculating [e]m/n*
speculation [u]m/n
sped [e]
speech [E]
speechless [e]
speed [E]
speedboat [O]
speeding [E]m/n
speeding [e]m/n*
speedster [er]
speedway [A]
speedy [E]
spell [e]l
spellbinding [E]m/n
spellbinding [e]m/n*
spellbound [ow]m/n
speller [er]
spelling [E]m/n
spelling [e]m/n*
spend [e]m/n
spender [er]
spending [E]m/n
spending [e]m/n*
spent [e]m/n
sperm [er]m/n
spew [oo]

spewing [E]m/n

spewing [e]m/n*

spice [I]

spicy [E]

spider [er]

spidery [E]

spiff [i]

spiffy [E]

spike [I]

spiking [E]m/n

spiking [e]m/n*

spiky [E]

spill [i]l

spilling [E]m/n

spilling [e]m/n*

spilt [i]l

spin [i]m/n

spinach [e]

spinal [u]l

spindle [u]l

spine [I]m/n

spineless [e]

spinner [er]

spinning [E]m/n

spinning [e]m/n*

spinoff [o]

spinster [er]

spiny [E]

spiral [u]l

spiraling [E]m/n

spiraling [e]m/n*

spirit [i]

spirited [e]

spiritual [u]l

spiritualism [e]m/n

spirituality [E]

spiritually [E]

spit [i]

spite [I]

spiteful [u]l

spitting [E]m/n

spitting [e]m/n*

splash [a]

splashdown [ow]m/n

splashing [E]m/n

splashing [e]m/n*

splashy [E]

splatter [er]

splattering [E]m/n

splattering [e]m/n*

splendid [i]

splendidly [E]

splendor [er]

splice [I]

splicing [E]m/n

splicing [e]m/n*

splint [i]m/n

splinted [e]

splinter [er]

splintering [E]m/n

splintering [e]m/n*

splinting [E]m/n

splinting [e]m/n*

split [i]

splitting [E]m/n

splitting [e]m/n*

splotchy [E]

splurge [er]

splurging [E]m/n

splurging [e]m/n*

spoil [Oi]l

spoiler [er]

spoiling [E]m/n

spoiling [e]m/n*

spoke [O]

spoken [e]m/n

sponge [u]m/n

spongy [E]

sponsor [er]

sponsoring [E]m/n

sponsoring [e]m/n*

spontaneity [E]

spontaneous [e]

spontaneously [E]

spook [oo]

spooking [E]m/n

spooking [e]m/n*

spooky [E]

spooky [e]*

spool [oo]l

spoon [oo]m/n

spoonful [u]l

spooning [E]m/n

spooning [e]m/n*

sporadic [i]

sporadically [E]

spore [O]r

sport [O]r

sporting [E]m/n

sporting [e]m/n*

sportscast [a]

sportscaster [er]

sporty [E]

spot [o]

spotless [e]

spotlessly [E]

spotlight [I]

spotted [e]

spotter [er]

spotting [E]m/n

spotting [e]m/n*

spotty [E]

spouse [ow]

spout [ow]

spouting [E]m/n

spouting [e]m/n*

sprain [A]m/n

spraining [E]m/n

spraining [e]m/n*

sprang [a]ng/k

sprawl [o]l

sprawling [E]m/n

sprawling [e]m/n*

spray [A]

sprayer [er]

spraying [E]m/n

spraying [e]m/n*

spread [e]

spreader [er]

spreading [E]m/n

spreading [e]m/n*

spreadsheet [E]

spree [E]

sprig [i]

spring [E]m/n

springing [E]m/n
springing [e]m/n*
springtime [I]m/n
springy [E]
sprinkle [u]l
sprinkler [er]
sprinkling [E]m/n
sprinkling [e]m/n*
sprint [i]m/n
sprinted [e]
sprinter [er]
sprinting [E]m/n
sprinting [e]m/n*
sprout [ow]
sprouted [e]
sprouting [E]m/n
sprouting [e]m/n*
spruce [oo]
sprucing [E]m/n
sprucing [e]m/n*
sprung [u]m/n
spun [u]m/n
spunk [u]m/n
spunky [E]
spur [er]
spurn [er]m/n
spurning [E]m/n
spurning [e]m/n*
spurring [E]m/n
spurring [e]m/n*
spurt [er]
spurting [E]m/n
spurting [e]m/n*
sputter [er]
sputtering [E]m/n
sputtering [e]m/n*
spy [I]
spyglass [a]
spying [E]m/n
spying [e]m/n*
squabble [u]l
squabbling [E]m/n
squabbling [e]m/n*
squad [o]
squadron [e]m/n

squalor [er]
squander [er]
squandering [E]m/n
squandering [e]m/n*
square [e]r
squarely [E]
squash [o]
squat [o]
squatted [e]
squatter [er]
squatting [E]m/n
squatting [e]m/n*
squatty [E]
squawk [o]
squawking [E]m/n
squawking [e]m/n*
squeak [E]
squeaking [E]m/n
squeaking [e]m/n*
squeaky [E]
squealer [er]
squealing [E]m/n
squealing [e]m/n*
squeamish [i]
squeamishly [E]
squeegee [E]
squeeze [E]
squeezing [E]m/n
squeezing [e]m/n*
squint [i]m/n
squinted [e]
squinting [E]m/n
squinting [e]m/n*
squinty [E]
squirm [er]m/n
squirming [E]m/n
squirming [e]m/n*
squirmy [E]
squirrel [u]l
squirt [er]
squirted [e]
squirting [E]m/n
squirting [e]m/n*
squishy [E]
stab [a]

stabber [er]
stabbing [E]m/n
stabbing [e]m/n*
stability [E]
stabilize [I]
stabilizing [E]m/n
stabilizing [e]m/n*
stable [u]l
staccato [O]
stack [a]
stacker [er]
stacking [E]m/n
stacking [e]m/n*
stadium [u]m/n
staff [a]
staffing [E]m/n
staffing [e]m/n*
stag [a]
stage [A]
stagger [er]
staggering [E]m/n
staggering [e]m/n*
staging [E]m/n
staging [e]m/n*
stagnate [A]
stagnated [e]
stagnating [E]m/n
stagnating [e]m/n*
stain [A]m/n
staining [E]m/n
staining [e]m/n*
stair [e]r
staircase [A]
stairway [A]
stairwell [e]l
stake [A]
stakeout [ow]
staking [E]m/n
staking [e]m/n*
stale [A]l
stalemate [A]
stalk [o]
stalker [er]
stalking [E]m/n
stalking [e]m/n*

stall [o]l
stalling [E]m/n
stalling [e]m/n*
stallion [e]m/n
stamina [u]
stammer [er]
stammering [E]m/n
stammering [e]m/n*
stamp [a]m/n
stampede [E]
stampeding [E]m/n
stampeding [e]m/n*
stamping [E]m/n
stamping [e]m/n*
stance [a]m/n
stand [a]m/n
standard [er]
standardize [I]
standardizing [E]m/n
standardizing [e]m/n*
standby [I]
standing [E]m/n
standing [e]m/n*
standoff [o]
standstill [i]l
staple [u]l
stapler [er]
stapling [E]m/n
stapling [e]m/n*
star [o]r
starch [o]r
starching [E]m/n
starching [e]m/n*
starchy [E]
stardom [u]m/n
stardust [u]
stare [e]r
starfish [i]
staring [E]m/n
staring [e]m/n*
starlet [e]
starlight [I]
starlit [i]
starring [E]m/n
starring [e]m/n*

starry [E]
start [o]r
starter [er]
starting [E]m/n
starting [e]m/n*
startle [u]l
startling [E]m/n
startling [e]m/n*
starvation [u]m/n
starve [o]r
starving [E]m/n
starving [e]m/n*
stash [a]
stashing [E]m/n
stashing [e]m/n*
state [A]
stated [e]
stately [E]
statement [e]m/n
stateside [I]
statewide [I]
static [i]
station [u]m/n
stationary [E]
stationery [E]
statistic [i]
statistical [u]l
statistically [E]
statue [oo]
stature [er]
status [e]
stay [A]
staying [E]m/n
staying [e]m/n*
stead [e]
steadfast [a]
steady [E]
steady [e]*
steak [A]
steal [E]l
stealer [er]
stealing [E]m/n
stealing [e]m/n*
stealth [e]l
stealthy [E]

steam [E]m/n
steamboat [O]
steamer [er]
steaming [E]m/n
steaming [e]m/n*
steamroll [O]l
steamy [E]
steel [E]l
steeling [E]m/n
steeling [e]m/n*
steep [E]
steeping [E]m/n
steeping [e]m/n*
steeple [u]l
steer [E]r
steering [E]m/n
steering [e]m/n*
stein [I]m/n
stellar [er]
stem [e]m/n
stemming [E]m/n
stemming [e]m/n*
stencil [u]l
step [e]
stepping [E]m/n
stepping [e]m/n*
stereo [O]
stereotype [I]
sterile [u]l
sterilize [I]
sterilizing [E]m/n
sterilizing [e]m/n*
sterling [E]m/n
sterling [e]m/n*
stern [er]m/n
sternly [E]
steroid [Oi]
stethoscope [O]
stew [oo]
stewing [E]m/n
stewing [e]m/n*
stick [i]
sticker [er]
sticking [E]m/n
sticking [e]m/n*

stickler [er]
stickpin [i]m/n
sticky [E]
stiff [i]
stiffen [e]m/n
stiffening [E]m/n
stiffening [e]m/n*
stiffer [er]
stiffly [E]
stifle [u]l
stifling [E]m/n
stifling [e]m/n*
stigma [u]
stiletto [O]
still [i]l
stimulate [A]
stimulated [e]
stimulating [E]m/n
stimulating [e]m/n*
stimulation [u]m/n
stimulus [e]
sting [E]m/n
stinger [er]
stinging [E]m/n
stinging [e]m/n*
stingray [A]
stingy [E]
stink [E]m/n
stinker [er]
stinking [E]m/n
stinking [e]m/n*
stinky [E]
stipulate [A]
stipulated [e]
stipulating [E]m/n
stipulating [e]m/n*
stipulation [u]m/n
stir [er]
stirring [E]m/n
stirring [e]m/n*
stirrup [u]
stitch [i]
stitching [E]m/n
stitching [e]m/n*
stock [o]

stockade [A]
stockbroker [er]
stocking [E]m/n
stocking [e]m/n*
stockpile [I]l
stocky [E]
stodgy [E]
stogie [E]
stoke [O]
stoking [E]m/n
stoking [e]m/n*
stole [O]l
stolen [e]m/n
stomach [e]
stomachache [A]
stomp [o]m/n
stomping [E]m/n
stomping [e]m/n*
stone [O]m/n
stony [E]
stood [oo/]
stool [oo]l
stop [o]
stoplight [I]
stopper [er]
stopping [E]m/n
stopping [e]m/n*
storage [e]
store [O]r
storewide [I]
storing [E]m/n
storing [e]m/n*
stork [O]r
storm [O]r
stormy [E]
story [E]
storybook [oo/]
storyteller [er]
stove [O]
stovepipe [I]
stow [O]
stowaway [A]
stowing [E]m/n
stowing [e]m/n*
straddle [u]l

straddling [E]m/n
straddling [e]m/n*
straggle [u]l
straggler [er]
straggling [E]m/n
straggling [e]m/n*
straight [A]
straighten [e]m/n
straightening [E]m/n
straightening [e]m/n*
straighter [er]
straightforward [er]
strain [A]m/n
strainer [er]
straining [E]m/n
straining [e]m/n*
strait [A]
strand [a]m/n
stranded [e]
strange [A]m/n
strangely [E]
stranger [er]
strangle [u]l
strangling [E]m/n
strangling [e]m/n*
strap [a]
strapping [E]m/n
strapping [e]m/n*
strategic [i]
strategically [E]
strategy [E]
straw [o]
stray [A]
straying [E]m/n
straying [e]m/n*
streak [E]
streaking [E]m/n
streaking [e]m/n*
streaky [E]
stream [E]m/n
streamer [er]
streaming [E]m/n
streaming [e]m/n*
streamline [I]m/n
street [E]

streetcar [o]r
streetlight [I]
streetwise [I]
strength [e]m/n
strengthen [e]m/n
strengthening [E]m/n
strengthening [e]m/n*
strenuous [e]
strenuously [E]
strep [e]
stress [e]
stressful [u]l
stressing [E]m/n
stressing [e]m/n*
stretch [e]
stretchable [u]l
stretcher [er]
stretching [E]m/n
stretching [e]m/n*
stretchy [E]
strewn [oo]m/n
stricken [e]m/n
strict [i]
stricter [er]
strictly [E]
stride [I]
striding [E]m/n
striding [e]m/n*
strike [I]
striking [E]m/n
striking [e]m/n*
string [E]m/n
stringy [E]
strip [i]
stripe [I]
striping [E]m/n
striping [e]m/n*
stripper [er]
stripping [E]m/n
stripping [e]m/n*
strive [I]
striving [E]m/n
striving [e]m/n*
strobe [O]
strode [O]

stroke [O]
stroking [E]m/n
stroking [e]m/n*
stroll [O]l
stroller [er]
strolling [E]m/n
strolling [e]m/n*
strong [o]m/n
stronger [er]
strongest [e]
strongly [E]
strongly [e]*
struck [u]
structure [er]
strudel [u]l
struggle [u]l
struggling [E]m/n
struggling [e]m/n*
strum [u]m/n
strumming [E]m/n
strumming [e]m/n*
strut [u]
strutting [E]m/n
strutting [e]m/n*
stub [u]
stubbing [E]m/n
stubbing [e]m/n*
stubborn [er]m/n
stubbornly [E]
stubby [E]
stucco [O]
stuck [u]
stud [u]
student [e]m/n
studio [O]
study [E]
studying [E]m/n
studying [e]m/n*
stuff [u]
stuffer [er]
stuffing [E]m/n
stuffing [e]m/n*
stuffy [E]
stumble [u]l
stumbling [E]m/n

stumbling [e]m/n*
stump [u]
stumper [er]
stun [u]m/n
stunk [u]m/n
stunning [E]m/n
stunning [e]m/n*
stunt [u]m/n
stunted [e]
stuntman [a]m/n
stupendous [e]
stupendously [E]
stupid [i]
stupidly [E]
stupor [er]
sturdy [E]
stutter [er]
stuttering [E]m/n
stuttering [e]m/n*
sty [I]
style [I]l
styling [E]m/n
styling [e]m/n*
stylish [i]
stylist [i]
stylize [I]
stylus [e]
suave [o]
suavely [E]
sub [u]
subbing [E]m/n
subbing [e]m/n*
subconscious [e]
subconsciously [E]
subdue [oo]
subduing [E]m/n
subduing [e]m/n*
subject [e]
subjecting [E]m/n
subjecting [e]m/n*
subjective [i]
subjectively [E]
sublet [e]
subletting [E]m/n
subletting [e]m/n*

sublime [I]m/n
subliminal [u]l
subliminally [E]
submarine [E]m/n
submerge [er]
submerging [E]m/n
submerging [e]m/n*
submerse [er]
submersing [E]m/n
submersing [e]m/n*
submission [u]m/n
submit [i]
submitting [E]m/n
submitting [e]m/n*
subscribe [I]
subscribing [E]m/n
subscribing [e]m/n*
subscription [u]m/n
subside [I]
subsiding [E]m/n
subsiding [e]m/n*
substance [e]m/n
substantial [u]l
substantially [E]
substitute [oo]
substituting [E]m/n
substituting [e]m/n*
substitution [u]m/n
subtle [u]l
subtly [E]
subtract [a]
subtracted [e]
subtracting [E]m/n
subtracting [e]m/n*
suburb [er]
suburban [e]m/n
subway [A]
succeed [E]
succeeding [E]m/n
succeeding [e]m/n*
success [e]
successful [u]l
successfully [E]
succulent [e]m/n
succumb [u]m/n

succumbing [E]m/n
succumbing [e]m/n*
such [u]
suck [u]
sucker [er]
sucking [E]m/n
sucking [e]m/n*
suction [u]m/n
sudden [e]m/n
suddenly [E]
suddenly [e]*
sue [oo]
suede [A]
suffer [er]
suffering [E]m/n
suffering [e]m/n*
sufficient [e]m/n
sufficiently [E]
suffix [i]
suffocate [A]
suffocated [e]
suffocating [E]m/n
suffocating [e]m/n*
sugar [er]
sugary [E]
suggest [e]
suggesting [E]m/n
suggesting [e]m/n*
suggestion [u]m/n
suggestive [i]
suicidal [u]l
suicide [I]
suing [E]m/n
suing [e]m/n*
suit [oo]
suitable [u]l
suitcase [A]
suite [E]
suited [e]
suiting [E]m/n
suiting [e]m/n*
suitor [er]
sulfur [er]
sulfuric [i]
sulk [u]l

sulking [E]m/n
sulking [e]m/n*
sulky [E]
sultry [E]
sum [u]m/n
summarize [I]
summarizing [E]m/n
summarizing [e]m/n*
summary [E]
summer [er]
summertime [I]m/n
summery [E]
summing [E]m/n
summing [e]m/n*
summit [i]
summon [e]m/n
summoning [E]m/n
summoning [e]m/n*
sumo [O]
sun [u]m/n
sunburn [er]m/n
sundae [A]
Sunday [A]
sundress [e]
sung [u]m/n
sunglasses [e]
sunk [u]m/n
sunken [e]m/n
sunlight [I]
sunlit [i]
sunning [E]m/n
sunning [e]m/n*
sunny [E]
sunrise [I]
sunscreen [E]m/n
sunset [e]
sunshade [A]
sunshine [I]m/n
sunspot [o]
sunstroke [O]
suntan [a]m/n
super [er]
superb [er]
superbly [E]
superficial [u]l

superficially [E]
superior [er]
superiority [E]
supermarket [e]
supersonic [i]
superstition [u]m/n
superstitious [e]
superstitiously [E]
supervise [I]
supervising [E]m/n
supervising [e]m/n*
supervision [u]m/n
supervisor [er]
supper [er]
supple [u]l
supplement [e]m/n
supplemental [u]l
supply [I]
supplying [E]m/n
supplying [e]m/n*
support [O]r
supported [e]
supporter [er]
supporting [E]m/n
supporting [e]m/n*
supportive [i]
suppose [O]
supposedly [E]
suppress [e]
suppressing [E]m/n
suppressing [e]m/n*
suppression [u]m/n
supreme [E]m/n
supremely [E]
surcharge [o]r
sure [er]
surely [E]
surely [e]*
surf [er]
surface [e]
surfboard [O]r
surfer [er]
surfing [E]m/n
surfing [e]m/n*
surge [er]

surgeon [e]m/n
surgery [E]
surgical [u]l
surgically [E]
surging [E]m/n
surging [e]m/n*
surpass [a]
surpassing [E]m/n
surpassing [e]m/n*
surplus [u]
surprise [I]
surprising [E]m/n
surprising [e]m/n*
surprisingly [E]
surreal [E]l
surrender [er]
surrendering [E]m/n
surrendering [e]m/n*
surround [ow]m/n
surrounding [E]m/n
surrounding [e]m/n*
survey [A]
surveying [E]m/n
surveying [e]m/n*
survival [u]l
survive [I]
surviving [E]m/n
surviving [e]m/n*
survivor [er]
sushi [E]
suspect [e]
suspecting [E]m/n
suspecting [e]m/n*
suspend [e]m/n
suspending [E]m/n
suspending [e]m/n*
suspense [e]m/n
suspenseful [u]l
suspicion [u]m/n
suspicious [e]
suspiciously [E]
sustain [A]m/n
sustaining [E]m/n
sustaining [e]m/n*
suture [er]

suturing [E]m/n
suturing [e]m/n*
swab [o]
swabbing [E]m/n
swabbing [e]m/n*
swag [a]
swagger [er]
swaggering [E]m/n
swaggering [e]m/n*
swallow [O]
swallowing [E]m/n
swallowing [e]m/n*
swam [a]m/n
swamp [o]m/n
swampy [E]
swan [o]m/n
swank [a]ng/k
swanky [E]
swap [o]
swapping [E]m/n
swapping [e]m/n*
swarm [O]r
swarming [E]m/n
swarming [e]m/n*
swat [o]
swatch [o]
swatted [e]
swatter [er]
swatting [E]m/n
swatting [e]m/n*
sway [A]
swaying [E]m/n
swaying [e]m/n*
swear [e]r
swearing [E]m/n
swearing [e]m/n*
sweat [e]
sweater [er]
sweating [E]m/n
sweating [e]m/n*
sweatshirt [er]
sweatshop [o]
sweaty [E]
sweaty [e]*
sweep [E]

sweeper [er]
sweeping [E]m/n
sweeping [e]m/n*
sweepstake [A]
sweet [E]
sweetbread [e]
sweeten [e]m/n
sweetening [E]m/n
sweetening [e]m/n*
sweeter [er]
sweetheart [o]r
sweetie [E]
sweetly [E]
sweetly [e]*
swell [e]l
swelling [E]m/n
swelling [e]m/n*
swept [e]
swerve [er]
swerving [E]m/n
swerving [e]m/n*
swift [i]
swifter [er]
swiftly [E]
swig [i]
swim [i]m/n
swimmer [er]
swimming [E]m/n
swimming [e]m/n*

swimsuit [oo]
swindler [er]
swindling [E]m/n
swindling [e]m/n*
swine [I]m/n
swing [E]m/n
swinger [er]
swinging [E]m/n
swinging [e]m/n*
swipe [I]
swiping [E]m/n
swiping [e]m/n*
swirl [u]l
swirling [E]m/n
swirling [e]m/n*
swirly [E]
swish [i]
swishy [E]
switch [i]
switchblade [A]
switching [E]m/n
switching [e]m/n*
swivel [u]l
swiveling [E]m/n
swiveling [e]m/n*
swollen [e]m/n
swoon [oo]m/n
swooning [E]m/n
swooning [e]m/n*

swoop [oo]
swooping [E]m/n
swooping [e]m/n*
sword [O]r
swordplay [A]
swore [O]r
sworn [O]r
syllable [u]l
symbol [u]l
symbolic [i]
symbolism [e]m/n
symbolize [I]
sympathetic [i]
sympathize [I]
sympathizing [E]m/n
sympathizing [e]m/n*
sympathy [E]
symphony [E]
symptom [e]m/n
syndrome [O]m/n
synthetic [i]
synthetically [E]
syringe [i]m/n
syrup [u]
system [e]m/n
systematic [i]
systematically [E]

T

tab [a]
tabby [E]
table [u]l
tablet [e]
tabloid [Oi]
taboo [oo]
tack [a]
tackle [u]l
tackling [E]m/n
tackling [e]m/n*
tacky [E]

taco [O]
tactful [u]l
tactfully [E]
tactic [i]
tactical [u]l
tactically [E]
tadpole [O]l
taffy [E]
tag [a]
tagging [E]m/n
tagging [e]m/n*

tail [A]l
tailbone [O]m/n
tailgate [A]
tailgated [e]
tailgating [E]m/n
tailgating [e]m/n*
tailing [E]m/n
tailing [e]m/n*
taillight [I]
tailor [er]
tailpipe [I]

tailspin [i]m/n
taint [A]m/n
tainted [e]
tainting [E]m/n
tainting [e]m/n*
take [A]
taken [e]m/n
takeoff [o]
taker [er]
taking [E]m/n
taking [e]m/n*
talcum [u]m/n
tale [A]l
talent [e]m/n
talented [e]
talk [o]
talkative [i]
talker [er]
talking [E]m/n
talking [e]m/n*
tall [o]l
taller [er]
tallest [e]
tally [E]
tallying [E]m/n
tallying [e]m/n*
talon [u]m/n
tamale [E]
tambourine [E]m/n
tame [A]m/n
taming [E]m/n
taming [e]m/n*
tamper [er]
tampering [E]m/n
tampering [e]m/n*
tan [a]m/n
tandem [e]m/n
tangerine [E]m/n
tangible [u]l
tangibly [E]
tangle [u]l
tangling [E]m/n
tangling [e]m/n*
tango [O]
tangy [E]

tank [a]ng/k
tanker [er]
tanking [E]m/n
tanking [e]m/n*
tanning [E]m/n
tanning [e]m/n*
tantalize [I]
tantalizing [E]m/n
tantalizing [e]m/n*
tantrum [u]m/n
tap [a]
tape [A]
taper [er]
tapering [E]m/n
tapering [e]m/n*
taping [E]m/n
taping [e]m/n*
tapping [E]m/n
tapping [e]m/n*
tar [o]r
tarantula [u]
tardy [E]
target [e]
targeting [E]m/n
targeting [e]m/n*
tarnish [i]
tarnishing [E]m/n
tarnishing [e]m/n*
taro [O]
tarring [E]m/n
tarring [e]m/n*
tart [o]r
tartar [er]
task [a]
tassel [u]l
taste [A]
tasted [e]
tasteful [u]l
tastier [er]
tasting [E]m/n
tasting [e]m/n*
tasty [E]
tater [er]
tattle [u]l
tattler [er]

tattling [E]m/n
tattling [e]m/n*
tattoo [oo]
tattooing [E]m/n
tattooing [e]m/n*
taught [o]
taunt [o]m/n
taunted [e]
taunting [E]m/n
taunting [e]m/n*
taupe [O]
taut [o]
tavern [er]m/n
tawdry [E]
tawny [E]
tax [a]
taxation [u]m/n
taxi [E]
taxicab [a]
taxing [E]m/n
taxing [e]m/n*
tea [E]
teabag [a]
teach [E]
teacher [er]
teaching [E]m/n
teaching [e]m/n*
teacup [u]
teal [E]l
team [E]m/n
teaming [E]m/n
teaming [e]m/n*
teammate [A]
teamster [er]
teamwork [er]
teapot [o]
tear [E]r
tear [e]r
teardrop [o]
teargas [a]
tearing [E]m/n
tearing [e]m/n*
teary [E]
tease [E]
teaser [er]

teasing [E]m/n
teasing [e]m/n*
tech [e]
technical [u]l
technically [E]
technician [e]m/n
technique [E]
technology [E]
teddy [E]
tedious [e]
tediously [E]
tee [E]
teeing [E]m/n
teeing [e]m/n*
teen [E]m/n
teenage [A]
teenager [er]
teeny [E]
teepee [E]
teeter [er]
teetering [E]m/n
teetering [e]m/n*
teeth [E]
teething [E]m/n
teething [e]m/n*
telecast [a]
telecasting [E]m/n
telecasting [e]m/n*
telemarketer [er]
telemarketing [E]m/n
telemarketing [e]m/n*
telepathy [E]
telephone [O]m/n
telescope [O]
telescopic [i]
television [u]m/n
tell [e]l
teller [er]
telling [E]m/n
telling [e]m/n*
temper [er]
temperament [e]m/n
temperamental [u]l
temperature [er]
tempering [E]m/n

tempering [e]m/n*
template [e]
temple [u]l
tempo [O]
temporarily [E]
temporary [E]
tempt [e]m/n
temptation [u]m/n
tempted [e]
tempting [E]m/n
tempting [e]m/n*
ten [e]m/n
tenant [e]m/n
tend [e]m/n
tended [e]
tendency [E]
tender [er]
tenderize [I]
tenderizing [E]m/n
tenderizing [e]m/n*
tenderloin [Oi]m/n
tenderly [E]
tending [E]m/n
tending [e]m/n*
tendon [e]m/n
tennis [i]
tenor [er]
tense [e]m/n
tensely [E]
tension [u]m/n
tentacle [u]l
tentative [i]
tentatively [E]
tenth [e]m/n
tenure [er]
tepid [i]
term [er]
terminal [u]l
terminally [E]
terminate [A]
terminated [e]
terminating [E]m/n
terminating [e]m/n*
termination [u]m/n
terminology [E]

termite [I]
terrace [e]
terrain [A]m/n
terrarium [u]m/n
terrestrial [u]l
terrible [u]l
terribly [E]
terrier [er]
terrific [i]
terrifically [E]
terrify [I]
terrifying [E]m/n
terrifying [e]m/n*
territorial [u]l
territory [E]
terror [er]
terrorize [I]
terrorizing [E]m/n
terrorizing [e]m/n*
terry [E]
test [e]
tester [er]
testify [I]
testifying [E]m/n
testifying [e]m/n*
testimonial [u]l
testimony [E]
testing [E]m/n
testing [e]m/n*
testy [E]
tether [er]
tethering [E]m/n
tethering [e]m/n*
text [e]
textbook [oo/]
textile [I]l
texting [E]m/n
texting [e]m/n*
texture [er]
than [a]m/n
thank [a]ng/k
thankful [u]l
thankfully [E]
thanking [E]m/n
thanking [e]m/n*

that [a]
thaw [o]
thawing [E]m/n
thawing [e]m/n*
the [E]
the [ʊ]
theater [er]
theatrical [ʊ]l
theatrically [E]
thee [E]
their [e]r
them [e]m/n
theme [E]m/n
themselves [e]l
then [e]m/n
theorize [I]
theorizing [E]m/n
theorizing [e]m/n*
theory [E]
therapeutic [i]
therapist [i]
therapy [E]
there [e]r
therefore [O]r
therein [i]m/n
thermal [ʊ]l
thermometer [er]
thermostat [a]
thesaurus [e]
these [E]
thesis [i]
they [A]
thick [i]
thicken [e]m/n
thickening [E]m/n
thickening [e]m/n*
thicker [er]
thickly [E]
thief [E]
thigh [I]
thimble [ʊ]l
thin [i]m/n
thing [E]m/n
think [E]m/n
thinker [er]

thinking [E]m/n
thinking [e]m/n*
thinner [er]
thinning [E]m/n
thinning [e]m/n*
third [er]
thirst [er]
thirsty [E]
thirsty [e]*
thirteen [E]m/n
thirty [E]
this [i]
thong [o]m/n
thorn [O]r
thorny [E]
thorough [O]
thoroughbred [e]
thoroughly [E]
those [O]
though [O]
thought [o]
thoughtful [ʊ]l
thoughtfully [E]
thousand [e]m/n
thread [e]
threadbare [e]r
threading [E]m/n
threading [e]m/n*
threat [e]
threaten [e]m/n
threatening [E]m/n
threatening [e]m/n*
three [E]
threefold [O]l
threesome [ʊ]m/n
threshold [O]l
threw [oo]
thrift [i]
thrifty [E]
thrill [i]l
thriller [er]
thrilling [E]m/n
thrilling [e]m/n*
thrive [I]
thriving [E]m/n

thriving [e]m/n*
throat [O]
throaty [E]
throb [o]
throbbing [E]m/n
throbbing [e]m/n*
throne [O]m/n
through [oo]
throughout [ow]
throw [O]
throwback [a]
throwing [E]m/n
throwing [e]m/n*
thrust [u]
thrusting [E]m/n
thrusting [e]m/n*
thug [u]
thumb [u]m/n
thumbhole [O]l
thumbnail [A]l
thumbprint [i]m/n
thumbtack [a]
thunder [er]
thunderbolt [O]l
thundering [E]m/n
thundering [e]m/n*
thunderous [e]
thunderstorm [O]r
Thursday [A]
thwart [O]r
thwarted [e]
thwarting [E]m/n
thwarting [e]m/n*
thyme [I]m/n
thyroid [Oi]
tick [i]
ticker [er]
ticket [e]
ticketing [E]m/n
ticketing [e]m/n*
ticking [E]m/n
ticking [e]m/n*
tickle [u]l
tickler [er]
tickling [E]m/n

tickling [e]m/n*
tidbit [i]
tide [I]
tidy [E]
tie [I]
tieback [a]
tier [E]r
tiff [i]
tiger [er]
tight [I]
tighten [e]m/n
tightening [E]m/n
tightening [e]m/n*
tighter [er]
tightrope [O]
tile [I]l
till [i]l
tilt [i]l
tilting [E]m/n
tilting [e]m/n*
timber [er]
time [I]m/n
timeless [e]
timer [er]
timesaving [E]m/n
timesaving [e]m/n*
timetable [u]l
timid [i]
timidly [E]
timing [E]m/n
timing [e]m/n*
tin [i]m/n
tinge [i]m/n
tingle [u]l
tingling [E]m/n
tingling [e]m/n*
tingly [E]
tinker [er]
tinkering [E]m/n
tinkering [e]m/n*
tinny [E]
tinsel [u]l
tint [i]m/n
tinted [e]
tinting [E]m/n

tinting [e]m/n*
tiny [E]
tip [i]
tipper [er]
tipping [E]m/n
tipping [e]m/n*
tipsy [E]
tiptoe [O]
tiptoeing [E]m/n
tiptoeing [e]m/n*
tiptop [o]
tirade [A]
tire [I]r
tiresome [u]m/n
tiring [E]m/n
tiring [e]m/n*
tissue [oo]
title [u]l
tizzy [E]
to [oo]
toad [O]
toadstool [oo]l
toast [O]
toaster [er]
toasting [E]m/n
toasting [e]m/n*
tobacco [O]
today [A]
toddle [u]l
toddler [er]
toddling [E]m/n
toddling [e]m/n*
toddy [E]
toe [O]
toenail [A]l
toffee [E]
together [er]
toggle [u]l
toggling [E]m/n
toggling [e]m/n*
toilet [e]
toiletry [E]
token [e]m/n
told [O]l
tolerable [u]l

tolerably [E]
tolerance [e]m/n
tolerant [e]m/n
tolerate [A]
tolerated [e]
tolerating [E]m/n
tolerating [e]m/n*
toll [O]l
tollgate [A]
tomato [O]
tomboy [Oi]
tomboyish [i]
tombstone [O]m/n
tomorrow [O]
ton [u]m/n
tonal [u]l
tone [O]m/n
tongue [u]m/n
tonic [i]
tonight [I]
toning [E]m/n
toning [e]m/n*
tonsil [u]l
tonsillitis [i]
too [oo]
took [oo/]
tool [oo]l
toolbox [o]
toot [oo]
tooth [oo]
toothache [A]
toothbrush [u]
toothpaste [A]
toothpick [i]
toothy [E]
tooting [E]m/n
tooting [e]m/n*
top [o]
topaz [a]
topic [i]
topical [u]l
topically [E]
topnotch [o]
topper [er]
topping [E]m/n

topping [e]m/n*
topside [I]
torchlight [I]
tore [O]r
torment [e]m/n
tormented [e]
tormenting [E]m/n
tormenting [e]m/n*
torn [O]r
tornado [O]
torpedo [O]
torque [O]r
torrential [u]l
torso [O]
torte [O]r
tortilla [u]
tortoise [i]
torture [er]
torturing [E]m/n
torturing [e]m/n*
toss [o]
tossing [E]m/n
tossing [e]m/n*
tostada [u]
tot [o]
total [u]l
totally [E]
totally [e]*
tote [O]
totem [e]m/n
toting [E]m/n
toting [e]m/n*
toucan [a]m/n
touch [u]
touchdown [ow]m/n
touching [E]m/n
touching [e]m/n*
touchy [E]
tough [u]
toughen [e]m/n
toughening [E]m/n
toughening [e]m/n*
tougher [er]
toughly [E]
toupee [A]

tour [er]
touring [E]m/n
touring [e]m/n*
tourism [e]m/n
tourist [i]
tournament [e]m/n
tow [O]
toward [O]r
towel [u]l
tower [er]
towering [E]m/n
towering [e]m/n*
towing [E]m/n
towing [e]m/n*
town [ow]m/n
townsfolk [O]l
township [i]
toxic [i]
toxicity [E]
toxin [i]m/n
toy [Oi]
toying [E]m/n
toying [e]m/n*
trace [A]
tracer [er]
tracing [E]m/n
tracing [e]m/n*
track [a]
tracker [er]
tracking [E]m/n
tracking [e]m/n*
traction [u]m/n
tractor [er]
trade [A]
traded [e]
trademark [o]r
tradeoff [o]
trader [er]
trading [E]m/n
trading [e]m/n*
tradition [u]m/n
traditional [u]l
traditionally [E]
traffic [i]
trafficking [E]m/n

trafficking [e]m/n*
tragedy [E]
tragic [i]
tragically [E]
trail [A]l
trailer [er]
trailing [E]m/n
trailing [e]m/n*
train [A]m/n
trainee [E]
trainer [er]
training [E]m/n
training [e]m/n*
trainload [O]
trait [A]
traitor [er]
tram [a]m/n
trample [u]l
trampling [E]m/n
trampling [e]m/n*
trampoline [E]m/n
trance [a]m/n
tranquil [i]l
tranquility [E]
transact [a]
transacted [e]
transaction [u]m/n
transcend [e]m/n
transcended [e]
transcending [E]m/n
transcending [e]m/n*
transcribe [I]
transcribing [E]m/n
transcribing [e]m/n*
transcript [i]
transcription [u]m/n
transfer [er]
transferring [E]m/n
transferring [e]m/n*
transform [O]r
transformation [u]m/n
transforming [E]m/n
transforming [e]m/n*
transit [i]
transition [u]m/n

transitional [u]l
translate [A]
translated [e]
translating [E]m/n
translating [e]m/n*
translucent [e]m/n
transmission [u]m/n
transmit [i]
transmitted [e]
transmitting [E]m/n
transmitting [e]m/n*
transparent [e]m/n
transparently [E]
transpire [I]r
transpiring [E]m/n
transpiring [e]m/n*
transplant [a]m/n
transplanted [e]
transplanting [E]m/n
transplanting [e]m/n*
transport [O]r
transportation [u]m/n
transported [e]
transporting [E]m/n
transporting [e]m/n*
transpose [O]
transposing [E]m/n
transposing [e]m/n*
trap [a]
trapeze [E]
trapper [er]
trapping [E]m/n
trapping [e]m/n*
trash [a]
trashing [E]m/n
trashing [e]m/n*
trashy [E]
trauma [u]
traumatic [i]
traumatizing [E]m/n
traumatizing [e]m/n*
travel [u]l
traveler [er]
traveling [E]m/n
traveling [e]m/n*

tray [A]
treacherous [e]
treachery [E]
tread [e]
treading [E]m/n
treading [e]m/n*
treadmill [i]l
treason [e]m/n
treasure [er]
treasurer [er]
treasuring [E]m/n
treasuring [e]m/n*
treasury [E]
treat [E]
treated [e]
treating [E]m/n
treating [e]m/n*
treaty [E]
treble [u]l
tree [E]
treetop [o]
trek [e]
trekking [E]m/n
trekking [e]m/n*
tremble [u]l
trembler [er]
trembling [E]m/n
trembling [e]m/n*
tremendous [e]
tremendously [E]
tremor [er]
trench [e]m/n
trend [e]m/n
trending [E]m/n
trending [e]m/n*
trendsetter [er]
trendsetting [E]m/n
trendsetting [e]m/n*
trendy [E]
trespass [a]
trespassing [E]m/n
trespassing [e]m/n*
triad [a]
trial [u]l
triangle [u]l

triangular [er]
triathlon [o]m/n
tribal [u]l
tribe [I]
tribute [oo]
triceps [e]
trick [i]
tricking [E]m/n
tricking [e]m/n*
trickle [u]l
trickling [E]m/n
trickling [e]m/n*
trickster [er]
tricky [E]
tricycle [u]l
trigger [er]
triggering [E]m/n
triggering [e]m/n*
trillion [e]m/n
trim [i]m/n
trimmer [er]
trimming [E]m/n
trimming [e]m/n*
trinket [e]
trio [O]
trip [i]
triple [u]l
triplicate [e]
tripling [E]m/n
tripling [e]m/n*
tripod [o]
tripping [E]m/n
tripping [e]m/n*
trite [I]
triumph [u]m/n
triumphant [e]m/n
triumphing [E]m/n
triumphing [e]m/n*
trivia [u]
trivial [u]l
trivialize [I]
troll [O]l
trolley [E]
trolling [E]m/n
trolling [e]m/n*

trombone [O]m/n
troop [oo]
trooper [er]
trophy [E]
tropic [i]
tropical [u]l
trot [o]
trotted [e]
trotter [er]
trotting [E]m/n
trotting [e]m/n*
trouble [u]l
troubling [E]m/n
troubling [e]m/n*
trough [o]
trouper [er]
trouser [er]
trousseau [O]
truancy [E]
truant [e]m/n
truck [u]
trucker [er]
trucking [E]m/n
trucking [e]m/n*
truckload [O]
true [oo]
truer [er]
truffle [u]l
truly [E]
trumpet [e]
trumpeting [E]m/n
trumpeting [e]m/n*
trunk [u]m/n
trust [u]
trusted [e]
trustee [E]
trusting [E]m/n
trusting [e]m/n*
trustworthy [E]
trusty [E]
truth [oo]
truthful [u]l
truthfully [E]
try [I]
trying [E]m/n

trying [e]m/n*
tub [u]
tuba [u]
tubby [E]
tube [oo]
tubing [E]m/n
tubing [e]m/n*
tubular [er]
tuck [u]
tucking [E]m/n
tucking [e]m/n*
Tuesday [A]
tug [u]
tugboat [O]
tugging [E]m/n
tugging [e]m/n*
tuition [u]m/n
tulip [i]
tumble [u]l
tumbler [er]
tumbling [E]m/n
tumbling [e]m/n*
tummy [E]
tumor [er]
tune [oo]m/n
tuner [er]
tunic [i]
tuning [E]m/n
tuning [e]m/n*
tunnel [u]l
tunneling [E]m/n
tunneling [e]m/n*
turbine [I]m/n
turbo [O]
turbulence [e]m/n
turbulent [e]m/n
turkey [E]
turmoil [Oi]l
turn [er]
turndown [ow]m/n
turning [E]m/n
turning [e]m/n*
turnkey [E]
turnoff [o]
turnstile [I]l

turntable [u]l
turpentine [I]m/n
turquoise [Oi]
tutor [er]
tutorial [u]l
tutoring [E]m/n
tutoring [e]m/n*
tux [u]
tuxedo [O]
TV [E]
tweak [E]
tweaking [E]m/n
tweaking [e]m/n*
tweed [E]
tweet [E]
tweeting [E]m/n
tweeting [e]m/n*
twelve [e]l
twenty [E]
twerp [er]
twice [I]
twig [i]
twilight [I]
twill [i]l
twin [i]m/n
twine [I]m/n
twinkle [u]l
twinkling [E]m/n
twinkling [e]m/n*
twirl [u]l
twirling [E]m/n
twirling [e]m/n*
twist [i]
twisted [e]
twister [er]
twisting [E]m/n
twisting [e]m/n*
twit [i]
twitch [i]
twitching [E]m/n
twitching [e]m/n*
twitter [er]
two [oo]
twosome [u]m/n
tying [E]m/n

tying [e]m/n*
type [l]
typecast [a]
typecasting [E]m/n
typecasting [e]m/n*

typeset [e]
typesetting [E]m/n
typesetting [e]m/n*
typewriter [er]
typical [u]l

typically [E]
typing [E]m/n
typing [e]m/n*
typo [O]
tyrant [e]m/n

U

udder [er]
ugh [u]
ugly [E]
ulcer [er]
ulcerate [A]
ulcerated [e]
ulcerating [E]m/n
ulcerating [e]m/n*
ulceration [u]m/n
ulterior [er]
ultimate [e]
ultimately [E]
ultimatum [u]m/n
ultra [u]
ultraviolet [e]
umber [er]
umbilical [u]l
umbrella [u]
umpire [l]r
unable [u]l
unaccustomed [u]m/n
unaffected [e]
unanimous [e]
unassuming [E]m/n
unassuming [e]m/n*
unauthorized [l]
unavailable [u]l
unavoidable [u]l
unaware [e]r
unbalanced [e]m/n
unbecoming [E]m/n
unbecoming [e]m/n*
unbelievable [u]l
unbending [E]m/n
unbending [e]m/n*

unbiased [e]
unbutton [e]m/n
unbuttoning [E]m/n
unbuttoning [e]m/n*
uncanny [E]
uncertain [i]m/n
uncertainty [E]
uncivilized [l]
uncle [u]l
uncomfortable [u]l
uncomfortably [E]
uncommitted [e]
uncommon [e]m/n
unconcerned [er]m/n
unconditional [u]l
unconditionally [E]
unconquerable [u]l
unconscious [e]
unconsciously [E]
uncontrollable [u]l
uncontrollably [E]
unconventional [u]l
unconvincing [E]m/n
unconvincing [e]m/n*
uncorrected [e]
undeniable [u]l
undeniably [E]
under [er]
underage [A]
underarm [o]r
underclassman [e]m/n
underclothes [O]
undercover [er]
undercurrent [e]m/n
underdog [o]

underfoot [oo/]
undergo [O]
undergraduate [e]
underground [ow]m/n
underline [l]m/n
underlying [E]m/n
underlying [e]m/n*
undermine [l]m/n
underneath [E]
underpass [a]
underprivileged [e]
underscore [O]r
undersell [e]l
undershirt [er]
underside [l]
understand [a]m/n
understood [oo/]
understudy [E]
undertaker [er]
undertone [O]m/n
undertow [O]
underwater [er]
underway [A]
underwear [e]r
underweight [A]
underwent [e]m/n
underworld [er]
underwrite [l]
underwritten [e]m/n
undesirable [u]l
undid [i]
undisturbed [er]
undo [oo]
undone [u]m/n
undoubtedly [E]

undress [e]
unearth [er]
unearthly [E]
uneasy [E]
unedited [e]
unemployed [Oi]
uneven [e]m/n
unexpected [e]
unexpectedly [E]
unexplored [O]r
unfair [e]r
unfairly [E]
unfamiliar [er]
unfavorable [u]l
unfavorably [E]
unfed [e]
unfit [i]
unfold [O]l
unfolded [e]
unfolding [E]m/n
unfolding [e]m/n*
unforeseen [E]m/n
unforgettable [u]l
unfortunate [e]
uniform [O]r
uniformity [E]
unify [I]
unifying [E]m/n
unifying [e]m/n*
uninhibited [e]
uninsured [er]
union [e]m/n
unionize [I]
unique [E]
uniquely [E]
unisex [e]
unison [e]m/n
unit [i]
unite [I]
united [e]
uniting [E]m/n
uniting [e]m/n*
unity [E]
universal [u]l
universally [E]

universe [er]
university [E]
unkind [I]m/n
unknowing [E]m/n
unknowing [e]m/n*
unknowingly [E]
unknown [O]m/n
unlawful [u]l
unlawfully [E]
unleash [E]
unleashing [E]m/n
unleashing [e]m/n*
unless [e]
unlike [I]
unlikely [E]
unlimited [e]
unlined [I]m/n
unload [O]
unloaded [e]
unloading [E]m/n
unloading [e]m/n*
unlock [o]
unlocking [E]m/n
unlocking [e]m/n*
unmanned [a]m/n
unnatural [u]l
unnecessary [E]
unnerve [er]
unnerving [E]m/n
unnerving [e]m/n*
unoccupied [I]
unofficial [u]l
unofficially [E]
unorthodox [o]
unpaid [A]
unparalleled [e]l
unpleasant [e]m/n
unprofitable [u]l
unqualified [I]
unquestionable [u]l
unravel [u]l
unraveling [E]m/n
unraveling [e]m/n*
unreal [E]l
unreasonable [u]l

unreasonably [E]
unrefined [I]m/n
unreliable [u]l
unruly [E]
unsafe [A]
unsatisfactory [E]
unsatisfied [I]
unsigned [I]m/n
unsociable [u]l
unsophisticated [e]
unspeakable [u]l
unspeakably [E]
unspoken [e]m/n
unstable [u]l
unsurpassed [a]
unthinkable [u]l
untidy [E]
until [i]l
untouchable [u]l
untruthful [u]l
unused [oo]
unusual [u]l
unusually [E]
unwanted [e]
unwarranted [e]
unwed [e]
unwind [I]m/n
unwinding [E]m/n
unwinding [e]m/n*
unwise [I]
unwisely [E]
unworthy [E]
unwritten [e]m/n
up [u]
upbringing [E]m/n
upbringing [e]m/n*
upcoming [E]m/n
upcoming [e]m/n*
update [A]
updated [e]
updating [E]m/n
updating [e]m/n*
upgrade [A]
upgraded [e]
upgrading [E]m/n

upgrading [e]m/n*
upheaval [u]l
upheld [e]l
uphill [i]l
uphold [O]
upholding [E]m/n
upholding [e]m/n*
upholster [er]
upholstering [E]m/n
upholstering [e]m/n*
upholstery [E]
upkeep [E]
uplift [i]
uplifting [E]m/n
uplifting [e]m/n*
upmost [O]
upon [o]m/n
upper [er]
uppercase [A]
upperclassman [e]m/n
uppercut [u]
upright [I]
uprising [E]m/n
uprising [e]m/n*
uproar [O]r
uproarious [e]

uproariously [E]
uproot [oo]
uprooted [e]
uprooting [E]m/n
uprooting [e]m/n*
upset [e]
upsetting [E]m/n
upsetting [e]m/n*
upside [I]
upstage [A]
upstaging [E]m/n
upstaging [e]m/n*
upstairs [e]r
upstate [A]
upswing [E]m/n
uptight [I]
uptown [ow]m/n
urban [e]m/n
urchin [i]m/n
urge [er]
urgency [E]
urgent [e]m/n
urgently [E]
urging [E]m/n
urging [e]m/n*
urine [i]m/n

us [u]
usable [u]l
usage [e]
use [oo]
useful [u]l
useless [e]
user [er]
username [A]m/n
usher [er]
ushering [E]m/n
ushering [e]m/n*
using [E]m/n
using [e]m/n*
usual [u]l
usually [E]
utensil [u]l
utility [E]
utilize [I]
utilizing [E]m/n
utilizing [e]m/n*
utmost [O]
utter [er]
uttering [E]m/n
uttering [e]m/n*
utterly [E]

V

vacancy [E]
vacant [e]m/n
vacate [A]
vacated [e]
vacating [E]m/n
vacating [e]m/n*
vacation [u]m/n
vacationing [E]m/n
vacationing [e]m/n*
vaccinate [A]
vaccinated [e]
vaccinating [E]m/n
vaccinating [e]m/n*
vaccination [u]m/n

vaccine [E]m/n
vacuum [oo]m/n
vacuuming [E]m/n
vacuuming [e]m/n*
vague [A]
vaguely [E]
vain [A]m/n
valance [e]m/n
valentine [I]m/n
valet [A]
valiant [e]m/n
valiantly [E]
valid [i]
validate [A]

validated [e]
validating [E]m/n
validating [e]m/n*
validation [u]m/n
valium [u]m/n
valley [E]
valor [er]
valuable [u]l
value [oo]
valve [a]l
vampire [I]r
van [a]m/n
vandal [u]l
vandalism [e]m/n

vandalize [l]
vanilla [u]
vanish [i]
vanishing [E]m/n
vanishing [e]m/n*
vanity [E]
vapor [er]
vaporize [l]
vaporizer [er]
vaporizing [E]m/n
vaporizing [e]m/n*
variable [u]l
variance [e]m/n
variant [e]m/n
variation [u]m/n
varicose [O]
variety [E]
various [e]
varnish [i]
varnishing [E]m/n
varnishing [e]m/n*
vary [E]
varying [E]m/n
varying [e]m/n*
vase [A]
vast [a]
vastly [E]
vault [o]l
vaulted [e]
vaulting [E]m/n
vaulting [e]m/n*
veal [E]l
vector [er]
vegan [e]m/n
vegetable [u]l
vegetarian [e]m/n
vegetate [A]
vegetation [u]m/n
vehicle [u]l
vehicular [er]
veil [A]l
vein [A]m/n
velocity [E]
velour [er]
velvet [e]

velvety [E]
vendetta [u]
vendor [er]
veneer [E]r
vengeance [e]m/n
vengeful [u]l
venom [u]m/n
venomous [e]
venous [e]
vent [e]m/n
vented [e]
ventilate [A]
ventilated [e]
ventilating [E]m/n
ventilating [e]m/n*
ventilation [u]m/n
ventilator [er]
venting [E]m/n
venting [e]m/n*
ventriloquist [i]
venture [er]
venturing [E]m/n
venturing [e]m/n*
venue [oo]
veranda [u]
verbal [u]l
verbalize [l]
verbalizing [E]m/n
verbalizing [e]m/n*
verbally [E]
verbatim [i]m/n
verdict [i]
verge [er]
verging [E]m/n
verging [e]m/n*
verification [u]m/n
verify [I]
verifying [E]m/n
verifying [e]m/n*
vermin [i]m/n
versatile [u]l
versatility [E]
verse [er]
version [u]m/n
versus [e]

vertical [u]l
vertically [E]
very [E]
very [e]*
vessel [u]l
vest [e]
vested [e]
vet [e]
veteran [e]m/n
veterinary [E]
veto [O]
vetoing [E]m/n
vetoing [e]m/n*
via [u]
viable [u]l
vial [I]l
vibrant [e]m/n
vibrantly [E]
vibrate [A]
vibrated [e]
vibrating [E]m/n
vibrating [e]m/n*
vibration [u]m/n
vibrato [O]
vibrator [er]
vice [I]
vicinity [E]
vicious [e]
viciously [E]
victim [i]m/n
victimize [l]
victimizing [E]m/n
victimizing [e]m/n*
victor [er]
victorious [e]
victoriously [E]
victory [E]
video [O]
videoing [E]m/n
videoing [e]m/n*
view [oo]
viewer [er]
viewing [E]m/n
viewing [e]m/n*
viewpoint [Oi]m/n

vigil [u]l
vigilant [e]m/n
vigilante [E]
vignette [e]
vigor [er]
vigorous [e]
vile [I]l
village [e]
villain [i]m/n
villainous [e]
vine [I]m/n
vinegar [er]
vineyard [er]
vintage [e]
violate [A]
violated [e]
violating [E]m/n
violating [e]m/n*
violence [e]m/n
violent [e]m/n
violently [E]
violet [e]
violin [i]m/n
viper [er]
viral [u]l
virtual [u]l
virtually [E]
virtue [oo]
virtuoso [O]
virus [e]
vise [I]
visibility [E]
visible [u]l
visibly [E]
vision [u]m/n
visionary [E]
visit [i]
visiting [E]m/n
visiting [e]m/n*
visitor [er]

visor [er]
vista [u]
visual [u]l
visualize [I]
visualizing [E]m/n
visualizing [e]m/n*
visually [E]
vital [u]l
vitality [E]
vitalize [I]
vitally [E]
vitamin [i]m/n
vivacious [e]
vivid [i]
vividly [E]
vixen [e]m/n
vocabulary [E]
vocal [u]l
vocalist [i]
vocalize [I]
vocalizing [E]m/n
vocalizing [e]m/n*
vocally [E]
vocation [u]m/n
vocational [u]l
vodka [u]
vogue [O]
voice [Oi]
voicing [E]m/n
voicing [e]m/n*
void [Oi]
voided [e]
voiding [E]m/n
voiding [e]m/n*
voila [o]
volatile [u]l
volcanic [i]
volcano [O]
volley [E]
volleyball [o]l

volleying [E]m/n
volleying [e]m/n*
voltage [e]
volume [oo]m/n
voluminous [e]
voluntarily [E]
voluntary [E]
volunteer [E]r
volunteering [E]m/n
volunteering [e]m/n*
voluptuous [e]
voluptuously [E]
vomit [i]
vomited [e]
vomiting [E]m/n
vomiting [e]m/n*
voodoo [oo]
vortex [e]
vote [O]
voted [e]
voter [er]
voting [E]m/n
voting [e]m/n*
votive [i]
vouch [ow]
voucher [er]
vouching [E]m/n
vouching [e]m/n*
vow [ow]
vowel [u]l
vowing [E]m/n
vowing [e]m/n*
voyage [e]
voyager [er]
vulgar [er]
vulgarity [E]
vulnerable [u]l
vulnerably [E]
vulture [er]

W

wacko [O]
wacky [E]
wad [o]
wadded [e]
waddle [u]l
waddling [E]m/n
waddling [e]m/n*
wade [A]
waded [e]
wading [E]m/n
wading [e]m/n*
wafer [er]
waffle [u]l
wag [a]
wage [A]
wager [er]
wagering [E]m/n
wagering [e]m/n*
wagging [E]m/n
wagging [e]m/n*
waging [E]m/n
waging [e]m/n*
wagon [e]m/n
waif [A]
waist [A]
waistline [I]m/n
wait [A]
waited [e]
waiter [er]
waiting [E]m/n
waiting [e]m/n*
waitress [e]
waive [A]
waiver [er]
waiving [E]m/n
waiving [e]m/n*
wake [A]
waken [e]m/n
wakening [E]m/n
wakening [e]m/n*
walk [o]

walker [er]
walking [E]m/n
walking [e]m/n*
walkway [A]
wall [o]l
wallop [u]
walloping [E]m/n
walloping [e]m/n*
wallow [O]
wallowing [E]m/n
wallowing [e]m/n*
wallpaper [er]
walnut [u]
walrus [e]
waltz [o]
waltzing [E]m/n
waltzing [e]m/n*
wander [er]
wandering [E]m/n
wandering [e]m/n*
want [o]m/n
wanting [E]m/n
wanting [e]m/n*
war [O]r
ward [O]r
warden [e]m/n
wardrobe [O]
ware [e]r
warehouse [ow]
warfare [e]r
warhead [e]
warily [E]
warlock [o]
warm [O]r
warmer [er]
warming [E]m/n
warming [e]m/n*
warmth [O]r
warn [O]r
warning [E]m/n
warning [e]m/n*

warp [O]r
warping [E]m/n
warping [e]m/n*
warrant [e]m/n
warranted [e]
warranting [E]m/n
warranting [e]m/n*
warranty [E]
warrior [er]
warship [i]
wart [O]r
wartime [I]m/n
wary [E]
wash [o]
washable [u]l
washbowl [O]l
washcloth [o]
washer [er]
washing [E]m/n
washing [e]m/n*
washrag [a]
wasn't [e]m/n
waste [A]
wasted [e]
wasteful [u]l
wasteland [a]m/n
wastepaper [er]
wasting [E]m/n
wasting [e]m/n*
watch [o]
watchdog [o]
watcher [er]
watchful [u]l
watching [E]m/n
watching [e]m/n*
watchman [e]m/n
watchtower [er]
water [er]
waterbed [e]
watercolor [er]
waterfall [o]l

waterfront [u]m/n
watering [E]m/n
watering [e]m/n*
watermark [o]r
watermelon [e]m/n
waterproof [oo]
waterproofing [E]m/n
waterproofing [e]m/n*
watertight [I]
watery [E]
watt [o]
wattage [e]
wave [A]
waver [er]
wavering [E]m/n
wavering [e]m/n*
waving [E]m/n
waving [e]m/n*
wavy [E]
wax [a]
waxing [E]m/n
waxing [e]m/n*
waxy [E]
way [A]
wayside [I]
wayward [er]
weak [E]
weaken [e]m/n
weakening [E]m/n
weakening [e]m/n*
weaker [er]
weakling [E]m/n
weakling [e]m/n*
weakly [E]
weakness [e]
wealth [e]l
wealthy [E]
weapon [e]m/n
weaponry [E]
wear [e]r
wearable [u]l
wearily [E]
wearing [E]m/n
wearing [e]m/n*
weary [E]

weasel [u]l
weaseling [E]m/n
weaseling [e]m/n*
weather [er]
weathering [E]m/n
weathering [e]m/n*
weatherproof [oo]
weatherproofing [E]m/n
weatherproofing [e]m/n*
weave [E]
weaver [er]
weaving [E]m/n
weaving [e]m/n*
web [e]
webbing [E]m/n
webbing [e]m/n*
website [I]
wed [e]
wedding [E]m/n
wedding [e]m/n*
wedge [e]
wedging [E]m/n
wedging [e]m/n*
Wednesday [A]
wee [E]
weed [E]
weeding [E]m/n
weeding [e]m/n*
week [E]
weekday [A]
weekly [E]
weeknight [I]
weepy [E]
weigh [A]
weighing [E]m/n
weighing [e]m/n*
weight [A]
weighted [e]
weightless [e]
weightlessly [E]
weighty [E]
weird [E]r
weirdly [E]
weirdo [O]
welcome [u]m/n

welcoming [E]m/n
welcoming [e]m/n*
weld [e]l
welder [er]
welding [E]m/n
welding [e]m/n*
welfare [e]r
well [e]l
wellness [e]
went [e]m/n
were [er]
werewolf [oo]l
west [e]
westbound [ow]m/n
westerly [E]
western [er]m/n
westward [er]
wet [e]
wetland [e]m/n
wetting [E]m/n
wetting [e]m/n*
whack [a]
whacking [E]m/n
whacking [e]m/n*
whale [A]l
wham [a]m/n
wharf [O]r
what [u]
whatever [er]
whatnot [o]
whatsoever [er]
wheat [E]
wheel [E]l
wheelbarrow [O]
wheelchair [e]r
wheeler [er]
wheelie [E]
wheeling [E]m/n
wheeling [e]m/n*
wheeze [E]
wheezing [E]m/n
wheezing [e]m/n*
wheezy [E]
when [e]m/n
whenever [er]

where [e]r
whereas [a]
whereby [I]
wherefore [O]r
wherein [i]m/n
wherever [er]
whet [e]
whether [er]
whetting [E]m/n
whetting [e]m/n*
whey [A]
which [i]
whichever [er]
whiff [i]
whiffing [E]m/n
whiffing [e]m/n*
while [I]l
whim [i]m/n
whimper [er]
whimpering [E]m/n
whimpering [e]m/n*
whimsical [u]l
whimsically [E]
whimsy [E]
whine [I]m/n
whiner [er]
whining [E]m/n
whining [e]m/n*
whinny [E]
whip [i]
whiplash [a]
whipping [E]m/n
whipping [e]m/n*
whirl [u]l
whirling [E]m/n
whirling [e]m/n*
whirlpool [oo]l
whirlwind [i]m/n
whirly [E]
whisk [i]
whisker [er]
whiskey [E]
whiskey [e]*
whisking [E]m/n
whisking [e]m/n*

whisper [er]
whispering [E]m/n
whispering [e]m/n*
whistle [u]l
whistler [er]
whistling [E]m/n
whistling [e]m/n*
white [I]
whitecap [a]
whiten [e]m/n
whitening [E]m/n
whitening [e]m/n*
whiter [er]
whittle [u]l
whittling [E]m/n
whittling [e]m/n*
whiz [i]
who [oo]
whoa [O]
whoever [er]
whole [O]l
wholehearted [e]
wholeheartedly [E]
wholesale [A]l
wholesaling [E]m/n
wholesaling [e]m/n*
wholesome [u]m/n
wholly [E]
whom [oo]m/n
whomever [er]
whoopee [E]
whopper [er]
whose [oo]
why [I]
wick [i]
wicked [e]
wicker [er]
wide [I]
widely [E]
widen [e]m/n
widening [E]m/n
widening [e]m/n*
wider [er]
widespread [e]
widow [O]

widower [er]
width [i]
wiener [er]
wife [I]
wig [i]
wiggle [u]l
wiggling [E]m/n
wiggling [e]m/n*
wild [I]l
wilder [er]
wilderness [e]
wildfire [I]r
wildlife [I]
wildly [E]
wile [I]l
will [i]l
willful [u]l
willing [E]m/n
willing [e]m/n*
willow [O]
willpower [er]
wilt [i]l
wilting [E]m/n
wilting [e]m/n*
wimp [i]m/n
wimpy [E]
win [i]m/n
wind [i]m/n
wind [I]m/n
windblown [O]m/n
winded [e]
windfall [o]l
winding [E]m/n
winding [e]m/n*
windmill [i]l
window [O]
windowsill [i]l
windpipe [I]
windproof [oo]
windshield [E]l
windsock [o]
windy [E]
wine [I]m/n
wineglass [a]
wing [E]m/n

wingback [a]
winging [E]m/n
winging [e]m/n*
wingspan [a]m/n
wink [E]m/n
winking [E]m/n
winking [e]m/n*
winner [er]
winning [E]m/n
winning [e]m/n*
winter [er]
winterize [I]
winterizing [E]m/n
winterizing [e]m/n*
wintertime [I]m/n
wintery [E]
wipe [I]
wiper [er]
wiping [E]m/n
wiping [e]m/n*
wire [I]r
wireless [e]
wiring [E]m/n
wiring [e]m/n*
wiry [E]
wisdom [u]m/n
wise [I]
wisecrack [a]
wisely [E]
wisely [e]*
wiser [er]
wish [i]
wishbone [O]m/n
wishful [u]l
wishfully [E]
wishing [E]m/n
wishing [e]m/n*
wisp [i]
wispy [E]
wit [i]
witch [i]
witchcraft [a]
witchy [E]
with [i]
withdraw [o]

withdrawal [o]l
withdrawn [o]m/n
withdrew [oo]
wither [er]
withering [E]m/n
withering [e]m/n*
withhold [O]l
withholding [E]m/n
withholding [e]m/n*
within [i]m/n
without [ow]
withstand [a]m/n
withstanding [E]m/n
withstanding [e]m/n*
witness [e]
witnessing [E]m/n
witnessing [e]m/n*
witty [E]
wizard [er]
wizardly [E]
woe [O]
woeful [u]l
wok [o]
woke [O]
woken [e]m/n
wolfhound [ow]m/n
wolverine [E]m/n
woman [e]m/n
womb [oo]m/n
women [e]m/n
won [u]m/n
won't [O]m/n
wonder [er]
wonderful [u]l
wondering [E]m/n
wondering [e]m/n*
wonderland [a]m/n
wondrous [e]
woo [oo]
wood [oo/]
wooden [e]m/n
woodshed [e]
woodsman [e]m/n
woodsy [E]
woodwork [er]

woodworking [E]m/n
woodworking [e]m/n*
woody [E]
wooing [E]m/n
wooing [e]m/n*
wool [oo]l
woolen [e]m/n
wooly [E]
woozy [E]
word [er]
worded [e]
wordplay [A]
wordy [E]
wore [O]r
work [er]
workable [u]l
workaholic [i]
workbook [oo/]
workday [A]
worker [er]
workforce [O]r
workhorse [O]r
working [E]m/n
working [e]m/n*
workload [O]
workman [e]m/n
workmanship [i]
workout [ow]
workplace [A]
workroom [oo]m/n
worksheet [E]
workshop [o]
workstation [u]m/n
world [er]
worldly [E]
worldwide [I]
worm [er]m/n
wormhole [O]l
wormy [E]
worn [O]r
worrisome [u]m/n
worry [E]
worry [e]*
worrying [E]m/n
worrying [e]m/n*

worse [er]
worsen [e]m/n
worsening [E]m/n
worsening [e]m/n*
worship [i]
worshipping [E]m/n
worshipping [e]m/n*
worst [er]
worth [er]
worthless [e]
worthwhile [I]l
worthy [E]
would [oo/]
wouldn't [e]m/n
wound [oo]m/n
wound [ow]m/n
wove [O]
woven [e]m/n
wow [ow]
wrack [a]
wracking [E]m/n

wracking [e]m/n*
wrangle [u]l
wrangler [er]
wrangling [E]m/n
wrangling [e]m/n*
wrap [a]
wrapper [er]
wrapping [E]m/n
wrapping [e]m/n*
wrath [a]
wreath [E]
wreck [e]
wreckage [e]
wrecking [E]m/n
wrecking [e]m/n*
wrench [e]m/n
wrenching [E]m/n
wrenching [e]m/n*
wrestle [u]l
wrestler [er]
wrestling [E]m/n

wrestling [e]m/n*
wretch [e]
wring [E]m/n
wringing [E]m/n
wringing [e]m/n*
wrinkle [u]l
wrinkling [E]m/n
wrinkling [e]m/n*
wrist [i]
wristwatch [o]
write [I]
writer [er]
writing [E]m/n
writing [e]m/n*
written [e]m/n
wrong [o]m/n
wrongful [u]l
wrote [O]
wrought [o]
wrung [u]m/n
wry [I]

x-ray [A]

xylophone [O]m/n

yacht [o]
yachting [E]m/n
yachting [e]m/n*
yak [a]
yam [a]m/n
yank [a]ng/k
yanking [E]m/n
yanking [e]m/n*
yard [o]r
yardage [e]
yardstick [i]
yarn [o]r

yawn [o]m/n
yawning [E]m/n
yawning [e]m/n*
yea [A]
year [E]r
yearbook [oo/]
yearling [E]m/n
yearly [E]
yearn [er]m/n
yearning [E]m/n
yearning [e]m/n*
yeast [E]

yell [e]l
yelling [E]m/n
yelling [e]m/n*
yellow [O]
yellowish [i]
yelp [e]l
yelping [E]m/n
yelping [e]m/n*
yen [e]m/n
yes [e]
yesterday [A]
yesteryear [E]r

yet [e]
yield [E]l
yielding [E]m/n
yielding [e]m/n*
yin [i]m/n
yippee [E]
yodel [u]l
yodeling [E]m/n
yodeling [e]m/n*
yoga [u]

yogi [E]
yogurt [er]
yoke [O]
yolk [O]
yonder [er]
you [oo]
young [u]m/n
younger [er]
youngest [e]
youngster [er]

your [O]r
yourself [e]l
youth [oo]
youthful [u]l
yuck [u]
yucky [E]
yuletide [I]
yum [u]m/n
yummy [E]

Z

zany [E]
zap [a]
zapping [E]m/n
zapping [e]m/n*
zeal [E]l
zealous [e]
zebra [u]
zero [O]
zeroing [E]m/n
zeroing [e]m/n*
zest [e]
zesty [E]
zigzag [a]

zigzagging [E]m/n
zigzagging [e]m/n*
zilch [i]l
zillion [u]m/n
zinc [E]m/n
zing [E]m/n
zinger [er]
zinging [E]m/n
zinging [e]m/n*
zingy [E]
zip [i]
zipper [er]
zipping [E]m/n

zipping [e]m/n*
zippy [E]
zit [i]
zombie [E]
zone [O]m/n
zoning [E]m/n
zoning [e]m/n*
zoology [E]
zoom [oo]m/n
zooming [E]m/n
zooming [e]m/n*
zucchini [E]

PART TWO

Abbreviated Rhyming Dictionary

[A]

[A]   as in: stay

a	annihilate	beige	cascade
abbreviate	anticipate	bellyache	case
ablaze	anyplace	beltway	castaway
accelerate	anyway	betray	castrate
accentuate	ape	birthday	causeway
acclimate	appraise	birthplace	cave
accommodate	appreciate	blade	celebrate
accumulate	appropriate	blasé	chalet
ace	arcade	blaze	chambray
acetate	archway	blockade	charade
ache	array	bookcase	chase
activate	ashtray	bouquet	cheapskate
administrate	assassinate	brace	checkmate
advocate	associate	braid	cheesecake
aerate	astray	brake	circulate
afraid	ate	brave	classmate
aftershave	authenticate	break	clay
aftertaste	automate	breezeway	cliché
agape	await	bridesmaid	collaborate
age	awake	briefcase	commemorate
aggravate	away	brigade	commentate
agitate	backache	brocade	commiserate
aid	backspace	buffet	commonplace
aide	backstage	cabaret	communicate
airwave	bait	café	compensate
airway	bake	cage	complicate
alienate	ballet	cake	concave
alleviate	barricade	calculate	concentrate
allocate	base	calibrate	confiscate
alternate	bass	candidate	congratulate
always	bathe	cape	congregate
amaze	bay	captivate	consolidate
animate	behave	carbohydrate	constipate

consummate	deviate	evacuate	glaze
contaminate	dictate	evade	gourmet
convey	differentiate	evaluate	grace
cooperate	dilate	evaporate	grade
coordinate	discriminate	everyday	graduate
cornflake	disgrace	everyplace	grape
crate	dislocate	exaggerate	grate
crave	dismay	exterminate	grave
craze	disobey	fabricate	gravitate
create	displace	face	gray
cremate	display	facilitate	graze
crepe	dissipate	fade	great
crochet	domesticate	fairway	grey
croquet	dominate	faith	gyrate
crusade	donate	fake	halfway
cultivate	doomsday	fascinate	hallucinate
cupcake	doorway	fate	hallway
cyberspace	downgrade	fiancé	handmade
daresay	downplay	fillet	handshake
database	drape	filtrate	haste
date	driveway	fireplace	hate
day	duplicate	fixate	hay
daybreak	earache	flake	haze
daze	earthquake	floodgate	headache
debate	educate	fluctuate	headway
decade	eight	foreplay	hearsay
decay	elaborate	forgave	heartache
decontaminate	elate	formulate	heartbreak
decorate	elevate	forsake	heavyweight
dedicate	eliminate	freeway	hesitate
deejay	elongate	freight	hey
deface	embrace	Friday	hibernate
deflate	engage	fruitcake	highway
degenerate	engrave	frustrate	holiday
degrade	enrage	fumigate	homemade
dehydrate	entrée	gait	hooray
delay	enunciate	gape	horseplay
delegate	equate	gate	hotcake
deliberate	eradicate	gateway	housebreak
demonstrate	erase	gauge	humiliate
depreciate	escalate	gave	hydrate
designate	escape	gay	illuminate
deteriorate	essay	gaze	illustrate
detonate	estate	generate	imitate
devastate	estimate	glade	incorporate

indicate
inflate
initiate
inlaid
inlay
inmate
innovate
insulate
intake
intimidate
intoxicate
inundate
invade
investigate
irate
irrigate
irritate
isolate
jade
jailbait
jailbreak
keepsake
lace
laid
lake
laminate
lampshade
landscape
late
lay
lemonade
liberate
lightweight
limeade
liquidate
locate
lubricate
made
magistrate
maid
mainstay
make
mandate
manipulate
manmade

masquerade
mate
may
mayday
maze
mediate
medicate
meditate
mermaid
microwave
midway
migrate
milkshake
misbehave
mislaid
misplace
misshape
mistake
moderate
Monday
motivate
mutate
naiveté
nameplate
namesake
narrate
navigate
nay
negligee
negotiate
nominate
notate
nowadays
nursemaid
obey
obligate
okay
opaque
operate
orchestrate
originate
ornate
oscillate
outbreak
outrage

outweigh
overpaid
overpay
overweight
pace
page
paid
palpitate
pancake
paperweight
parade
parfait
parkway
parlay
partake
participate
partway
passageway
paste
pathway
pave
pay
payday
penetrate
perforate
permeate
perpetrate
persuade
phase
phrase
pillowcase
place
plague
plate
play
playmate
pollinate
populate
portray
postdate
praise
pray
precipitate
premeditate
prepay

prey
primate
probate
procrastinate
promenade
prorate
prostate
prostrate
protégé
pulsate
punctuate
puree
race
raceway
radiate
rage
raid
railway
raise
rake
rape
rate
rattlesnake
rave
ray
rebate
reciprocate
recuperate
redecorate
refrigerate
reggae
regulate
rehabilitate
reinstate
rejuvenate
relate
relay
remake
renovate
repaid
repay
replace
replay
reshape
restate

resume
retake
retaliate
retrace
ricochet
risqué
roadway
roommate
rotate
runway
sachet
safe
sake
sashay
saturate
Saturday
sauté
save
say
schoolmate
scintillate
scrape
screenplay
seascape
sedate
segregate
separate
serenade
shade
shake
shape
shave
shipshape
shockwave
shoelace
shortcake
shortwave
sideways

simulate
situate
skate
slate
slave
slay
sleigh
snake
snowflake
someday
someway
soufflé
space
spay
speculate
speedway
spray
stage
stagnate
staircase
stairway
stake
stalemate
state
stay
steak
stimulate
stingray
stipulate
stockade
stomachache
stowaway
straight
strait
stray
subway
suede
suffocate

suitcase
sundae
Sunday
sunshade
survey
sway
sweepstake
switchblade
swordplay
tailgate
take
tape
taste
teammate
teenage
terminate
they
Thursday
tirade
today
tolerate
tollgate
toothache
toothpaste
toupee
trace
trade
trait
translate
tray
Tuesday
ulcerate
underage
underway
underweight
unpaid
unsafe
update

upgrade
uppercase
upstage
upstate
vacate
vaccinate
vague
valet
validate
vase
vegetate
ventilate
vibrate
violate
wade
wage
waif
waist
wait
waive
wake
walkway
waste
wave
way
Wednesday
weekday
weigh
weight
whey
wordplay
workday
workplace
x-ray
yea
yesterday

[A]l

as in: scale

airmail
ale

avail
bail

bale
blackmail

cattail
coattail

cocktail
curtail
derail
detail
doornail
dovetail
ducktail
entail
exhale
fail

fairytale
female
frail
hail
inhale
mail
male
nail
nightingale
pail

pale
prevail
quail
rail
retail
sail
sale
scale
snail
stale

tail
tale
thumbnail
toenail
trail
veil
whale
wholesale

[A]m/n

as in: **same**

abstain
acclaim
acquaint
aim
ain't
airplane
arraign
arrange
ashamed
attain
became
birdbrain
blame
bloodstain
brain
butane
came
campaign
cane
cellophane
chain
champagne
change
claim
cocaine
complain
complaint

constrain
contain
deranged
detain
disclaim
disdain
domain
drain
entertain
exchange
exclaim
explain
eyestrain
faint
fame
flame
frame
gain
game
grain
humane
hurricane
inflame
insane
lame
lamebrain
lane

main
mainframe
maintain
mane
membrane
migraine
mundane
name
nickname
obtain
octane
overcame
pain
paint
pane
pertain
plain
plane
pregame
proclaim
profane
propane
quaint
rain
range
rearrange
reclaim

refrain
regain
reign
rein
remain
rename
restrain
restraint
retain
saint
same
sane
shame
slain
sprain
stain
strain
strange
sustain
taint
tame
terrain
train
username
vain
vein

[a]

[a] as in: staff

aback
acrobat
act
ad
adapt
add
aftermath
aircraft
alas
almanac
amass
apt
artifact
ask
ass
attach
attack
attract
autograph
ax
back
backlash
backpack
backtrack
bad
badge
bag
bareback
bask
bass
bat
batch
bath

beanbag
beeswax
behalf
birdbath
blab
black
blackjack
blast
bluegrass
brag
brass
broadcast
bureaucrat
burlap
bypass
cab
cache
cad
calf
callback
cap
carafe
cardiac
cash
cast
cat
cataract
catch
catnap
chap
chitchat
clack
clap

clash
clasp
class
climax
cognac
collapse
colorfast
combat
comeback
compact
comrade
contact
contract
contrast
copycat
counteract
crab
crabgrass
crack
craft
crap
crash
crass
cutback
dab
dad
dash
deathtrap
detach
diplomat
dishrag
dispatch
distract

doodad
doormat
downcast
drab
draft
drag
drawback
earwax
enact
entrap
exact
extract
eyelash
fact
fad
fast
fat
fax
feedback
fiberglass
firetrap
flab
flack
flag
flap
flapjack
flash
flashback
flask
flat
fleabag
forecast
format

fullback	jazz	outlast	sac
gab	kayak	overcast	sack
gag	keypad	overdraft	sad
gap	kickback	overlap	sag
gas	kidnap	overpass	sandbag
giraffe	knack	pack	sandblast
glad	knapsack	pad	sap
glass	kneecap	pap	sass
grab	knickknack	paragraph	sassafras
grad	lab	pass	sat
graph	lack	past	scab
grasp	lad	pat	schoolbag
grass	lag	patch	scrap
greenback	lap	path	scratch
habitat	lapse	payback	scratchpad
hack	lass	perhaps	setback
had	last	photograph	shack
hag	latch	piggyback	shag
half	laugh	pizzazz	shellac
halfback	lilac	plaid	sidetrack
handbag	mad	plaque	skullcap
handicap	mailbag	playback	slab
harass	maniac	prefab	slack
hardback	map	quack	slap
has	mask	quarterback	slapjack
hat	mass	racetrack	smack
hatch	mast	rack	smash
hatchback	mat	raft	smokestack
have	match	rag	snack
haystack	math	ransack	snag
hijack	miscast	rap	snap
homeopath	mishap	rapt	snatch
horseback	mousetrap	rash	snowcap
hourglass	mustache	rat	soundtrack
hubcap	nab	react	splash
humpback	nag	recap	sportscast
hunchback	nap	recast	spyglass
icecap	newscast	rehab	stab
icepack	nightcap	relapse	stack
impact	nomad	relax	staff
impasse	nonfat	repack	stag
intact	notepad	retract	stash
jab	outback	rickrack	steadfast
jack	outcast	riffraff	strap
jackass	outclass	rollback	subtract

surpass
swag
tab
tack
tag
tap
task
tax
taxicab
teabag
teargas
telecast

that
thermostat
throwback
thumbtack
tieback
topaz
track
transact
trap
trash
trespass
triad

typecast
underpass
unsurpassed
vast
wag
washrag
wax
whack
whereas
whiplash
whitecap
wineglass

wingback
wisecrack
witchcraft
wrack
wrap
wrath
yak
zap
zigzag

[a]l   as in: shall

canal
corral
decal

gal
locale
morale

pal
rationale
shall

valve

[a]m/n   as in: slam

advance
advance
ant
aunt
avalanche
backhand
ban
band
bandstand
beforehand
began
bland
bran
branch
brand
broadband
businessman
camp
can

caravan
cardigan
champ
chance
chant
circumstance
clam
clamp
clan
command
craftsman
cram
cramp
dam
damn
damp
dance
deadpan
demand

diagram
disband
dishpan
doorjamb
doorman
dreamland
dustpan
eggplant
enchant
enhance
exam
expand
expanse
fan
farmland
finance
glance
gland
gram

grand
grandstand
grant
ham
hand
happenstance
implant
jam
lamb
lamp
land
ma'am
madman
mailman
man
milkman
monogram
outran
pan

pant	sand	span	transplant
pecan	sandman	stamp	understand
plan	saucepan	stance	unmanned
plant	scam	stand	van
preplan	scan	strand	wasteland
program	scram	stuntman	wham
ram	sedan	suntan	wingspan
ramp	sham	swam	withstand
ran	sideman	tan	wonderland
ranch	slam	than	yam
rattan	slant	toucan	
recant	snowman	tram	
romance	spaceman	trance	

[a]ng/k   as in: sang

bang	dang	plank	sprang
bank	drank	prank	swank
blank	frank	rang	tank
boomerang	gang	rank	thank
clang	hang	sang	yank
crank	mustang	sank	

[E]

[E]

as in: **see**

ability
abnormality
abnormally
abruptly
absentee
absolutely
absorbency
absurdity
abundantly
academically
academy
accessory
accidentally
accompany
accordingly
accountability
accuracy
accurately
accusatory
achieve
achy
acidity
acne
acoustically
acrobatically
actively
activity
actuality
actually
acutely
adamantly
adaptability
additionally

adeptly
adequacy
adequately
adobe
adultery
adversary
adversity
advisory
aerodynamically
aesthetically
affordably
agency
aggressively
agility
agony
agree
aimlessly
airy
alarmingly
algae
alimony
allergy
alley
almighty
already
amazingly
ambitiously
amnesty
amply
anatomy
ancestry
anchovy
angrily

angry
animosity
anniversary
annually
ante
antibody
antifreeze
antique
antsy
anxiety
anxiously
any
anybody
apiece
apology
apparently
appropriately
approximately
aptly
archery
arguably
army
arrogantly
artery
artfully
artificially
artillery
artistically
artistry
artsy
asleep
assembly
astonishingly

astoundingly
astrology
astronomically
astronomy
astutely
athlete
athletically
atrociously
atrocity
attendee
attentively
attorney
attractively
audacity
audibly
authentically
authenticity
authority
autobiography
automatically
auxiliary
availability
awfully
awkwardly
baby
backseat
badly
baggy
bakery
balcony
balmy
baloney
bankruptcy

barely	blotchy	buckwheat	catastrophe
barley	blueberry	buddy	catchy
basically	bluntly	budgetary	category
battery	blurry	buggy	catty
batty	blustery	bulky	cautionary
bayberry	bodily	bully	cautiously
be	body	bumblebee	cavalry
beach	bogey	bumpy	cavity
bead	boldly	bungee	cease
beady	bony	bunny	celebrity
beanie	boogie	buoy	celery
beast	bookie	bureaucracy	cemetery
beat	bootie	burglary	centerpiece
beautifully	booty	burgundy	centipede
beauty	bossy	bury	century
bee	botany	bushy	ceremony
beef	bouncy	busily	certainly
beep	boundary	busty	certainty
beet	bounty	busy	chalky
belief	boutique	busybody	chamois
believe	brainy	buttery	chaotically
belligerently	brandy	cabby	charitably
belly	brassy	caddy	charity
beneath	bratty	cagey	chassis
beneficiary	bravely	calamity	chatty
berry	bravery	calligraphy	cheap
bigamy	brawny	calmly	cheaply
bikini	brazenly	calorie	cheat
bimonthly	breach	camaraderie	cheek
biography	breathe	canary	cheeky
biology	breed	candidly	cheerfully
birdie	breeze	candy	cheery
birdseed	breezy	cannery	cheese
bitchy	brewery	canopy	cheesy
bittersweet	bribery	capability	chemistry
bitty	brief	capacity	cherry
biweekly	briefly	captivity	chewy
blackberry	brightly	cardiology	chickpea
blarney	brilliantly	carefree	chief
bleach	briskly	carefully	chiefly
bleed	broccoli	carelessly	chili
blindly	brotherly	carpentry	chimney
blissfully	brownie	carry	chimpanzee
bloodthirsty	brutality	casually	chintzy
bloody	brutally	casualty	choosy

choppy
choreography
chubby
chummy
chunky
chutney
cinematography
circuitry
circulatory
city
clammy
clarity
classy
clearly
clergy
clingy
clinically
cloudy
clumpy
clumsy
clunky
coarsely
cockney
cocky
coffee
colicky
colleague
collie
colony
comedy
comfy
comically
commentary
committee
commodity
community
company
comparatively
compassionately
compatibility
compatibly
compete
complete
completely
complexity

complimentary
compulsively
concede
conceit
conceive
concisely
conclusively
concrete
conditionally
confectionery
confetti
confidentiality
confidentially
confidently
conformity
conscientiously
consciously
conservatory
consistency
consistently
conspicuously
conspiracy
constantly
contemporary
contently
continually
continuity
contrary
controversy
conveniently
cookie
cootie
copy
cordially
corny
coronary
cosmetically
cosmetology
cosmically
country
county
courageously
courteously
courtesy
coyly

coyote
cozy
crabby
crafty
cranberry
cranky
cranny
crappy
crazily
crazy
creak
creaky
creamy
credibility
creek
creep
creepy
criminally
crispy
critically
critique
croaky
crony
crookedly
crossbreed
croupy
crucially
cruddy
crudely
cruelly
cruelty
crummy
crunchy
crusty
cryptically
cubby
culinary
curiosity
curiously
currency
currently
curry
curtsy
curvy
cushy

custody
customary
cutely
cutesy
cutie
cutlery
cynically
daddy
daffy
daily
daintily
dainty
dairy
daisy
dally
dandy
dangerously
deadly
dearly
deathly
debrief
debris
deceased
deceit
deceive
decency
decently
decisively
decrease
decree
deed
deep
deeply
defeat
defensively
defiantly
deficiency
deficiently
deformity
degree
delete
deli
deliberately
delicacy
delicately

delightfully
delinquency
delinquently
deliriously
democracy
democratically
demography
densely
density
dentistry
dependability
deplete
deputy
derby
dermatology
derogatory
deservedly
desperately
despicably
destiny
destructively
detainee
dewy
dexterity
diagonally
diametrically
diary
dictionary
dietary
differently
difficulty
dignity
diligently
dilly
dimly
dimply
dingy
dinky
diplomacy
diplomatically
dippy
directly
directory
dirty
disability

disagree
disbelief
disbelieve
disciplinary
discovery
discreet
discreetly
discrepancy
disease
disgracefully
dishonestly
dishonorably
disloyally
disobediently
disorderly
displease
dissatisfactory
distantly
distinctly
ditty
diversity
divinely
divvy
dizzy
documentary
dodgy
doggy
doily
dolly
donkey
dopey
dormitory
doubtfully
doubtlessly
doughy
dowdy
downbeat
downy
dowry
draftee
drafty
drapery
drastically
dreadfully
dreamy

dreary
dressy
drippy
droopy
drowsy
drudgery
drumbeat
duality
ducky
duly
dummy
dumpy
durability
dusky
dusty
duty
dynasty
each
eagerly
early
earnestly
earthly
earthy
ease
easily
east
easy
eat
eaves
ebony
eccentricity
ecologically
ecology
economically
economy
ecstasy
edgy
eerie
eerily
effectively
efficiency
efficiently
effortlessly
eighty
elasticity

electricity
elegantly
elementary
eligibility
elite
eloquently
embassy
embody
embroidery
emcee
emergency
empathy
employee
empty
endlessly
enemy
energy
enormity
enormously
entirely
entity
entry
enviously
environmentally
envy
epiphany
equality
equally
erotically
erratically
essentially
eternally
eternity
ethically
eulogy
evasively
eve
evenly
eventually
every
everybody
evidently
exactly
exceed
exceptionally

excessively	feasibly	fleshy	frivolously
exclusively	feast	flexibility	frizzy
exclusivity	feat	flexibly	frosty
exemplary	feathering	flighty	frothy
exotically	feathery	flimsy	frugally
expensively	February	flirty	fruity
expertise	fee	floozy	frumpy
expertly	feebly	floppy	fumy
explanatory	feed	flossy	fundamentally
explicitly	feet	flouncy	funky
exploratory	feisty	flowery	funny
expressively	felony	fluently	furiously
exquisitely	femininity	fluffy	furry
extensively	ferociously	flunky	fury
externally	ferry	flurry	fussy
extraordinarily	fertility	foamy	futility
extraordinary	festivity	foggy	fuzzy
extravagantly	fidelity	fogy	gabby
extremely	fidgety	folksy	galaxy
extremity	fiercely	folly	gallantly
exuberantly	fiery	fondly	gallery
fabulously	fifty	foolishly	galley
facility	filly	forcefully	gamey
factory	filmy	foresee	garlicky
faculty	filthy	formality	gassy
faintly	finale	formally	gaudy
fairly	finality	fortunately	gee
fairy	finally	forty	generally
faithfully	finely	foxy	generosity
falsely	finicky	frankly	generously
falsie	firmly	frantically	genie
family	fishy	freak	gently
famously	fizzy	freaky	genuinely
fanatically	flabby	free	ghostly
fancy	flaky	freebie	giddy
fanny	flamboyantly	freeze	gimmicky
fantastically	flashy	frenzy	gingerly
fantasy	flatly	frequency	girly
fashionably	flattery	frequently	gladly
fatherly	flaunty	freshly	glamorously
fatigue	flea	friendly	glassy
fatty	flee	frightfully	glee
faulty	fleece	frigidly	glittery
fearfully	fleecy	frilly	glitzy
fearlessly	fleet	frisky	globally

gloomy	guilty	history	identity
glory	gummy	hoagie	iffy
glossy	guppy	hoarsely	illegally
glumly	gurney	hobby	imaginary
goalie	gushy	hockey	immaculately
goatee	gusty	hokey	immediately
golly	gutsy	holistically	immensely
goody	gypsy	holly	immortality
gooey	habitually	holy	immunity
goofy	hairy	homey	impatiently
gorgeously	handsomely	honestly	impeccably
gory	handy	honesty	imperfectly
gracefully	hanky	honey	impolitely
graciously	haphazardly	honky	importantly
gradually	happily	honorably	impossibility
grainy	happy	honorary	impressively
grandly	hardly	hooky	improperly
granny	hardy	hopefully	impulsively
graphically	harmony	hopelessly	inaccurately
grassy	harshly	horizontally	inadequately
gravely	hastily	horny	incidentally
gravity	hasty	horribly	incomplete
gravy	hazardously	horrifying	increase
grease	hazy	hosiery	indecently
greasy	he	hospitality	indeed
greatly	healthy	hostility	indestructibly
greed	heap	hotly	indirectly
greedy	heartily	hourly	individually
greet	hearty	howdy	industry
grimy	heat	hubby	ineffectively
gritty	heave	huffy	inefficiently
grizzly	heavenly	hugely	inevitably
grocery	heavy	humanely	inexpensively
groggy	heed	humanly	infinitely
groovy	hefty	humbly	informally
grossly	helplessly	humidity	injury
grouchy	hereditary	humility	innocently
groupie	heroically	hungry	insanely
grubby	hesitantly	hurry	insanity
grudgingly	hickey	husky	insincerity
gruffly	highly	hussy	instantly
grumpy	hilariously	hypnotically	instinctively
grungy	hilly	icky	integrity
guacamole	hippie	icy	intellectually
guarantee	historically	ideally	intelligently

intensely	karate	leisurely	manatee
intently	keenly	lemony	mandatory
internally	keep	lengthy	manly
intimacy	key	lethally	many
intimately	khaki	levee	marquee
intravenously	kidney	liability	marry
intricately	kindheartedly	liberally	martini
intrigue	kindly	library	marvelously
intuitively	kinky	lightheartedly	masculinity
inventory	kitty	lightly	massively
invisibly	kiwi	likely	masterpiece
involuntarily	klutzy	lily	maternally
involuntary	knead	linguine	maternity
irony	knee	literally	matrimony
irrationally	knobby	lively	matronly
irregularity	knotty	lobby	maturely
irregularly	kooky	locally	maturity
irresistibly	laboratory	lofty	maxi
irresponsibly	lacy	logically	maybe
itchy	lady	lonely	me
ivory	lanky	loony	mealy
ivy	larceny	loopy	measly
jaggedly	largely	loosely	meat
jamboree	lastly	lottery	meaty
January	lately	loudly	mechanically
jazzy	laundry	lousy	mediating
jealously	lavishly	lovely	medically
jelly	lawfully	lowly	medley
jeopardy	lazily	loyally	meet
jerky	lazy	loyalty	melancholy
jewelry	lead	lucidity	melodically
jiffy	leaf	lucidly	melodramatically
jittery	leafy	luckily	melody
jockey	league	lucky	memory
jointly	leak	lumpy	mentality
jolly	leaky	lusciously	mentally
journey	leap	luxury	mercifully
jubilantly	lease	macaroni	mercy
jubilee	least	madly	merely
juicy	leave	magically	merry
jumpy	leery	magnificently	messy
junkie	lefty	mainly	methodically
junky	legally	majestically	meticulously
jury	legendary	majesty	mighty
justly	legitimately	majority	mildly

military
milky
mini
minority
minty
miserably
miserly
misery
mislead
missionary
mistakenly
misty
mockery
modality
moderately
modestly
modesty
moldy
momentarily
momentary
mommy
monetary
money
monkey
monopoly
monotony
monstrosity
monumentally
moody
morally
morbidity
morbidly
mortality
mortally
mossy
mostly
motherly
motif
motley
mousy
mouthy
movie
moxie
muddy
muggy

multi
mummy
munchies
murky
mushy
musicality
musically
musky
musty
mutiny
mutually
mysteriously
mystery
mystically
mystique
naive
naively
namely
nanny
nappy
narrowly
nasally
nastily
nasty
nationality
nationally
naturally
naughty
navy
nearly
neat
neatly
necessarily
necessary
necessity
need
needy
negatively
negativity
neighborly
nerdy
nervously
nervy
neurosis
neurotically

newly
nicely
niche
niece
nifty
nightly
nimbly
ninety
ninny
nippy
nobility
nobly
nobody
nocturnally
noisily
noisy
nominally
nominee
nonchalantly
normalcy
normally
northerly
nosy
notoriously
novelty
nubby
nudity
numerically
nursery
nutty
obediently
obese
obesity
obituary
objectively
objectivity
obligatory
obscenely
obscenity
obscurity
observatory
obsessively
obsolete
obviously
occasionally

occupancy
oddity
oddly
offbeat
offensively
officially
oily
oldie
ominously
only
oozy
opacity
openly
opportunity
orally
orderly
ordinarily
ordinary
organically
orgy
originally
ornery
outrageously
overeat
overly
overseas
oversee
painfully
painstakingly
painterly
paisley
panicky
pansy
pantry
panty
parakeet
parody
parsley
partially
particularly
partly
party
passionately
passively
pastrami

pastry	photography	potpourri	productivity
pasty	physically	pottery	profanity
patchy	physique	potty	professionally
paternally	picky	poultry	proficiently
paternity	piece	poverty	profoundly
pathetically	piggy	powdery	progressively
patiently	pinky	powerfully	prominently
patsy	pitchy	practically	promiscuity
payee	pitifully	prairie	promissory
pea	pity	preach	proofread
peace	pixie	preachy	properly
peacefully	plainly	precariously	property
peach	planetary	precede	prophecy
peachy	playfully	precisely	proportionately
peak	plea	preconceive	proprietary
peculiarity	plead	predatory	prosperity
peculiarly	pleasantly	predominantly	proudly
pedigree	pleasantries	preemie	proximity
pee	please	preferably	proxy
peek	pleat	preheat	psyche
peeve	plenty	preliminary	psychiatry
peewee	podiatry	prematurely	psychologically
penalty	poetry	preparatory	psychology
penny	pointy	preppy	psychotically
pepperoni	poky	presently	puberty
peppy	police	presidency	publicity
perceive	policy	prestige	publicly
perfectly	politely	presumably	pudgy
periphery	politically	pretty	puffy
perjury	pompously	previously	pulley
perky	pony	prickly	punchy
permanently	poorly	priest	punctuality
perpetually	poppy	primarily	punctually
persistently	popularity	primary	puny
personality	porky	primitively	puppetry
personally	pornography	priority	puppy
pesky	positively	prissy	purely
petite	posse	privacy	purity
petty	possessively	privately	purposely
pharmacy	possibility	privy	pushy
phenomenally	possibly	probability	putty
philosophy	posterity	probably	pygmy
phony	posy	proceed	quackery
phooey	potency	prodigy	quaintly
photocopy	potentially	productively	quality

quantity
queasy
query
quickie
quickly
quietly
quirky
rabies
racially
racy
radiantly
radically
radiology
raggedy
ragweed
rainy
rally
rampantly
randomly
rapidly
rarely
rarity
rashly
raspberry
raspy
ratty
raunchy
ravenously
ravioli
reach
read
readily
ready
reality
really
realty
reasonably
recede
receipt
receive
recently
recipe
recklessly
recovery
reef

reek
referee
refugee
registry
regularly
relatively
relativity
release
relentlessly
reliability
reliably
relief
relieve
reluctantly
remedy
remotely
repeat
respectfully
responsibility
responsibly
restlessly
retreat
retrieve
revolutionary
rhythmically
rickety
ridiculously
rightfully
rigidly
rigorously
risky
ritzy
rivalry
roadie
robbery
rocky
romantically
rookie
roomy
rosary
rosy
rotary
roughly
routinely
rowdy

royally
royalty
ruby
rudely
rugby
ruggedly
runny
rusty
sacredly
sadly
safely
safety
saggy
saintly
salary
salty
sanctuary
sandy
sanitary
sanity
sappy
sarcastically
sassy
satisfactory
saucy
savagely
savory
savvy
scampi
scantily
scanty
scarcely
scary
scenery
scenically
scholarly
scholastically
scientifically
scrappy
scratchy
scrawny
screech
screechy
screwy
scrimpy

scruffy
scrutiny
scummy
scurry
sea
seamy
seat
secondary
secrecy
secretary
secretly
securely
security
sedately
see
seed
seedy
seek
seemingly
seize
selectively
senility
seniority
sensibilities
sensibly
sensitively
sensitivity
sensory
sensuality
sensually
sensuously
sentimentally
sentry
separately
serendipity
serenely
serenity
series
seriously
seventy
severely
severity
sexuality
sexually
sexy

shabby	skivvy	solemnly	squarely
shadowy	slavery	solidarity	squatty
shady	sleazy	solidly	squeak
shaggy	sleek	solitary	squeaky
shaky	sleep	somberly	squeamishly
shapely	sleepy	somebody	squeegee
sharpie	sleeve	sorcery	squeeze
sheet	slimy	sorely	squinty
shifty	slink	sorority	squirmy
shimmy	slinky	sorrowfully	squishy
shiny	slippery	sorry	stability
shoddy	slivery	soupy	stampede
showy	sloppy	southerly	starchy
shrewdly	slowly	spaghetti	starry
shriek	slummy	sparkly	stately
shrilly	slurry	speak	stationary
shrubbery	slushy	specialty	stationery
shyly	slutty	species	statistically
sickly	slyly	specifically	steady
siege	smartly	spectacularly	stealthy
sightsee	smarty	speech	steamy
significantly	smiley	speed	steep
silently	smoggy	speedy	sternly
silly	smoky	spicy	sticky
silvery	smoothly	spidery	stiffly
similarity	smugly	spiffy	stingy
similarly	smutty	spiky	stinky
simplicity	snappy	spiny	stocky
simply	snazzy	spirituality	stodgy
simultaneously	sneak	spiritually	stogie
sincerely	sneaky	splashy	stony
sincerity	sneeze	splendidly	stormy
sinfully	snippy	splotchy	story
singularity	snobby	spongy	strangely
sinisterly	snooty	spontaneity	strategically
sissy	snotty	spontaneously	strategy
sisterly	snowy	spooky	streak
sixty	snugly	sporadically	streaky
skeptically	soapy	sporty	street
sketchy	socially	spotlessly	strenuously
ski	society	spotty	stretchy
skillfully	softie	spreadsheet	strictly
skimpy	softly	spree	stringy
skinny	soggy	springy	strongly
skis	solely	spunky	stubbornly

stubby
study
stuffy
stupendously
stupidly
sturdy
suavely
subconsciously
subjectively
subliminally
substantially
subtly
succeed
successfully
suddenly
sufficiently
sugary
suite
sulky
sultry
summary
summery
sunny
superbly
superficially
superiority
superstitiously
supposedly
supremely
surely
surgery
surgically
surprisingly
sushi
suspiciously
swampy
swanky
sweaty
sweep
sweet
sweetie
sweetly
swiftly
swirly
swishy

sympathy
symphony
synthetically
systematically
tabby
tacky
tactfully
tactically
taffy
tally
tamale
tangibly
tangy
tardy
tasty
tawdry
tawny
taxi
tea
teach
teary
tease
technically
technique
technology
teddy
tediously
tee
teeny
teepee
teeth
telepathy
temporarily
temporary
tendency
tenderly
tensely
tentatively
terminally
terminology
terribly
terrifically
territory
terry
testimony

testy
thankfully
the
theatrically
thee
theory
therapy
these
thickly
thief
thirsty
thirty
thorny
thoroughly
thoughtfully
three
thrifty
throaty
tidy
timidly
tingly
tinny
tiny
tipsy
tizzy
toddy
toffee
toiletry
tolerably
toothy
topically
totally
touchy
toughly
toxicity
traditionally
tragedy
tragically
trainee
tranquility
transparently
trapeze
trashy
treachery
treasury

treat
treaty
tree
tremendously
trendy
tricky
trolley
trophy
truancy
truly
trustee
trustworthy
trusty
truthfully
tubby
tummy
turkey
turnkey
TV
tweak
tweed
tweet
twenty
typically
ugly
ultimately
uncanny
uncertainty
uncomfortably
unconditionally
unconsciously
uncontrollably
undeniably
underneath
understudy
undoubtedly
unearthly
uneasy
unexpectedly
unfairly
unfavorably
uniformity
unique
uniquely
unity

universally	verbally	waxy	wiry
university	versatility	weak	wisely
unknowingly	vertically	weakly	wishfully
unlawfully	very	wealthy	wispy
unleash	veterinary	weaponry	witchy
unlikely	vibrantly	wearily	witty
unnecessary	vicinity	weary	wizardly
unofficially	viciously	weave	woodsy
unreasonably	victoriously	wee	woody
unruly	victory	weed	wooly
unsatisfactory	vigilante	week	woozy
unspeakably	violently	weekly	wordy
untidy	virtually	weepy	worksheet
unusually	visibility	weightlessly	worldly
unwisely	visibly	weighty	wormy
unworthy	visionary	weirdly	worry
upholstery	visually	westerly	worthy
upkeep	vitality	wheat	wreath
uproariously	vitally	wheelie	yearly
urgency	vividly	wheeze	yeast
urgently	vocabulary	wheezy	yippee
usually	vocally	whimsically	yogi
utility	volley	whimsy	yucky
utterly	voluntarily	whinny	yummy
vacancy	voluntary	whirly	zany
vaguely	voluptuously	whiskey	zesty
valiantly	vulgarity	wholeheartedly	zingy
valley	vulnerably	wholly	zippy
vanity	wacky	whoopee	zombie
variety	warily	widely	zoology
vary	warranty	wildly	zucchini
vastly	wary	wimpy	
velocity	watery	windy	
velvety	wavy	wintery	

[E]l   as in: steel

appeal	feel	meal	repeal
backfield	field	ordeal	reveal
battlefield	heal	outfield	seal
conceal	heel	peel	shield
cornmeal	ideal	real	steal
deal	kneel	reel	steel

surreal	unreal	wheel	yield
teal	veal	windshield	zeal

[E]m/n

as in: **seem**

abandoning	adopting	annoying	assuring
abbreviating	adoring	answering	astonishing
abducting	adorning	antagonizing	astounding
abiding	advancing	anticipating	atoning
aborting	advertising	anything	attaching
absorbing	advising	apologizing	attacking
abstaining	advocating	appealing	attaining
abusing	affecting	appearing	attempting
accelerating	affirming	appetizing	attending
accepting	affixing	applauding	attracting
accessing	afflicting	applying	attributing
accessorizing	aggravating	appointing	auctioning
acclimating	aging	appraising	auditing
accommodating	agonizing	appreciating	augmenting
accompanying	agreeing	apprehending	authoring
accomplishing	aiding	approaching	authorizing
according	aiming	approving	autographing
accounting	alarming	aquamarine	automating
accumulating	alerting	arching	avenging
accusing	aligning	archiving	averting
achieving	alleging	arguing	avoiding
aching	alleviating	arising	awaiting
acing	allocating	arousing	awakening
acknowledging	allotting	arraigning	awarding
acquiring	allowing	arranging	awning
acting	alluding	arresting	backbreaking
activating	alluring	arriving	backing
adapting	altering	asking	backpacking
addicting	alternating	aspiring	backswing
adding	amazing	assassinating	baffling
addressing	amending	assaulting	bailing
adhering	amplifying	assembling	baiting
adjoining	amusing	asserting	baking
adjourning	analyzing	assessing	balancing
adjusting	anchoring	assigning	balding
administering	angering	assisting	balking
admiring	annihilating	assorting	balling
admitting	announcing	assuming	banding

banging
banishing
banking
bankrolling
bankrupting
banning
bantering
baptizing
barking
barreling
barricading
barring
bartering
basking
bathing
battering
batting
bawling
beading
beam
beaming
bean
bearing
beating
beckoning
becoming
bedazzling
bedding
beefing
beeping
befriending
begging
beginning
begrudging
behaving
beholding
behooving
being
believing
belittling
belonging
belting
benching
bending
benefitting

bestowing
betraying
betting
between
beveling
bewildering
bewitching
bidding
biking
binding
birthing
biting
blabbing
blaming
blasting
blazing
bleaching
bleeding
blending
blessing
blinding
blink
blinking
blistering
bloating
blocking
bloodcurdling
blooming
blossoming
blotting
blowing
bludgeoning
bluffing
blundering
blurring
blurting
boarding
boasting
boating
bobbing
bobsledding
boggling
boiling
bolting
bombarding

bombing
bonding
booking
bookkeeping
booming
boosting
booting
bootlegging
boozing
bordering
boring
borrowing
bossing
botching
bothering
bottlenecking
bottling
bouncing
bounding
bowing
bowling
boxing
bracing
bracketing
bragging
braiding
brainstorming
brainwashing
braking
branching
branding
breaching
breaking
breathing
breathtaking
breeding
breezing
brewing
bribing
bridging
briefing
brightening
brimming
bring
bringing

brink
broaching
broadcasting
broadening
broiling
bronzing
brooding
brownnosing
browsing
bruising
brushing
bubbling
bucking
budding
budgeting
buffering
buffing
bugging
building
bulging
bulldozing
bulletproofing
bullfighting
bullying
bumming
bumping
bunching
bunking
burdening
burglarizing
burning
burping
burrowing
bursting
busting
bustling
buying
buzzing
bypassing
caffeine
calcifying
calculating
calibrating
calling
camouflaging

campaigning	challenging	clean	commencing
camping	changing	cleaning	commending
canceling	channeling	cleansing	commenting
canning	chanting	clearing	commissioning
canoeing	chaperoning	clicking	committing
canteen	charging	climbing	communicating
canvassing	charming	cling	commuting
capitalizing	chartering	clinging	compacting
capping	charting	clipping	comparing
capsizing	chasing	cloaking	compelling
captivating	chattering	clocking	compensating
capturing	cheapening	clogging	competing
caramelizing	cheating	cloning	compiling
careen	checking	closing	complaining
careening	cheering	clotting	completing
caressing	cherishing	clowning	complicating
caring	chewing	clubbing	complimenting
caroling	childbearing	clucking	complying
carpeting	childproofing	cluing	composing
carpooling	chilling	clumping	composting
carrying	chiming	clutching	compounding
carting	chipping	cluttering	comprehending
carving	chirping	coaching	compressing
cascading	chiseling	coasting	comprising
cashing	chlorine	coating	compromising
casing	choking	coaxing	computerizing
casting	choosing	codeine	computing
castrating	chopping	coding	concealing
cataloging	chuckling	coexisting	conceding
catching	chugging	coiling	conceiving
categorizing	churning	coining	concentrating
catering	cinching	collaborating	concerning
caulking	circling	collapsing	concluding
causing	circuiting	collecting	concocting
cautioning	circulating	colliding	condemning
caving	civilizing	colonizing	condensing
cavorting	clacking	coloring	condescending
ceasing	claiming	combating	condoning
ceiling	clamping	combing	conducting
celebrating	clanging	combining	confessing
cementing	clapping	comforting	confiding
censoring	clashing	coming	configuring
centering	clasping	commandeering	confining
centralizing	clattering	commanding	confirming
chaining	clawing	commemorating	confiscating

conflicting
conforming
confronting
confusing
congratulating
congregating
conjuring
connecting
conning
conniving
conquering
consenting
conserving
considering
consigning
consisting
consolidating
consoling
conspiring
constraining
constricting
constructing
consulting
consuming
contacting
containing
contaminating
contending
contesting
contorting
contracting
contradicting
contrasting
contributing
controlling
convene
convening
converging
conversing
converting
conveying
convicting
convincing
cooing
cooking

cooling
cooperating
coordinating
coping
copping
copying
coring
cornering
corralling
correcting
corresponding
corroding
corrupting
cosigning
costing
coughing
counseling
counteracting
counterfeiting
counting
courting
covering
cowering
cracking
crackling
cradling
crafting
cramming
cramping
cranking
crashing
crating
craving
crawling
creaking
cream
creating
creeping
cremating
cringing
crinkling
crippling
crisscrossing
criticizing
critiquing

croaking
crocheting
cropping
crossbreeding
crossing
crowding
crowing
crowning
crucifying
cruising
crumbling
crumpling
crunching
crusading
crushing
crying
crystallizing
cuddling
cueing
cuffing
cuisine
cultivating
cupping
curbing
curdling
curing
curling
cursing
curtailing
curtsying
curving
cushioning
customizing
cutting
cycling
dabbing
dabbling
damaging
dampening
dancing
dangling
daring
darkening
darling
darning

darting
dashing
dating
daunting
dawning
daydream
daydreaming
dazzling
deadening
deafening
dealing
debating
debriefing
debugging
debunking
debuting
decaying
deceiving
deciding
deciphering
decking
declaring
declining
decoding
decontaminating
decorating
decreasing
dedicating
deducting
defacing
defaulting
defeating
defecting
defending
deferring
defining
deflating
deflecting
defrosting
defying
degenerating
degrading
dehydrating
delaying
delegating

deleting
deliberating
delighting
delivering
deluding
demanding
demean
demeaning
demolishing
demonstrating
demoting
denouncing
denting
denying
deodorizing
departing
depending
depicting
depleting
deploring
deploying
deporting
depositing
depreciating
depressing
depriving
deputizing
derailing
deriving
descending
describing
desensitizing
deserting
deserving
designing
desiring
despairing
despising
destroying
detaching
detailing
detaining
detecting
deteriorating
determining

deterring
dethroning
detonating
detouring
devastating
developing
deviating
devising
devoting
devouring
diagnosing
dialing
dicing
dickering
dictating
dieting
differentiating
differing
diffusing
digesting
digging
digitizing
dignifying
digressing
dilating
diluting
diminishing
dimming
dining
dipping
directing
disabling
disagreeing
disappearing
disappointing
disapproving
disarming
disassembling
disbanding
disbarring
disbelieving
disbursing
discarding
discharging
disciplining

disclaiming
disclosing
discoloring
discomforting
disconnecting
discontinuing
discounting
discouraging
discovering
discrediting
discriminating
discussing
disfiguring
disguising
disgusting
dishing
dishonoring
disinfecting
disliking
dislocating
dislodging
dismantling
dismissing
dismounting
disobeying
disorganizing
disowning
dispatching
dispelling
dispensing
dispersing
displacing
displaying
displeasing
disposing
disproving
disputing
disqualifying
disregarding
disrespecting
disrobing
disrupting
dissecting
dissipating
dissolving

distilling
distinct
distorting
distracting
distributing
disturbing
diverting
dividing
diving
divorcing
divulging
divvying
docking
doctoring
documenting
dodging
dogging
doing
domesticating
dominating
domineering
donating
doting
dotting
doubling
doubting
dousing
downgrading
downloading
downplaying
downsizing
dozing
drafting
dragging
draining
dramatizing
draping
drawing
dreading
dream
dreaming
dredging
drenching
dressing
dribbling

drifting
drilling
drink
drinking
dripping
driving
drizzling
droning
drooling
drooping
dropkicking
dropping
drowning
drudging
drugging
drumming
drying
dubbing
duckling
dulling
dumping
dumpling
dunking
duplicating
during
dusting
dwelling
dwindling
dying
earning
earring
earthling
easing
easygoing
eating
eavesdropping
eclipsing
edging
editing
educating
egging
eighteen
ejecting
elaborating
elbowing

electing
electrifying
electrocuting
elevating
eliminating
elongating
eloping
eluding
embarking
embarrassing
embedding
embellishing
embezzling
embossing
embracing
emceeing
emerging
emitting
employing
empowering
emptying
enabling
enacting
enchanting
enclosing
encoding
encompassing
encountering
encouraging
encrypting
endangering
endeavoring
ending
endorsing
enduring
energizing
enforcing
engaging
engineering
engraving
enhancing
enjoying
enlarging
enlightening
enlisting

enraging
enriching
enrolling
entailing
entangling
entering
enterprising
entertaining
enthralling
enticing
entitling
entrapping
entwining
enunciating
enveloping
envisioning
envying
equaling
equating
equipping
eradicating
erasing
erecting
eroding
erupting
escalating
escaping
escorting
establishing
esteem
estimating
etching
evacuating
evading
evaluating
evaporating
evening
everlasting
everything
evoking
evolving
exaggerating
examining
exceeding
excelling

exchanging
exciting
exclaiming
excluding
excusing
executing
exempting
exercising
exerting
exhaling
exhausting
exhibiting
existing
exiting
expanding
expecting
expediting
expelling
experiencing
experimenting
expiring
explaining
exploding
exploiting
exploring
exporting
exposing
expressing
extending
exterminating
extinct
extinguishing
extorting
extracting
extreme
extruding
eyeing
facilitating
facing
fading
failing
faking
falling
falsifying
faltering

familiarizing
fanning
fantasizing
farming
fascinating
fasting
fathering
fattening
faulting
favoring
fawning
faxing
feasting
featuring
feeding
feeling
fencing
fermenting
fertilizing
festering
fetching
feuding
fibbing
fiddling
fielding
fiend
fifteen
fighting
figurine
filling
filtering
finalizing
financing
finding
fingering
finishing
fireproofing
firing
fishing
fitting
fixing
fizzling
flaking
flaming
flapping

flaring
flashing
flattering
flaunting
fleeing
fleeting
flexing
flickering
flicking
flinching
fling
flipping
flirting
floating
flocking
flooding
flooring
flopping
flossing
floundering
flourishing
flowing
flubbing
fluctuating
fluffing
flunking
flushing
flustering
fluttering
flying
foaming
focusing
folding
following
fooling
footing
forbidding
forcing
forecasting
foreclosing
foregoing
foreseeing
foretelling
forewarning
forfeiting

forgetting
forgiving
formalizing
formatting
forming
formulating
forsaking
forthcoming
fortifying
forwarding
fostering
fouling
founding
fourteen
fracturing
fragmenting
framing
freaking
freeing
freeloading
freezing
freshening
fretting
frightening
frolicking
frosting
frowning
frustrating
frying
fudging
fueling
fulfilling
fumbling
fumigating
functioning
funding
furnishing
fussing
gagging
gaining
galloping
gambling
gaming
gaping
gardening

gargling
garnishing
gasoline
gathering
gauging
gawking
gazing
gearing
generating
gesturing
getting
gifting
giggling
giving
glancing
glaring
glazing
gliding
glimmering
glimpsing
glistening
glittering
gloating
globetrotting
glorifying
glossing
glowing
gnawing
goading
going
golfing
goofing
gossiping
governing
grabbing
grading
graduating
grandstanding
granting
grasping
gratifying
grating
gravitating
graying
grazing

green	harmonizing	hogging	impairing
greeting	harnessing	hoisting	implementing
grilling	harping	holding	imploding
grinding	harvesting	hollering	imploring
grinning	hassling	homing	implying
gripping	hastening	honeymooning	importing
gritting	hatching	honing	imposing
groaning	hating	honking	impressing
grooming	hauling	honoring	improving
grooving	haunting	hooking	improvising
groping	having	hoping	inching
grounding	hawking	hopping	inclining
grouping	hazing	hosting	including
growing	heading	hounding	increasing
growling	healing	housebreaking	incurring
grueling	heaping	housing	indenting
grumbling	hearing	hovering	indexing
grunting	heartbreaking	howling	indicating
guarding	heating	huddling	indicting
guiding	heaving	hugging	indulging
gumming	heckling	humiliating	infecting
gunning	hedging	humming	inflaming
gushing	heeding	humoring	inflating
guzzling	heeling	hunching	inflicting
gyrating	heightening	hunkering	influencing
hacking	helping	hunting	informing
haggling	hemming	hurdling	inhaling
hailing	herding	hurrying	inheriting
hairstyling	hesitating	hurting	inhibiting
Halloween	hibernating	hushing	initiating
hallucinating	hiccuping	hustling	injecting
halting	hiding	hydrating	injuring
hammering	highlighting	hygiene	ink
hamming	hijacking	hypnotizing	inning
hampering	hiking	icing	inquiring
handcuffing	hindering	identifying	inserting
handing	hinging	idling	insisting
handling	hinting	igniting	inspecting
handwriting	hiring	ignoring	inspiring
hanging	hissing	illuminating	installing
happening	hitchhiking	illustrating	instilling
harassing	hitting	imagining	instinct
harboring	hoarding	imitating	instructing
hardening	hobnobbing	immersing	insulting
harming	hocking	impacting	intending

intensifying	judging	leering	loving
interesting	juggling	legalizing	lowering
interning	jumbling	lending	lubricating
interpreting	jumping	lengthening	lugging
interrupting	kayaking	lessening	lumbering
intersecting	keen	lettering	lumping
interviewing	keeping	letting	lurking
intimidating	kenneling	leveling	lying
intoxicating	kicking	leveraging	machine
intriguing	kidding	liberating	maddening
introducing	kidnapping	licensing	magazine
intruding	killing	licking	magnifying
invading	king	lien	mailing
inventing	kink	lifting	mainstream
inverting	kissing	lightening	mainstreaming
investigating	kneading	lightning	maintaining
investing	kneeling	limiting	majoring
inviting	knitting	limousine	making
invoicing	knocking	limping	managing
involving	knowing	lingering	mandating
irking	laboring	lining	maneuvering
ironing	lacing	link	manicuring
irrigating	lacquering	linking	manipulating
irritating	lagging	liquidating	manufacturing
isolating	laminating	listening	mapping
issuing	landing	listing	marching
itching	landscaping	littering	marine
itemizing	lapping	living	marketing
jabbing	lasting	loading	marking
jamming	latching	loafing	marring
jarring	lathering	loaning	marrying
jaywalking	laughing	lobbying	masking
jeopardizing	launching	locating	masquerading
jerking	laundering	locking	massaging
jetting	layering	lodging	mastering
jiggling	laying	logging	matching
jilting	leading	loitering	materializing
jinx	leaking	longing	matting
jinxing	lean	looking	maturing
jogging	leaning	looping	mauling
joining	leaping	loosening	maximizing
joking	learning	looting	mean
jolting	leasing	lopping	meaning
jotting	leaving	losing	measuring
joyriding	lecturing	lounging	meddling

meditating
meeting
melting
menacing
mending
mentioning
mentoring
merchandising
merging
mesmerizing
messing
metering
mewing
microwaving
migrating
milking
milling
mimicking
mincing
minding
mingling
miniaturizing
minimizing
mining
mirroring
misbehaving
misconstruing
misguiding
misjudging
misleading
misplacing
misreading
missing
misspelling
misting
mixing
moaning
mobbing
mobilizing
mocking
modeling
modifying
moistening
moisturizing
molding

molesting
monitoring
monogramming
mooning
moping
mopping
morning
mothering
motioning
motivating
motorcycling
mounding
mourning
mouthwatering
moving
mowing
mucking
muffling
mugging
multiplying
munching
murdering
murmuring
mustering
mutating
muttering
nabbing
nagging
nailing
naming
napping
narrating
narrowing
navigating
nearing
necking
nectarine
needing
needling
neglecting
negotiating
neighboring
netting
networking
neutering

neutralizing
nibbling
nicking
nicotine
nineteen
nipping
nitpicking
nixing
nodding
nominating
normalizing
notating
nothing
noticing
notifying
noting
nourishing
nudging
nuking
numbing
nursing
nurturing
nuzzling
obeying
objecting
obscene
obscuring
observing
obsessing
obstructing
obtaining
occupying
occurring
offending
offering
offsetting
okaying
omitting
ongoing
oozing
opening
operating
opposing
opting
ordering

organizing
originating
oscillating
ousting
outbidding
outfoxing
outgrowing
outing
outlasting
outlining
outliving
outmaneuvering
outnumbering
outpouring
outselling
outshining
outsmarting
outstanding
outweighing
outwitting
overcharging
overcoming
overdrawing
overeating
overflowing
overgrowing
overpowering
overruling
overseeing
overwhelming
owing
owning
pacing
packaging
packing
padding
paddling
paging
painstaking
painting
pairing
pampering
paneling
panhandling
panicking

panting	persecuting	plopping	premiering
parachuting	persevering	plotting	preparing
parading	persisting	plugging	prepaying
paralyzing	perspiring	plumbing	preplanning
pardoning	persuading	plumping	prepping
parenting	pertaining	plundering	prescribing
parking	perturbing	plunging	presenting
paroling	pestering	plying	preserving
partaking	petitioning	poaching	preshrink
participating	petting	pointing	preshrinking
parting	phasing	poking	presiding
partnering	phoning	polarizing	presoaking
passing	photographing	polishing	pressing
pasteurizing	phrasing	pollinating	pressuring
pasting	picketing	polling	pressurizing
patching	picking	polluting	presuming
patenting	pickling	pondering	pretending
patrolling	picturing	pooling	prevailing
patting	piecing	popping	preventing
pausing	piercing	populating	previewing
paving	piling	portraying	preying
pawing	pilling	posing	pricing
pawning	pimping	positioning	pricking
paying	pinching	possessing	prickling
peaking	pink	posting	priming
pecking	pinning	postponing	printing
pedaling	pinpointing	posturing	pristine
peddling	pioneering	potting	probing
peeing	piping	pounding	proceeding
peeking	pitching	pouring	processing
peeling	pitting	pouting	proclaiming
peering	pitying	powering	procrastinating
pegging	pivoting	praising	prodding
penetrating	placing	praying	producing
perceiving	plaguing	preaching	professing
perching	planning	preceding	profiling
perfecting	planting	precinct	profiting
performing	plastering	precipitating	programming
perishing	playing	predicting	progressing
perjuring	plaything	predisposing	prohibiting
perking	pleading	preempting	projecting
permeating	pleasing	preexisting	prolonging
permitting	pleating	prefacing	promenading
perpetrating	pledging	preferring	promising
perplexing	plodding	preheating	promoting

prompting	qualifying	rearing	reforming
pronouncing	quarantine	rearranging	refraining
proofing	quarreling	reasoning	refreshing
proofreading	quartering	reassuring	refrigerating
propelling	queen	rebating	refrying
proposing	questioning	rebelling	refueling
propositioning	quilting	rebuilding	refunding
propping	quitting	recalling	refurbishing
prorating	quivering	recanting	refusing
prosecuting	quizzing	recapping	regaining
prospering	quoting	receding	regarding
protecting	racing	receiving	regime
protein	racketeering	recessing	registering
protesting	racking	rechecking	regressing
protruding	radiating	reciprocating	regretting
providing	raffling	reciting	rehabilitating
proving	rafting	reckoning	rehearsing
prowling	raging	reclaiming	reigning
pruning	raiding	reclining	reimbursing
prying	railing	recognizing	reinforcing
publishing	raining	recoiling	reining
puckering	raising	recollecting	reinstating
pudding	raking	recommending	rejecting
puffing	rambling	reconciling	rejoicing
puking	ramming	reconfirming	rejoining
pulling	ramping	reconsidering	rejuvenating
pulsating	ranging	recording	relapsing
pulverizing	ranking	recouping	relating
pummeling	ransacking	recovering	relaxing
pumping	raping	recruiting	relaying
punching	rappelling	recuperating	releasing
punctuating	rapping	recurring	relieving
puncturing	ratcheting	recycling	relishing
punishing	rating	redecorating	reliving
punting	rationalizing	redeem	reloading
purchasing	rationing	redeeming	relying
purging	rattling	redefining	remaining
purifying	ravaging	redoing	remaking
purring	raveling	reducing	remarking
pursing	ravine	reeking	remembering
pursuing	raving	reeling	reminding
pushing	reaching	referring	reminiscing
putting	reacting	refilling	remitting
puzzling	reading	refining	remodeling
quacking	realizing	reflecting	removing

renaming
rendering
renewing
renovating
renting
reorganizing
repacking
repairing
repaying
repealing
repeating
repelling
replacing
replaying
replenishing
replying
reporting
representing
repressing
reprising
reproducing
requesting
requiring
rerunning
rescuing
researching
reselling
resembling
resenting
reserving
resetting
reshaping
residing
resigning
resisting
resolving
resorting
respecting
responding
restarting
resting
restoring
restraining
restricting
resulting

resuming
retailing
retaining
retaking
retaliating
rethink
rethinking
retiring
retouching
retracing
retracting
retreating
retrieving
returning
reuniting
reusing
revealing
revenging
reversing
reverting
reviewing
revising
revitalizing
revoking
revolting
revolutionizing
revolving
rewarding
rewinding
rewriting
rhyming
ribbing
ricocheting
ridding
riding
rifling
rigging
righting
ring
ringing
rink
rinsing
ripening
ripping
rippling

rising
risking
rivaling
roaming
roaring
roasting
robbing
rocketing
rocking
rolling
romancing
romping
roofing
rooming
roosting
rooting
roping
rotating
rotting
roughening
roughing
rounding
routine
roving
rowing
rubbing
ruffling
ruining
ruling
rumbling
rummaging
running
rupturing
rushing
rusting
rustling
sabotaging
sacking
sacrificing
saddling
safeguarding
sagging
sailing
saline
saltine

saluting
salvaging
sampling
sanctioning
sandblasting
sanding
sapping
sardine
sashaying
satisfying
saturating
sauntering
sautéing
saving
savoring
sawing
saying
scabbing
scaffolding
scalding
scaling
scalloping
scamming
scampering
scanning
scaring
scarring
scathing
scattering
scavenging
scene
scheduling
scheme
scheming
schlepping
schooling
scintillating
scoffing
scolding
scooping
scooting
scoping
scorching
scoring
scorning

scouring	sending	shoveling	skinning
scouting	sensationalizing	shoving	skipping
scowling	sensing	showing	skirting
scrambling	sentencing	shrieking	skydiving
scraping	separating	shrink	skyrocketing
scrapping	sequencing	shrinking	skywriting
scratching	serenading	shriveling	slackening
scrawling	serene	shrugging	slacking
scream	serving	shuddering	slamming
screaming	setting	shuffling	slandering
screeching	settling	shunning	slanting
screen	seventeen	shutting	slapping
screening	severing	sibling	slaughtering
screwing	sewing	sickening	slaving
scribbling	shacking	sidelining	slaying
scrimping	shading	sidestepping	sledding
scrolling	shagging	sidetracking	sleeping
scrounging	shaking	siding	sleepwalking
scrubbing	shampooing	sighing	slenderizing
scrunching	shaping	sighting	slicing
scrutinizing	sharing	sightseeing	sliding
scuffing	sharpening	signaling	slimming
scuffling	shattering	signifying	slinking
scurrying	shaving	signing	slipping
sealing	shearing	simmering	slithering
seam	shedding	simplifying	slitting
searching	sheen	simulating	slobbering
searing	sheeting	sing	sloping
seasoning	shelling	singing	slouching
seating	sheltering	sink	slugging
seconding	shelving	sinking	slumming
securing	shielding	sinning	slumping
sedating	shifting	siphoning	slurring
seducing	shilling	sipping	smacking
seeding	shimmering	sitting	smashing
seeing	shining	sixteen	smattering
seeking	shipping	sizing	smearing
seem	shirking	sizzling	smelling
seeming	shivering	skating	smiling
seen	shocking	sketching	smirking
segmenting	shooting	skewing	smithereens
segregating	shopping	skidding	smoking
seizing	shortening	skiing	smoldering
selecting	shorting	skimming	smoothing
selling	shouting	skimping	smothering

smudging
snacking
snagging
snaking
snapping
snatching
sneaking
sneering
sneezing
snickering
sniffing
snipping
snoozing
snoring
snorkeling
snorting
snowing
snubbing
snuffing
snuggling
soaking
soaping
soaring
sobering
socking
softening
soiling
soldering
soliciting
soloing
solving
something
soothing
sorting
sounding
sowing
soybean
spacing
spanning
sparing
sparking
sparring
spattering
spawning
spaying

speaking
spearing
specializing
specifying
speculating
speeding
spellbinding
spelling
spending
spewing
spiking
spilling
spinning
spiraling
spitting
splashing
splattering
splicing
splintering
splinting
splitting
splurging
spoiling
sponsoring
spooking
spooning
sporting
spotting
spouting
spraining
sprawling
spraying
spreading
spring
springing
sprinkling
sprinting
sprouting
sprucing
spurning
spurring
spurting
sputtering
spying
squabbling

squandering
squatting
squawking
squeaking
squealing
squeezing
squinting
squirming
squirting
stabbing
stabilizing
stacking
staffing
staggering
staging
stagnating
staining
staking
stalking
stalling
stammering
stampeding
stamping
standardizing
standing
stapling
starching
staring
starring
starting
startling
starving
stashing
staying
stealing
steam
steaming
steeling
steeping
steering
stemming
stepping
sterilizing
sterling
stewing

sticking
stiffening
stifling
stimulating
sting
stinging
stink
stinking
stipulating
stirring
stitching
stocking
stoking
stomping
stopping
storing
stowing
straddling
straggling
straightening
straining
strangling
strapping
straying
streaking
stream
streaming
strengthening
stressing
stretching
striding
striking
string
striping
stripping
striving
stroking
strolling
struggling
strumming
strutting
stubbing
studying
stuffing
stumbling

stunning	suturing	tarnishing	throwing
stuttering	swabbing	tarring	thrusting
styling	swaggering	tasting	thundering
subbing	swallowing	tattling	thwarting
subduing	swapping	tattooing	ticketing
subjecting	swarming	taunting	ticking
subletting	swatting	taxing	tickling
submarine	swaying	teaching	tightening
submerging	swearing	team	tilting
submersing	sweating	teaming	timesaving
submitting	sweeping	tearing	timing
subscribing	sweetening	teasing	tingling
subsiding	swelling	teeing	tinkering
substituting	swerving	teen	tinting
subtracting	swimming	teetering	tipping
succeeding	swindling	teething	tiptoeing
succumbing	swing	telecasting	tiring
sucking	swinging	telemarketing	toasting
suffering	swiping	telling	toddling
suffocating	swirling	tempering	toggling
suggesting	switching	tempting	tolerating
suing	swiveling	tenderizing	toning
suiting	swooning	tending	tooting
sulking	swooping	terminating	topping
summarizing	sympathizing	terrifying	tormenting
summing	tackling	terrorizing	torturing
summoning	tagging	testifying	tossing
sunning	tailgating	testing	toting
sunscreen	tailing	tethering	touching
supervising	tainting	texting	toughening
supplying	taking	thanking	touring
supporting	talking	thawing	towering
suppressing	tallying	theme	towing
supreme	tambourine	theorizing	toying
surfing	taming	thickening	tracing
surging	tampering	thing	tracking
surpassing	tangerine	think	trading
surprising	tangling	thinking	trafficking
surrendering	tanking	thinning	trailing
surrounding	tanning	thirteen	training
surveying	tantalizing	threading	trampling
surviving	tapering	threatening	trampoline
suspecting	taping	thrilling	transcending
suspending	tapping	thriving	transcribing
sustaining	targeting	throbbing	transferring

transforming
translating
transmitting
transpiring
transplanting
transporting
transposing
trapping
trashing
traumatizing
traveling
treading
treasuring
treating
trekking
trembling
trending
trendsetting
trespassing
tricking
trickling
triggering
trimming
tripling
tripping
triumphing
trolling
trotting
troubling
trucking
trumpeting
trusting
trying
tubing
tucking
tugging
tumbling
tuning
tunneling
turning
tutoring
tweaking
tweeting
twinkling
twirling

twisting
twitching
tying
typecasting
typesetting
typing
ulcerating
unassuming
unbecoming
unbending
unbuttoning
unconvincing
underlying
unfolding
unforeseen
unifying
uniting
unknowing
unleashing
unloading
unlocking
unnerving
unraveling
unwinding
upbringing
upcoming
updating
upgrading
upholding
upholstering
uplifting
uprising
uprooting
upsetting
upstaging
upswing
urging
ushering
using
utilizing
uttering
vacating
vacationing
vaccinating
vaccine

vacuuming
validating
vanishing
vaporizing
varnishing
varying
vaulting
ventilating
venting
venturing
verbalizing
verging
verifying
vetoing
vibrating
victimizing
videoing
viewing
violating
visiting
visualizing
vocalizing
voicing
voiding
volleying
volunteering
vomiting
voting
vouching
vowing
waddling
wading
wagering
wagging
waging
waiting
waiving
wakening
walking
walloping
wallowing
waltzing
wandering
wanting
warming

warning
warping
warranting
washing
wasting
watching
watering
waterproofing
wavering
waving
waxing
weakening
weakling
wearing
weaseling
weathering
weatherproofing
weaving
webbing
wedding
wedging
weeding
weighing
welcoming
welding
wetting
whacking
wheeling
wheezing
whetting
whiffing
whimpering
whining
whipping
whirling
whisking
whispering
whistling
whitening
whittling
wholesaling
widening
wiggling
willing
wilting

winding
wing
winging
wink
winking
winning
winterizing
wiping
wiring
wishing
withering
withholding
withstanding

witnessing
wolverine
wondering
woodworking
wooing
working
worrying
worsening
worshipping
wracking
wrangling
wrapping
wrecking

wrenching
wrestling
wring
wringing
wrinkling
writing
yachting
yanking
yawning
yearling
yearning
yelling
yelping

yielding
yodeling
zapping
zeroing
zigzagging
zinc
zing
zinging
zipping
zoning
zooming

[E]r

as in: **sincere**

adhere
appear
atmosphere
beard
beer
biosphere
brassiere
career
cashier
cashmere
cavalier
cheer
clear
commandeer

dear
deer
disappear
domineer
ear
engineer
fear
fierce
gear
hear
here
insincere
leer
mere

near
overhear
peer
persevere
pier
pierce
pioneer
premier
racketeer
rear
reindeer
sear
severe
shear

sheer
sincere
smear
sneer
souvenir
spear
steer
tear
tier
veneer
volunteer
weird
year
yesteryear

[e]

[e]   as in: step

Includes alternate pronunciations, as in sexy* pronounced sex-eh.

abbreviated	adopted	ambitious	associate
abducted	advantage	amended	associated
abided	advantageous	amorous	assorted
aborted	adventurous	amounted	astounded
abreast	advocate	animated	atrocious
abscess	advocated	anklet	attempted
accelerated	aerated	annex	attended
accented	affect	annihilated	attracted
accentuated	affectionate	anonymous	attributed
accept	affiliate	anticipated	audited
access	affiliated	anxious	August
acclimated	afflicted	anybody*	authenticated
accommodated	ageless	apparatus	automated
accounted	aggravated	applauded	averted
accumulated	agitated	appointed	avoided
accurate	ahead	appreciated	awaited
acknowledge	aided	apprehended	awarded
acquainted	aimless	appropriate	baby*
acreage	airhead	appropriated	bachelorette
acted	alerted	approximate	backhanded
activated	alias	architect	backrest
actress	alienated	armrest	backstretch
adapted	allege	arrest	badly*
added	alleviated	asparagus	baggage
addicted	allocated	aspect	baited
address	allotted	assassinated	ballad
adept	alluded	assaulted	ballot
adequate	alphabet	asserted	bandage
adjusted	already*	assess	banded
administrated	alternate	asset	bankrupted
admitted	alternated	assisted	banquet

barely*
barrack
barricaded
basinet
basket
bassinet
batted
beaded
bearded
bed
bedspread
befriended
beg
belated
beloved
belted
bended
benefitted
best
bet
beverage
bias
biceps
biggest
bigot
bishop
bitterness
blanket
blasted
bled
blended
bless
blinded
bloated
blockhead
bloodshed
blotted
blurted
boarded
boasted
bobsled
body*
bogus
boisterous
bolted

bombarded
bonded
bonehead
boniest
bonnet
bonus
booklet
boosted
booted
bootleg
bossiest
bottleneck
bottomless
bounciest
bounded
boundless
boycotted
bracelet
bracket
braided
brainless
branded
bravest
bread
breakfast
breakneck
breast
breath
breathless
bred
brightest
brightness
broadcasted
brokerage
brooded
brunette
bucket
budded
budget
bullet
burlesque
business
busted
cabbage
cabinet

cactus
cadet
calculated
calibrated
callous
calmness
campus
cantankerous
canvas
captivated
carbonated
carded
careless
caress
carob
carpet
carriage
carrot
carted
cascaded
casket
cassette
castrated
cautious
cavorted
celebrated
celibate
cemented
census
certificate
chanted
charted
cheated
check
chef
chess
chocolate
choicest
chorus
Christmas
cigarette
circulated
circus
cited
citrus

clarinet
cleanest
cleanliness
clearest
cleavage
climate
closeness
closest
closet
clotted
clouded
clueless
coasted
coated
cobweb
coded
coed
coldest
collaborated
collect
college
collegiate
collided
colorless
combated
comet
comforted
commanded
commemorated
commended
commentated
commented
commiserated
committed
communicated
commuted
compacted
compass
compassionate
compensated
competed
completed
complex
complicated
complimented

composted
compounded
comprehended
compress
computed
conceded
conceited
concentrated
concept
concluded
concocted
condescended
conducted
confederate
confess
confided
confiscated
conflicted
confronted
congest
conglomerate
congratulated
congregated
congress
connect
conquest
conscientious
conscious
consciousness
consented
considerate
consisted
consolidated
conspicuous
constipated
constricted
constructed
consulted
consummate
consummated
contacted
contagious
contaminated
contended
contest

context
continuous
contorted
contracted
contradicted
contrasted
contributed
converted
convex
convicted
coolest
cooperated
coordinate
coordinated
corded
cornbread
corporate
correct
corresponded
corroded
corrupted
cottage
counted
counteracted
counterfeited
countless
courageous
courted
courteous
crafted
crated
crazy*
creaminess
created
credited
cremated
cricket
crooked
croquette
crossbred
crowded
crusaded
crusted
cultivated
curious

cutest
cutlet
daddy*
damage
dangerous
darkness
darted
dated
daybed
dead
deadhead
deaf
death
deathbed
debated
debt
decaffeinated
decided
deck
decoded
decontaminated
decorated
dedicated
deducted
deepest
defaulted
defeated
defect
defended
deflated
deflect
defrosted
degenerate
degenerated
degraded
dehydrated
delegate
delegated
deleted
deliberate
deliberated
delicate
delicious
delighted
delirious

deluded
demanded
demented
demonstrated
demoted
dented
departed
depended
depicted
depleted
deported
deposited
depreciated
depress
deserted
designated
desk
desolate
desperate
detect
deteriorated
detest
detonated
devastated
deviated
devious
devoted
diabetes
dictated
diet
differentiated
digest
digress
dilated
diluted
dimwitted
dinette
direct
disadvantage
disappointed
disastrous
disbanded
discarded
disconnect
discounted

discourage
discredited
discriminated
disgusted
dishonest
disinfect
diskette
dislocated
dismounted
disproportionate
disputed
disregarded
disrespect
disrupted
dissect
dissipated
distorted
distracted
distress
distributed
diverted
divided
doctorate
documented
domesticated
dominated
donated
doorstep
doted
dotted
doubted
doubtless
downgraded
downloaded
drafted
dragnet
drainage
dread
dredge
dress
drifted
dryness
dubious
duet
dullest

duplex
duplicate
duplicated
dusted
earliest
earnest
easiest
edge
educated
effect
effortless
egg
egghead
eject
elaborate
elaborated
elated
eldest
elect
elevated
eliminated
elongated
eluded
embarrass
embed
emitted
enacted
enchanted
encoded
encompass
encourage
encrypted
ended
endless
enlisted
enormous
enthusiast
enunciated
envious
equated
eradicated
erect
eroded
erupted
escalated

escorted
esophagus
estimate
etch
etiquette
evacuated
evaded
evaluated
evaporated
everybody*
evicted
exaggerated
exceeded
except
excess
excited
excluded
executed
exerted
exhausted
exhibited
existed
exited
expanded
expect
expedited
experimented
exploded
exploited
exported
express
extended
exterminated
extorted
extracted
extruded
eyeglasses
eyewitness
fabricated
fabulous
facet
facilitated
faded
fainted
famous

farfetched
farmstead
farsighted
farthest
fascinated
fasted
fated
faucet
fearless
fed
fermented
ferocious
ferret
fetch
fetus
fictitious
filtrated
finale *
finesse
finest
fishnet
fitness
fitted
fixated
flatbed
flathead
flaunted
flawless
fleck
fled
flesh
flex
flirtatious
flirted
floated
flooded
fluctuated
focus
folded
footstep
forecasted
forehead
forest
forfeited
forget

forgiven
forgiveness
formatted
formulated
fortunate
founded
fragmented
frequented
fresh
fret
frivolous
frosted
frustrated
fumigated
funded
fungus
funny*
furious
furnace
gadget
gaited
garbage
gated
gazette
generated
generous
genius
gently*
get
gifted
glamorous
glided
gloated
glorious
goaded
goblet
goddess
goodness
gooseneck
gorgeous
gracious
graded
graduate
graduated
grandstanded

granted
grated
gravitated
greeted
gritted
grounded
grunted
guarded
guess
guest
guided
gyrated
hairless
hallucinated
halted
hammock
handcrafted
handed
handset
happiness
happy*
hardest
hardhead
harness
harvest
hated
hatred
haunted
havoc
hazardous
head
headdress
headset
heated
heavy*
heck
hedge
heeded
helmet
helpless
herded
hesitated
hex
hiatus
hibernated

highness
hilarious
hinted
hoarded
hoisted
honest
hooded
hopeless
hornet
hostage
hosted
hostess
hounded
humiliated
humorous
hundred
hungry*
hunted
hurry*
hydrated
idiot
ignited
illness
illuminated
illustrated
image
imitated
immaculate
immediate
impacted
imperfect
implanted
implemented
imploded
imported
impress
inaccurate
inadequate
included
inconsiderate
incorporated
indebted
indented
index
indicated

indicted
indirect
infect
inflated
inflicted
infrared
ingenious
inherited
inhibited
initiated
inject
innovated
insect
inserted
insisted
inspect
instead
instep
instructed
insulated
insulted
intellect
intended
interest
intermediate
interpret
interrupted
intersect
intimate
intimidated
intoxicated
intravenous
intricate
inundated
invaded
invented
inverted
invest
investigated
invited
irrigated
irritated
isolated
jacket
jaded

jagged	limitless	message	net
jealous	lioness	met	newest
jet	liquidated	method	newlywed
jilted	listed	meticulous	next
jolted	listless	migrated	nicest
jotted	loaded	mildest	nobody*
joyous	located	mileage	nodded
jutted	locket	minded	nominated
keg	loneliness	minted	nonetheless
kept	lonely*	minus	nosy*
kidded	longest	minute	notated
kindhearted	looted	miraculous	noted
kindly*	loudest	miscellaneous	notorious
kindness	lousiest	mischievous	nucleus
kismet	lousy*	misguided	nugget
kneaded	lovely*	misled	numerous
knighted	lubricated	misread	nutmeg
knitted	luggage	misstep	nutritious
knotted	luminous	mistress	object
knowledge	luscious	moderate	obligated
lady*	lusted	moderated	oblivious
laminate	lustrous	modest	obsess
laminated	luxurious	molded	obvious
landed	magnet	molest	octave
language	manage	money*	offended
largest	mandated	monotonous	offset
lasted	manipulated	monstrous	oldest
lately*	market	moped	omelet
latest	marriage	mortgage	ominous
layette	marry*	motivated	only*
lazy*	marvelous	murderous	onset
lead	masqueraded	mutated	operated
leanest	mated	mysterious	orchestrated
led	matted	naked	oriented
ledge	mattress	nameless	originated
leg	meanest	narrated	orphanage
legitimate	mediated	nasty*	outfitted
less	medicated	navigated	outlasted
let	meditated	nearsighted	outlet
letterhead	melted	neck	outrageous
lettuce	menace	necklace	outwitted
leverage	mended	needed	overhead
liberated	mercy*	neglect	overzealous
lighthearted	merriment	negotiated	package
likeness	mess	nervous	packet

padded	pledge	prospect	recommended
painted	plodded	prosperous	recorded
palace	plotted	protect	recruited
palate	pocket	protest	recuperated
palette	poet	provided	red
pallet	pointed	pulsated	redecorated
palpitated	pointless	punctuated	redhead
panted	poisonous	puppet	redneck
paperless	pollinated	purchase	reflect
paraded	pomegranate	purebred	reflex
parrot	pompous	purely*	refresh
participated	populated	purpose	refrigerated
party*	porous	quartet	refunded
passage	possess	quiet	regarded
passionate	postage	quilted	regardless
pasted	postdated	quintet	regress
patriot	pothead	quintuplet	regret
patted	pounded	racket	regulated
paycheck	powerless	radiated	rehabilitated
peck	precarious	radius	reinstated
peg	precious	rafted	reject
pellet	preface	ragged	rejuvenated
penetrated	premed	raided	related
penniless	premeditated	rally*	relent
pent	prep	rambunctious	relentless
pep	preset	rarely*	religious
perfect	press	ratchet	reloaded
perforated	prestigious	rated	reminded
perilous	presumptuous	ratted	remitted
permeated	pretty*	ravage	renovated
perplex	previous	ravenous	rented
persuaded	priceless	reacted	repeated
perverted	priestess	read	repetitious
pest	princess	ready*	reported
pet	private	really*	represented
picket	privilege	rebated	repress
pilgrimage	process	rebellious	reputed
pilot	procrastinated	recanted	request
pinhead	profess	receded	resented
planet	progress	recess	reset
planted	project	recheck	resided
plated	promenaded	reciprocated	resisted
plated	promiscuous	recited	resorted
pleated	proportionate	reckless	respect
pled	prorated	recollect	responded

rest	saturated	shorted	spinach
restarted	savage	shred	spineless
restated	says	shrinkage	spirited
restless	scalded	shrouded	splinted
restricted	scandalous	sickbed	spontaneous
resulted	scarlet	sickness	spooky*
retaliated	scary*	sidestep	spotless
retracted	scented	sighted	spotted
retreated	schlep	silhouette	spread
retrospect	scolded	silly*	sprinted
reunited	scooted	simulated	sprouted
reverted	scouted	simultaneous	squatted
revolted	scripted	sincerely*	squinted
rewarded	scrumptious	sinus	squirted
ridiculous	seabed	situated	stagnated
righteous	seated	skated	starlet
rigorous	secluded	sketch	stated
roasted	secret	skidded	status
rocket	sedated	skinhead	stead
roosted	seeded	skirted	steady*
rosette	segmented	skyrocket	step
rotated	segregated	slanted	stimulated
rotted	select	slated	stimulus
roughage	senate	sled	stipulated
roughneck	senseless	sleepless	stomach
roulette	sensuous	sleeveless	storage
rounded	separate	slept	stranded
rowdy*	separated	slighted	strenuous
rugged	serenaded	slotted	strep
rummage	serious	slowly*	stress
rusty*	set	smallest	stretch
ruthless	sewage	smartest	strongest
sacred	sex	socket	strongly*
saddest	sexy*	solicited	stunted
safeguarded	shaded	somebody*	stupendous
safely*	shady*	sophisticated	stylus
safest	shameless	sorted	subconscious
said	shed	sounded	subject
salad	shielded	spacious	sublet
salted	shifted	spearhead	subtracted
saluted	shiny*	spec	success
salvage	shipwreck	speck	suddenly*
sandblasted	shirtless	speculated	suffocated
sanded	shortage	sped	suggest
sapped	shortbread	speechless	suited

sundress	tolerated	unloaded	voted
sunglasses	tormented	unsophisticated	voyage
sunset	totally*	unwanted	wadded
supermarket	traded	unwarranted	waded
superstitious	transacted	unwed	waited
supported	transcended	updated	waitress
suppress	translated	upgraded	walrus
surely*	transmitted	uproarious	warhead
surface	transplanted	uprooted	warranted
suspect	transported	upset	wasted
suspicious	treacherous	usage	waterbed
swatted	tread	useless	wattage
sweat	treated	vacated	weakness
sweaty*	trek	vaccinated	web
sweetbread	tremendous	validated	wed
sweetly*	triceps	various	wedge
swept	trinket	vaulted	weighted
tablet	triplicate	velvet	weightless
tailgated	trotted	venomous	wellness
tainted	trumpet	venous	west
talented	trusted	vented	wet
tallest	twisted	ventilated	whet
target	typeset	versus	whiskey*
tasted	ulcerated	very*	wholehearted
taunted	ultimate	vest	wicked
tech	ultraviolet	vested	widespread
tedious	unaffected	vet	wilderness
template	unanimous	vibrated	winded
tempted	unbiased	vicious	wireless
tended	uncommitted	victorious	wisely*
terminated	unconscious	vignette	witness
terrace	uncorrected	vigorous	wondrous
test	undergraduate	village	woodshed
text	underprivileged	villainous	worded
thesaurus	undress	vintage	worry*
thirsty*	unedited	violated	worthless
thoroughbred	unexpected	violet	wreck
thread	unfed	virus	wreckage
threat	unfolded	vivacious	wretch
thunderous	unfortunate	voided	yardage
thwarted	uninhibited	voltage	yes
ticket	unisex	voluminous	yet
timeless	united	voluptuous	youngest
tinted	unless	vomited	zealous
toilet	unlimited	vortex	zest

[e]l

as in: **sell**

barbell
bell
belle
belt
bombshell
bookshelf
caramel
carousel
cartel
cell
clamshell
clientele
compel
cowbell
dealt
dell
dispel
doorbell
dumbbell
dwell
eggshell

elf
else
excel
expel
farewell
fell
felt
foretell
gazelle
gel
health
heartfelt
held
hell
help
herself
himself
hotel
itself
lapel
melt

misspell
morsel
motel
myself
Noel
nutshell
ourselves
outsell
overwhelm
parallel
pastel
personnel
propel
quarrel
quell
rappel
realm
repel
resell
seashell
self

sell
shelf
shell
smell
spell
stairwell
stealth
swell
tell
themselves
twelve
undersell
unparalleled
upheld
wealth
weld
well
yell
yelp
yourself

[e]m/n

as in: **stem**

Includes alternate pronunciations, as in saving* pronounced save'n.

abandon
abandoning*
abbreviating*
abdomen
abducting*
abiding*
aborting*
absence
absent
absorbance
absorbent
absorbing*

abstaining*
abstinence
abundance
abundant
abusing*
accelerating*
accent
acceptance
accepting*
accessing*
accessorizing*
accident

acclimating*
accommodating*
accompaniment
accompanying*
accomplishing*
accomplishment
accordance
according*
accountant
accounting*
accumulating*
accusing*

achievement
achieving*
aching*
acing*
acknowledging*
acquaintance
acquiring*
acting*
activating*
adamant
adapting*
addicting*

adding*	alignment	apparent	assigning*
addressing*	allegiance	appealing*	assignment
adhering*	alleging*	appearance	assistance
adjacent	alleviating*	appearing*	assistant
adjoining*	alliance	appetizing*	assisting*
adjourning*	allocating*	applauding*	assorting*
adjusting*	allotment	appliance	assortment
adjustment	allotting*	applicant	assuming*
administering*	allowance	applying*	assurance
admiring*	allowing*	appointing*	assuring*
admitting*	alluding*	appointment	astonishing*
adolescence	alluring*	appraising*	astonishment
adolescent	almond	appreciating*	astounding*
adopting*	altering*	apprehend	astringent
adoring*	alternating*	apprehending*	atonement
adorning*	amazement	approaching*	atoning*
advancement	amazing*	approving*	attaching*
advancing*	ambiance	apron	attachment
advertisement	ambient	arching*	attacking*
advertising*	ambulance	archiving*	attaining*
advisement	amen	arguing*	attempt
advising*	amend	argument	attempting*
advocating*	amending*	arisen	attend
affecting*	amendment	arising*	attendance
affirming*	amplifying*	arousing*	attendant
affixing*	amusement	arraigning*	attending*
afflicting*	amusing*	arraignment	attracting*
affluent	analyzing*	arrangement	attributing*
again	anchoring*	arranging*	auctioning*
against	ancient	arresting*	audience
aggravating*	angering*	arriving*	auditing*
aging*	annihilating*	arrogance	augment
agonizing*	announcement	arrogant	augmenting*
agreeing*	announcing*	arson	authoring*
agreement	annoyance	artisan	authorizing*
ahem	annoying*	ashen	autism
aiding*	answering*	asking*	autographing*
ailment	antagonizing*	aspen	automating*
aiming*	anthem	aspiring*	avenge
airman	anticipating*	assassinating*	avenging*
alarming*	antioxidant	assaulting*	averting*
alcoholism	antiperspirant	assembling*	avoiding*
alerting*	anything*	asserting*	awaiting*
alien	apartment	assessing*	awaken
aligning*	apologizing*	assessment	awakening*

awarding*
awning*
awoken
backbreaking*
backing*
backpacking*
backswing*
bacon
baffling*
bailing*
baiting*
baking*
balance
balancing*
balding*
balling*
banding*
bandwagon
banging*
banishing*
banking*
bankrolling*
bankrupting*
banning*
bantering*
baptism
baptizing*
barbarian
barking*
barreling*
barren
barricading*
barring*
bartering*
basement
basking*
bathing*
battering*
batting*
bawling*
beacon
beading*
beaming*
bearing*
beaten

beating*
beckon
beckoning*
becoming*
bedazzling*
bedding*
bedridden
beefing*
been
beeping*
befriend
befriending*
begging*
beginning*
begrudging*
behaving*
beholding*
behooving*
being*
believing*
belittling*
belligerent
bellman
belonging*
belting*
bench
benching*
bend
bending*
benefitting*
bent
bereavement
bestowing*
betraying*
betting*
beveling*
bewildering*
bewitching*
bidding*
biking*
binding*
bipartisan
birthing*
biting*
bitten

blabbing*
blacken
blaming*
blasting*
blazing*
bleaching*
bleeding*
blend
blending*
blessing*
blinding*
blinking*
blistering*
bloating*
blocking*
bloodcurdling*
blooming*
blossoming*
blotting*
blowing*
bludgeon
bludgeoning*
bluffing*
blundering*
blurring*
blurting*
boarding*
boasting*
boating*
bobbing*
boggling*
boiling*
bolting*
bombarding*
bombing*
bonding*
bookend
booking*
bookkeeping*
booming*
boosting*
booting*
bootlegging*
boozing*
bordering*

boring*
borrowing*
bossing*
botching*
bothering*
bottlenecking*
bottling*
bouncing*
bounding*
bowing*
bowling*
boxing*
boyfriend
bracing*
bragging*
braiding*
brainstorming*
brainwashing*
braking*
branching*
branding*
brazen
breaching*
breaking*
breathing*
breathtaking*
breeding*
breezing*
brethren
brewing*
bribing*
bridging*
briefing*
brighten
brightening*
brilliance
brilliant
brimming*
bringing*
broaching*
broadcasting*
broaden
broadening*
broiling*
broken

bronzing*
brooding*
brownnosing*
browsing*
bruising*
brushing*
bubbling*
bucking*
budding*
budgeting*
buffering*
buffing*
bugging*
building*
bulging*
bulldozing*
bulletproofing*
bullfighting*
bullying*
bumming*
bumping*
bunching*
bunking*
buoyant
burden
burdening*
burglarizing*
burning*
burping*
burrowing*
bursting*
businesswoman
busting*
bustling*
button
buying*
buzzing*
bypassing*
calcifying*
calculating*
calibrating*
calling*
camouflaging*
campaigning*
camping*

canceling*
canning*
cannon
canoeing*
canon
canvassing*
capitalism
capitalizing*
capping*
capsizing*
captain
captivating*
capturing*
caramelizing*
carbon
careening*
caressing*
caring*
caroling*
carpeting*
carpooling*
carrying*
carting*
carton
carving*
cascading*
cashing*
casing*
casting*
castrating*
cataloging*
catching*
categorizing*
catering*
cauldron
caulking*
causing*
cautioning*
caving*
cavorting*
cayenne
ceasing*
ceiling*
celebrating*
cement

cementing*
censoring*
cent
centering*
centralizing*
certain
chaining*
chairman
challenge
challenging*
chameleon
champion
changing*
channeling*
chanting*
chaperoning*
charging*
charming*
chartering*
charting*
chasing*
chattering*
chauvinism
cheapen
cheapening*
cheating*
checking*
cheering*
cherishing*
chewing*
chicken
childbearing*
childproofing*
children
chilling*
chiming*
chipping*
chirping*
chiseling*
choking*
choosing*
chopping*
chosen
christen
Christian

chuckling*
chugging*
churning*
cinching*
circling*
circuiting*
circulating*
circumference
citizen
civilian
civilizing*
clacking*
claiming*
clairvoyance
clairvoyant
clamping*
clanging*
clapping*
clashing*
clasping*
clattering*
clawing*
cleaning*
cleanse
cleansing*
clearance
clearing*
clicking*
client
climbing*
clinging*
clipping*
cloaking*
clocking*
clogging*
cloning*
closing*
clowning*
clubbing*
clucking*
cluing*
clumping*
clutching*
cluttering*
coaching*

coasting*	compartment	confiding*	contestant
coating*	compelling*	configuring*	contesting*
coaxing*	compensating*	confinement	continent
coding*	competent	confining*	contorting*
coexisting*	competing*	confirming*	contracting*
coiling*	compiling*	confiscating*	contradicting*
coincidence	complaining*	conflicting*	contrasting*
coincident	completing*	conforming*	contributing*
coining*	compliant	confronting*	controlling*
collaborating*	complicating*	confusing*	convalescence
collapsing*	compliment	congratulating*	convalescent
collecting*	complimenting*	congregating*	convenient
colliding*	complying*	conjuring*	convening*
colonizing*	component	connecting*	convent
coloring*	composing*	conning*	converging*
combating*	composting*	conniving*	conversing*
combing*	compounding*	conquering*	converting*
combining*	comprehend	conscience	conveying*
comedian	comprehending*	consent	convicting*
comedienne	compressing*	consenting*	convincing*
comforting*	comprising*	consequence	cooing*
coming*	compromising*	conserving*	cooking*
commandeering*	computerizing*	considering*	coolant
commanding*	computing*	consigning*	cooling*
commandment	concealing*	consignment	cooperating*
commemorating*	conceding*	consistent	coordinating*
commence	conceiving*	consisting*	coping*
commencement	concentrating*	consolidating*	copping*
commencing*	concerning*	consoling*	copying*
commend	concluding*	conspiring*	coring*
commending*	concocting*	constant	cornering*
comment	condemn	constraining*	corralling*
commenting*	condemning*	constricting*	correcting*
commercialism	condense	constructing*	correspondence
commissioning*	condensing*	consulting*	correspondent
commitment	condescend	consuming*	corresponding*
committing*	condescending*	contacting*	corroding*
common	condiment	containing*	corrupting*
commonsense	condolence	containment	cosigning*
communicating*	condoning*	contaminant	cosmopolitan
communism	conducting*	contaminating*	costing*
commuting*	conference	contempt	cotton
compacting*	confessing*	contend	coughing*
comparing*	confidence	contending*	couldn't
comparison	confident	content	counseling*

counteracting*
counterfeiting*
counting*
courting*
covering*
cowering*
cracking*
crackling*
cradling*
crafting*
cramming*
cramping*
cranking*
crashing*
crating*
craving*
crawling*
creaking*
creating*
creeping*
cremating*
crescent
crimson
cringing*
crinkling*
crippling*
crisscrossing*
criticism
criticizing*
critiquing*
croaking*
crocheting*
cropping*
crossbreeding*
crossing*
crowding*
crowing*
crowning*
crucifying*
cruising*
crumbling*
crumpling*
crunching*
crusading*
crushing*

crying*
crystallizing*
cuddling*
cueing*
cuffing*
cultivating*
cupping*
curbing*
curdling*
curing*
curling*
current
cursing*
curtailing*
curtain
curtsying*
curving*
cushioning*
custodian
customizing*
cutting*
cycling*
cynicism
dabbing*
dabbling*
damaging*
dampen
dampening*
dancing*
dangling*
daring*
darken
darkening*
darling*
darning*
darting*
dashing*
dating*
daunting*
dawning*
daydreaming*
dazzling*
deaden
deadening*
deafen

deafening*
dealing*
debating*
debriefing*
debugging*
debunking*
debuting*
decadence
decadent
decaying*
deceiving*
decent
deciding*
deciphering*
decking*
declaring*
declining*
decoding*
decongestant
decontaminating*
decorating*
decreasing*
dedicating*
deducting*
deepen
defacing*
defaulting*
defeating*
defecting*
defend
defendant
defending*
defense
deferring*
defiance
defiant
deficient
defining*
deflating*
deflecting*
defrosting*
defying*
degrading*
dehydrating*
delaying*

delegating*
deleting*
deliberating*
delighting*
delinquent
delivering*
deluding*
demanding*
demeaning*
demolishing*
demon
demonstrating*
demoting*
den
denouncing*
dense
dent
denting*
denying*
deodorant
deodorizing*
departing*
department
depend
dependence
dependent
depending*
depicting*
depleting*
deploring*
deploying*
deporting*
depositing*
depreciating*
depressing*
depriving*
deputizing*
derailing*
deriving*
descend
descendant
descending*
descent
describing*
desensitizing*

deserting*
deserving*
designing*
desiring*
despairing*
despising*
destined
destroying*
detaching*
detailing*
detaining*
detecting*
detergent
deteriorating*
determining*
deterrent
deterring*
dethroning*
detonating*
detouring*
detriment
devastating*
developing*
development
deviating*
devising*
devoting*
devouring*
diagnosing*
dialing*
diamond
dicing*
dickering*
dictating*
dieting*
difference
different
differentiating*
differing*
diffusing*
digesting*
digging*
digitizing*
dignifying*
digressing*

dilating*
diligence
diligent
diluting*
diminishing*
dimming*
dining*
dipping*
directing*
disabling*
disagreeing*
disagreement
disappearance
disappearing*
disappointing*
disappointment
disapproving*
disarming*
disassembling*
disbanding*
disbarring*
disbelieving*
disbursement
disbursing*
discarding*
discharging*
disciplining*
disclaiming*
disclosing*
discoloring*
discomforting*
disconnecting*
discontinuing*
discounting*
discouragement
discouraging*
discovering*
discrediting*
discriminating*
discussing*
disfiguring*
disguising*
disgusting*
dishing*
dishonoring*

disillusionment
disinfectant
disinfecting*
disliking*
dislocating*
dislodging*
dismantling*
dismissing*
dismounting*
disobedience
disobedient
disobeying*
disorganizing*
disowning*
dispatching*
dispelling*
dispense
dispensing*
dispersing*
displacing*
displaying*
displeasing*
disposing*
disproving*
disputing*
disqualifying*
disregarding*
disrespecting*
disrobing*
disrupting*
dissecting*
dissipating*
dissolving*
distance
distant
distilling*
distorting*
distracting*
distributing*
disturbing*
diverting*
dividend
dividing*
diving*
divorcing*

divulging*
divvying*
docking*
doctoring*
document
documenting*
dodging*
dogging*
doing*
domesticating*
dominance
dominant
dominating*
domineering*
dominion
donating*
dormant
doting*
dotting*
doubling*
doubting*
dousing*
downgrading*
downloading*
downplaying*
downsizing*
dozen
dozing*
drafting*
draftsman
dragging*
dragon
draining*
dramatizing*
draping*
drawing*
dreading*
dreaming*
dredging*
drench
drenching*
dressing*
dribbling*
drifting*
drilling*

drinking*
dripping*
driven
driving*
drizzling*
droning*
drooling*
drooping*
dropkicking*
dropping*
drowning*
drudging*
drugging*
drumming*
drunken
drying*
dubbing*
duckling*
dulling*
dumping*
dumpling*
dungeon
dunking*
duplicating*
during*
dusting*
dwelling*
dwindling*
dying*
earning*
earthling*
easing*
easygoing*
eaten
eating*
eavesdropping*
eclipsing*
ecosystem
edging*
editing*
educating*
efficient
egging*
ejecting*
elaborating*

elbowing*
electing*
electrifying*
electrocuting*
elegance
elegant
element
elephant
elevating*
eleven
eliminating*
elongating*
eloping*
eloquence
eloquent
eluding*
embarking*
embarrassing*
embarrassment
embedding*
embellishing*
embezzling*
emblem
embossing*
embracing*
emceeing*
emerging*
emitting*
employing*
employment
empowering*
emptying*
enabling*
enacting*
enchanting*
enchantment
enclosing*
encoding*
encompassing*
encountering*
encouragement
encouraging*
encrypting*
end
endangering*

endeavoring*
ending*
endorsing*
endurance
enduring*
energizing*
enforcing*
engagement
engaging*
engineering*
engraving*
enhancing*
enjoying*
enlargement
enlarging*
enlighten
enlightening*
enlightenment
enlisting*
enraging*
enriching*
enrolling*
enrollment
entailing*
entangling*
entering*
enterprising*
entertaining*
entertainment
enthralling*
enthusiasm
enticing*
entitling*
entrance
entrapment
entrapping*
entwining*
enunciating*
enveloping*
environment
envisioning*
envying*
equaling*
equating*
equestrian

equipment
equipping*
equivalent
eradicating*
erasing*
erecting*
eroding*
errand
erupting*
escalating*
escaping*
escorting*
essence
establishing*
establishment
estimating*
estrogen
etching*
evacuating*
evading*
evaluating*
evaporating*
even
evening*
event
everlasting*
everything*
evidence
evident
evoking*
evolving*
exaggerating*
examining*
exceeding*
excellence
excellent
excelling*
exchanging*
excitement
exciting*
exclaiming*
excluding*
excusing*
executing*
exempt

exempting*
exercising*
exerting*
exhaling*
exhausting*
exhibiting*
existence
existing*
exiting*
expanding*
expectant
expecting*
expedient
expediting*
expelling*
expense
experience
experiencing*
experiment
experimenting*
expiring*
explaining*
exploding*
exploiting*
exploring*
exporting*
exposing*
expressing*
extend
extending*
extent
exterminating*
extinguishing*
extorting*
extracting*
extravagance
extravagant
extruding*
exuberant
eyeing*
facilitating*
facing*
fading*
failing*
faking*

fallen
falling*
falsifying*
faltering*
familiarizing*
fanning*
fantasizing*
farming*
fascinating*
fasting*
fathering*
fatten
fattening*
faulting*
favoring*
favoritism
fawning*
faxing*
feasting*
featuring*
feeding*
feeling*
felon
femme
fence
fencing*
ferment
fermenting*
fertilizing*
festering*
fetching*
feuding*
fibbing*
fiddling*
fielding*
fighting*
figment
filling*
filtering*
finalizing*
financing*
finding*
fingering*
finishing*
fireman

fireproofing*
firing*
fisherman
fishing*
fitting*
fixing*
fizzling*
flaking*
flamboyant
flaming*
flapping*
flaring*
flashing*
flatten
flattering*
flaunting*
fleeing*
fleeting*
flexing*
flickering*
flicking*
flinching*
flipping*
flirting*
floating*
flocking*
flooding*
flooring*
flopping*
flossing*
floundering*
flourishing*
flowing*
flubbing*
fluctuating*
fluent
fluffing*
flunking*
flushing*
flustering*
fluttering*
flying*
foaming*
focusing*
folding*

following*
fooling*
footing*
forbidden
forbidding*
forcing*
forecasting*
foreclosing*
foregoing*
foreign
foreman
foreseeing*
foretelling*
forewarning*
forfeiting*
forgetting*
forgiving*
forgotten
formalizing*
formatting*
forming*
formulating*
forsaken
forsaking*
forthcoming*
fortifying*
fortune
forwarding*
fostering*
fouling*
founding*
fountain
fracturing*
fragment
fragmenting*
fragrance
fragrant
framing*
freaking*
freeing*
freeloading*
freezing*
frequent
freshen
freshening*

freshman
fretting*
friend
frighten
frightening*
frolicking*
frosting*
frowning*
frozen
frustrating*
frying*
fudging*
fueling*
fulfilling*
fumbling*
fumigating*
functioning*
funding*
furnishing*
fussing*
gagging*
gaining*
gallant
galloping*
gambling*
gaming*
gaping*
garden
gardening*
gargling*
garland
garment
garnishing*
gathering*
gauging*
gawking*
gazing*
gearing*
gem
generating*
gesturing*
getting*
giant
gifting*
giggling*

gingham
girlfriend
given
giving*
glancing*
glaring*
glazing*
glen
gliding*
glimmering*
glimpsing*
glisten
glistening*
glittering*
gloating*
globetrotting*
glorifying*
glossing*
glowing*
gnawing*
goading*
going*
golden
golfing*
goofing*
gossiping*
gotten
governing*
grabbing*
grading*
graduating*
grandchildren
grandstanding*
granting*
grasping*
gratifying*
grating*
gravitating*
graying*
grazing*
greeting*
grilling*
grinding*
grinning*
gripping*

gritting*
groaning*
grooming*
groomsman
grooving*
groping*
grounding*
grouping*
growing*
growling*
grueling*
grumbling*
grunting*
guardian
guarding*
guiding*
gumming*
gunman
gunning*
gushing*
guzzling*
gyrating*
hacking*
haggling*
hailing*
hairstyling*
hallucinating*
halting*
hammering*
hamming*
hampering*
handcuffing*
handing*
handling*
handwriting*
handwritten
hanging*
happen
happening*
harassing*
harboring*
harden
hardening*
harem
harming*

harmonizing*
harnessing*
harping*
harvesting*
hassling*
hasten
hastening*
hatching*
hating*
hauling*
haunting*
haven
having*
hawking*
hazing*
heading*
healing*
heaping*
hearing*
heartbreaking*
heartbroken
heathen
heating*
heaven
heaving*
heckling*
hedging*
heeding*
heeling*
heighten
heightening*
helping*
hem
hemming*
hen
herding*
heroism
hesitant
hesitating*
hibernating*
hiccuping*
hidden
hiding*
highlighting*
hijacking*

hiking*	hustling*	inefficient	intimidating*
hindering*	hydrating*	infant	intoxicating*
hinging*	hypnotizing*	infecting*	intriguing*
hinting*	icing*	inflaming*	introducing*
hiring*	identifying*	inflating*	intruding*
hissing*	idling*	inflicting*	invading*
hitchhiking*	igniting*	influence	invent
hitting*	ignorance	influencing*	inventing*
hoarding*	ignorant	informing*	inverting*
hobnobbing*	ignoring*	inhaling*	investigating*
hocking*	illuminating*	inheriting*	investing*
hogging*	illustrating*	inhibiting*	investment
hoisting*	imagining*	initiating*	inviting*
holding*	imbalance	injecting*	invoicing*
hollering*	imitating*	injuring*	involving*
homing*	immense	inning*	irking*
honeymooning*	immersing*	innocence	ironing*
honing*	impacting*	innocent	irrelevant
honking*	impairing*	inquiring*	irrigating*
honoring*	impatient	inserting*	irritating*
hooking*	implement	insisting*	island
hoping*	implementing*	inspecting*	isolating*
hopping*	imploding*	inspiring*	issuing*
horizon	imploring*	installing*	itching*
hosting*	implying*	installment	item
hounding*	important	instant	itemizing*
housebreaking*	importing*	instilling*	jabbing*
housebroken	imposing*	instructing*	jamming*
housing*	impressing*	instrument	jarring*
hovering*	improvement	insufficient	jaywalking*
howling*	improving*	insulting*	jeopardizing*
huddling*	improvising*	insurance	jerking*
hugging*	inching*	intelligence	jetting*
human	incident	intelligent	jiggling*
humiliating*	inclining*	intend	jilting*
humming*	including*	intending*	jinxing*
humoring*	increasing*	intense	jogging*
hunching*	incurring*	intensifying*	joining*
hunkering*	indecent	intent	joking*
hunting*	indent	interesting*	jolting*
hurdling*	indenting*	interning*	jotting*
hurrying*	indexing*	interpreting*	journalism
hurting*	indicating*	interrupting*	joyriding*
husband	indicting*	intersecting*	jubilant
hushing*	indulging*	interviewing*	judging*

juggling*
jumbling*
jumping*
junction
kayaking*
keeping*
kenneling*
kicking*
kidding*
kidnapping*
killing*
kindergarten
kissing*
kitchen
kitten
kneading*
kneeling*
knitting*
knocking*
knowing*
laboring*
lacing*
lacquering*
lagging*
laminating*
landing*
landscaping*
lapping*
lasting*
latching*
lathering*
laughing*
launching*
laundering*
layering*
laying*
leading*
leaking*
leaning*
leaping*
learning*
leasing*
leaving*
lecturing*
leering*

legalizing*
legend
lemon
lend
lending*
length
lengthen
lengthening*
lenient
lens
lent
lessen
lessening*
lesson
lettering*
letting*
leveling*
leveraging*
liberating*
librarian
license
licensing*
licking*
lifting*
lighten
lightening*
lightning*
limiting*
limping*
linen
lingering*
lining*
linking*
lion
liquidating*
listen
listening*
listing*
littering*
liven
living*
loading*
loafing*
loaning*
lobbying*

locating*
locking*
lodging*
logging*
loitering*
longing*
looking*
looping*
loosen
loosening*
looting*
lopping*
losing*
lounging*
loving*
lowering*
lubricant
lubricating*
lugging*
lumbering*
lumping*
luncheon
lurking*
lying*
madam
maddening*
magician
magnetism
magnificent
magnifying*
maiden
mailing*
mainstreaming*
maintaining*
majoring*
making*
management
managing*
mandating*
maneuvering*
manicuring*
manipulating*
mannequin
mannerism
mansion

manufacturing*
mapping*
marching*
marketing*
marking*
marksman
marring*
marrying*
masking*
masquerading*
massaging*
mastering*
matching*
materializing*
mathematician
matron
matting*
maturing*
mauling*
maximizing*
mayhem
meaning*
meant
measurement
measuring*
meddling*
meditating*
meeting*
melon
melting*
men
menacing*
mend
mending*
mentioning*
mentoring*
merchandising*
merchant
merging*
mesmerizing*
messing*
metering*
mewing*
microwaving*
migrating*

milking*
milling*
mimicking*
mincing*
minding*
mingling*
miniaturizing*
minimizing*
mining*
mirroring*
misbehaving*
misconstruing*
misfortune
misguiding*
misjudging*
misleading*
misplacing*
misreading*
misshapen
missing*
misspelling*
mistaken
misting*
mitten
mixing*
moaning*
mobbing*
mobilizing*
mocking*
modeling*
modem
modifying*
moisten
moistening*
moisturizing*
molding*
molesting*
molten
moment
monitoring*
monogramming*
monument
mooning*
moping*
mopping*

morning*
mothering*
motioning*
motivating*
motorcycling*
mounding*
mourning*
mouthwatering*
movement
moving*
mowing*
mucking*
muffling*
mugging*
multiplying*
munching*
murdering*
murmuring*
mustering*
mutating*
muttering*
nabbing*
nagging*
nailing*
naming*
napping*
narrating*
narrowing*
navigating*
nearing*
necking*
needing*
needling*
neglecting*
negotiating*
neighboring*
netting*
networking*
neutering*
neutralizing*
nibbling*
nicking*
nipping*
nitpicking*
nitrogen

nixing*
nodding*
nominating*
nonsense
nonviolent
normalizing*
notating*
nothing*
noticing*
notifying*
noting*
nourishing*
nourishment
nudging*
nuisance
nuking*
numbing*
nursing*
nurturing*
nutrient
nuzzling*
obedience
obedient
obeying*
objecting*
obscuring*
observant
observing*
obsessing*
obstetrician
obstructing*
obtaining*
occupant
occupying*
occurrence
occurring*
ocean
offend
offending*
offense
offering*
offsetting*
often
okaying*
olden

omen
omitting*
ongoing*
onion
oozing*
open
opening*
operating*
opinion
opponent
opposing*
optician
optimism
opting*
orange
ordering*
ordinance
organ
organizing*
orient
originating*
ornament
orphan
oscillating*
ousting*
outbidding*
outfoxing*
outgrowing*
outing*
outlasting*
outlining*
outliving*
outmaneuvering*
outnumbering*
outpouring*
outselling*
outshining*
outsmarting*
outspoken
outstanding*
outweighing*
outwitting*
oven
overcharging*
overcoming*

overdrawing*
overeating*
overflowing*
overgrowing*
overpowering*
overruling*
overseeing*
overwhelming*
owing*
owning*
oxen
oxygen
pacing*
packaging*
packing*
padding*
paddling*
paging*
painstaking*
painting*
pairing*
pampering*
paneling*
panhandling*
panicking*
panting*
parachuting*
parading*
paralyzing*
parchment
pardoning*
parent
parenting*
parking*
parliament
paroling*
partaking*
participant
participating*
parting*
partnering*
passing*
pasteurizing*
pasting*
patching*

patent
patenting*
patience
patient
patriotism
patrolling*
patron
patting*
pausing*
pavilion
paving*
pawing*
pawning*
paying*
payment
peaking*
peasant
pecking*
pedaling*
peddling*
pedestrian
pediatrician
peeing*
peeking*
peeling*
peering*
pegging*
pelican
pen
penchant
pendant
pendent
penetrating*
pennant
perceiving*
percent
perching*
perfecting*
performance
performing*
perishing*
perjuring*
perking*
permanent
permeating*

permitting*
perpetrating*
perplexing*
persecuting*
perseverance
persevering*
persistence
persistent
persisting*
person
perspiring*
persuading*
pertaining*
perturbing*
pessimism
pestering*
petitioning*
petting*
phasing*
pheasant
phlegm
phoning*
photographing*
phrasing*
physician
picketing*
picking*
pickling*
picturing*
piecing*
piercing*
pigeon
pigment
piling*
pilling*
pimping*
pinching*
pinning*
pinpointing*
pioneering*
piping*
piston
pitching*
pitting*
pitying*

pivoting*
placement
placing*
plaguing*
plankton
planning*
planting*
plastering*
playing*
playpen
pleading*
pleasant
pleasing*
pleating*
pledging*
plodding*
plopping*
plotting*
plugging*
plumbing*
plumping*
plundering*
plunging*
plying*
poaching*
poem
pointing*
poison
poking*
polarizing*
policeman
policewoman
polishing*
politician
pollen
pollinating*
polling*
polluting*
pondering*
pooling*
popping*
populating*
portraying*
posing*
positioning*

possessing*
posting*
postman
postponing*
posturing*
potent
potting*
pounding*
pouring*
pouting*
powering*
praising*
praying*
preaching*
precedent
preceding*
precipitating*
predicament
predicting*
predisposing*
predominance
predominant
preempt
preempting*
preexisting*
prefacing*
preference
preferring*
pregnant
preheating*
premiering*
preparing*
prepaying*
preplanning*
prepping*
prescribing*
presence
present
presenting*
preserving*
preshrinking*
president
presiding*
presoaking*
pressing*

pressuring*
pressurizing*
presuming*
pretend
pretending*
pretense
prevailing*
prevalence
prevalent
prevent
preventing*
previewing*
preying*
pricing*
pricking*
prickling*
priming*
printing*
prison
probing*
problem
proceeding*
processing*
proclaiming*
procrastinating*
prodding*
producing*
professing*
professionalism
proficient
profiling*
profiting*
programming*
progressing*
prohibiting*
projecting*
prolonging*
promenading*
prominence
prominent
promising*
promoting*
prompting*
pronouncing*
proofing*

proofreading*
propellant
propelling*
proposing*
propositioning*
propping*
prorating*
prosecuting*
prospering*
protecting*
protestant
protesting*
protruding*
proven
providing*
proving*
prowling*
pruning*
prying*
publishing*
puckering*
pudding*
puffing*
puking*
pulling*
pulsating*
pulverizing*
pummeling*
pumping*
punching*
punctuating*
puncturing*
pungent
punishing*
punishment
punting*
purchasing*
purging*
purifying*
purring*
pursing*
pursuant
pursuing*
pushing*
putting*

puzzling*
quacking*
quadrant
qualifying*
quarreling*
quartering*
questioning*
quicken
quilting*
quitting*
quivering*
quizzing*
racing*
racism
racketeering*
racking*
radiance
radiant
radiating*
raffling*
rafting*
raging*
raiding*
railing*
raining*
raising*
raking*
rambling*
ramming*
rampant
ramping*
ranging*
ranking*
ransacking*
raping*
rappelling*
rapping*
ratcheting*
rating*
rationalizing*
rationing*
rattling*
ravaging*
raveling*
raven

raving*
reaching*
reacting*
reading*
realizing*
rearing*
rearranging*
reasoning*
reassurance
reassuring*
rebating*
rebelling*
rebellion
rebuilding*
recalling*
recanting*
recapping*
receding*
receiving*
recent
recessing*
rechecking*
recipient
reciprocating*
reciting*
reckon
reckoning*
reclaiming*
reclining*
recognizing*
recoiling*
recollecting*
recommend
recommending*
reconciling*
reconfirming*
reconsidering*
recording*
recouping*
recovering*
recruiting*
recuperating*
recurring*
recycling*
redecorating*

redeeming*
redefining*
redoing*
reducing*
redundant
reeking*
reeling*
reference
referring*
refilling*
refining*
reflecting*
reforming*
refraining*
refreshing*
refreshment
refrigerating*
refrying*
refueling*
refunding*
refurbishing*
refusing*
regaining*
regarding*
regimen
region
registering*
regressing*
regretting*
rehabilitating*
rehearsing*
reigning*
reimbursement
reimbursing*
reinforcement
reinforcing*
reining*
reinstating*
rejecting*
rejoicing*
rejoining*
rejuvenating*
relapsing*
relating*
relaxing*

relaying*
releasing*
relevance
relevant
relieving*
religion
relishing*
reliving*
reloading*
reluctance
reluctant
relying*
remaining*
remaking*
remarking*
remembering*
remembrance
reminding*
reminiscent
reminiscing*
remitting*
remnant
remodeling*
removing*
renaming*
rendering*
renewing*
renovating*
rent
renting*
reorganizing*
repacking*
repairing*
repaying*
repealing*
repeating*
repelling*
replacement
replacing*
replaying*
replenishing*
replying*
reporting*
represent
representing*

repressing*
reprising*
reproducing*
republican
requesting*
requirement
requiring*
rerunning*
rescuing*
researching*
reselling*
resembling*
resent
resenting*
resentment
reserving*
resetting*
reshaping*
residence
resident
residing*
resigning*
resistance
resisting*
resolving*
resorting*
respecting*
responding*
restarting*
resting*
restoring*
restraining*
restricting*
resulting*
resuming*
retailing*
retaining*
retaking*
retaliating*
rethinking*
retirement
retiring*
retouching*
retracing*
retracting*

retreating*	roaming*	salmon	scorching*
retrieving*	roaring*	saluting*	scoring*
returning*	roasting*	salvaging*	scorning*
reunion	robbing*	sampling*	scorpion
reuniting*	rocketing*	sanctioning*	scouring*
reusing*	rocking*	sandblasting*	scouting*
revealing*	rodent	sanding*	scowling*
revenge	rolling*	sapping*	scrambling*
revenging*	romancing*	sarcasm	scraping*
reverence	romping*	sashaying*	scrapping*
reverend	roofing*	satisfying*	scratching*
reverent	rooming*	saturating*	scrawling*
reversing*	roosting*	sauntering*	screaming*
reverting*	rooting*	sautéing*	screeching*
reviewing*	roping*	saving*	screening*
revising*	rotating*	savoring*	screwing*
revitalizing*	rotten	sawing*	scribbling*
revoking*	rotting*	saying*	scrimping*
revolting*	roughen	scabbing*	scrolling*
revolutionizing*	roughening*	scaffolding*	scrounging*
revolving*	roughing*	scalding*	scrubbing*
rewarding*	rounding*	scaling*	scrunching*
rewinding*	roving*	scallion	scrutinizing*
rewriting*	rowing*	scalloping*	scuffing*
rhyming*	rubbing*	scamming*	scuffling*
rhythm	ruffling*	scampering*	scurrying*
ribbing*	ruining*	scanning*	sealing*
ribbon	ruling*	scaring*	searching*
ricocheting*	rumbling*	scarring*	searing*
ridden	rummaging*	scathing*	season
ridding*	running*	scattering*	seasoning*
riding*	rupturing*	scavenge	seating*
rifling*	rushing*	scavenging*	second
rigging*	rusting*	scent	seconding*
righting*	rustling*	scheduling*	securing*
ringing*	sabotaging*	scheming*	sedating*
rinsing*	sacking*	schlepping*	sediment
ripen	sacrificing*	schooling*	seducing*
ripening*	sadden	science	seeding*
ripping*	saddling*	scintillating*	seeing*
rippling*	safeguarding*	scoffing*	seeking*
risen	sagging*	scolding*	seeming*
rising*	sailing*	scooping*	segment
risking*	salesman	scooting*	segmenting*
rivaling*	salesperson	scoping*	segregating*

seizing*
selecting*
selling*
semblance
send
sending*
sensationalizing*
sense
sensing*
sent
sentence
sentencing*
sentiment
separating*
sequence
sequencing*
serenading*
serpent
serving*
setting*
settlement
settling*
seven
seventh
severance
severing*
sewing*
shacking*
shading*
shagging*
shaken
shaking*
shampooing*
shaping*
sharing*
sharpen
sharpening*
shattering*
shaven
shaving*
shearing*
shedding*
sheeting*
shelling*
sheltering*

shelving*
shielding*
shifting*
shilling*
shimmering*
shining*
shipping*
shirking*
shivering*
shocking*
shooting*
shopping*
shorten
shortening*
shorting*
shouting*
shoveling*
shoving*
showing*
shrieking*
shrinking*
shriveling*
shrugging*
shrunken
shuddering*
shuffling*
shunning*
shutting*
sibling*
sicken
sickening*
sidelining*
sidestepping*
sidetracking*
siding*
sighing*
sighting*
sightseeing*
signaling*
significance
significant
signifying*
signing*
silent
silken

simmering*
simpleton
simplifying*
simulating*
singing*
sinking*
sinning*
siphon
siphoning*
sipping*
siren
sitting*
sizing*
sizzling*
skating*
skeleton
sketching*
skewing*
skidding*
skiing*
skimming*
skimping*
skinning*
skipping*
skirting*
skydiving*
skyrocketing*
skywriting*
slacken
slackening*
slacking*
slamming*
slandering*
slanting*
slapping*
slaughtering*
slaving*
slaying*
sledding*
sleeping*
sleepwalking*
slenderizing*
slicing*
sliding*
slimming*

slinking*
slipping*
slithering*
slitting*
slobbering*
slogan
sloping*
slouching*
slugging*
slumming*
slumping*
slurring*
smacking*
smarten
smashing*
smattering*
smearing*
smelling*
smiling*
smirking*
smitten
smoking*
smoldering*
smoothing*
smothering*
smudging*
snacking*
snagging*
snaking*
snapping*
snatching*
sneaking*
sneering*
sneezing*
snickering*
sniffing*
snipping*
snoozing*
snoring*
snorkeling*
snorting*
snowing*
snubbing*
snuffing*
snuggling*

soaking*
soaping*
soaring*
sobering*
socking*
soften
softening*
soiling*
soldering*
solemn
soliciting*
soloing*
solving*
something*
soothing*
sorting*
sounding*
sowing*
spacing*
spanning*
sparing*
sparking*
sparring*
spasm
spattering*
spawning*
spaying*
speaking*
spearing*
specializing*
specifying*
specimen
speculating*
speeding*
spellbinding*
spelling*
spend
spending*
spent
spewing*
spiking*
spilling*
spinning*
spiraling*
spiritualism

spitting*
splashing*
splattering*
splicing*
splintering*
splinting*
splitting*
splurging*
spoiling*
spoken
sponsoring*
spooking*
spooning*
sporting*
spotting*
spouting*
spraining*
sprawling*
spraying*
spreading*
springing*
sprinkling*
sprinting*
sprouting*
sprucing*
spurning*
spurring*
spurting*
sputtering*
spying*
squabbling*
squadron
squandering*
squatting*
squawking*
squeaking*
squealing*
squeezing*
squinting*
squirming*
squirting*
stabbing*
stabilizing*
stacking*
staffing*

staggering*
staging*
stagnating*
staining*
staking*
stalking*
stalling*
stallion
stammering*
stampeding*
stamping*
standardizing*
standing*
stapling*
starching*
staring*
starring*
starting*
startling*
starving*
stashing*
statement
staying*
stealing*
steaming*
steeling*
steeping*
steering*
stem
stemming*
stepping*
sterilizing*
sterling*
stewing*
sticking*
stiffen
stiffening*
stifling*
stimulating*
stinging*
stinking*
stipulating*
stirring*
stitching*
stocking*

stoking*
stolen
stomping*
stopping*
storing*
stowing*
straddling*
straggling*
straighten
straightening*
straining*
strangling*
strapping*
straying*
streaking*
streaming*
strength
strengthen
strengthening*
stressing*
stretching*
stricken
striding*
striking*
striping*
stripping*
striving*
stroking*
strolling*
struggling*
strumming*
strutting*
stubbing*
student
studying*
stuffing*
stumbling*
stunning*
stuttering*
styling*
subbing*
subduing*
subjecting*
subletting*
submerging*

submersing*
submitting*
subscribing*
subsiding*
substance
substituting*
subtracting*
suburban
succeeding*
succulent
succumbing*
sucking*
sudden
suffering*
sufficient
suffocating*
suggesting*
suing*
suiting*
sulking*
summarizing*
summing*
summon
summoning*
sunken
sunning*
supervising*
supplement
supplying*
supporting*
suppressing*
surfing*
surgeon
surging*
surpassing*
surprising*
surrendering*
surrounding*
surveying*
surviving*
suspecting*
suspend
suspending*
suspense
sustaining*

suturing*
swabbing*
swaggering*
swallowing*
swapping*
swarming*
swatting*
swaying*
swearing*
sweating*
sweeping*
sweeten
sweetening*
swelling*
swerving*
swimming*
swindling*
swinging*
swiping*
swirling*
switching*
swiveling*
swollen
swooning*
swooping*
symbolism
sympathizing*
symptom
system
tackling*
tagging*
tailgating*
tailing*
tainting*
taken
taking*
talent
talking*
tallying*
taming*
tampering*
tandem
tangling*
tanking*
tanning*

tantalizing*
tapering*
taping*
tapping*
targeting*
tarnishing*
tarring*
tasting*
tattling*
tattooing*
taunting*
taxing*
teaching*
teaming*
tearing*
teasing*
technician
teeing*
teetering*
teething*
telecasting*
telemarketing*
telling*
temperament
tempering*
tempt
tempting*
ten
tenant
tend
tenderizing*
tending*
tendon
tense
tenth
terminating*
terrifying*
terrorizing*
testifying*
testing*
tethering*
texting*
thanking*
thawing*
them

then
theorizing*
thicken
thickening*
thinking*
thinning*
thousand
threading*
threaten
threatening*
thrilling*
thriving*
throbbing*
throwing*
thrusting*
thundering*
thwarting*
ticketing*
ticking*
tickling*
tighten
tightening*
tilting*
timesaving*
timing*
tingling*
tinkering*
tinting*
tipping*
tiptoeing*
tiring*
toasting*
toddling*
toggling*
token
tolerance
tolerant
tolerating*
toning*
tooting*
topping*
torment
tormenting*
torturing*
tossing*

totem
toting*
touching*
toughen
toughening*
touring*
tourism
tournament
towering*
towing*
toying*
tracing*
tracking*
trading*
trafficking*
trailing*
training*
trampling*
transcend
transcending*
transcribing*
transferring*
transforming*
translating*
translucent
transmitting*
transparent
transpiring*
transplanting*
transporting*
transposing*
trapping*
trashing*
traumatizing*
traveling*
treading*
treason
treasuring*
treating*
trekking*
trembling*
trench
trend
trending*
trendsetting*

trespassing*
tricking*
trickling*
triggering*
trillion
trimming*
tripling*
tripping*
triumphant
triumphing*
trolling*
trotting*
troubling*
truant
trucking*
trumpeting*
trusting*
trying*
tubing*
tucking*
tugging*
tumbling*
tuning*
tunneling*
turbulence
turbulent
turning*
tutoring*
tweaking*
tweeting*
twinkling*
twirling*
twisting*
twitching*
tying*
typecasting*
typesetting*
typing*
tyrant
ulcerating*
unassuming*
unbalanced
unbecoming*
unbending*
unbutton

unbuttoning*
uncommon
unconvincing*
underclassman
undercurrent
underlying*
underwent
underwritten
uneven
unfolding*
unifying*
union
unison
uniting*
unknowing*
unleashing*
unloading*
unlocking*
unnerving*
unpleasant
unraveling*
unspoken
unwinding*
unwritten
upbringing*
upcoming*
updating*
upgrading*
upholding*
upholstering*
uplifting*
upperclassman
uprising*
uprooting*
upsetting*
upstaging*
urban
urgent
urging*
ushering*
using*
utilizing*
uttering*
vacant
vacating*

vacationing*
vaccinating*
vacuuming*
valance
valiant
validating*
vandalism
vanishing*
vaporizing*
variance
variant
varnishing*
varying*
vaulting*
vegan
vegetarian
vengeance
vent
ventilating*
venting*
venturing*
verbalizing*
verging*
verifying*
veteran
vetoing*
vibrant
vibrating*
victimizing*
videoing*
viewing*
vigilant
violating*
violence
violent
visiting*
visualizing*
vixen
vocalizing*
voicing*
voiding*
volleying*
volunteering*
vomiting*
voting*

vouching*
vowing*
waddling*
wading*
wagering*
wagging*
waging*
wagon
waiting*
waiving*
waken
wakening*
walking*
walloping*
wallowing*
waltzing*
wandering*
wanting*
warden
warming*
warning*
warping*
warrant
warranting*
washing*
wasn't
wasting*
watching*
watchman
watering*
watermelon
waterproofing*
wavering*

waving*
waxing*
weaken
weakening*
weakling*
weapon
wearing*
weaseling*
weathering*
weatherproofing*
weaving*
webbing*
wedding*
wedging*
weeding*
weighing*
welcoming*
welding*
went
wetland
wetting*
whacking*
wheeling*
wheezing*
when
whetting*
whiffing*
whimpering*
whining*
whipping*
whirling*
whisking*
whispering*

whistling*
whiten
whitening*
whittling*
wholesaling*
widen
widening*
wiggling*
willing*
wilting*
winding*
winging*
winking*
winning*
winterizing*
wiping*
wiring*
wishing*
withering*
withholding*
withstanding*
witnessing*
woken
woman
women
wondering*
wooden
woodsman
woodworking*
wooing*
woolen
working*
workman

worrying*
worsen
worsening*
worshipping*
wouldn't
woven
wracking*
wrangling*
wrapping*
wrecking*
wrench
wrenching*
wrestling*
wringing*
wrinkling*
writing*
written
yachting*
yanking*
yawning*
yearning*
yelling*
yelping*
yen
yielding*
yodeling*
zapping*
zeroing*
zigzagging*
zinging*
zipping*
zoning*
zooming*

[e]r   as in: swear

affair
air
airfare
anywhere
armchair
aware
backstairs

bare
bear
beware
billionaire
care
chair
compare

concessionaire
concierge
dare
debonair
declare
despair
dinnerware

disrepair
downstairs
elsewhere
everywhere
fair
fare
flair

flare
glare
hair
impair
millionaire
nightmare
nowhere
pair
pear
prepare

questionnaire
rare
repair
scarce
scare
share
silverware
solitaire
somewhere
spare

square
stair
stare
swear
tear
their
there
threadbare
unaware
underwear

unfair
upstairs
ware
warfare
wear
welfare
wheelchair
where

[er]

[er]   as in: smarter

abductor
absurd
abuser
accelerator
accuser
achiever
acre
actor
acupressure
acupuncture
adapter
adjuster
administer
administrator
adventure
adverb
adverse
advertiser
advisor
after
afterward
agitator
aglitter
agriculture
alert
alligator
allure
altar
alter
alternator
altogether
amateur
ambassador

amber
amour
analyzer
ancestor
anchor
anger
angular
animator
announcer
another
answer
antler
appetizer
applicator
appraiser
arbor
architecture
armor
arranger
artwork
assert
assure
astrologer
astronomer
attacker
author
avenger
avert
aviator
awkward
babysitter
bachelor
backer

backpacker
backward
badger
bagger
baker
banister
banker
banner
banter
barber
barrier
bartender
barter
batter
beachcomber
beadwork
beaker
beaver
beeper
beggar
beginner
behavior
believer
berserk
bestseller
better
bettor
bewilder
bicker
bigger
biker
billiard
binder

binocular
bipolar
bird
birth
bitter
bladder
blazer
bleacher
blender
blinder
blinker
blister
blizzard
blockbuster
blocker
bloodsucker
bloomer
blooper
blotter
blower
bluebird
bluer
blunder
blur
blurb
blurt
boarder
boiler
bolder
bomber
bookkeeper
boomer
booster

bootlegger	cabdriver	checker	comforter
border	cadaver	cheddar	commander
bother	calculator	cheeseburger	commentator
boulder	calendar	childbirth	commerce
bouncer	caliber	chiropractor	commissioner
bowler	caller	chirp	commoner
boxer	calmer	choker	commuter
bragger	camper	chooser	compactor
brainpower	cancer	chopper	competitor
breaker	candor	choreographer	complainer
breather	canister	chowder	composer
breeder	canker	church	composure
brightener	caper	cider	computer
brighter	captor	cinder	concert
broadcaster	capture	circular	conductor
broader	carburetor	clatter	confer
brochure	caregiver	cleaner	configure
broiler	caretaker	cleanser	conjure
broker	caricature	clearer	connoisseur
brother	caroler	cleaver	conquer
browser	carpenter	clerk	conserve
bruiser	carrier	clever	consider
brushwork	carver	clicker	conspirator
bubbler	catcher	cliffhanger	consumer
buffer	cater	climber	container
bugger	caterpillar	clincher	contender
builder	cauliflower	clipper	contour
bulldozer	cedar	clobber	contractor
bullfighter	cellar	clockwork	contributor
bummer	cellular	closer	controller
bumper	censor	closure	converge
bunker	center	clover	converse
burger	centimeter	clunker	convert
burglar	challenger	cluster	cooler
burner	chamber	clutter	coordinator
burp	chapter	coaster	copier
burst	character	cobbler	copper
buster	charger	cocker	copywriter
butcher	charmer	colander	corner
butler	charter	colder	cornflower
butter	chaser	collaborator	coroner
buyer	chatter	collar	cougar
buzzer	chauffeur	collector	counselor
buzzword	cheaper	color	counter
bystander	cheater	comfort	courier

cover
covert
cower
coworker
cracker
crasher
crater
crawler
creamer
creator
creature
creditor
crisper
critter
crooner
cruiser
crusher
cucumber
culture
cupboard
curb
cure
curler
curse
cursor
curve
custard
customer
cuter
cutter
cyber
cycler
cylinder
dagger
damper
dancer
dander
danger
darker
dasher
daughter
dealer
decanter
December
decipher

decoder
decorator
deeper
defender
defer
defroster
dehydrator
deliver
demeanor
demonstrator
denominator
denture
deodorizer
departure
desert
deserter
deserve
designer
dessert
destroyer
deter
detonator
detour
developer
devour
diameter
diaper
dicker
dictator
differ
dimmer
diner
dinner
dipper
director
dirt
disaster
disbeliever
disburse
disclaimer
disclosure
discolor
discomfort
discover
disfigure

dishonor
dishwasher
dishwater
disorder
disperse
distemper
disturb
diver
diverse
divert
divider
doctor
dodger
doer
dogcatcher
dollar
donor
doodler
downer
downward
dreamer
dresser
dressmaker
dribbler
drifter
driller
drinker
driver
dropper
drummer
drunkard
drunker
druthers
dryer
duller
dumber
dumpster
duplicator
duster
dweller
eager
earlier
earth
easier
edger

editor
educator
effort
either
elder
elevator
ember
emerge
empower
enabler
enclosure
encounter
endanger
endeavor
endure
energizer
ensure
enter
entrepreneur
equator
eraser
error
escalator
ether
ever
exert
expert
exposure
exterior
exterminator
extracurricular
eyedropper
factor
failure
faker
falter
familiar
farmer
farther
fastener
faster
father
fatter
favor
feather

feature	former	goner	helper
feeder	forward	governor	her
feeler	foster	grader	herb
femur	founder	grammar	herd
fender	foyer	granddaughter	higher
fertilizer	fracture	grander	highlighter
fester	framer	grandfather	hiker
fever	framework	grandmother	hinder
fewer	freeloader	grantor	hipster
fiber	freer	grater	hitter
fiddler	freezer	greater	holder
fieldwork	freighter	greener	holler
fighter	fresher	greeter	homer
figure	friendlier	grinder	homework
filler	friskier	grocer	honker
filmmaker	fritter	groomer	honor
filter	fryer	grower	hooker
finder	fuller	guesswork	horror
finer	fur	gusher	hotter
finger	furniture	gutter	hour
firecracker	further	guzzler	housework
fireworks	future	hacker	hover
first	gambler	halter	however
fixer	gamer	hamburger	hugger
fixture	gangster	hammer	humor
flatter	garner	hamper	hunger
flaunter	garter	hamster	hunker
flavor	gather	handiwork	hunter
flicker	gator	handler	hurt
flipper	gazer	hangar	hustler
flirt	geezer	hanger	hyper
floater	gender	haphazard	immature
flounder	generator	harbor	immerse
flour	gentler	hardener	impostor
flower	gesture	harder	improper
fluster	geyser	harsher	incur
flutter	ginger	hazard	indicator
flyer	giver	healer	inferior
folder	glacier	heard	injure
follower	glamour	heater	inner
footer	glider	heather	insert
footwork	glimmer	heavier	insider
foreclosure	glitter	heeler	inspector
foreigner	globular	heifer	installer
forever	golfer	helicopter	instructor

insure	leaner	major	mower
interior	leather	maker	muffler
inverse	lecture	maneuver	mugger
invert	ledger	manicure	murder
inward	legwork	manner	murmur
irk	leisure	manor	muscular
irregular	lender	manufacture	mustard
janitor	leopard	manure	muster
jerk	leper	marker	mutter
jester	lesser	martyr	narrower
jeweler	letter	master	nature
jitter	lever	matcher	naysayer
jogger	lighter	matter	nearer
joker	limber	mature	neater
juggler	liner	mayor	nectar
juicer	linger	meager	neighbor
jumper	liqueur	meaner	neither
junior	liquor	measure	nerd
juror	listener	meddler	nerve
keener	liter	mediocre	network
keeper	literature	member	neuter
kicker	litter	merge	never
killer	liver	merger	newer
kilometer	loafer	messenger	newscaster
kilter	loaner	meter	newsletter
kinder	lobster	milder	newspaper
kisser	locker	miner	nicer
knocker	lodger	miniature	November
kosher	logger	minor	number
labor	loiter	mirror	nurse
laborer	loner	miser	nurture
lackluster	longer	mister	obscure
lacquer	looker	mixer	observe
ladder	looser	mixture	occur
larger	loser	mobster	October
laser	louder	moderator	odor
later	lounger	modular	offer
lather	lousier	moisture	officer
laughter	lover	molar	ogre
launcher	lower	molecular	older
launder	lumber	monitor	operator
lavender	lunar	monster	orchard
lawyer	lurk	mother	order
layer	luster	motor	organizer
leader	mailer	mover	other

our	perverse	preregister	rambler
outburst	pervert	preschooler	rancher
outer	pester	preserve	ranger
outmaneuver	pewter	pressure	rapper
outnumber	philosopher	prettier	rapture
outsider	photographer	primer	rather
outward	picker	printer	rattler
over	picture	prisoner	razor
overheard	piecework	procedure	reactor
overpower	pillar	procrastinator	reader
overture	piper	producer	reassure
owner	pitcher	professor	recapture
oyster	planner	projector	receiver
pager	planter	promoter	recliner
painkiller	plaster	prompter	reconsider
painter	platter	propeller	record
pamper	player	proper	recover
panther	pleaser	proprietor	rectangular
paper	pleasure	prosecutor	recur
paperwork	plumber	prospector	reefer
parishioner	plumper	prosper	refer
parlor	plunder	protector	reflector
particular	plunger	prouder	refrigerator
partner	pointer	proverb	register
passenger	poker	provider	regular
password	polar	prowler	regulator
pastor	ponder	publisher	rehearse
pasture	popper	pucker	reimburse
patchwork	popular	puncher	remainder
patter	porter	puncture	remember
pauper	poser	pure	render
paver	poster	purge	renter
pecker	posterior	purr	reporter
peculiar	posture	purse	research
peddler	potter	pusher	reserve
pedicure	powder	putter	retailer
pedometer	power	quarter	retainer
peeler	practitioner	quicker	reverse
peeper	prankster	quirk	revert
pepper	prayer	quitter	richer
per	preacher	quiver	rider
perch	predator	racer	ringer
perjure	predecessor	radiator	riper
perk	prefer	rafter	riser
perturb	premature	raider	river

roadwork	scribbler	shrewder	slugger
roaster	scripture	shudder	slumber
robber	scrounger	shutter	slur
rocker	scrubber	shyster	smaller
roller	sculptor	sicker	smarter
romper	sculpture	sideburn	smatter
roofer	sealer	sifter	smirk
rooster	search	signature	smoker
roper	sector	signer	smolder
roster	secure	silver	smoother
rougher	seeker	similar	smother
rounder	seer	simmer	snapper
router	seizure	simpler	snatcher
rover	seller	singer	sneaker
rubber	seltzer	singular	snicker
rudder	semester	sinister	snifter
ruler	senator	sinner	sniper
rumor	sender	sir	sober
runner	senior	sister	soccer
rupture	sensor	sitter	softer
rustler	September	sizzler	solar
saber	serve	skater	solder
sadder	server	sketcher	soldier
safer	setter	skewer	solicitor
sailor	settler	skier	solver
salesclerk	sever	skimmer	somber
sampler	sewer	skipper	sooner
sandpaper	shaker	skirt	sorcerer
saucer	sharper	slacker	sour
saunter	shatter	slammer	sparkler
savior	shaver	slander	spatter
savor	shelter	slapper	speaker
scamper	shimmer	slaughter	spectacular
scanner	shipper	slayer	speedster
scatter	shirk	sleeper	speller
scavenger	shirt	slender	spender
scholar	shiver	slicer	spider
schoolwork	shocker	slicker	spinner
scissors	shooter	slider	spinster
scooter	shopper	slimmer	splatter
scorcher	shorter	slipper	splendor
scour	shoulder	slither	splinter
scratcher	shouter	sliver	splurge
screamer	shower	slobber	spoiler
screener	shredder	slower	sponsor

sportscaster	stronger	taper	torture
spotter	structure	tartar	tougher
sprayer	stuffer	tastier	tour
spreader	stumper	tater	tower
sprinkler	stupor	tattler	tracer
sprinter	stutter	teacher	tracker
spur	submerge	teamster	tractor
spurt	submerse	teamwork	trader
sputter	suburb	teaser	trailer
squalor	sucker	teenager	trainer
squander	suffer	teeter	traitor
squatter	sugar	telemarketer	transfer
squealer	suitor	teller	trapper
squirt	sulfur	temper	traveler
stabber	summer	temperature	treasure
stacker	super	tender	treasurer
stagger	superb	tenor	trembler
stalker	superior	tenure	tremor
stammer	supervisor	term	trendsetter
standard	supper	terrier	triangular
stapler	supporter	terror	trickster
starter	sure	tester	trigger
stature	surf	tether	trimmer
stealer	surfer	texture	trooper
steamer	surge	theater	trotter
stellar	surrender	thermometer	trouper
sticker	survivor	thicker	trouser
stickler	suture	thinker	trucker
stiffer	swagger	thinner	truer
stinger	swatter	third	tubular
stinker	sweater	thirst	tumbler
stir	sweatshirt	thriller	tumor
stockbroker	sweeper	thunder	tuner
stopper	sweeter	ticker	turn
storyteller	swerve	tickler	tutor
straggler	swifter	tiger	twerp
straighter	swimmer	tighter	twister
straightforward	swindler	timber	twitter
strainer	swinger	timer	typewriter
stranger	tailor	tinker	udder
streamer	taker	tipper	ulcer
stretcher	talker	toaster	ulterior
stricter	taller	toddler	umber
stripper	tamper	together	under
stroller	tanker	topper	undercover

undershirt
undertaker
underwater
underworld
undisturbed
unearth
unfamiliar
uninsured
universe
unnerve
upholster
upper
urge
user
usher
utter
valor
vapor
vaporizer
vector
vehicular
velour
vendor
ventilator
venture
verge
verse
vibrator

victor
viewer
vigor
vinegar
vineyard
viper
visitor
visor
voter
voucher
voyager
vulgar
vulture
wafer
wager
waiter
waiver
walker
wallpaper
wander
warmer
warrior
washer
wastepaper
watcher
watchtower
water
watercolor

waver
wayward
weaker
weather
weaver
welder
were
westward
whatever
whatsoever
wheeler
whenever
wherever
whether
whichever
whimper
whiner
whisker
whisper
whistler
whiter
whoever
whomever
whopper
wicker
wider
widower
wiener

wilder
willpower
winner
winter
wiper
wiser
wither
wizard
wonder
woodwork
word
work
worker
world
worse
worst
worth
wrangler
wrapper
wrestler
writer
yogurt
yonder
younger
youngster
zinger
zipper

[er]l   as in: schoolgirl

cowgirl
curl

girl
hurl

pearl
playgirl

salesgirl
schoolgirl

[er]m/n   as in: stern

adjourn
affirm
auburn
bookworm

burn
cavern
churn
concern

confirm
downturn
earn
earthworm

eastern
fern
firm
germ

govern	midterm	southern	tavern
heartburn	modern	sperm	unconcerned
inchworm	northern	spurn	western
intern	pattern	squirm	worm
iron	perm	stern	yearn
lantern	reconfirm	stubborn	
learn	return	sunburn	

[I]

[I]   as in: slide

abide	baptize	chloride	defy
accessorize	beautify	cite	delight
advertise	bedside	civilize	demise
advice	beehive	clarify	deny
advise	beside	classify	deodorize
afterlife	bike	clockwise	depressurize
agonize	bite	cockeyed	deprive
airtight	bonsai	cockfight	deputize
alibi	bribe	coincide	derive
alike	bride	collide	describe
alive	bright	colonize	desensitize
ally	broadside	commercialize	despise
alongside	brutalize	comply	despite
alphabetize	bullfight	comprise	device
alright	burglarize	compromise	devise
amplify	butterfly	computerize	dice
analyze	buy	conceptualize	die
antagonize	bye	concise	digitize
anti	byte	confide	dignify
apologize	cacti	connive	dike
appetite	calcify	copyright	disguise
apply	campsite	counterclockwise	dislike
archive	candlelight	countryside	disorganize
arise	capitalize	cowhide	disqualify
arrive	capsize	criticize	dissatisfied
aside	caramelize	crosswise	dive
astride	categorize	crucify	divide
authorize	cellulite	cry	dockside
awry	centralize	crystallize	dogfight
aye	certify	curbside	downright
backside	characterize	customize	downside
backslide	chastise	daylight	downsize
banzai	childlike	decide	dragonfly

drainpipe	fry	inside	nationwide
dramatize	gaslight	insight	nearby
drive	ghostwrite	institutionalize	necktie
dry	glide	intensify	neutralize
dye	glorify	invite	nice
dynamite	goodbye	itemize	night
economize	goodnight	jeopardize	nighttime
edgewise	graphite	joyride	normalize
electrify	gratify	July	nosedive
emphasize	gripe	justify	notify
energize	guide	kite	occupy
enterprise	gunfight	knife	optimize
entice	guy	knight	organize
equalize	harmonize	lamplight	otherwise
excite	hayride	landslide	outright
exercise	headlight	legalize	outside
expedite	height	lie	overnight
eye	hereby	life	oversight
eyesight	hi	light	oversize
falsify	hide	like	pacify
familiarize	high	likewise	paradise
fantasize	highlight	live	paralyze
fertilize	hike	lullaby	parasite
fight	hillside	magnify	passerby
finalize	hindsight	materialize	pasteurize
finite	hitchhike	maximize	patronize
firefly	hive	memorialize	penalize
fireside	homelike	memorize	penlight
fisheye	horrify	merchandise	percentile 'l
fistfight	horsefly	mesmerize	peroxide
five	housefly	meteorite	personalize
flashlight	humidify	midnight	pesticide
fleabite	hype	might	pie
flight	hypnotize	miniaturize	pigsty
floodlight	I	minimize	pike
fluoride	ice	misguide	pinkeye
fly	idealize	mobilize	pinstripe
foresight	identify	modernize	pipe
formalize	idolize	modify	playwright
forthright	ignite	moisturize	plight
fortify	immortalize	moonlight	ply
fortnight	imply	moonrise	polarize
franchise	impolite	multiply	polite
fright	improvise	my	poltergeist
frostbite	indict	mystify	poolside

potpie	rye	standardize	tonight
precise	sacrifice	standby	topside
preoccupy	safelight	starlight	torchlight
prescribe	satellite	stateside	transcribe
preside	satisfy	statewide	tribe
pressurize	scandalize	stereotype	trite
price	scrutinize	sterilize	trivialize
pride	searchlight	stoplight	try
prize	seaside	storewide	twice
prizefight	sensationalize	stovepipe	twilight
prototype	sensitize	streetlight	type
provide	shuteye	streetwise	unauthorized
pry	shy	stride	uncivilized
publicize	side	strike	underside
pulverize	sigh	stripe	underwrite
purify	sight	strive	unify
qualify	signify	sty	unionize
quite	simplify	stylize	unite
rabbi	site	subscribe	unlike
rationalize	size	subside	unoccupied
rawhide	skintight	suicide	unqualified
realize	sky	summarize	unsatisfied
recite	skydive	sunlight	unwise
recognize	skylight	sunrise	upright
refried	skywrite	supervise	upside
refry	slice	supply	uptight
rely	slide	surprise	utilize
reorganize	slight	survive	vandalize
reply	sly	swipe	vaporize
reprise	smite	symbolize	verbalize
reside	snakebite	sympathize	verify
reunite	snide	taillight	vice
revise	snipe	tailpipe	victimize
revitalize	socialize	tantalize	vise
revive	solidify	tenderize	visualize
revolutionize	spaceflight	termite	vitalize
rewrite	specialize	terrify	vocalize
ride	specify	terrorize	watertight
right	spice	testify	wayside
ringside	spike	theorize	website
ripe	spite	thigh	weeknight
riptide	splice	thrive	whereby
rise	spotlight	tide	white
rite	spy	tie	why
roadside	stabilize	tight	wide

wife	winterize	worldwide	yuletide
wildlife	wipe	write	
windpipe	wise	wry	

[I]l

as in: **smile**

agile	freestyle	mile	style
aisle	gentile	misfile	textile
argyle	godchild	pile	tile
awhile	grandchild	profile	turnstile
brainchild	hairstyle	projectile	vial
child	infantile	reconcile	vile
compile	isle	reptile	while
crocodile	juvenile	rile	wild
dial	lifestyle	senile	wile
exile	meanwhile	smile	worthwhile
file	mild	stockpile	

[I]m/n

as in: **shrine**

airline	clothesline	feline	mealtime
airtime	coastline	find	meantime
align	combine	fine	mind
alkaline	confine	grapevine	mine
alpine	consign	grime	moonshine
anytime	cosign	grind	neckline
asinine	crime	guideline	nine
assign	dateline	hairline	ninth
baseline	daytime	halftime	online
bedtime	deadline	headline	outline
beeline	decline	hemline	outshine
behind	define	hind	pastime
benign	design	incline	peacetime
bind	dime	kind	pine
blind	dine	lifeline	pipeline
borderline	divine	lifetime	playtime
byline	downtime	lime	porcupine
canine	entwine	line	prime
chime	enzyme	mainline	recline
climb	equine	mankind	redefine

refine
remind
resign
rewind
rhyme
rind
shine
shoreline
shrine
sideline
sign

skyline
slime
sometime
spine
springtime
stein
streamline
sublime
summertime
sunshine
swine

thyme
time
turbine
turpentine
twine
underline
undermine
unkind
unlined
unrefined
unsigned

unwind
valentine
vine
waistline
wartime
whine
wind
wine
wintertime

[I]r
as in: satire

acquire
admire
afire
amplifier
aspire
attire
backfire
bonfire
choir
conspire

crier
desire
dire
empire
entire
expire
fire
flier
hire
inquire

inspire
liar
misfire
pacifier
perspire
pliers
prior
require
retire
sapphire

satire
tire
transpire
umpire
vampire
wildfire
wire

[i]

[i]

as in: sit

abrasive
abusive
academic
accomplice
accomplish
acid
acidic
acoustic
acrobatic
acrylic
active
addict
addictive
additive
adhesive
administrative
admit
adoptive
adrift
aerobic
aerodynamic
aesthetic
affirmative
affix
afflict
aggressive
airsick
airstrip
alarmist
alcoholic
allergic
alternative
amateurish

amethyst
amid
amiss
analysis
anemic
anesthetic
angelfish
angelic
anguish
animalistic
anorexic
antacid
antagonistic
antibiotic
antic
anticlimactic
antiseptic
apologetic
appendix
appreciative
apprehensive
apprentice
apprenticeship
aquatic
arctic
argumentative
armpit
aromatic
arsenic
arthritic
arthritis
artist
artistic

assertive
assist
astonish
astronomic
athletic
atmospheric
atomic
attentive
attic
attractive
audit
authentic
autistic
automatic
automotive
avid
backstitch
ballistic
bandit
bandwidth
banish
barbaric
basic
basis
benefit
bewitch
bib
bid
big
biscuit
bit
bitch
blemish

bliss
bluish
bodice
botanic
boyish
brandish
brick
bridge
brisk
bronchitis
broomstick
caloric
candid
candlestick
capitalist
captive
cardiologist
carsick
cartridge
catfish
catnip
caustic
censorship
ceramic
cervix
championship
chaotic
characteristic
charismatic
chauvinist
chauvinistic
checklist
chemist

cherish
chick
childish
chip
chiropractic
chopstick
chromatic
chronic
cinematic
circuit
citizenship
civic
classic
claustrophobic
click
cliff
climactic
clinic
clip
clique
cockpit
coexist
colic
collective
columnist
comedic
comic
commemorative
commit
communicative
communist
companionship
comparative
competitive
composite
comprehensive
compulsive
conclusive
conducive
conflict
conservative
consist
constrict
constrictive
constructive

contradict
convict
cooperative
corrective
corrosive
cosmetic
cosmetologist
cosmic
counterfeit
courage
courtship
cowlick
creative
credit
crevice
crib
crisis
crisp
critic
crucifix
crypt
cryptic
cubic
culprit
cumulative
cupid
cursive
cyclist
cynic
cyst
debit
deceptive
decisive
decorative
decrepit
defective
defensive
deficit
definite
definitive
degenerative
demerit
democratic
demographic
demolish

demonic
demonstrative
dentist
depict
deposit
derelict
descriptive
destructive
detective
diabetic
diabolic
diagnosis
diagnostic
dialysis
diametric
did
dig
digit
diminish
dimwit
dip
diplomatic
dipstick
directive
disc
discredit
dish
disk
dismiss
disservice
distinctive
distinguish
domestic
dominatrix
dramatic
drastic
drawbridge
drift
drip
dropkick
drumstick
dynamic
eccentric
eclipse
economic

economist
ecstatic
edit
effective
elastic
elective
electric
electronic
elitist
elusive
embellish
embryonic
emit
emotive
empathetic
emphasis
encrypt
energetic
enlist
enrich
enthusiastic
epic
epidemic
episodic
equip
erosive
erotic
erratic
esoteric
establish
ethics
ethnic
euphoric
evasive
evict
excessive
exclusive
executive
exhaustive
exhibit
exist
exit
exotic
expansive
expensive

explicit	futuristic	humid	limerick
explosive	garlic	hybrid	limit
expressive	garnish	hydraulic	lip
exquisite	generic	hypnosis	lipstick
extensive	ghoulish	hypnotic	liquid
extinguish	gibberish	idiotic	list
eyelid	gift	imaginative	lit
fabric	gig	imperialistic	live
fanatic	gigantic	impressive	livid
fantastic	gimmick	impulsive	logic
favorite	girlish	inactive	lovesick
festive	give	incentive	lucid
fetish	glitch	ineffective	lunatic
feverish	gossip	inexpensive	lyric
fib	gothic	infinite	magic
fiendish	granite	inflict	magnetic
fifth	graphic	informative	majestic
fig	grid	inherit	manic
figurative	grip	inhibit	manuscript
filmstrip	grit	innovative	massive
fin	gymnastic	insist	materialistic
finalist	habit	instinctive	mathematics
fingertip	hairstylist	intuitive	matrix
finish	handpick	ironic	maverick
fish	hardship	itch	mechanic
fit	heartsick	jiff	medic
fix	hectic	jig	melodic
flagship	hellish	journalist	melodramatic
flick	hermit	journalistic	membership
flip	heroic	justice	merit
florist	hick	karmic	metallic
flourish	hid	kick	metric
fluid	hip	kid	microscopic
foolish	his	kinship	mid
forbid	Hispanic	kiss	mimic
forfeit	hiss	kit	minimalist
forgive	historic	knit	minimalistic
frantic	hit	lattice	mischief
fridge	hitch	lavish	misfit
friendship	holistic	leadership	miss
frigid	homeopathic	legit	mist
frizz	homesick	lick	mitt
frolic	horrid	licorice	mix
fugitive	horrific	lid	moonlit
furnish	housesit	lift	morbid

moronic	outbid	pit	pubic
mosaic	outdid	pitch	public
motive	outfit	pivot	publicist
music	outlive	plaintiff	publish
mystic	outwit	plastic	punish
myth	oversensitive	platonic	punitive
narcotic	panelist	podiatrist	purist
native	panic	poetic	purplish
negative	panoramic	polish	putrid
neurosis	paralysis	politics	pyramid
neurotic	paramedic	polyp	quick
niche	parish	porpoise	quip
nick	parsnip	porridge	quit
nip	partnership	portrait	quiz
nit	partridge	positive	rabbit
nitpick	passive	possessive	rabid
nitwit	pathetic	practice	radish
nix	patriotic	pragmatic	rancid
nomadic	pediatrics	predict	rapid
nonskid	pelvic	preexist	realistic
nostalgic	pelvis	prefix	receptionist
notice	perceptive	prehistoric	receptive
nourish	period	prejudice	redid
novelist	periodic	premise	reflective
novice	perish	preventative	refurbish
numeric	permissive	preventive	relationship
oasis	permit	prick	relative
objective	persist	primitive	relic
obsessive	perspective	problematic	relish
obstetric	persuasive	productive	relive
oceanic	pessimistic	profit	reminisce
offensive	pharmacist	prognosis	remit
office	phobic	progressive	repetitive
olive	phonetic	prohibit	replenish
omit	phonics	prohibitive	republic
onyx	photogenic	prolific	repulsive
operatic	photographic	promise	resist
opposite	physics	prospective	restrict
optic	pianist	prosthetic	retrospective
optimistic	pick	protagonist	rhinoceros
orbit	picnic	provocative	rhythmic
orchid	pig	prudish	rib
organic	pinkish	psychiatric	rich
orthopedic	pinprick	psychic	rid
osmosis	pip	psychotic	ridge

riff	skirmish	suggestive	transit
rig	skit	sulfuric	transmit
rigid	skittish	summit	traumatic
rip	slapstick	sunlit	trick
risk	slick	supersonic	trip
robotic	slid	supportive	tropic
romantic	slip	swift	tulip
rubbish	slit	swig	tunic
rustic	sluggish	swish	twig
sandwich	sniff	switch	twist
sarcastic	snip	symbolic	twit
scenic	snobbish	sympathetic	twitch
schematic	solicit	synthetic	undid
schizophrenic	solid	systematic	unfit
scholarship	solstice	tactic	unit
scholastic	sonic	talkative	uplift
scientific	sordid	tarnish	valid
scientist	spaceship	telescopic	vanish
script	spastic	tennis	varnish
seasick	specialist	tentative	ventriloquist
secretive	specific	tepid	verdict
sedative	spiff	terrific	visit
seductive	spirit	therapeutic	vivid
seismic	spit	therapist	vocalist
selective	splendid	thesis	volcanic
selfish	split	thick	vomit
sensitive	sporadic	this	votive
septic	sprig	thrift	warship
service	squeamish	tick	which
sheepish	starfish	tidbit	whiff
shellfish	starlit	tiff	whip
sheriff	static	timid	whisk
shift	statistic	tip	whiz
shindig	stick	tomboyish	wick
ship	stiff	tonic	width
shtick	stitch	tonsillitis	wig
sick	strategic	toothpick	wish
sidekick	strict	topic	wisp
sieve	strip	tortoise	wit
sip	stupid	tourist	witch
sit	stylish	township	with
six	stylist	toxic	workaholic
skeptic	subjective	traffic	workmanship
skid	submit	tragic	worship
skip	suffix	transcript	wrist

yardstick   yellowish   zip   zit

[i]l   as in: skill

anthill   fulfill   nil   still
bill   gill   pill   thrill
build   goodwill   quilt   till
built   grill   rebuild   tilt
buttermilk   guild   rebuilt   tranquil
chenille   guilt   refill   treadmill
chill   hill   sawmill   twill
daffodil   ill   shill   until
distill   instill   shrill   uphill
downhill   jilt   silk   will
drill   kill   sill   wilt
fill   landfill   skill   windmill
foothill   milk   spill   windowsill
freewill   mill   spilt   zilch
frill   molehill   standstill

[i]m/n   as in: slim

adrenaline   coffin   genuine   jasmine
aspirin   convince   gin   kin
assassin   cousin   glimpse   limb
bargain   cringe   goblin   limp
basin   cumin   grim   margarine
begin   denim   grin   margin
bin   determine   gym   masculine
binge   dim   hairpin   medicine
blueprint   din   herein   mince
brim   discipline   him   mint
bulletin   dolphin   hinge   moccasin
bumpkin   downwind   hint   mountain
cabin   engine   hymn   muffin
chaplain   examine   imagine   muslin
chin   famine   in   napkin
cinch   feminine   inch   noggin
clinch   flinch   inn   origin
clothespin   fringe   intestine   paraffin

penguin	rinse	splint	urchin
penicillin	robin	sprint	urine
peppermint	ruin	squint	verbatim
pilgrim	satin	stickpin	vermin
pimp	scrimp	swim	victim
pin	sequin	syringe	villain
pinch	shin	tailspin	violin
porcelain	shrimp	therein	vitamin
predetermine	sin	thin	wherein
prim	since	thumbprint	whim
prince	singe	tin	whirlwind
print	skim	tinge	wimp
prism	skimp	tint	win
pumpkin	skin	toxin	wind
raisin	slim	trim	within
resin	spearmint	twin	yin
rim	spin	uncertain	

[O]

[O]

as in: snow

abode	bistro	choke	depot
afloat	bloat	chose	devote
afterglow	blow	cloak	diagnose
aglow	boast	close	disclose
ago	boat	clothes	disco
airflow	bongo	clove	dispose
albino	borrow	coach	disrobe
alcove	both	coast	ditto
almost	bow	coat	domino
aloe	bravado	coax	dope
also	bravo	cockroach	dote
although	breaststroke	cocoa	dough
alto	broach	code	download
antelope	broke	comatose	doze
antidote	bronco	combo	dreamboat
approach	brooch	commando	drove
armadillo	brownnose	commode	duo
armload	buffalo	compose	dynamo
arrow	bulldoze	compost	earlobe
artichoke	bungalow	concerto	echo
audio	bureau	condo	ego
auto	burrito	cope	elbow
avocado	burrow	corrode	elope
awoke	calico	cosmos	embryo
backstroke	cameo	cove	enclose
banjo	cantaloupe	cowpoke	encode
bathrobe	cappuccino	croak	envelope
beau	cargo	crossroad	episode
bedfellow	carload	crow	erode
behold	caseload	cutthroat	escrow
below	casino	deco	espresso
bestow	cello	decode	evoke
bingo	chateau	demote	explode

expo	horoscope	mono	presoak
expose	hose	mope	presto
fellow	host	mosquito	primrose
fiasco	houseboat	most	pro
float	housecoat	motto	probe
flow	household	mow	promote
follow	implode	mumbo	pronto
footnote	impose	narrow	propose
foreclose	indigo	no	prose
forego	info	node	provoke
fro	innermost	nope	psycho
froze	joke	nose	pueblo
furlough	jumbo	note	quote
furrow	kaleidoscope	oaf	radio
gazebo	keynote	oak	railroad
gecko	keystroke	oath	rainbow
ghetto	kilo	ode	raincoat
ghost	know	oh	ratio
gizmo	lasso	oppose	reload
gloat	libido	outgrow	remote
globe	lifeboat	overcoat	revoke
glow	limbo	overflow	rewrote
go	limo	overgrow	road
goad	lingo	overload	roast
goat	load	owe	robe
goes	loaf	payload	rode
grope	loco	periscope	rodeo
gross	logo	photo	rogue
grotto	lotto	piano	rope
grove	low	piccolo	rose
grow	macho	pillow	rove
growth	macro	pimento	row
gumbo	maestro	pistachio	rowboat
gusto	mango	placebo	sailboat
gyro	marshmallow	plateau	scapegoat
halo	mayo	poach	scarecrow
heatstroke	meadow	poke	scenario
hello	mellow	polo	scope
hero	memo	poncho	sew
hippo	metro	porno	shadow
hoax	micro	portfolio	shallow
hoe	microscope	pose	shipload
hollow	mistletoe	post	show
honcho	moat	potato	showboat
hope	mode	predispose	sideshow

silo
slideshow
slope
slow
slowpoke
smoke
snow
so
soak
soap
solo
soprano
sorrow
sourdough
sow
sparrow
speedboat
spoke
staccato
steamboat
stereo
stethoscope
stiletto
stoke
stove
stow

strobe
strode
stroke
stucco
studio
sumo
sunstroke
suppose
swallow
taco
tango
taro
taupe
telescope
tempo
thorough
those
though
throat
throw
tightrope
tiptoe
toad
toast
tobacco
toe

tomato
tomorrow
tornado
torpedo
torso
tote
tow
trainload
transpose
trio
trousseau
truckload
tugboat
turbo
tuxedo
typo
underclothes
undergo
undertow
unload
uphold
upmost
utmost
varicose
veto
vibrato

video
virtuoso
vogue
volcano
vote
wacko
wallow
wardrobe
weirdo
wheelbarrow
whoa
widow
willow
window
woe
woke
workload
wove
wrote
yellow
yoke
yolk
zero

[O]l

as in: **sole**

armhole
bankroll
billfold
blindfold
bold
bolt
bowl
buttonhole
camisole
casserole
charcoal
coal
cold
console

control
enroll
fishbowl
flagpole
foal
fold
folk
foxhole
goal
gold
hellhole
hold
hole
insole

jolt
keyhole
knoll
knothole
loophole
marigold
mold
mole
old
parole
patrol
payroll
peephole
pinhole

pole
poll
pothole
revolt
role
roll
scaffold
scold
scroll
sinkhole
sold
sole
soul
steamroll

stole	threshold	toll	washbowl
stroll	thumbhole	townsfolk	whole
tadpole	thunderbolt	troll	withhold
threefold	told	unfold	wormhole

[O]m/n   as in: stone

alone	dethrone	hormone	rhinestone
atone	disown	ingrown	roam
backbone	dome	jawbone	sandstone
baritone	don't	keystone	scone
birthstone	drone	known	shinbone
blown	earphone	limestone	sown
bone	flagstone	loan	stone
breastbone	flown	lone	syndrome
brownstone	foam	metronome	tailbone
chaperon	gallstone	microphone	telephone
cheekbone	gemstone	milestone	throne
chrome	gnome	moan	tombstone
clone	groan	moonstone	tone
cobblestone	grown	outgrown	trombone
collarbone	halftone	overgrown	undertone
cologne	headphone	own	unknown
comb	headstone	ozone	windblown
condone	hipbone	phone	wishbone
cone	home	pinecone	won't
cornerstone	homegrown	postpone	xylophone
cyclone	hone	prone	zone

[O]r   as in: store

aboard	airport	blackboard	cavort
abort	anymore	board	chord
absorb	ashore	bookstore	chore
accord	assort	bore	coarse
acorn	award	born	cohort
adore	backdoor	brainstorm	conform
adorn	baseboard	bullhorn	contort
afford	before	cardboard	cord
airborne	billboard	carport	core

cork	four	pitchfork	sort
corn	fourscore	platform	source
corpse	fourth	poor	spore
corridor	furthermore	popcorn	sport
course	galore	pore	store
court	gore	pork	stork
dashboard	guarantor	porn	storm
decor	hardcore	port	support
deform	hoard	postwar	surfboard
deplore	hoarse	pour	swarm
deport	horn	quart	sword
dinosaur	horse	quartz	swore
discourse	ignore	racehorse	sworn
distort	implore	rapport	therefore
divorce	import	reborn	thorn
door	indoor	record	thunderstorm
dorm	inform	recourse	thwart
downpour	keyboard	reform	tore
drawer	landlord	reinforce	torn
drugstore	longhorn	remorse	torque
encore	lovelorn	report	torte
endorse	lukewarm	reservoir	toward
enforce	mentor	resort	transform
escort	meteor	resource	transport
evermore	more	restore	underscore
explore	mourn	reward	unexplored
export	newborn	roar	uniform
extort	nor	sawhorse	uproar
eyesore	norm	scorch	war
firstborn	north	score	ward
floor	oar	scoreboard	warm
foghorn	offshore	scorn	warmth
folklore	or	seahorse	warn
for	orb	seashore	warp
force	ore	shore	wart
fore	outdoor	short	wharf
forevermore	outpour	skateboard	wherefore
forewarn	outscore	snore	wore
fork	outworn	snort	workforce
forlorn	overboard	snowstorm	workhorse
form	passport	soar	worn
fort	peppercorn	sophomore	your
forth	perform	sore	

[Oi]

[Oi]   as in: steroid

ahoy	cowboy	hoist	schoolboy
android	coy	invoice	soy
annoy	decoy	joy	steroid
asteroid	deploy	killjoy	tabloid
avoid	destroy	moist	thyroid
bellboy	devoid	noise	tomboy
boy	employ	overjoyed	toy
busboy	enjoy	playboy	turquoise
choice	envoy	ploy	unemployed
convoy	exploit	poise	voice
corduroy	hemorrhoid	rejoice	void

[Oi]l   as in: soil

boil	foil	soil
broil	oil	spoil
coil	recoil	turmoil

[Oi]m/n   as in: sirloin

adjoin	disappoint	needlepoint	tenderloin
appoint	groin	pinpoint	viewpoint
ballpoint	join	point	
checkpoint	joint	rejoin	
coin	loin	sirloin	

[o]

[o]   as in: spot

abroad
across
adopt
aftershock
afterthought
ah
allot
aloft
analog
antilock
applaud
applause
apricot
astronaut
atop
aught
awe
backdrop
backlog
backstop
backwash
barbershop
beanstalk
bellhop
blacktop
blah
blastoff
blob
block
bloodshot
blot
blotch
boardwalk

bob
boondocks
boss
botch
bought
box
boycott
bra
brainwash
broad
broth
brought buckshot
bulldog
bullfrog
butterscotch
bylaw
camouflage
cannot
carwash
castoff
catalog
caught
cause
cellblock
chalk
chaos
chatterbox
cheesecloth
chock
chop
clause
claw
clock

clog
clot
cloth
cob
cock
coffeepot
cog
coleslaw
collage
concoct
cop
corncob
cornstalk
corsage
cost
cot
cough
countertop
crackpot
crisscross
crop
cross
crosswalk
cutoff
deadlock
defrost
desktop
dewdrop
dialogue
dishcloth
dislodge
distraught
doc

dock
dodge
dog
doorknob
doorstop
dot
draw
drop
eardrop
earshot
eavesdrop
eggnog
emboss
entourage
exhaust
flattop
flaw
flock
flop
floss
flowerpot
fog
forethought
forgot
fought
fox
foxtrot
fraught
frock
frog
frost
garage
gauze

gawk	knot	outbox	showoff
gearbox	lapdog	outfox	shutoff
glob	law	outlaw	sidewalk
gloss	layoff	overdraw	sleepwalk
gnaw	leapfrog	ox	slingshot
gob	liftoff	pa	slipknot
gosh	lob	padlock	slob
got	lock	pause	slot
grandma	lodge	paw	smock
grandpa	loft	pawnshop	smog
gridlock	log	payoff	snapshot
groundhog	lollipop	peacock	snob
gumdrop	lop	pilaf	snot
gunshot	loss	pillbox	soapbox
hacksaw	lost	playoff	sock
hah	lot	plod	sod
hardtop	lox	plop	soft
hatbox	ma	plot	sought
hawk	mailbox	pop	southpaw
headlock	mascot	pot	spa
heartthrob	massage	potshot	spacewalk
hemlock	mauve	pox	spinoff
hilltop	melodrama	prod	spot
hobnob	mirage	prologue	squad
hock	mob	prop	squash
hog	mock	raindrop	squat
hoopla	moonwalk	raw	squawk
hop	mop	roadblock	stalk
hot	moss	rob	standoff
hotshot	mountaintop	robot	stock
hurrah	mouthwash	rock	stop
icebox	naught	rod	straw
inkblot	nighthawk	rooftop	suave
jackpot	nightspot	rot	sunspot
jaw	nod	sabotage	swab
jaywalk	nonstop	sandbox	swap
jigsaw	not	sauce	swat
job	notch	saw	swatch
jock	o'clock	scoff	sweatshop
jog	odd	sendoff	takeoff
jot	off	sexpot	talk
kickoff	onslaught	shamrock	taught
knob	opt	shock	taut
knock	orthodox	shop	teapot
knockoff	ought	shot	teardrop

thaw	tradeoff	voila	watt
thought	treetop	wad	whatnot
throb	tripod	walk	windsock
tiptop	trot	waltz	withdraw
toolbox	trough	warlock	wok
top	turnoff	wash	workshop
topnotch	underdog	washcloth	wristwatch
toss	unlock	watch	wrought
tot	unorthodox	watchdog	yacht

[o]l   as in: solve

absolve	default	haul	recall
aerosol	dissolve	highball	resolve
alcohol	doll	install	revolve
all	downfall	involve	salt
asphalt	drawl	landfall	scald
assault	drywall	mall	scrawl
bald	enthrall	malt	screwball
balk	evolve	maul	shawl
ball	eyeball	meatball	shortfall
baseball	fall	menthol	small
basketball	false	mothball	snowfall
bawl	fault	Neanderthal	softball
blackball	fireball	nightfall	solve
brawl	football	oddball	sprawl
call	gall	overall	stall
calm	golf	overhaul	tall
catchall	goofball	palm	vault
caulk	hairball	pinball	volleyball
cholesterol	hall	pitfall	wall
cobalt	halt	protocol	waterfall
cornball	handball	qualm	windfall
crawl	hardball	rainfall	withdrawal

[o]m/n   as in: song

along	belong	bomb	bouillon
aunt	beyond	bonbon	bronze
baton	blond	bond	bygone

chiffon
con
confidante
correspond
coupon
crayon
croissant
crouton
dawn
debutante
doggone
drawn
eon
fawn
flaunt
fond
font
foregone
gone

haunt
hexagon
honk
icon
intercom
launch
lawn
lifelong
long
marathon
mom
moron
neon
nonchalant
nylon
oblong
octagon
on
overdrawn

Parmesan
paunch
pawn
pecan
pentagon
phenomenon
pond
prawn
predawn
prolong
prom
prompt
pylon
python
rayon
renaissance
respond
response
restaurant

romp
saffron
salon
sitcom
song
spawn
stomp
strong
swamp
swan
taunt
thong
triathlon
upon
want
withdrawn
wrong
yawn

[o]r   as in: star

afar
ajar
alarm
apart
arc
arch
are
ark
arm
art
backyard
ballpark
bankcard
bar
bark
barn
barnyard
bazaar
benchmark
birthmark
bizarre

bombard
bookmark
boudoir
boulevard
brickyard
car
card
cart
carve
caviar
charge
charm
chart
cigar
cornstarch
courtyard
crowbar
dark
darn
dart
depart

disarm
disbar
discard
discharge
disregard
embark
enlarge
far
farce
farm
guard
guitar
handlebar
hard
harm
harp
harsh
heart
jar
landmark
large

lifeguard
mar
march
mark
memoir
outsmart
overcharge
par
park
part
postcard
radar
regard
registrar
remark
restart
rhubarb
safeguard
sandbar
scar
scarf

seminar

shark

sharp

smart

sonar

spar

spark

star

starch

start

starve

streetcar

surcharge

sweetheart

tar

tart

trademark

underarm

watermark

yard

yarn

[oo/]

[oo/]   as in: **stood**

afoot	driftwood	notebook	soot
ambush	foot	octopus	stood
barefoot	good	outlook	storybook
book	handbook	overlook	textbook
brook	hood	parenthood	took
brotherhood	hook	plywood	underfoot
bush	input	push	understood
checkbook	likelihood	put	wood
childhood	look	scrapbook	workbook
cook	neighborhood	shook	would
could	nook	should	yearbook

[oo]

[oo]   as in: scoot

absolute	burglarproof	disapprove	group
abuse	caboose	discontinue	hairdo
accuse	canoe	disprove	hoop
acute	cashew	dispute	hue
allude	chew	distribute	huge
altitude	childproof	do	improve
amuse	choose	drew	include
anew	chute	droop	institute
approve	clue	dude	interview
aptitude	commute	due	into
argue	compute	electrocute	introduce
askew	conclude	elude	intrude
astute	confuse	enthused	issue
attitude	construe	exclude	juice
attribute	continue	excuse	kangaroo
avenue	contribute	execute	knew
bamboo	coo	extrude	kook
barbecue	corkscrew	feud	latitude
behoove	crew	few	lawsuit
blew	croup	fireproof	lewd
blue	crude	flew	loop
blues	cruise	flu	loose
boo	cube	fluke	loot
boost	cuckoo	flute	lose
boot	cue	food	lube
booth	curfew	foolproof	menu
booze	cute	fortitude	mew
breakthrough	debut	fruit	mildew
brew	delude	glue	minute
brood	destitute	goof	misconstrue
bruise	dew	gratitude	mood
brute	diffuse	grew	moose
bulletproof	dilute	groove	moot

move	recruit	shampoo	too
multitude	redo	shoe	toot
mute	reduce	shoot	tooth
nephew	refuge	shrewd	tribute
new	refuse	skew	troop
nude	refute	smooth	true
nuke	remove	snafu	truth
ooze	rendezvous	snoot	tube
outdo	renew	snooze	two
outgrew	reproduce	solitude	undo
overdue	rescue	soothe	unused
overview	residue	soundproof	uproot
papoose	reuse	soup	use
parachute	revenue	spew	value
persecute	review	spook	venue
pew	revue	spruce	view
pollute	roof	statue	virtue
prelude	roost	stew	voodoo
preview	root	subdue	waterproof
produce	rouge	substitute	weatherproof
proof	route	sue	who
prosecute	rude	suit	whose
prostitute	salute	swimsuit	windproof
protrude	scoop	swoop	withdrew
prove	scoot	taboo	woo
prude	screw	tattoo	you
puke	scrooge	threw	youth
pursue	seafood	through	
pursuit	seclude	tissue	
recoup	seduce	to	

[oo]l   as in: school

armful	dual	mouthful	ridicule
barstool	fool	mule	rule
bull	footstool	nodule	school
capsule	fuel	overrule	spool
carpool	full	perceptual	stool
cesspool	ghoul	pool	toadstool
cool	gruel	preschool	tool
cruel	handful	pull	werewolf
cupful	module	refuel	whirlpool
drool	molecule	residual	wool

[oo]m/n

as in: **soon**

afternoon	classroom	lagoon	saloon
assume	cocoon	moon	showroom
baboon	commune	mushroom	soon
balloon	consume	noon	spoon
ballroom	costume	opportune	strewn
bathroom	courtroom	perfume	swoon
bedroom	darkroom	platoon	tune
bloom	elbowroom	plume	vacuum
boardroom	gloom	presume	volume
boom	groom	prune	whom
bridegroom	heirloom	raccoon	womb
broom	honeymoon	restroom	workroom
buffoon	immune	resume	wound
cartoon	June	room	zoom

[ow]

[ow]   as in: somehow

about
allow
aloud
anyhow
arouse
bailout
birdhouse
blackout
blouse
blowout
bow
breakout
brow
browse
burnout
checkout
chow
cloud
clout
clubhouse

cookout
couch
courthouse
cow
crowd
doghouse
doubt
douse
drought
dugout
eyebrow
farmhouse
greenhouse
house
how
jailhouse
lighthouse
loud
louse
luau

madhouse
mouse
mouth
now
nuthouse
ouch
oust
out
outhouse
ow
penthouse
playhouse
poorhouse
pouch
pout
proud
roughhouse
route
schoolhouse
scout

shout
shroud
slouch
smokehouse
somehow
south
spouse
spout
sprout
stakeout
throughout
vouch
vow
warehouse
without
workout
wow

[ow]l   as in: scowl

afoul
bowel
dishtowel

foul
fowl
growl

howl
owl
scowl

[ow]m/n

as in: sound

abound	crown	meltdown	shutdown
account	denounce	mound	slowdown
aground	discount	nightgown	sound
amount	dismount	noun	spellbound
announce	down	ounce	splashdown
around	downtown	playground	surround
astound	drown	pound	touchdown
background	found	profound	town
bounce	frown	pronoun	turndown
bound	gown	pronounce	underground
breakdown	ground	putdown	uptown
brown	hometown	renown	westbound
campground	hound	round	wolfhound
clown	knockdown	rubdown	wound
compound	letdown	rundown	
count	lounge	scrounge	
countdown	lowdown	shakedown	
crackdown	markdown	showdown	

[u]

[u]   as in: shut

Includes alternate pronunciations, as in sister* pronounced sis-tuh.

a	because	chug	destruct
abduct	bedbug	cinema	develop
above	begrudge	claustrophobia	diarrhea
abrupt	blood	cleanup	dilemma
adjust	blowup	club	diploma
agenda	bluff	cluck	discuss
airbrush	blush	clutch	disgust
algebra	bonanza	cobra	disrupt
amnesia	breakup	coconut	does
amok	brother*	coma	dollop
anemia	brush	comma	doughnut
anesthesia	buck	conduct	dove
anorexia	bud	construct	drama
another*	budge	cornea	drudge
antenna	buff	corrupt	drug
aqua	bug	crackup	dub
area	buildup	criteria	duck
arena	bus	crud	dud
aroma	bust	crush	dug
asthma	but	crust	dumbstruck
aura	butt	cub	dust
awestruck	buzz	cud	earmuff
azalea	cabana	cuff	earplug
backup	cafeteria	cup	eczema
bacteria	camera	cut	enchilada
ballerina	candelabra	dandruff	enough
banana	charisma	data	era
bandana	checkup	debug	erupt
bankrupt	cherub	deduct	extravaganza
barracuda	chestnut	deluxe	father*
bathtub	chuck	dementia	fiesta

flood	luck	plug	sister*
flub	lug	plus	sludge
fluff	lush	plush	slug
flush	lust	pneumonia	slush
formula	makeup	polka	slut
fudge	mama	potluck	smudge
fuss	media	product	smug
fuzz	misjudge	propaganda	smut
gallop	mocha	pub	snub
gamut	mother*	puck	snuff
gardenia	mozzarella	puff	snug
glove	much	pug	soda
gondola	muck	pup	somewhat
gorilla	mud	pushup	spatula
grownup	mug	putt	stamina
grub	multimedia	quota	stardust
grudge	mush	replica	stigma
gruff	musk	retina	stirrup
gush	must	retouch	struck
gut	mutt	robust	strut
haircut	nausea	rosebud	stub
handcuff	nebula	rotunda	stuck
Hanukkah	nightclub	rough	stud
hiccup	nostalgia	roundup	stuff
holdup	nub	rub	stump
hub	nudge	rug	sub
hubbub	nut	rush	such
huff	obstruct	rust	suck
hug	of	rut	surplus
humbug	opera	saga	syrup
hush	orchestra	saliva	tarantula
hut	paintbrush	sauna	teacup
hutch	pajama	scallop	the
idea	panorama	schmuck	thrust
instruct	papa	scrub	thug
interrupt	papaya	scruff	toothbrush
judge	pasta	scuff	tortilla
jug	peanut	setup	tostada
just	petunia	shakeup	touch
jut	phobia	shortcut	tough
ketchup	piecrust	shove	trauma
ladybug	piñata	shrub	trivia
lineup	pizza	shrug	truck
love	pizzeria	shut	trust
lover*	plaza	siesta	tub

tuba	umbrella	veranda	what
tuck	up	via	yoga
tug	uppercut	vista	yuck
tux	us	vodka	zebra
ugh	vanilla	wallop	
ultra	vendetta	walnut	

[u]l   as in: skull

abdominal	annul	barnacle	buckle
able	answerable	barrel	bugle
abnormal	antisocial	bashful	bulge
abominable	apparel	basil	bulk
acceptable	apple	battle	bundle
accessible	applicable	beagle	burial
accidental	appraisal	bearable	bushel
accountable	approachable	beautiful	bustle
achievable	approval	bedazzle	cable
actual	April	beetle	camel
adaptable	architectural	believable	cancel
additional	archival	belittle	candle
adjustable	arguable	beneficial	capable
admirable	arousal	betrayal	capital
admiral	arrival	bevel	capitol
admissible	arsenal	biannual	cardinal
adoptable	artful	bible	careful
adorable	article	biblical	carnival
adult	artificial	bicycle	carol
advisable	assemble	bifocal	castle
aerial	astral	bilingual	casual
affordable	astronomical	biodegradable	cathedral
agreeable	attainable	blissful	cattle
agricultural	atypical	boggle	celestial
allowable	audible	botanical	centennial
alphabetical	audiovisual	bottle	central
ample	available	breakable	cereal
analytical	avoidable	bridal	cerebral
ancestral	awful	bridle	ceremonial
angel	axle	brindle	channel
angle	bacterial	brittle	chapel
animal	baffle	bronchial	charitable
ankle	bagel	brutal	cheerful
annual	bangle	bubble	chemical

chisel
choral
chronicle
chuckle
circle
circumstantial
civil
classical
clerical
clinical
coincidental
collapsible
collateral
collectible
colonel
colonial
colorful
colossal
combustible
comfortable
comical
commendable
commercial
comparable
compatible
conceivable
conceptual
conditional
confessional
confidential
congressional
conical
consensual
consequential
considerable
constable
consult
consumable
contemptible
contextual
continental
continual
contractual
controversial
conventional

convertible
convulse
coral
cordial
council
counsel
couple
crackle
cradle
credential
credible
criminal
crinkle
cripple
critical
crucial
crumble
crumple
crystal
cubicle
cuddle
cultural
curable
curdle
custodial
cuticle
cycle
cynical
dabble
dangle
daredevil
dazzle
debatable
deceitful
decimal
deductible
delectable
delightful
delusional
denial
dental
dependable
deplorable
desirable
despicable

destructible
detectable
detestable
detrimental
devotional
diabolical
diagonal
diesel
difficult
digestible
digital
dimensional
dimple
disable
disagreeable
disapproval
disassemble
disgraceful
disgruntle
dishonorable
disloyal
dismantle
disposable
disposal
disrespectful
divulge
docile
double
doubtful
dowel
dreadful
dribble
drinkable
drizzle
dull
durable
dwindle
dysfunctional
eagle
easel
eatable
ecological
economical
edible
editorial

educational
electrical
elemental
eligible
embezzle
emerald
emotional
enable
enamel
enforceable
enjoyable
ensemble
entangle
entitle
entrepreneurial
environmental
equal
essential
eternal
ethical
eventful
eventual
example
exceptional
excitable
experimental
external
facial
factual
faithful
fanatical
fanciful
fashionable
favorable
fearful
feasible
feeble
fertile
festival
fickle
fictional
fiddle
finagle
final
financial

fiscal	harmful	insult	marital
fizzle	hassle	intellectual	material
flannel	hazel	intentional	maternal
flavorful	heckle	internal	mathematical
flexible	helpful	intestinal	matrimonial
floral	herbal	invincible	measles
focal	honeysuckle	invisible	mechanical
forceful	honorable	irrational	medal
forgettable	hopeful	irresistible	meddle
formal	horizontal	irresponsible	medical
fossil	hormonal	irreversible	medieval
fractional	horrible	irritable	memorable
fragile	hospitable	janitorial	memorial
freckle	hospital	jewel	mental
frightful	hostile	jiggle	merciful
frontal	huddle	jingle	metal
frugal	huggable	journal	methodical
fumble	humble	joyful	middle
functional	hurdle	juggle	mineral
fundamental	hustle	jumble	mingle
funeral	icicle	jungle	minimal
funnel	identical	kennel	miracle
futile	idle	knowledgeable	miserable
gainful	idol	knuckle	missile
gamble	illegal	label	mobile
gargle	imbecile	laughable	model
gavel	immoral	lawful	monumental
general	immortal	legal	moral
gentle	impeccable	legible	mortal
giggle	imperial	lethal	motivational
global	impossible	level	motorcycle
gobble	impractical	liable	muddle
graceful	incidental	liberal	muffle
gradual	indestructible	likable	multilevel
gravel	individual	little	multiple
gravitational	indulge	local	mural
griddle	industrial	logical	muscle
gristle	inevitable	lovable	musical
grovel	influential	loyal	mutual
grumble	informal	lustful	muzzle
gulf	initial	lyrical	mystical
guzzle	inspirational	magical	nasal
habitual	institutional	maniacal	national
haggle	instructional	marble	natural
handle	instrumental	marginal	nautical

naval
needle
neutral
nibble
nickel
nimble
noble
nocturnal
nominal
nonverbal
noodle
normal
nostril
noticeable
novel
numerical
numskull
nuzzle
obstacle
occasional
occult
official
operational
optical
optimal
optional
oral
orbital
orchestral
oriental
original
ornamental
oval
overindulge
paddle
painful
palatable
palpable
panel
panhandle
paralegal
parcel
parental
partial
particle

paternal
peaceful
pebble
pedal
peddle
pedestal
penal
pencil
people
perceptible
perennial
peril
peripheral
perishable
permissible
perpetual
personal
petal
pharmaceutical
phenomenal
philosophical
physical
pickle
pimple
pineapple
pinnacle
pistol
pitiful
pivotal
pixel
playful
pleasurable
plentiful
pliable
plural
political
poodle
portable
portal
possible
postal
potential
powerful
practical
predictable

preferable
preferential
prejudicial
prenatal
presentable
presumable
pretzel
prickle
primeval
principal
principle
printable
probable
procedural
professional
profitable
promotional
proposal
proverbial
provincial
provisional
prowl
psychological
puddle
pulp
pulse
pummel
pumpernickel
punctual
punishable
pupil
purple
puzzle
quadruple
questionable
quintessential
quizzical
racial
radial
radical
raffle
ramble
ramshackle
rascal
rational

rattle
ravel
reasonable
rebel
rebuttal
receptacle
reciprocal
recital
recreational
rectangle
recycle
referral
refusal
regal
regional
rehearsal
reliable
remarkable
remedial
remodel
remorseful
removable
removal
rental
reprisal
repulse
reputable
resemble
resentful
residential
resourceful
respectable
respectful
responsible
result
retinal
reversal
reversible
revival
revocable
riddle
rifle
rightful
ripple
rival

royal
rubble
ruffle
rumble
rural
rustle
saddle
sample
sandal
scalpel
scandal
schedule
scoundrel
scramble
scribble
scuffle
seagull
seasonal
sectional
semiformal
senatorial
sensational
sensible
sensual
sentimental
sequel
sequential
serial
settle
several
sexual
shackle
shamble
shameful
shovel
shrivel
shuffle
signal
simple
sinful
single
sizable
sizzle
skeletal
skeptical

skillful
skull
smuggle
snorkel
snuggle
sociable
social
sorrowful
soulful
sparkle
special
speckle
spectacle
spinal
spindle
spiral
spiritual
spiteful
spoonful
sprinkle
squabble
squirrel
stable
staple
startle
statistical
steeple
stencil
sterile
stifle
straddle
straggle
strangle
stressful
stretchable
strudel
struggle
stumble
subliminal
substantial
subtle
successful
suicidal
suitable
sulk

superficial
supple
supplemental
surgical
survival
suspenseful
swirl
swivel
syllable
symbol
table
tackle
tactful
tactical
tangible
tangle
tassel
tasteful
tattle
technical
temperamental
temple
tentacle
terminal
terrestrial
terrible
territorial
testimonial
thankful
theatrical
thermal
thimble
thoughtful
tickle
timetable
tingle
tinsel
title
toddle
toggle
tolerable
tonal
tonsil
topical
torrential

total
towel
traditional
trample
transitional
travel
treble
tremble
trial
triangle
tribal
trickle
tricycle
triple
trivial
tropical
trouble
truffle
truthful
tumble
tunnel
turntable
tutorial
twinkle
twirl
typical
umbilical
unable
unavailable
unavoidable
unbelievable
uncle
uncomfortable
unconditional
unconquerable
uncontrollable
unconventional
undeniable
undesirable
unfavorable
unforgettable
universal
unlawful
unnatural
unofficial

unprofitable
unquestionable
unravel
unreasonable
unreliable
unsociable
unspeakable
unstable
unthinkable
untouchable
untruthful
unusual
upheaval
usable
useful
usual

utensil
valuable
vandal
variable
vegetable
vehicle
vengeful
verbal
versatile
vertical
vessel
viable
vigil
viral
virtual
visible

visual
vital
vocal
vocational
volatile
vowel
vulnerable
waddle
waffle
washable
wasteful
watchful
wearable
weasel
whimsical
whirl

whistle
whittle
wiggle
willful
wishful
woeful
wonderful
workable
wrangle
wrestle
wrinkle
wrongful
yodel
youthful

[u]m/n   as in: sun

abbreviation
abduction
abortion
abrasion
absorption
acceleration
accommodation
accordion
accumulation
accusation
accustom
action
activation
adaptation
addendum
addiction
addition
administration
admiration
admission
adoption
adoration
adventuresome
affection
affiliation

affirmation
affliction
aggravation
aggression
agitation
album
allegation
alleviation
allocation
alteration
aluminum
ambition
ammunition
among
amongst
amplification
animation
annihilation
anticipation
anyone
application
appreciation
apprehension
approximation
aquarium

assassination
association
assumption
asylum
atom
attention
attraction
auction
audition
auditorium
augmentation
authorization
autumn
aviation
awesome
beachfront
beautician
become
begun
billion
blossom
blunt
boredom
bosom
bothersome

bottom
bourbon
brunch
brunt
bullion
bum
bump
bun
bunch
bunk
burdensome
buxom
calcification
calcium
calculation
calibration
cancellation
canyon
caption
carnation
caution
celebration
certification
chipmunk
chum

chunk
cinnamon
circulation
citation
civilization
clarification
classification
clump
clunk
coliseum
collaboration
collection
collision
colon
column
combination
combustion
come
commemoration
commission
commotion
communication
communion
companion
compassion
compensation
competition
compilation
complexion
complication
composition
comprehension
compression
compulsion
concentration
concession
conclusion
concussion
condensation
condition
condom
confection
confession
configuration
confirmation
confront
confrontation

confusion
congestion
conglomeration
congratulation
congregation
connection
conservation
consideration
consolation
consolidation
constellation
constipation
constriction
construction
consultation
contagion
contamination
continuation
contraception
contraction
contradiction
contraption
contribution
convention
conversation
conviction
convulsion
cooperation
coordination
corporation
correction
corrosion
corruption
cranium
creation
crumb
crunch
cumbersome
curriculum
cushion
custom
dandelion
debunk
deception
decision
declaration
decontamination

decoration
dedication
deduction
definition
deforestation
defunct
dehydration
delegation
deliberation
delusion
demolition
demonstration
denomination
deportation
deposition
depreciation
depression
description
designation
desolation
desperation
destination
destruction
detection
detention
deterioration
determination
deviation
devotion
dictation
diction
dietitian
digestion
dimension
direction
discoloration
disconnection
discretion
discrimination
discussion
disillusion
dislocation
disposition
dissatisfaction
distinction
distribution
documentation

domination
donation
done
drum
drunk
dumb
dumdum
dump
dunk
duplication
duration
dysfunction
eardrum
edition
education
elation
election
electrician
electrocution
elevation
elimination
emission
emotion
emporium
envision
equation
equilibrium
eradication
erosion
eruption
evacuation
evaluation
evaporation
everyone
evolution
exaggeration
examination
exception
exclamation
excursion
exemption
exertion
exhaustion
exhibition
expectation
expedition
expiration

explanation
exploration
explosion
expression
expulsion
extension
extinction
extraction
fabrication
fascination
fashion
fathom
fearsome
fertilization
fiction
filtration
fixation
flunk
forefront
formation
forum
foundation
foursome
fraction
freedom
friction
from
front
frustration
fun
function
fund
fusion
gallon
generation
geranium
glum
graduation
grandson
gravitation
gruesome
grunt
gum
gumption
gun
gunk
gymnasium

gypsum
handgun
handsome
helium
hesitation
homespun
hum
humdrum
humiliation
hunch
hunk
hunt
illusion
illustration
imagination
imitation
imperfection
imposition
impression
inclination
income
indecision
indentation
indication
indigestion
infection
inflammation
inflation
infliction
information
inhibition
injection
innovation
insertion
inspection
inspiration
installation
institution
instruction
instrumentation
insulation
intention
intermission
interpretation
interruption
intersection
intimidation

intoxication
introduction
intrusion
intuition
invasion
invention
investigation
invitation
irrigation
irritation
isolation
jump
junk
kingdom
limitation
linoleum
liquidation
loathsome
location
lonesome
lotion
lump
lunch
maximum
medallion
mediation
medication
meditation
medium
mention
millennium
million
minimum
mission
moderation
molestation
momentum
monk
month
motion
motivation
mum
munch
museum
musician
mutation
narration

nation
navigation
negotiation
none
nonfiction
notation
notification
notion
numb
nun
nutrition
objection
obligation
oblivion
observation
obsession
obstruction
occasion
occupation
one
operation
opposition
optimum
option
orchestration
organization
orientation
outcome
outdone
outrun
ovation
overcome
palpitation
pardon
participation
partition
passion
pendulum
pension
perception
percussion
perfection
perforation
permission
persecution
perspiration
persuasion

perversion
petition
petroleum
phantom
pincushion
planetarium
plantation
platinum
plum
plump
plunge
plunk
podium
pollution
population
portion
position
possession
possum
postpartum
potassium
potion
precaution
precipitation
precision
preconception
prediction
premeditation
premium
premonition
preparation
prescription
presentation
preservation
preshrunk
presumption
prevention
probation
procrastination
production
progression
promotion
pronunciation
proportion
proposition
propulsion
prosecution

prostitution
protection
protrusion
provision
provocation
publication
pump
pun
punch
punctuation
punk
punt
purification
qualification
quantum
question
quotation
radiation
ramification
random
ransom
ration
reaction
realization
reason
reception
recession
recognition
recommendation
reconciliation
recondition
recreation
redemption
redone
reduction
reflection
refrigeration
refund
registration
regression
regulation
rehabilitation
reincarnation
rejection
relation
relaxation
remediation

renovation
repetition
repulsion
reputation
rerun
reservation
restoration
restriction
retaliation
retention
revelation
revision
revolution
rotation
rum
run
rung
salvation
sanction
sanitation
satisfaction
saturation
scrunch
scum
seclusion
section
sedation
seduction
segregation
seldom
selection
sensation
separation
sermon
serum
session
shotgun
shrunk
shun
simulation
situation
skunk
slum
slump
slunk
sodium
solicitation

solution
some
someone
son
sophistication
specification
spectrum
speculation
sponge
sprung
spun
spunk
stadium
stardom
starvation
station
stimulation
stipulation
strum
stun
stunk
stunt
submission
subscription
substitution
succumb
suction
suggestion
sum
sun
sung
sunk
superstition
supervision
suppression
suspicion
talcum
talon
tantrum
taxation
television
temptation
tension
termination
terrarium
threesome
thumb

tiresome	triumph	valium	welcome
ton	trunk	variation	wholesome
tongue	tuition	vegetation	wisdom
traction	twosome	venom	won
tradition	ulceration	ventilation	workstation
transaction	ultimatum	verification	worrisome
transcription	unaccustomed	version	wrung
transformation	undone	vibration	young
transition	vacation	vision	yum
transmission	vaccination	vocation	zillion
transportation	validation	waterfront	

More Books by Linda A. Bell

"REAL Words for Writers: Alphabetical Word List"
by Linda A. Bell
www.RealWordsForWriters.com

Even the most prolific writers and bloggers get stuck from time to time and need some words! I don't mean a bunch of hoity-toity words that fill up traditional reference books, like *malapropos, usufruct, compendious, dishabille,* and *valetudinarian.* I'm talking about **REAL Words**; words that people actually use in **real-life** conversations!

"REAL Words for Writers: Alphabetical Word List" is the ultimate QUICK-REFERENCE book for writing blogs, books, booklets, advertising copy, marketing materials, newsletters, website content, and more! It contains over 15,000 REAL Words, including base words and derivatives, to help you get unstuck and keep your creativity flowing!

"10 Great Reasons to Write and Self-Publish a Little Booklet!"
by Linda A. Bell
www.iHeartBooklets.com

Having a nice business card is important, but let's face it, most people are going to lose it as fast as you can give it to them. Tri-fold brochures tend to go straight into the trash without even being opened, and they can be quite expensive to make. When you hand someone a professionally designed booklet, however, with information that is interesting and relevant to their needs, their response is quite different. People perceive these as a gift; something of value! They hang onto them and read them over and over. Using a booklet as a marketing tool is the fastest, most cost-effective way to establish credibility and position yourself as an expert in your field!

Linda A. Bell specializes in helping clients find creative ways to market and promote their products and services through blogging, social media, advertising jingles, and self-publishing books and booklets. To learn more, visit: www.BellCreativeStudio.com

Please take a few moments to give "REAL Words for Songwriters: Alphabetical Word List and Abbreviated Rhyming Dictionary" a positive review on Amazon. *Thank you!*

www.RealWordsForSongwriters.com